Educating
Children with
Severe Maladaptive Behaviors

Educating
Children with
Severe Maladaptive Behaviors

SUSAN STAINBACK, Ed.D.

Associate Professor
Department of Special Education
College of Education
University of Northern Iowa
Cedar Falls, Iowa

WILLIAM STAINBACK, Ed.D.
Professor
Department of Special Education
College of Education
University of Northern Iowa
Cedar Falls, Iowa

Grune & Stratton
A Subsidiary of Harcourt Brace Jovanovich, Publishers
New York   London   Toronto   Sydney   San Francisco

Library of Congress Cataloging in Publication Data

Stainback, Susan Bray.
    Educating children with severe maladaptive behaviors.

    Bibliography: p.
    Includes index.
        1. Problem children—Education. 2. Mentally ill
children—Education. I.   Stainback, William C., joint
author. II.   Title. [DNLM: 1. Child behavior
disorders. 2. Education, Special. LC4801 S782e]
LC4801.S78   371.94   80-18747
ISBN 0-8089-1269-0

Grune & Stratton, Inc.
111 Fifth Avenue
New York, New York 10003

Distributed in the United Kingdom by
Academic Press, Inc. (London) Ltd.
24/28 Oval Road, London NW1

Library of Congress Catalog Number 80-18747
International Standard Book Number 0-8089-1269-0

Printed in the United States of America

Contents

PART I

PART II

PART III

v

PART IV

Acknowledgment

We would like to express our appreciation for the support that numerous people provided during the preparation of this text. We wish to especially thank the faculty and staff in the Department of Special Education at the University of Northern Iowa. In addition, we would like to acknowledge Diane Wagner and the many others who spent numerous hours typing, copying, collating, and retyping the manuscript. For the pictures in the book, we owe thanks to the children and to their parents and teachers, as well as to Dr. Charles Vaughn and Sid Morris who made the arrangements for the pictures to be taken and to Bob Coleman who took the pictures.

Finally, we would like to thank all those individuals who were kind enough to give us permission to utilize materials from their publications. They include Dr. Dennis Russo and Dr. Robert Koegel whose work documents the feasibility of teaching at least some children who have been labeled "autistic" in a public school classroom, thereby utilizing several of the programming procedures discussed in this text; and Dr. Andrew Meyers and Dr. Edward Craighead whose studies on classroom treatment of children who have been labeled "psychotic" also support the trends and programming techniques endorsed in this book. In addition, we would like to thank Dr. Polsgrove for his critical evaluation of the research literature on self-control. We would also like to thank the officials of the Council for Children with Behavior Disorders who gave us permission to integrate some of the material we have published as articles in *Behavioral Disorders* into various chapters of this text.

Dr. Susan Stainback is an associate professor in the Department of Special Education at the University of Northern Iowa. She received her doctorate in Special Education from the University of Virginia. Her research and writings have been widely published. Before becoming a university professor, she was a classroom teacher of elementary age severely handicapped students. In addition to teaching and conducting research at the University of Northern Iowa, Dr. Stainback has served as a consultant to many agencies and has conducted workshops throughout the United States.

Dr. William Stainback is a professor in the Department of Special Education at the University of Northern Iowa. He received his doctorate in Special Education from the University of Virginia. His professional experience includes teaching elementary and junior high school level children with mild and severe behavior problems. At the University of Northern Iowa he conducts research and teaches courses in classroom organization and management. Dr. Stainback has published extensively on systematic ways of changing maladaptive behavior. He also has conducted workshops and has made numerous presentations regarding educational methods for children who display maladaptive behavior.

Preface

This book focuses on the educational needs of children who exhibit severe maladaptive behaviors. It is an advanced text designed for school and support personnel (including potential and practicing teachers, psychologists, administrators, and other resource personnel) who are or will be either directly or indirectly involved in the education of these children.

Children who display maladaptive behavior, such as that of extreme withdrawal, self-mutilation, or aggressive responses, have been labeled "sick," "seriously emotionally disturbed," and "psychotic" and, for the most part, have not been educated within the public school system. This, however, is rapidly changing, and therefore it is the intent of this text to make educators and resource personnel more aware of the programming trends and techniques for teaching children with severe maladaptive behaviors.

PART I

In all three chapters of Part I, background information is provided to aid the reader in gaining a general perspective of the education of children who exhibit severe maladaptive behavior.

The first chapter provides an introduction and overview. The common definitions, classification systems, characteristics, and prevalence figures are included. These descriptive data concerns are discussed with traditionally used categorical labels such as "emotional disturbance" and "behavior disorders," since these are the terms that professionals generally use to describe and discuss children with maladaptive behavior. Chapter 1 focuses on children who exhibit mild as well as severe patterns. Hopefully, this will assist the reader in gaining perspective of the educational area concerned with children who display maladaptive behavior and how those children who display severe maladaptive behavior fit into the total picture.

Chapter 2 traces the development of the educational area dealing with children who exhibit maladaptive behavior. As in the first chapter, the focus is on children with both mild and severe maladaptive behaviors in order to provide a more integrated background.

In chapter 3 the authors analyze and interpret some of the current trends in special education, particularly as they relate to the education of children who display severe maladaptive behavior.

In summary, Part I presents the necessary background information for a general understanding of why some children end up being labeled behaviorally disordered or emotionally disturbed and describes briefly the evolution of educational programs designed to assist these children.

1
What Is Maladaptive Behavior?

This book concerns the education of children and youth whose behaviors do not meet the expectations of parents, siblings, teachers, peers, and others. Their behaviors are in excess of what is expected or are to a lesser degree than what is expected. Children who exhibit such behavior patterns have had their behaviors labeled as being deviant, extreme, maladjusted, or abnormal. In some cases the children themselves have been labeled as being sick, psychotic, emotionally disturbed, insane, or behaviorally disordered.

Whether a behavior is considered to be maladaptive depends on many factors. One of these relates to the differing expectations of others. It is well known that expectations vary among different social and cultural groups. A particular behavior in one group may be considered "maladaptive," while in another group the *same* behavior might be considered "normal." For example, the frequent display of fighting and aggressive behaviors on the part of the child growing up within an inner-city environment may not be considered maladaptive. Quite to the contrary, such behaviors may be considered "normal" by peers or gang members within that environment. The same behaviors, however, probably would be considered maladaptive or deviant if displayed by a child growing up in a middle-class, suburban environment by the persons in that particular environment or social/cultural group.

Another factor that can influence whether or not a behavior is considered maladaptive is its intensity, duration, and/or frequency. It is not likely that a child who only briefly displayed a few maladaptive behaviors would be classified as disturbed. If the child frequently displayed severe forms of maladaptive behavior over a long period of time, however, he/ she might be diagnosed as "emotionally disturbed," "behaviorally disordered," or "psychotic." One problem with this particular factor is just how often, for how long, and/or at what intensity does an individual have to display attention-seeking, boisterous, rude behavior before the behavior is labeled as being maladaptive or before the individual is labeled as being sick, disturbed, disordered or insane? If such behavior occurs 75 times within three years, do we say that this is too often for too long a period of time and therefore maladaptive and that the individual is probably behaviorally disordered? Or, does it have to occur 250 times? Another example would be the individual who fails to interact with others. How often, for how long, at what intensity does this have to occur before we say the behavior is maladaptive or before the individual is labeled withdrawn, shy, or autistic. That is, how many times does he have to fail to interact when confronted with the opportunity to do so?

The specific situation or stimulus conditions under which a behavior is displayed also influences whether or not it is considered maladaptive or deviant. Doing a great deal of loud talking at parties and other social gatherings is considered normal by most people, but if the same individual talks constantly during study hall and under similar stimulus conditions such as in church or the library, this talking behavior may be considered maladaptive and/or the individual labeled behaviorally disordered or emotionally disturbed. Another example would be the individual who talks and mumbles to himself while practicing a speech in the privacy of his home versus the individual who talks and mumbles to himself in many varied situations, such as in department stores, on street corners, in classrooms, and at social gatherings.

The age of the child displaying the behavior(s) has an influence on whether or not the behavior is labeled as being maladaptive. Researchers (e.g., MacFarlane, Allen, & Honzik, 1955) have found that most children are excessively modest and have specific fears between three and four years of age. Therefore, the excessive modesty and fears of a three-year-old generally would not be considered extreme or maladaptive behavior since most children are excessively modest and have fears at that age. On the other hand, such behaviors might be labeled maladaptive if displayed frequently for a long period of time by a fifteen-year-old. In other words, a behavior that might be viewed as normal at one age may be designated maladaptive at a younger or older age. Another example points this out very clearly. Many babies display rocking motions and engage in some forms of head banging very early in life, and this often is considered to be within normal patterns of development. If such behaviors persist and occur at later ages, however, it is usually considered to be abnormal, deviant, extreme, or maladaptive.

Several additional factors should be recognized when attempting to define maladaptive behaviors or children with behavioral disorders. One is that the maladaptive behaviors that have earned some children the label emotionally disturbed or behaviorally disordered are displayed by many nonlabeled children. All children in fact, are likely to experience some emotional problems to some degree at some time. Lapouse and Monk (1964) studied a large group of children between the ages of 6 and 12 from randomly selected homes. They found that (1) about 50 percent demonstrated many temper tantrums and fears, (2) over 30 percent chewed their fingernails and had nightmares, and (3) about 15 percent sucked their thumbs and wet their beds. A second factor that should be recognized is that there are no widely accepted, standardized measures for behaviors deemed maladaptive, deviant, or extreme. While intelligence tests are often used to define mental retardation, there are no comparable tests available to define maladaptive behavior, a behavioral disability, or emotional disability (Kauffman, 1977).

As the above discussion would indicate, whether a behavior is labeled maladaptive or an individual is labeled as disordered or disturbed is not a simple matter. Despite the complexities and difficulties involved, various authors and researchers have attempted to define and classify behaviors and/or individuals as being extreme, deviant, disordered or disturbed. In this chapter, a sample of the terms, definitions, and classification approaches that are currently employed by educators are reviewed. Also included are discussions related to the characteristics of children who display maladaptive behaviors and the prevalence of children who display these behaviors in the school-age population.

TERMS AND DEFINITIONS

A variety of terms have been employed by educators to refer to children who exhibit maladaptive behaviors. Some of the most popular are: *emotionally handicapped, emotionally disturbed, behaviorally disordered, behaviorally disabled, socially maladjusted, delinquent, psychologically disordered, severely* or *seriously emotionally disturbed, severely handicapped, autistic, schizophrenic,* and/or *psychotic.* There also has been a large number of definitions formulated to explain what is meant by the various terms. A few of the most prevalent terms and definitions are reviewed here.

Terms and definitions employed to refer to children's maladaptive behaviors in a generic or overall way are discussed first. In defining these terms no distinction is made between mild/moderate and severe/profound disorders, although the authors of the definitions appeared to have the more mildly/moderately handicapped in mind when discussing their definitions. Next definitions are examined that differentiate between the mildly/moderately disordered and the severely/profoundly disordered. Finally, terms and definitions related to severe emotional or behavioral disorders are reviewed.

Generic Terms and Definitions

Many authors in their description of children who exhibit deviant behavior do not discriminate on the basis of degree of severity of the behavior exhibited. In their definitions, however, there is a tendency to focus on the more mildly handicapped since there is a higher incidence of children exhibiting the milder forms of maladaptive behavior and it is that group that the community and the public schools have been held more directly responsible for in the past. (Children with severe forms of maladaptive behavior have traditionally been institutionalized or placed in residential centers, although this tradition is now changing rapidly.)

Bower (1969) recommends the term "emotionally handicapped" to describe those individuals who exhibit "maladaptive" behaviors, because he believes that the word "handicapped" implies a lasting and persistent quality. He feels that terms such as "emotionally disturbed" or "socially maladjusted" are misleading since they do not imply a lasting quality. In other words, there is a need to differentiate between those who have transient or temporary behavioral or emotional problems from those who are truly handicapped. Bower (1969) defines emotionally handicapped children as those who display one or more of the following characteristics *to a marked degree over a period of time:*

1 An inability to learn which cannot be explained by intellectual, sensory, or health factors.
2 An inability to build or maintain satisfactory interpersonal relationships with peers and teachers.
3 Inappropriate types of behavior or feelings under normal conditions.
4 A general, pervasive mood of unhappiness or depression.
5 A tendency to develop physical symptoms, pains, or fears associated with personal or school problems. (pp. 22-23)

Bower's definition provides a method of identifying children who are emotionally handicapped by the behaviors that they display. Generally speaking, Bower does not attempt to deal with the causes of the emotional handicap, although certain causes are excluded in the first statement cited above.

Smith and Neisworth (1975), in contrast to Bower, do not believe that the terms "socially maladjusted" and "emotionally disturbed" are misleading. In their definition they differentiate between those who should be defined as emotionally disturbed and those who should be defined as socially maladjusted. According to Smith and Neisworth (1975):

> There are two very broad categories of adjustment problems: emotional disturbance and social maladjustment. Almost everyone experiences instances of maladjustment in his lifetime. These transitional time periods are normal if they are relatively brief and infrequent. They may very well be situation-specific, that is, related to a certain trying or disturbing event, place, or person. Hence, there is no clear line of demarcation between normal and abnormal personal-social behaviors. "Emotional disturbance" is a general term that is used to include numerous imprecisely defined conditions such as "mental illness," "psychosis," "neurosis," "schizophrenia," "phobia," "obsession," "compulsion," "autism," and so on. Each of these categories of disturbance has characteristics that separate it from the others. Fundamentally, children who exhibit emotionally disturbed behaviors are excessively aggressive, withdrawn, or both. Their central problem usually is not violation of social roles or the mores and folkways of the culture; they are, however, usually very unhappy people. Social maladjustment, in contrast, involves behavior which violates rules. The behavior may be acceptable within the context of the child's subculture, but not in society at large. In fact, within the child's immediate social milieu rule-violating behavior (e.g., throwing stones at school windows) may be rewarded. (pp. 26–27)

In their definition Smith and Neisworth recognized, as Bower did in his definition, that all children display inappropriate behaviors at times. They attempted to deal with this by excluding transient problems that may be situational in nature, that is, related to specific events, places, and/or persons.

Graubard (1973) recommends that special educators use the term "behavioral disabilities" to refer to children traditionally classified as being emotionally disturbed, socially maladjusted, and/or juvenile delinquent. In contrast to Smith and Neisworth, Graubard does not see the necessity of differentiating the emotionally disturbed from the socially maladjusted. He defines behavioral disabilities as "a variety of excessive, chronic, deviant behaviors ranging from impulsive and aggressive to depressive and withdrawal acts (1) which violate the perceiver's expectation of appropriateness and (2) which the perceiver wishes to see stopped" (p. 246).

It should be noted that Graubard's definition is derived from an ecological perspective. In the ecological approach what is considered deviant or maladaptive is seen as much a function of the perceiver as of the behaver. While the child of concern is the behaver, it is the teachers, peers, and parents who are among the perceivers.

"Juvenile delinquency" is often included in discussions of children who display behavior disorders. The term is used to refer to children and youth who have violated the law. According to Kvaraceus and Miller (1959), juvenile delinquency is "behavior by nonadults which violates specific legal norms or the norms of a particular societal institution with sufficient frequency and/or seriousness so as to provide a firm basis for legal action against the behaving individual or group" (p. 54). In their definition Kvaraceus and Miller recognize that most children occasionally break rules or sometimes fail to follow regulations; therefore, they indicated that the norm-violating behavior must occur frequently and be of a serious nature. It also should be stressed that these authors' definition is based on "legal rules and regulations."

Mild/Moderate versus Severe/Profound Disorders

Definitions have appeared recently that differentiate between children who exhibit different degrees or severity of maladaptive behavior(s). Kauffman (1977) proposed a definition of children with emotional or behavioral disorders that differentiates those with mild and moderate disorders from those with severe and profound disorders. His definition is formulated from a learning theory perspective. Kauffman recognizes in the definition the role of social expectations in determining when behavior is disordered. He also acknowledges that the child's own self-perceptions can be involved in determining when behavior is disordered by including in the definition those children who respond to their environment in personally unsatisfying ways.

> Children with behavior disorders are those who chronically and markedly respond to their environment in socially unacceptable and/ or personally unsatisfying ways but who can be taught more socially acceptable and personally gratifying behavior. Children with mild and moderate behavior disorders can be taught effectively with their normal peers (if their teachers receive appropriate consultative help) or in special resource or self-contained classes with reasonable hope of quick reintegration with their normal peers. Children with severe and profound behavior disorders require intensive and prolonged intervention and must be taught at home or in special classes, special schools, or residential institutions. (Kauffman, 1977, p. 23)

It is important to note that this definition is one of the first to differentiate between the mildly/moderately and severely/profoundly behaviorally disordered. Kauffman made the differentiation by the type of special education programming most likely needed to improve the child's behavior.

Since Kauffman's definition, several other definitions have appeared that attempt to make a distinction between mild and severe disorders. Bryan and Bryan (1979) defined a behavior disorder as:

affective, emotional or behavior problems that interfere with the child's learning and/or social functioning. Such problems include over-action, like excessive and inappropriate aggression, and inaction, like excessive and inappropriate withdrawal. Extreme cases of behavior disorders include various types of psychoses, such as *schizophrenia* and *autism*. (p. 25)

These attempts to differentiate between mild and severe disorders is a reflection of the growing interest and responsibility of education for children considered to be seriously emotionally or behaviorally disordered.

Severe/Profound Disorders

While Kauffman was one of the first educators specifically to include in a formal definition of behavioral disorders children with severe disorders, members of other disciplines (e.g., psychiatry) have employed specific terms to refer to children who display extremely maladaptive behavior. The best known term is "psychotic." It is used in a generic way to refer to children who display serious, debilitating childhood emotional or behavioral disorders. The symptoms or behaviors displayed are frequently bizarre or grossly inappropriate. Unresponsiveness to others, avoidance of eye contact, severe speech and language disturbances, pathological preoccupation with manipulating objects, self-stimulation, self-injurious behavior, stereotyped movements, and/or disturbances in biological functions (eating, sleeping, and eliminating) are some of the behaviors that have been identified as characteristic of children labeled as being psychotic.

There are various specific conditions that come under the general term psychotic. Traditionally, childhood schizophrenia and infantile autism are two conditions or major forms of psychotic disturbances in children.

The major characteristics associated with childhood schizophrenia include:

1 Lack of contact with reality.
2 Development of own world.

3   Apparent denial of the human quality of people.
4   Inappropriate affect—either too flat or too explosive.
5   Body movements that appear bizarre—for example, robotlike walking or fluid, graceful gyrations.
6   Stereotyped actions—for example, twirling objects, flapping arms, or rocking back and forth in a repetitive fashion.
7   Special knowledge about particular subjects—for example, detailed information of the city's transportation system.
8   Distorted time orientation—a child may relate events that happened years ago in a manner suggesting they are part of his current existence.
9   Inappropriate speech structure and content—for example, parroting or speaking in fragments of sentences and/or displaying asynchronism of affect, verbal content, and tone of voice.

The major characteristics associated with infantile autism include:

1   Extreme withdrawal of contact with others including parents—for example, some autistic babies fail to reach out to be picked up and remain stiff and unaccommodating in their mother's arms.
2   Speech usually absent or severely impaired—many will answer a question with the same question, demonstrate pronominal reversal, and/or echolalia.
3   Likely to show an intelligent, pensive facial expression, which fosters the impression of high intelligence despite a low level of intellectual functioning.
4   Usually relates well to objects—may spin or twirl an object for hours; however, rarely uses an object for its intended purpose.
5   An intense desire to preserve the status quo—may become extremely upset by even small changes in a familiar routine.
6   Special skills in memory—for example, able to remember long lists of names or long passages of conversation.

Some professionals believe that autism is not a unique disorder that is different from childhood schizophrenia (Blau, 1962); others disagree (Rimland, 1964). The differences that have been postulated include the following:

1   Autism is present at birth or soon afterward whereas childhood schizophrenia usually makes its appearance after a period of at least five or six years of normal development.
2   Autistic children do not show signs of having visual and auditory hallucinations whereas schizophrenic children do, with many eventually developing signs of the delusions and hallucinations associated with adult schizophrenia.

3 Autistic children appear detached from, and indifferent to, their surroundings whereas schizophrenic children appear anxious and confused about their relationships to their surroundings.
4 Autistic children appear healthy whereas schizophrenic children are
typically of poor health.
5 Autism is more common in twins than is childhood schizophrenia.

On the other hand, as mentioned, there are professionals who contend that it is not feasible to distinguish between autism, schizophrenia,
and other forms of severe emotional or behavioral disorders (Blau, 1962;
Kauffman, 1977). These professionals believe that designations such as
the following are more or less synonymous: psychotic, atypical, seriously
deviant child, schizophrenic, autistic, symbiotic, brain injured, incipient
schizophrenic, pseudopsychoses, pseudoneurotic psychoses, abnormal
child, schizoid personality, and impulse-ridden character. For them research has not demonstrated that subcategories of seriously disturbed
children can be reliably distinguished.

Most of the information to date in regard to terminology and definitions related to children who exhibit very severe forms of maladaptive
behavior has come from disciplines such as psychiatry. Psychiatry has
been the source of many of the terms and definitions regarding severe/
profound disorders because education traditionally has dealt with the mild
behavioral disorders, leaving the severe disorders to psychiatry. This will
be changing in the future since educators are becoming more involved
with this population, and thus more information from an educational perspective is likely to become available. It appears, however, that educators
are going to be less interested in terminology and definition than other
disciplines have been; instead educators will be more interested in how to
change, through the teaching/learning process, whatever behaviors the
child displays.* (See Chapter 3 for an explanation.)

CLASSIFICATION APPROACHES

When reviewing classification systems in special education and psychology, it becomes apparent that there are many different ways and degrees of classifying individuals who exhibit disordered behavior. First,

---

*The terms "behaviorally disordered" and "emotionally disturbed" are used inter-
changeably in the first section of this book to refer to children who exhibit deviant or maladaptive behavior(s). This is consistent with the way most professionals currently refer to this
population of children, although some professionals use the term behaviorally disordered to
refer to children who exhibit "mild behavior problems" while reserving the term emotionally disturbed for those who exhibit serious or severe emotional difficulties.

the child is usually classified into a handicapped group (e.g., mentally retarded, learning disabled, behaviorally disordered). Second, he is usually further classified within the handicap group; for example, within behavioral disorders there are many possible classifications or categories—conduct disorder, schizophrenic, neurotic, psychotic. The purpose here is to review some of the ways of classifying children within the behavioral disorders category.

Psychiatric Descriptive System

The third edition of the *Diagnostic and Statistical Manual of Mental Disorders* (DSM–III), published by the American Psychiatric Association (1979), contains a section on children's disorders based upon a multiaxial approach to diagnosis. While special educators are not generally expected to be highly versed in the American psychiatric classification, they are usually expected to be familiar with it. It is often employed by psychiatrists and psychologists, especially by those who adhere to the psychoanalytically oriented perspective. The terminology used in the system is also sometimes referred to by educators in their work with children who have been labeled emotionally disturbed or behaviorally disordered.

The psychiatric system of the DSM–III lists ten conditions that are usually considered to be first evident in infancy, childhood, or adolescence. These are briefly described below.

1. Mental Retardation. This category includes those individuals who exhibit significant subaverage general intellectual functioning. Four subtypes of this category reflect the degree of intellectual impairment. They are: *mild, moderate, severe,* and *profound.*

2. Attention Deficit Disorder. This classification includes inattentive, impulsive, and/or hyperactive behaviors that are developmentally inappropriate for the mental and chronological age of the individual who is diagnosed as such. Variations under this category include the presence or absence of hyperactive and residual effects based upon the functioning of an individual who has previously exhibited these specific behaviors.

3. Conduct Disorders. There are five subtypes in this category to classify repetitive and persistant behavior. They include: *undersocialized aggression, undersocialized nonaggression, socialized aggression, socialized nonaggression,* and *atypical conduct disorder.*

4. Anxiety Disorders of Childhood or Adolescence. Such symptoms as excessive anxiety, withdrawal and/or worry is indicative of the behavior of individuals included in this category. The subtypes in this category are: *separation anxiety disorder, avoidant disorder of childhood or ado-lescence,* and *overanxious disorder.*

5. *Other Disorders of Infancy, Childhood or Adoles-cence.* Behaviors in this category include those of poor social and envi-ronmental adaptation (e.g., *social isolation, negativism, distress*). Sub-types of this caegory include: *reactive attachment disorder of infancy, schizoid disorder of childhood or adolescence, elective mutism, opposi-tional disorder,* and *identity disorder.*

6. *Eating Disorders.* There are five subtypes in this category: *ano-rexia nervosa, bulimia, pica rumination disorder of infancy* and *atypical eating disorder.*

7. *Stereotyped Movement Disorders.* Recurrent involuntary, repet-itive, rapid, purposeless motor movement (tics) and/or nonspasmotic, stereotyped voluntary purposeless movements (e.g., headbanging, rock-ing, handwaving) are included in this category. Subtypes under this cate-gory include: *transient tic disorder, chronic motor tic disorder, Tourette's disorder, atypical tic disorder* and *atypical stereotyped movement disor-der.*

8. *Other Disorders with Physical Manifestations.* This category in-cludes abnormal physical behavior with no evident underlying physiologi-cal problem. Such behavior includes *stuttering, functional enuresis, func-tional encopresis, sleepwalking disorder,* and *sleep-terror disorder.*

9. *Pervasive Developmental Disorders.* Abnormal behaviors in-cluded in this category are those of *bizarre responses to stimuli, impaired social relationships,* and *deficits in social skill, affect, speech and/or lan-guage development,* which tend to influence many if not all aspects of functioning. Defined within this category are those disorders of *infantile autism, childhood onset pervasive developmental disorder,* and *atypical pervasive developmental disorder.* A further breakdown is used for the first two subtypes—that of *full syndrome present* and *residual state.*

10. *Specific Developmental Disorders.* This category includes be-haviors in which performance is significantly below the expected level based on chronological and mental age and degree of schooling in particu-lar subject areas. *Developmental reading disorders, developmental arithmetic disorder, developmental language disorder* (expressive type and receptive type), *developmental articulation disorder, mixed specific developmental disorder* and *atypical specific developmental disorder* are subtypes within this category.

It should be noted that we have only reviewed the major psychiatric syndromes that are first evident in infancy, childhood, or adolescence. There are many subclassifications or categories under the major categories. Also, there are other adult categories to which children can be assigned.

Before leaving this discussion of the psychiatric classification system, a few remarks about some of the major problems that have been encountered with the system might be in order. Some of the remarks made here are based on research findings related to what is outlined in the second edition of the *Diagnostic and Statistical Manual of Mental Disorders* rather than the third edition. However, because the basic assumptions are the same for the second and third editions, it is likely that the findings would remain true. According to Bryan and Bryan (1979) one major problem is that the assignment of individuals to categories has been found to be unreliable. In other words, if two or more independent psychiatrists see the same individual, there is a good chance they will assign or classify him or her into different categories. Also, it has been found that social class, areas of residence, and other presumably irrelevant factors influence the diagnostic classification of a person (Redlich and Hollingshead, 1958). Another problem with the psychiatric classification is that once a person is diagnosed and labeled, he is likely to keep that label for a long time (Rosenhan, 1973). If the person should get better, the label might be modified slightly from "schizophrenia" to that of to say, for example, "schizophrenia in remission." Finally, there is little or no evidence that relevant information is provided in regard to the selection of a treatment strategy. This is a serious problem since this is a major reason for engaging in diagnosis and classification (Kanfer and Saslow, 1969).

It is not too surprising that the psychiatric classification is fraught with numerous problems since the system is not based on scientific, systematically gathered data. In other words, the categories are based on personal, clinical experiences rather than on objective, scientific evidence.

Empirical or Research Approach

The second approach to classification that we shall examine is the empirical or research approach. Herbert Quay (1972) has followed this approach in his attempts to classify problem behaviors. He and his colleagues have studied the problem behaviors of children in a variety of settings, including the public schools, institutions, hospitals, and child guidance clinics. They have used multivariate statistical procedures (factor-analytic techniques) to pinpoint behaviors that occur together to form a dimension, syndrome, or cluster. They have analyzed information or data obtained from sources such as ratings, checklists, and questionnaires.

Quay and associates have identified through research four behavioral patterns or dimensions among children who display problem behaviors that are fairly stable and pervasive:

1. Conduct disorders
2. Personality disorders
3. Inadequate/immature
4. Socialized delinquency

Children in the *conduct disorders* group are characterized by restlessness, attention seeking, disruptiveness, boisterousness, disobedience, irresponsibility, temper tantrums, fighting, bossiness, and destructiveness. In the *personality disorders* (anxious/withdrawn) group are children who exhibit anxiety, feelings of inferiority, lack of self-confidence, self-consciousness, fear, passivity, perfectionism, limited verbal responsiveness, and social isolation. Those in the *inadequate/immature* group are characterized by clumsiness, preoccupation, passivity, daydreaming, sluggishness, drowsiness, masturbation, reticence, lack of interest, excessive giggling, and failure to complete assignments. Those in the *socialized delinquency* group actively participate in gang activities, group acts of delinquency, truancy from school, and cooperative stealing; and they fail to conform to middle-class standards and values.

After reviewing Quay's and similar cluster-type approaches (e.g., Jenkins & Hewitt, 1944; Spivack, Swift, & Prewitt, 1972), Kirk and Gallagher (1979) concluded that for the most part maladaptive behavior seems to divide into two major groups:

> The first is an impulsive, hyperactive antisocial pattern that, at its most extreme, becomes dangerous to others and is labeled delinquent behavior. The second pattern is of a fearful, withdrawn unhappy child with many vague concerns and anxieties. The more extreme version of that pattern is the autistic or schizophrenic child. (p. 425)

As with almost any approach to classification, there are benefits and limitations to "cluster-type approaches." One benefit is that such an approach helps organize the vast myriad of possible maladaptive behaviors into smaller and more manageable clusters or dimensions. One limitation, however, is that no one has been able to show empirically that knowing the various clusters of behaviors can assist the teacher or anyone else in the selection of an appropriate treatment strategy.

Evaluation of the Classification Approaches

The two classification systems—the psychiatric descriptive and Quay's empirical approach—reviewed in this section are compared in Table 1-1. The psychiatric system is employed most widely in psychiatry to describe the type of difficulty a person is exhibiting and is often referred to by special educators in their work with children who display extreme behaviors.

Quay's (1972) classification system is, of course, more educational or school related in nature than the psychiatric descriptive system. Quay believes that differential educational programs can be designed to correspond to his four-way classification system. In other words, classroom instructional strategies and techniques could be based on the type of behavioral difficulty exhibited. One problem is that children are seldom "pure" anything, for example, delinquent or conduct disorder. Also, to date, no one has empirically demonstrated the efficacy of differential programming based on Quay's groupings.

In regard to severity, the psychiatric descriptive system covers the entire range from healthy to very severely disturbed or disordered individuals. Quay's system, however, does not make a differentiation between the mildly and severely disordered. This was probably not done by Quay because the public schools were not, in the past, required to educate children who displayed very extreme forms of maladaptive behavior.

CHARACTERISTICS OF BEHAVIORALLY DISORDERED CHILDREN

In attempts to describe children who display maladaptive behaviors numerous characteristics have been cited; among these are intelligence, academic achievement, attention, hyperactivity, withdrawal, aggression, and helplessness, which we shall consider here. Other characteristics of children with behavior disorders such as language disturbances, unresponsiveness to social stimuli, and inappropriate affect will become evident when reading later chapters of this book, particularly the chapters in Part II.

There is marked heterogeneity among "behaviorally disordered" children. No one child is likely to display all of the characteristics discussed. Indeed, some of the characteristics might be considered the reverse of each other, for example, impulsivity versus reflectivity (discussed under hyperactivity). Thus, one child may be hyperactive, impulsive and/or aggressive while another child may be shy and withdrawn. Not only can children within the category of behavioral disorders demonstrate almost opposite characteristics, but also the number of char-

Table 1–1
Comparison of Classification Approaches

Type	Author and Publication Date	Purpose	Range	Classification Components	Limitations
Psychiatric descriptive approach	American Psychiatric Association, 1979	To provide psychiatrists with a standard way of classifying mental disorders.	Entire spectrum: healthy to severe deviations	*Mental Retardation:* general subaverage intellectual functioning *Attention Deficit Disorder:* inattentive, impulsive and/or hyperactive behaviors that are developmental inappropriate *Conduct Disorders:* repetitive and persistent pattern of inappropriate conduct *Anxiety Disorders of Childhood or Adolescence:* excessive anxiety, withdrawal and/or worry *Other Disorders of Infancy, Childhood or Adolescence:* can include behavior indicative of poor social and environmental adaptation *Eating Disorders:* various types of abnormal eating behaviors *Stereotyped Movement Disorders:* recurrent, involuntary, repetitive, rapid, purposeless motor movement (tics) and/or nonspasmotic, stereotyped voluntary purposeless movements (e.g. headbanging, rocking, handwaving)	1. Assignments to groups have been found to be unreliable 2. Irrelevant factors (e.g., socioeconomic status, area of residence) have been found to influence classification. 3. Label is often retained by an individual for a long time regardless of behavior change 4. Classification provides little information regarding treatment

Table 1–1 (continued)
Comparison of Classification Approaches

Type	Author and Publication Date	Purpose	Range	Classification Components	Limitations
				Other Disorders with Physical Manifestations: abnormal physical behaviors with no evident underlying physiological problem	
				Pervasive Developmental Disorders: pervasive abnormal behaviors such as bizarre responses to stimuli, impaired social relationships and deficits in social skill, affect, speech or language development	
				Specific Developmental Disorders: performance is significantly below expected level based on chronological age, mental age and schooling in particular subject areas.	
Empirical or research approach	Herbert Quay, 1972	To develop a classification system based on empirical data	Classifies only deviant behaviors with no delineation between mild and severe problems	*Conduct disorders:* acting out behaviors such as restlessness, attention seeking, disruptiveness, boisterousness, disobedience, irresponsibility, temper tantrums, fighting, bossiness, and destructiveness.	1. Classification usefulness in program planning or treatment not yet shown
				Personality disorders: anxious/withdrawn behaviors such as anxiousness,	2. Does not cover all ranges of children who exhibit deviant behavior

feelings of inferiority, lack of self-confidence, self-consciousness, fear, passivity, perfectionism, limited verbal responses, and social isolation.

Inadequate/immature: clumsiness, preoccupation, passivity, daydreaming, sluggishness, drowsiness, masturbation, reticence, lack of interest, giggling, and failure to complete assignments.

Socialized delinquency: characterized by gang activities, group acts of delinquence, truancy, cooperative stealing, and failure to conform to middle class values and standards.

acteristics displayed may vary. While one child may exhibit many of the characteristics discussed, another child may exhibit only a few of the characteristics. It should be noted that before a child is given the label of "behaviorally disordered," most professionals look for a cluster of characteristics that occur together. Most professionals are very hesitant to give a child any label based on only one or two characteristics that might be indicative of a handicapping condition.

Intelligence

Children who have been designated as mildly disturbed or disordered range in intelligence from the retarded to gifted levels. The weight of the evidence, however, tends to indicate that the *average* IQ for childen who display mild maladaptive or deviant behaviors falls within the low normal range of intelligence as measured by standardized intelligence test (Bower, 1969; Graubard, 1964; Lyons & Powers, 1963; Motto & Wilkins, 1968; Stone & Rowley, 1964). Thus while many disturbed children score average or above on various intelligence tests, more of them score in the dull-normal, retarded range when compared to children who do not exhibit emotional difficulties. Whether children labeled behaviorally disordered have "real" IQs slightly below average is still not clear. It might be that their "behavior disorder" is causing them to score less than their actual or real IQ level. (Of course, it could be argued that the reverse is true—their low intelligence causes or contributes to the "behavior disorder.")

Most severely disturbed children, on the other hand, score well below the average on IQ measures. Some professionals believe that the measured scores do not reflect the actual intellectual level of severely disturbed children. Kanner (1943) contended that many autistic children are of normal or above intelligence even if they often fail to demonstrate their ability on intelligence tests. More recently, Rimland (1978) has described some autistic children as being able to "perform mental feats that far surpass the powers of ordinary people" (p. 69). Such statements and descriptions have led some professionals to speculate that many severely disturbed children who function at a retarded level are not really retarded. Others who have conducted research in this area have concluded, however, that the IQs of most severely disturbed children can be accurately measured and that the average IQ is probably somewhere within the 25–75 range (Bartak & Rutter, 1973; DeMyer, 1975; Lovaas, Koegel, Simmons, & Long, 1973). After completing an extensive review of the recent research regarding the cognitive functioning of psychotic children, Baker (1979) concluded:

The premise that psychotic children possess normal innate intelligence is challenged by the emergence of recent research dealing with measurement and stability of psychotic children's cognitive level. An analysis of recent and relevant research suggests that psychotic children do not differ from mentally retarded children in terms of cognitive functioning. (p. 344)

Regardless of the real IQ level, severely disturbed children do show large variations in measured IQ. After studying 97 psychotic children, Gittelman and Birch (1967) concluded that 56 percent scored below 69, 26 percent between 70 and 90, and 18 percent above 90.

Academic Achievement

Most studies of academic achievement of behaviorally disordered children have been confined to standardized test measures of reading and arithmetic. Few studies have been done in other subject areas.

For the mildly disturbed or disordered wide variations in academic achievement have been found. Some are brilliant, while others function below the average in comparison to their peers. Overall, however, the research evidence indicates that the majority are behind their peers in both academic achievement and grade level (Bower, 1969; Graubard, 1964; Motto & Wilkins, 1968; Stone & Rowley, 1964). This holds true even when expected achievement level is based on mental age rather than chronological age. In other words, they achieve at a lower level than their IQ level would predict.

When the data are further analyzed, there is some evidence that children classified as being conduct disordered (Graubard, 1971) and/or delinquent (Silberberg & Silberberg, 1971) are further behind academically than other categories of behaviorally disordered children, such as withdrawn and shy children. A few studies (Bower, 1969; Stone & Rowley, 1964) have found arithmetic achievement to be lower than reading achievement; others (Graubard, 1971; Motto & Wilkins, 1968), though, have found no discrepancy between these two academic areas.

In regard to severely disturbed children, most are markedly deficient in academic areas. As pointed out by Clarizio and McCoy (1976), success in reading, arithmetic, and other academics requires assertiveness, cooperation with others, concentration, and an interest in one's surroundings or external environment. Extremely withdrawn or aggressive/acting-out children usually lack several of these characteristics. Such children often function at a level wherein instruction is given in basic language skills, grooming, toileting, eating skills, and rudimentary reading and arithmetic skills rather than functional academics. There are exceptions. A few psychotic children do perform well in some academic areas, but their performance is usually erratic. Occasionally, they correctly complete a difficult academic assignment while having failed a simple assignment earlier.

The vast majority of seriously disturbed children, however, function far below their peers in most, if not all, academic areas. There are very few children labeled as being psychotic or seriously disturbed who function even close to adequate in school-related tasks.

Attention to Task

Mildly disturbed children are often described as being inattentive. They have difficulty focusing their attention on a task long enough to engage purposefully in the task. In addition to not focusing on the task at hand, there is some evidence that when mildly handicapped children do attend, or at least look at, a task, they may have problems attending to the "relevant" aspects. That is, they may have difficulty focusing on the important or "relevant" aspects of a task while screening out or ignoring the unimportant or "irrelevant" aspects. They have problems learning or responding correctly to a task because they focus on nearly everything other than the important, relevant aspects. They are *under*selective in regard to what they attend to.

Severely disturbed children show marked problems in attending behavior although in a different way than do mildly handicapped children. It is interesting that many professionals believe that the problem with severely disturbed children is too much attention to *limited aspects of a task*. There is some research evidence related to this phenomenon. Schreibam and Lovaas (1973), for example, found that severely disturbed children tend to respond to a single or limited number of features of a task or stimulus to such a degree that they fail to see other important or relevant aspects of the task. Rimland's (1978) description of the autistic savant explains this overselective characteristic of at least some severely disturbed children. Many are able to "zero in on whatever has attracted their attention. But these children lack the capacity to 'zero out,' to expand their focus and comprehend the context of whatever they are focusing on" (p. 80).

In short, the research evidence indicates that severely disturbed children tend to be *over*selective while mildly handicapped children tend to be *under*selective. More research is needed in this area before anything but tentative speculations can be accepted with any degree of confidence.

Another characteristic of severely disordered children, which is related to attentional behaviors, is what has been termed "gaze aversion."

Some behaviorally disordered children, especially those labeled as being "autistic," seem to avoid establishing eye contact with others. They appear to "look through" or beyond the person(s) around them. They do not focus on the face or maintain eye contact. For a more detailed account of gaze aversion, the reader is referred to Hutt and Hutt (1969).

Hyperactivity

Although for the most part hyperactivity has been researched and discussed in relation to children designated as "learning disabled," it is a characteristic frequently displayed by both mildly and severely behaviorally disordered children. As a result, some behaviorally disordered children have been characterized as being hyperactive; that is, they have been called "hyperactive" as well as "behaviorally disordered." Traditionally, hyperactivity has been explained as an inappropriate high level of motor activity or as heightened, persistent, sustained physical action.

These types of explanations, or at least some of the specifics of these types of explanations, have begun to be questioned. After reviewing the research findings, Whalen and Henker (1976) concluded that hyperactive children do not exhibit a heightened level of motor activity in unstructured situations (i.e., situations where the child is not required to concentrate on tasks imposed by others). If it is true that such children are generally not more active than their nonlabeled counterparts in unstructured situations, do they differ from other children in regard to motor activity in any types of situations? According to Whalen and Henker, such children may show atypically high levels of motor restlessness when the teacher requires performance on a structured task. In short, the problem appears to be an inability to modulate motor behavior in accordance with the demands of the situation rather than a general problem with inordinately high motor activity across all situations. Whalen and Henker, however, assert that hyperactive children do not wiggle or jiggle excessively, even when confronted with a structured task situation. Instead, they appear to lack the ability to keep their attention on the task at hand.

Impulsivity, which is often associated with hyperactivity, has received considerable attention from numerous researchers. It is characterized by quick and almost instantaneous response to stimulation. Responses appear to be made before thinking or planning occur. In short, the symptoms are rapid and inappropriate responses to tasks and situations. Children who exhibit this characteristic seem to be at the mercy of their impulses. They are "impulse ridden." The opposite of impulsivity is reflectivity. Reflectivity is the tendency to look, think, and consider alternatives before responding.

In summary, many severely and mildly behaviorally disordered children are described as having an abnormally high level of motor activity or as lacking the ability to modulate their motor activity. They also have been described as being impulsive in their actions.

Withdrawal

Behaviors indicative of withdrawal range from not making any special effort to make friends and engage in play activities or conversation to an intense dislike of contact with other people. In addition to withdrawal from human contact, some children display behaviors that indicate a general, overall withdrawal of interest in the environment as a whole—not just social interactions with other people. This can range from simply not being too concerned about what is occurring to complete detachment, indifference, and lack of recognition toward whatever is happening.

Mildly behaviorally disordered children may consistently, in many situations, refrain from initiating conversation, refrain from playing with others, or show unconcern and lack of interest in their environment. These children are frequently referred to as being shy, immature, anxious, socially fearful, reticent, nonentities, and/or wallflowers. Although they may either lack interest in their environment and/or be unconcerned, anxious, or fearful about socially interacting with others, they do not appear oblivious to others and their surroundings as is the case with many very severely disturbed, withdrawn children.

Extremely withdrawn children are often referred to as autistic, schizophrenic, or psychotic. They may show a lack of contact with reality and the subsequent development of their own world. These children may deny the human quality of other people, appear almost totally preoccupied with daydreams or fantasy, and demonstrate an intense disdain for human contact.

It should be noted that depression is sometimes associated with withdrawal. Some children can withdraw from all social contact and display behaviors indicative of extreme unhappiness.

Some mildly and severely behaviorally disordered children do exhibit behaviors indicative of withdrawal from their surroundings and/or parents, peers, and teachers. The degree of severity can range from "unreachable" psychotics to being shy, anxious, and fearful in social situations.

Aggressive Behavior

There are generally two categories assigned to aggressive behavior—physical or verbal (Stainback & Stainback, 1979). Physical aggression includes destructive activities against self or others and/or property—behaviors such as hitting, biting, scratching self or others, knocking holes in walls, grabbing, and spitting. Verbal aggression, on the other hand, involves yelling, cursing, abusive language, threats, and/or self-destructive statements such as "I'm stupid," "I'm dumb," "I'm bad," and/or "God made me a no-good."

If a child is obnoxious, negative, oppositional, and/or generally "nasty," he/she might be labeled mildly behaviorally disordered. Such children may use abusive language, say things in negative tones, not do what is requested of them, cry, tease others, yell, and/or make negative self statements, but they generally are not violent, brutal, destructive of property, or assaultive to the point of physically damaging other people or themselves.

Children who hit, bite, or scratch themselves or others, knock holes in walls, break furniture, and/or seriously threaten others are usually considered to be severely behaviorally disordered. While there are no clear lines of demarcation, children who display aggressive behaviors of less intensity, frequency, consistency, and/or seriousness are usually considered mildly behaviorally disordered, while those who frequently, consistently and over a long period of time display aggressive behaviors of a more "serious" nature generally are classified as being "severely" disordered.

It should be pointed out that "normal" children too display aggressive behaviors such as hitting, verbal assault, teasing, and stealing. The main difference is that aggressive children perform such behaviors at a much higher rate and at a much later age. It also should be added that the more onerous the deed, the higher the frequency and the longer the behavior is displayed, the more severe the problem or "disorder" is generally considered to be.

Helplessness

Some children display behaviors indicative of what has been referred to as "helplessness." They do not appear interested in trying to do anything. They do not establish goals for themselves. When confronted with tasks, they do not respond. They are often described as being depressed, bored, withdrawn, or as having "feelings of hopelessness." Perhaps the main characteristic is the inability to act. This probably stems from the expectation that actions will be unsuccessful—"No matter what I do, it's no use." "This attitude pervades the individual's thinking to such an extent that he perceives even his adequate performances as failures" (Mordock, 1975, p. 396).

The mildly behaviorally disordered child may demonstrate a lack of joy and interest in life. In addition, he may fail to perform academic or complex daily life skills that he previously performed without any assistance.

Table 1-2
Characteristics of Children Who Exhibit Maladaptive Behavior

Definition	Mildly Disturbed	Severely Disturbed	Comment
Intellectual or cognitive ability: as measured by a standardized intelligence	Average IQ score in low normal or dull normal range	Average IQ in mentally retarded range	Actual range for both groups is from retarded to gifted
Achievement: as measured by achievement test scores predominately in reading and arithmetic	Generally achieve at a lower level than their IQ level would infer Children classified as conduct disordered or delinquents further behind than other categories	Markedly deficient in academic areas Generally function at basic levels in language, toileting, eating, rudimentary reading & math	Both levels range the spectrum but most are generally below average Any seriously disturbed high achievers are usually erratic in responding
Underselectivity: difficulty focusing on relevant stimuli and screening out irrelevant stimuli *Overselectivity*: attention to limited aspects of a task, lacks ability to zero out	Difficulty focusing on task at hand Tend to be underselective	Tend to be overselective Often exhibits "gaze aversion," will not make or maintain eye contact	Both levels as a group have attending problems; however, research indicates that the type of attending problem may be different depending upon the seriousness of the emotional disturbance
Hyperactivity: inability to modulate motor behavior in accordance with the demands of a situation *Impulsivity*: quick, almost instantaneous response to stimulation	Frequently exhibit hyperactivity and impulsivity	Frequently exhibit hyperactivity and impulsivity	Reflectivity, the tendency to look, think and consider alternatives, is the reverse of impulsivity

Withdrawal: includes withdrawal from human contact and or general overall withdrawal of interest in the environment	May consistently refrain from initiating conversation, refrain from play with others, or exhibit lack of concern or interest in the environment—shy, immature, wallflower, but not oblivious to surroundings	May lack contact with reality and subsequently develop own world—often called autistic, schizophrenic, psychotic	Depression is sometimes associated with withdrawal
Physical aggression: destructive actions against self and other people and things	May be obnoxious, negative, oppositional and/or generally nasty	May frequently, consistently over a long period of time, display aggressive behaviors of a serious nature	"Normal" children also display aggressive behaviors but usually less onerous and at a lower rate.
Verbal aggression: Includes yelling, cursing, abusive language, threats and self-destructive statements	Generally *not* violent, brutal, destructive, assaultive, or physially damaging to others and self		
Helplessness: does not appear to be interested in trying to do anything, does not set goals for self, often does not respond to assigned tasks	May exhibit lack of joy and interest in life, fail to perform tasks previously exhibited, unwillingness to try, tends to give up quickly	May be highly dependent, pessimistic, and suicidal, may be unable to perform basic life skills	Teacher's task is to provide appropriate training that is based on the level the child is actually functioning

He appears unwilling to try or to put forth even minimal effort. He simply fails to respond or if he does try, he may give up quickly and say, "I just can't do it."

If a child is helpless to the point that he becomes highly dependent, pessimistic about everything, and/or suicidal, he will likely be classified as being psychotic, severely disturbed, or severely behaviorally disordered. The youngster may be unable to perform even basic life skills, such as eating, toileting, dressing, and bathing. When a child is this helpless, he usually fits the pattern or characteristics of the severely retarded child. In such cases it is appropriate to teach self-help or basic daily life skills to these severely disturbed children in the same way one teaches such skills to the severely retarded.

The reader should not conclude that all children with behavior disorders display the characteristics discussed in this section. They show wide variations in the number and type of behaviors exhibited. Some display many of the characteristics discussed; others, only a few or possibly different characteristics than these reviewed. Table 1-2 summarizes the characteristics of children who display maladaptive behavior.

THE PREVALENCE OF CHILDREN WITH BEHAVIOR DISORDERS

No one really knows how many children display behaviors that are out of synchronization with the expectations of those around them. Researchers who have attempted to determine the prevalence of such problems have obtained widely differing results, the main reason being that there is no universally agreed upon definition of the problem. Therefore, different definitions have been employed, and thus differing prevalence figures have resulted. Wood and Zabel (1979) have given another possible explanation for the wide descrepancies in studies of prevalence. They speculated that the particular figure that is obtained depends somewhat on whether the researchers ask classroom teachers (1) to rate children in their classes with behavior problems at that point in time on a "one-shot" screening or (2) to rate those children who have recurrent or persistent problems. The lower figures obtained probably represent those students who exhibit problems *over an extended period of time,* whereas the higher figures are obtained in those studies that tend to identify children who display problem behaviors *at any one point in time.* In other words, there appear to be many students who will exhibit behavior problems at one time or another. There are fewer students, however, who display persistent problems over an extended period of time. Unfortunately, it has not always been clear in the studies conducted to date exactly how the researchers defined "behavioral problems" or whether or not they were attempting (1) to identify children who have at one time or another in their school careers displayed behavioral problems or (2) to identify those children who display persistent problems.

Wichman (1928) conducted one of the first studies designed to estimate the prevalence of children who exhibit problem or abnormal behaviors. Teachers in selected school districts in New York State were requested to rate their pupils' behaviors. The pupils ranged in age from 6 to 12 years. It was concluded that 42 percent of the children had mild adjustment problems and 7 percent were seriously maladjusted. On the other hand, based on extensive surveys conducted in California, Bower (1961) estimated that teachers can expect to find three children in an average class of 30 pupils (10 percent) to show signs of emotional problems. Estimates published by the US Office of Education are much lower than either Bower's or Wichman's figures. Considering the school-age population in the United States as a whole, the U.S. Office of Education (1975) estimates that 2 percent have emotional problems. Schultz, Hirshoren, Manton, and Henderson (1971) reported the results of a survey of state education agencies in regard to estimates of emotional disturbance. They found that estimates range from .5 percent to 15 percent. Kelly, Bullock, and Dykes (1977) studied the perceptions of regular-class teachers in regard to the number of children in their classes displaying behavioral problems. The teachers reported that about 20 percent exhibited behavior problems. Of this number, 12 percent were reported to be mild problems. 6 percent moderate problems, and only 2 percent were seen as having severe problems. After reviewing many studies, Kirk (1972) concluded that most estimates range from 2 percent to 22 percent.

One of the most recent and extensive studies of prevalence was reported by Rubin and Balow (1978). Teachers rated the behaviors of 1586 children from kindergarten through grade six who were participants in an Education Follow-up Project in Minnesota. The children were reported to be similar to the "general" school-age population on measures of IQ, socioeconomic status (SES), and school achievement.

In any single year from 23 percent to 31 percent of the subjects were judged by their teachers as manifesting behavior problems. Long term cumlative prevalence rates were much higher. Among subjects receiving three or more annual ratings, 59 percent were considered as having a behavior problem by at least one teacher and 7.4 percent were considered as having behavior problems by every teacher who rated them. Results indicate that behavior that at least one teacher is willing to classify as a problem is the norm rather than the exception for elementary school children . . . . (Rubin & Balow, 1978, p. 102)

Regardless of how many children display behavioral or emotional problems, several facts have been ascertained from the studies conducted. One, males are more likely to be considered mildly disturbed or having behavior problems than females. It has been estimated that males outnumber females somewhere between 3 to 1 and 7 to 1 (Reinert, 1976). Two, children who display problem behaviors or who are "emotionally disturbed" are not distributed evenly throughout the general population. While "disturbed children can be found in all social classes, lower sociocultural classes produce far more than their share" (Pate, 1963, pp. 244–245).

Within the overall estimates of behavioral difficulties, estimates of the prevalence of severe problems indicate that few children display behaviors that are so different from what is expected that their behaviors are considered abnormally maladaptive or they are considered to be psychotic or seriously disturbed. There are, however, differing figures as to the rate of prevalence. Hermelin and O'Connor (1970) estimate that only 4 or 4.5 per 10,000 school-age children are considered to display such deviant behavior. According to Hintgen and Bryson (1972), the range is from 2 per 10,000 to 4.5 per 10,000 school-age children. It should be noted that reported psychotic conditions are more prevalent among adolescents and the least prevalent for children under five years of age (Clarizio & McCoy, 1976). It is not clear if there is an actual increase with age or whether the differences are a reflection of other factors, such as the inability of parents or teachers to deal with severe problems in the older child, that cause them to refer the child and which results in the child being identified and counted in prevalence figures.

In regard to sex differences, there are more males who manifest severe difficulties than females. The estimates for severe cases range somewhere between 2 to 1 to 5 to 1. In addition, there is some interesting information in regard to the relationship between socioeconomic status and prevalence. Those children classified as psychotic at a young age are likely to have high achieving, intelligent parents whereas children identified as being psychotic at a later age are likely to come from low socioeconomic status families in the marginal IQ range.

Before concluding our discussion of the prevalence of behavioral disorders, it should be noted that there is a high incidence of mild and severe behavioral and emotional problems among children labeled as being mentally retarded, learning disabled, blind, deaf, or otherwise handicapped. In fact, there is probably a much higher incidence of such problems among children who have been given various labels than the so-called "normal" population (Gardner, 1977).

SUMMARY

Terms such as deviant, maladjusted, abnormal, and extreme have been used to refer to the behaviors of children that are significantly out of synchronization with expectations of others. Such children have often been termed "sick," "insane," "emotionally disturbed," "behaviorally disordered," and/or "psychologically disordered." After a child's behavior is determined to be deviant and he is labeled as being behaviorally disordered or emotionally disturbed, he is usually further classified and/or characterized as being, for example, psychoneurotic, psychotic, a conduct disorder, hyperactive, withdrawn, aggressive, socially maladjusted, and/or seriously disturbed.

The characteristics of children tagged emotionally disturbed or behaviorally disordered have been studied and discussed by many researchers and authors. These include such characteristics as withdrawal, hyperactivity, poor academic achievement, aggression, and helplessness. It was stressed that not only can children within the category of behavioral disorders demonstrate almost opposite characteristics but the number of characteristics displayed may vary also.

There is disagreement in regard to the number of school-age children who display maladaptive behaviors. Estimates range from 2 percent (U.S. Office of Education, 1975) to 59 percent (Rubin & Balow, 1978). While the exact number of children who display maladaptive behavior is not known, it is clear that boys outnumber girls. It also is clear that a relatively small percentage of children with behavior disorders have problems so serious as to be labeled psychotic or severely disturbed. Estimates range from 2 to 4.5 per 10,000.

Finally, it was pointed out that most children exhibit antisocial, aggressive, or acting-out behavior at one time or another, and/or withdrawn, anxious or fearful behavior. The major difference between children labeled disturbed and other children relates to how often, how strongly, how long, and in what situations are the behaviors exhibited. There are, however, no clear guidelines in regard to just how often, how strong or intense, and how inappropriate to the situation the behaviors should be before they are designated maladaptive or the child is considered as having a behavioral or emotional disorder.

REFERENCES

American Psychiatric Association. *Diagnostic and Statistical Manual of Mental Disorders* (3rd ed). Washington, DC: American Psychiatric Association, 1979.

Baker, A.M. Cognitive functioning of psychotic children: A reappraisal. *Exceptional Children*, 1979, *45*, 344–348.

Bartak, L., & Rutter, M., Special educational treatment of autistic children: A comparative study—I. Design of study and characteristics of units. *Journal of Child Psychology and Psychiatry*, 1973, *14*, 161–179.

Blau, A. The nature of childhood schizophrenia. *Journal of the American Academy of Child Psychiatry*, 1962, *2*, 225–235.

Bower, E.M. *The education of emotionally handicapped children: A report to the California Legislature*. Sacramento: California State Department of Education, 1961.

Bower, E.M. *Early identification of emotionally handicapped children in school* (2nd ed.). Springfield: Thomas, 1969.

Bryan, J.H., & Bryan, T.H. *Exceptional children*. Sherman Oaks, CA: Alfred, 1979.

Clarizio, H.F., & McCoy, G.F. *Behavior disorders in children*. New York: Crowell, 1976.

DeMyer, M.K. The nature of neuropsychological disability in autistic children. *Journal of Autism and Childhood Schizophrenia*, 1975, *5*, 109–128.

Deno, E.N. *Educating children with emotional, learning and behavior problems*. Minneapolis: Leadership Training Institute/Special Education, University of Minnesota, 1978.

Gardner, W.I. *Learning and behavior characteristics of exceptional children and Youth*. Boston: Allyn & Bacon, 1977.

Gittelman, M., & Birch, G. Childhood schizophrenia, intellect, neurologic status, perinatal risk, prognosis, and family pathology. *Archives of General Psychiatry*, 1967, *17*, 16–25.

Graubard, P.S. The extent of academic retardation in a residential treatment center. *Journal of Educational Research*, 1964, *58*, 78–80.

Graubard, P.S. The use of indigenous grouping as the reinforcing agent in teaching disturbed delinquents to learn. In N.J. Long, W.C. Morse, & R.G. Newman (Eds.), *Conflict in the classroom* (2nd ed.). Belmont, CA: Wadsworth, 1971.

Graubard, P.S. Children with behavioral disabilities. In L.M. Dunn (Ed.), *Exceptional children in the schools* (2nd ed.). New York: Holt, Rinehart, & Winston, 1973.

Group for the Advancement of Psychiatry (GAP), Committee on Child Psychiatry. *Psychopathological disorders in childhood: Theoretical consideration and a proposed classification* (Vol. VI). Report No. 62. New York: GAP, June 1966.

Hermelin, B., & O'Connor, N. *Psychological experiments with autistic children*. Elmsford, NY: Pergamon, 1970.

Hintgen, J.M., & Bryson, C.Q. Recent developments in the study of early childhood psychoses: Infantile autism, childhood schizophrenia, and related disorders. *Schizophrenia Bulletin*, 1972, *5*, 8–54.

Hutt, C., & Hutt, S.J. Biological studies of autism. *Journal of Special Education,* 1969, *3,* 3–14.

Jenkins, R.L., & Hewitt, L. Types of personality structure encountered in child guidance clinics. *American Journal of Orthopsychiatry,* 1944, *14,* 83–94.

Kanfer, F.H., & Saslow, G. Behavioral diagnosis. In C.M. Franks (Ed.), *Behavior therapy: Appraisal and status.* New York: McGraw-Hill, 1969.

Kanner, L. Autistic disturbances of affective contact. *Nervous Child,* 1943, *2,* 217–250.

Kauffman, J.M. *Characteristics of children's behavior disorders.* Columbus, OH: Merrill, 1977

Kelly, T., Bullock, L., & Dykes, M. Behavioral disorders: Teachers' perceptions. *Exceptional Children,* 1977, *43,* 316–318.

Kirk, S.A. *Educating exceptional children* (2nd ed.). Boston: Houghton Mifflin, 1972.

Kirk, S.A., & Gallagher, J.J. *Educating exceptional children.* (3rd ed). Boston: Houghton Mifflin, 1979.

Kvaraceus, W.C. & Miller, W.B. *Delinquent behavior* (Vol. 1). Washington, DC: National Education Association, 1959.

Lapouse, R., & Monk, M.A. Behavior deviations in a representative sample of children: Variations by sex, age, race, social class and family size. *American Journal of Orthopsychiatry,* 1964, *34,* 436–446.

Lovaas, O.I., Koegel, R.L., Simmons, J.Q., & Long, J.S. Some generalization and follow-up measures on autistic children in behavior therapy. *Journal of Applied Behavior Analysis,* 1973, *6,* 131–166.

Lyons, D.F., & Powers, V. Follow-up study of elementary school children exempted from Los Angeles City Schools during 1960–1961. *Exceptional Children,* 1963, *30,* 155–162.

MacFarlane, J., Allen, L., & Honzik, M. *A developmental study of the behavior problems of normal children between 21 months and 14 years.* Berkeley: University of California Press, 1955.

Mordock, J.B. *The other children: An introduction to exceptionality.* New York: Harper & Row, 1975.

Motto, J.J., & Wilkins, G.S. Educational achievement of institutionalized emotionally disturbed children. *Journal of Educational Research,* 1968, *61,* 218–221.

O'Leary, K.D. The assessment of psychopathology in children. In H.C. Quay & J.S. Werry (Eds.), *Psychopathological disorders of childhood.* New York: Wiley, 1972.

Pate, J.E. Emotionally disturbed and socially maladapted children. In L.M. Dunn (Ed.), *Exceptional children in the schools.* New York: Holt, Rinehart & Winston, 1963.

Prugh, D. G., Engel, M., & Morse, W.C. Emotional disturbance in children. In N. Hobbs (Ed.), *Issues in the classification of Children* (Vol. I). San Francisco: Jossey-Bass, 1975.

Quay, H.C. Patterns of aggression, withdrawal and immaturity. In H.C. Quay & J.S. Werry (Eds.), *Psychopathological disorders of childhood.* New York: Wiley, 1972.

Redlich, F., & Hollingshead, A.B. *Social class and mental illness.* New York: Wiley, 1958.

Reinert, H.R. *Children in conflict.* St. Louis: Mosby, 1976.

Rhodes, W.C. The disturbing child. A problem of ecological management. *Exceptional Children,* 1967, *33,* 449–455.

Rimland, B. *Infantile autism.* New York: Appleton-Century-Crofts, 1964.

Rimland, B. Inside the mind of the autistic savant. *Psychology Today,* 1978, *12,* 69–80.

Robinson, N.M., & Robinson, H.B. *The mentally retarded child: A psychological approach* (2nd ed.). New York: McGraw-Hill, 1976.

Rosenhan, D.L. On being sane in insane places. *Science,* 1973, 179, 250–258.

Rubin, R., & Balow, B. Prevalence of teacher-identified behavior problems: A longitudinal study. *Exceptional Children,* 1978, *45,* 102–111.

Schreibman, L., & Lovaas, O.I. Overselective response to social stimuli by autistic children. *Journal of Abnormal Child Psychology,* 1973, *1,* 152–168.

Schultz, E.W., Hirshoren, A., Manton, A.B., & Henderson, R.A. Special education for the emotionally disturbed. *Exceptional Children,* 1971, *38,* 313–319.

Shea, T.M. *Teaching children and youth with behavior disorders.* St. Louis: Mosby, 1978.

Silberberg, N.E., & Silberberg, M.C. School achievement and delinquency. *Review of Educational Research,* 1971, *41,* 17–32.

Smith, R.M. & Neisworth, J.T. *The exceptional child: A functional approach.* New York: McGraw-Hill, 1975.

Spivack, G., Swift, M., & Prewitt, J. Syndromes of disturbed classroom behavior: A behavioral diagnostic system for elementary schools. *Journal of Special Education,* 1971, *5,* 269–292.

Stainback, W.C., & Stainback, S.B. Controlling severe forms of maladaptive behavior. *Behavioral Disorders,* 1979, *4,* 99–115.

Stone, F., & Rowley, V.N. Educational disability in emotionally disturbed children. *Exceptional Children,* 1964, *30,* 423–426.

Swanson, H.L., & Reinert, H.R. *Teaching strategies for children in conflict.* St. Louis: Mosby, 1979.

U.S. Office of Education. *Estimated number of handicapped children in the United States, 1974–1975.* Washington, DC: The Office, 1975.

Whalen, C.K., & Henker, B. Psychostimulants and children: A review and analysis. *Psychological Bulletin,* 1976, *83,* 1113–1130.

Wichman, E.K. *Children's behavior and teachers' attitudes.* New York: Commonwealth Fund, 1928.

Wood, F.W., & Zabel, R.H. *Making sense of reports on the incidence of behavioral disorders/emotional disturbance in school populations.* Minneapolis: University of Minnesota, 1979.

SELECTED READINGS FOR FURTHER STUDY

Deno, E.N. *Educating children with emotional, learning and behavior problems.* Minneapolis: Leadership Training Institute/Special Education, University of Minnesota, 1978.

Kauffman, J.M. *Characteristics of children's behavior disorders*. Columbus, OH: Merrill, 1977.

Kelly, T., Bullock, L., & Dykes, M. Behavioral disorders: Teachers' perceptions. *Exceptional Children,* 1977, *43,* 316–318.

Prugh, D.G., Engel, M., & Morse, W.C. Emotional disturbance in children. In N. Hobbs (Ed.), *Issues in the classification of children* (Vol. I). San Francisco: Jossey-Bass, 1975.

Rubin R., & Balow, B. Prevalence of teacher-identified behavior problems: A longitudinal study. *Exceptional Children,* 1978, *45,* 102–111.

U.S. Office of Education. *Estimated number of handicapped children in the United States, 1974–1975*. Washington, DC: The Office, 1975.

Wood, F.W., & Zabel, R.H. *Making sense of reports on the incidence of behavioral disorders/emotional disturbance in school populations*. Minneapolis: University of Minnesota, 1979.

Woods, D.J. Carving nature at its joints? Observations on a revised psychiatric nomenclature. *Journal of Clinical Psychology,* 1979, *35,* (4), 912–920.

2

Historical Development of Treatments for Maladaptive Behavior

A historical perspective is important when attempting to understand, build, and expand upon past and current practices in order to foster future progress. As pointed out by Blatt (1975), "from history flows more than knowledge, more than prescriptions, more than how it was—how we might try to make it become" (p. 402). This chapter takes note of many of the landmark events within the past three centuries regarding the treatment of children who exhibit maladaptive behaviors, including those labeled seriously emotionally disturbed.

1700s

During the first half of the 1700s children who displayed maladaptive behaviors experienced a difficult life. Although a few people tried to protect them, generally they experienced abuse, neglect, excessive punishment, and cruelty under the guise of treatment. Due to the idea of demon possession, religious individuals were often sought as a source of treatment. Often treatment involved beatings with a cat-o-nine tails, isolation, and food deprivation, which frequently resulted in death rather than cure.

The following description by a clergyman in 1713 of what happened to a seven-year-old girl describes the treatment that children who displayed maladaptive behaviors sometimes received.

She was placed in the custody of a minister known for his rigid orthodoxy. The minister, who saw in her ways the machinations of a "baneful and infernal" power, used a number of would-be therapeutic devices. He laid her on a bench and beat her with a cat-o-nine tails. He locked her in a dark pantry. He subjected her to a period of starvation. He clothed her in a frock of burlap. Under these circumstances, the child did not last long. She died after a few months, and everybody felt relieved. The minister was amply rewarded for his efforts. . . . (Kanner, 1962 p. 98)

The maladaptive behavior of the child described consisted of her refusal to join others in prayer and a demonstrated fear of the black-robed preacher. If the same child was born in the late 1700s after the American and French revolutions, she might have received better treatment. During this period there was a lot of discussion and emphasis on the rights of each individual. At about this time Phillipe Pinel, a distinguished French physician, became interested in the handicapped. He strongly believed in individual freedom and human dignity for all people. Pinel unchained many of the "idiots" (retarded) and "insane" (disturbed) who had been confined and brutalized for years in the Bicetre Hospital in Paris. The behavior of these severely deranged individuals improved remarkably after being treated with respect and given humane and kind treatment. Pinel's approach was termed "moral" treatment (psychological, not religious). It became widely known in Europe and America and was used in lunatic asylums in the treatment of children as well as adults.

Toward the end of the 1700s and during the early 1800s, the study and work of Jean Itard, who studied under Pinel, received wide recognition. Itard was known for his work with Victor,[1] a wild boy about 12 years old who was found living alone in the woods near Averyon, France. According to Itard (1962), he was a "scared, inarticulate creature who trotted and grunted like the beasts of the fields" (p. vi). Itard's methods of treatment influenced many of today's approaches to the treatment and education of the retarded and disturbed. His approach involved sensory stimulation, application of reinforcement principles, and the development of speech through imitation.

By the end of the 1700s professionals in American were becoming interested in the treatment and education of idiots and the insane. One of the most noted was Benjamin Rush, considered by many to be the father of American psychiatry. Rush disliked punishment that inflicted severe pain. He advocated kind and prudent methods of behavior control and emphasized the need for education and training.

---

*According to John Wing (1976) Victor showed most of the features of severe emotional disturbance, although many professionals have described Victor as probably being severely retarded.

1800s

During the 1800s individuals who were considered insane were often placed in lunatic asylums or locked away in back rooms or closets in the family home. While some were subjected to cruel and inhumane treatment, others received kind and effective treatment. Some asylums initiated "moral" treatment programs during the first half of the 1800s, including therapeutic activities and minimum restraint and kindness because many professionals felt that the insane could be helped. Indicative of this attitude was a statement made by Brigham in 1845: "There is no case incapable of some amendment. . ." (p. 335).

By the middle of the nineteenth century, individuals who were emotionally or intellectually disordered had gained many friends in the United States. Dorothea Dix, the great reformer, worked hard for improvements in conditions in asylums. Samuel Howe pushed for the education of all children, including those who today would be considered retarded and/or disturbed. Interest in the emotional disturbance of children, particularly serious emotional disturbance, was further fostered during this period by a chapter entitled "Insanity of Early Life" included in a text by Henry Maudsley, written originally in 1867 and revised in 1880, that reported accounts of maladaptive behavior in young children. Maudsley (1880) suggested infantile psychoses as a classification. There was, however, opposition to Maudsley's writings from those who continued to deny the existence of mental illness in young children.

Unfortunately, cruel and inhumane treatment was intertwined with much of the positive practices of the early and middle 1800s. Many of the insane were warehoused in large, isolated institutions and forgotten, without the benefits of treatment. They were sometimes beaten, restrained for days, or isolated in bare cells because of their strange and uncontrollable behavior. In addition, some professionals held bizarre ideas about the causes of insanity. For instance, many believed that masturbation caused or at least aggravated insanity. As a result, castration and ovariotomy were practiced in order to stop masturbation in idiotic, insane, and epileptic children.

Fortunately, not all professionals believed that masturbation caused insanity. According to Kauffman (1977), some psychiatrists in the early 1800s identified etiological factors in children's disturbing behaviors that today are given serious consideration. Parkinson in 1807 wrote about the interaction of the different temperaments children are born with and parental rearing practices, such as overprotection, overindulgence, and inconsistent discipline.

There was an increased interest in the mid 1800s in regard to possible explanations of maladaptive behavior other than on "pseudotheologic and pseudomoralistic grounds" (Kanner, 1962). This is evident from some of the anecdotal writings of that time. Kanner (1962) gives an account of a case presented by Descuret (1841):

> [A] boy who lived with a nurse during the first two years of his life. When he was taken to his home, he grew pale, sad and morose, refused to eat, and did not respond to his parents. The usual toys and diversions had no effect. On medical advice, the nurse was called back and, in the father's words, "from that moment on he began to live again." Eventually, he was separated from the nurse, first for a few hours, then for a whole day, then for a week, until finally the child was accustomed to her absence. (pp. 98–99)

In the latter part of the century, the focus was directed primarily to diagnosis and classification. In 1883 Emil Kraepelin published his text, *Lehrfuch der Psychiatric (Theories of Psychology)*, which is considered by many to have established the basis for the present psychiatric classification system. This period became known as the "descriptive era"; the main emphasis was on diagnosing and labeling rather than treatment. Indicative of this emphasis was the legal distinction made between feeblemindedness (mental retardation) and insanity (emotional disturbance) in England in 1886.

In the last half of the 1800s many professionals developed an attitude of fatalism. As Kanner (1962) stated, "There was a tendency toward fatalism which saw in the disorders the irreversible results of heredity, degeneracy, masturbation, overwork, religious preoccupation, intestinal parasites, or sudden changes of temperature" (p. 99). The prevailing belief was that insanity was irreversible, and this fact precluded effective treatment. Many asylums had become by the end of the 1800s large warehouses where the insane and idiots could be placed so as to be isolated from the rest of society.

While there was an attitude of fatalism prevalent at the close of the 1800s, it should not be concluded that nothing was being done in regard to treatment. There were some attempts. The writings of two Frenchmen, Paul Moreau De Tours (1888) and Marcel Manheimer (1899), stressed the importance of preventative treatment for children; they exemplify the concern on the part of at least some professionals for treatment. Other texts by H. Emminghaus (1887) in Germany and S. S. Ireland (1898) in Great Britain also were attempts to collect and organize information regarding mental diseases of children.

1900s

The twentieth century is popularly regarded by professionals as the "era of concern" for all children, including the handicapped. Lewis (1974) points out that "the 1900s was indeed an era of awakening not only in the areas of psychology and psychiatry, but also in education" (p. 8). Ellen Key, the Swedish sociologist, forecast this concern for children with the publication of her widely read book *Century of the Child* in 1909. Her prediction appears to have been an accurate one. (It is interesting to note that 1979 was designated as the "Year of the Child" by the United Nations.) Many advances have been made on the behalf of children during the 1900s.

A few examples of early developments concerning child welfare include the Clinic for Child Development at Yale University, founded in 1911 by Arnold Gesell. In 1909 William Healy established in Chicago the Juvenile Psychopathic Institute for the psychological and sociological study of juvenile delinquents. In 1912 the U.S. Children's Bureau was created by Congress to deal with all matters related to the welfare of children. In 1931 the first psychiatric hospital for children, the Bradley Home, was opened in Rhode Island.

At the beginning of the twentieth century the work done on testing and evaluation of children in France by Alfred Binet, working with Theodore Simon, led to the development of an intelligence test in 1905 that enabled a better discrimination to be made between the disturbed and retarded. Shortly thereafter, in 1921, Herman Rorschach, a Swiss psychiatrist, attempted to measure emotional and personality variables in a formal way by focusing on an individual's "inner life"; from his work came the present-day projective tests. There has been a proliferation of tests and evaluation instruments in the twentieth century, particularly since World War II. In addition to tests of intelligence and personality, there were screening and other evaluation instruments. These were widely used not only in education, psychiatry, and other professions, but also in industry and government. Development of screening instruments profoundly affected the identification of the behaviorally handicapped. Probably, the best known screening instrument was that by Bower and Lambert (1962) to identify children with emotional handicaps in the public schools of California. It should be mentioned here that, historically speaking, within the testing field there has been a growing disenchantment over the years since Binet's time with the norm-referenced test of the variety developed by Binet and a growing interest in what has been called criterion-referenced test (see Chapter 3).

The early 1900s saw the establishment of community child guidance clinics to meet the needs of emotionally disturbed children and the offering of mental hygiene courses in the public schools as a preventative measure for emotional disturbance. The story of Clifford Beers contributed greatly to the mental hygiene movement. Beers was a law student who after several asylum placements was cured at the home of a friendly attendant. He wrote a book that gained considerable acclaim, *A Mind That Found Itself* (1908), about the agonies of his ordeal. Subsequently, Beers, with Adolph Meyer and William James, founded the National Committee for Mental Hygiene (1909). In light of the present trends in special education (see Chapter 3), it is interesting to note that in 1920 one of the committee members, Thomas Haines (1925), stated that he believed the public schools should be concerned about the welfare of all exceptional children including the "psychopathic" (seriously disturbed) as well as those who exhibit more mild behavior problems.

Teacher training for the education of handicapped children was begun in 1914 in Michigan. Legislation regarding the care and education of the handicapped was enacted in many states in the first half of the century, and funds were appropriated for the extra cost involved (Henry, 1950). In addition, in the early 1900s several associations to meet the needs of the handicapped were organized such as the Council for Exceptional Children in 1922. National organizations concerned for the handicapped were founded throughout the century, including, to name only a few, the Council for Children with Behavioral Disorders (1964), National Society for Autistic Children (1965), and the American Association for the Education of the Severely/Profoundly Handicapped (1974).

Much literature was becoming available in the 1920s on childhood schizophrenia (e.g., De Sanctis, 1925; Hamburger, 1926; Ziehen, 1926). The looseness of the term "childhood schizophrenia," however, created diagnosis problems, and in 1933 Potter more specifically delineated the concept so that there could be greater consensus among professionals. During the 1930s and early 1940s information in the literature regarding emotionally disturbed children began to appear increasingly (Baker & Stullken, 1938). In the 1930s there were consistent attempts to study seriously emotionally disturbed children in regard to diagnosis, etiology, therapy, and prognosis (Kanner, 1962). It was also during this time that Leo Kanner of Johns Hopkins University published the first edition in 1935 of his now famous textbook *Childhood Psychiatry* (Kanner, 1972).

Just as the literature flourished so did the categories and classification systems for emotionally handicapped children (Despert, 1938, 1968; Kanner, 1943; Potter, 1933). The focus was on identifying symptom patterns that could be lumped together. Writings regarding the onset of symptoms to distinguish patterns or categories of disturbances became popular. This topic was addressed internationally by Ssucharewa (1932) in Russia, Lutz (1937) in Switzerland, and Despert (1938) in the United States. It was felt that once the exact disorder could be delineated, there would be a better chance of determining the etiology or cause of the disorder. The rationale was that if the cause could be uncovered, knowledge of how to proceed with treatment would follow (Kazdin, 1975); then treatment should be based on the unique characteristics and underlying pathology of different types of disorders (the medical model).

Among the most notable of categories for seriously disturbed children were childhood schizophrenia (Potter, 1933), Kanner's syndrome or early infantile autism (Kanner, 1943, 1972), and symbiotic infantile psychosis (Mahler, 1952). These and other severe disorders were subsumed under the general category childhood psychosis (Bergman & Escalona, 1949; Robinson & Vitale, 1954). The terms "insane" (emotionally disturbed) and "idiot" (mentally retarded) had by the 1930s fallen into disrepute. The term "emotionally disturbed" crept into the literature during this period; however, there is no definitive information available regarding the origin of the term or its definition. According to Kanner (1962), the term has been sometimes used "as a generality with no terminologic boundaries whatever and sometimes with reference to certain psychotic and near psychotic conditions" (p. 101).

With the multiplying of categories, a group of professionals advocated a return to the pre-Kreaepelin era of indefinite labeling (Rank, 1949). As Szurek (1956) stated, "We are beginning to consider it clinically fruitless, and even unnecessary, to draw any sharp dividing lines between a condition that one could consider psychoneurotic and another that one could call psychosis, autism, atypical development, or schizophrenia" (p. 522). It should be noted, however, that some professionals have vehemently reacted to the idea of reducing the emphasis on categories and labels. For example, Kanner (1962) stated:

> A historical survey teaches us that progress has always consisted of a breaking down of diffuse generic concepts into specific categories. We no longer speculate about fevers generically; bacteriology knows of totally different varieties of febrile illness. We no longer speak about insanity generically; we recognize a variety of psychotic reaction types. We no longer speak about feeblemindedness generically; we know that there is a vast difference between mongolism, microcephaly, and phenylketonuria; it would not occur to anyone to lump them together in any meaningful investigation. I believe that the time has come to acknowledge the heterogeneity of the many conditions comprised under the generic term, "emotionally disturbed children." (p. 101–102)

(In special education the controversy regarding labels and categories has not been resolved to date. While many professionals still adhere to categories, others question the practice.)

Along with the growing literature on childhood emotional disorders, there was an increased interest in the education of these children. In regard to school arrangements, a new concept introduced at the beginning of the 1900s was the visiting teacher. This concept became widely recognized and flourished in the United States during this period as a way of dealing with handicapped and/or troublesome children.

In 1953 the first day school program (private) for seriously emotionally disturbed children was founded by Carl Fenichel in New York. Other programs set up for the emotionally disturbed were residential in nature, such as Pionner House for delinquents in Detroit (Redl & Wineman, 1951, 1952), the children's program at Bellevue Psychiatric Hospital organized in 1934 by Bender in New York City (Berkowitz, 1974; Rothman, 1974), and the Sonja Shankman Orthogenic School at the University of Chicago (Bettelheim, 1950; Bettelheim & Sylvester, 1948). In 1946 New York City instituted school programs for emotionally disturbed children through the "600" schools. Berkowitz and Rothman (1967) have provided a description of the program.

> Although the first "600" schools were day schools located in regular school buildings in the community, almost immediately a number of residential diagnostic and treatment settings for disturbed children were accepted into the division, and "600" schools were organized for them. These schools were created to provide a therapeutic school environment for children who could not be taught effectively in regular schools and whose behavior, whether aggressive, bizarre, or withdrawn, could not be tolerated in the ordinary classroom. (p. 18)

In regard to intervention approaches, psychoanalysis held the forefront during the early years of the twentieth century. Except for a "radical" named John B. Watson who, based on the animal studies of Pavlov, made a statement in 1913 "Psychology as a Behaviorist Views It" regarding the placement of focus on conscious observable behaviors rather than subconscious ones, little was done in the first half of the 1900s that did not have a psychoanalytic flavor. The psychoanalytic approach is based on the writings of Sigmund Freud. Professionals who follow his approach, mostly psychiatrists, attempt to understand the individual's emotional difficulties in terms of his/her inner "psyche" and subconscious sexual motivations, instincts, drives, and conflicts. In short, maladaptive behavior is viewed as symptomatic of underlying causes that are thought to originate in traumatic childhood events and conflicts, which are subsequently repressed (Kirk & Gallagher, 1979). It was (and is) basically a cathartic or "talking-out-your-problems" form of therapy. The focus is on helping the individual uncover and understand or gain insight into his/her unconscious conflicts and motivations. Play therapy (Axline, 1947) and art-and-craft activities, rather than talking about past events and problems, are often employed to provide children with a way of expressing and bringing to the surface their inner conflicts. A permissive environment is usually established wherein the child will feel accepted and free to express inner feelings.

During the middle of the century several educational approaches, which remain popular to date, evolved from psychoanalytical concepts. Among others, Bettelheim (1950), Redl and Wineman (1951, 1952), Morse (1967), and Berkowitz and Rothman (1960) developed and employed educational methods based on psychoanalytic concepts. Bettelheim (1950) proposed "milieu therapy," which involves establishing an environment that fosters good mental health. "Milieu," a word of French derivation, in Bettelheim's terms means treatment by environment. Redl and Wineman (1951, 1952) proposed the "life-space interviewing (LSI)" approach, in which an interview or discussion is held with the child at the time of a crisis or conflict in order to help the child understand the causes of the problem. It is essentially a cathartic technique in which the teacher talks through with the child the crisis or problem at the time it occurs. Morse (1967) proposed the "crisis-teacher" concept; this involves the school employing an "extra" teacher who is not only trained in education, but is also competent in psychological interventions, such as LSI, individual counseling, and group interaction. In other words, the crisis teacher is an extra staff member who is trained to interact with a child during a crisis situation. Berkowitz and Rothman developed a variety of educational methods for emotionally disturbed children based on psychoanalytic concepts and published a description of these in their now classic book, *The Disturbed Child: Recognition and Psychoeducational Therapy in the Classroom* (1960). Essentially, they believe that a child must feel accepted and secure in his relationship with his teacher so that he will feel free to express his inner thoughts and conflicts and gradually, as a result, come to understand and gain insight about himself and his emotions and behaviors.

While these pioneers evolved much of their thinking and work from basic psychoanalytical concepts, they have modified their views over the years to incorporate structure and behavioral control concepts within their approaches. Also, most of the approaches that have been mentioned take an educational slant and focus toward present factors in the child's environment and his affective and cognitive behaviors with a de-emphasis on deep-seated, sexually latent, underlying conflicts and causes. There is still a focus, however, on getting the child to "understand" or "gain insight" about the causes of his behavior. Many of these ideas gained wider acceptance and practice in special-education circles after the publication of Long, Morse, and Newman's *Conflict in the Classroom* in 1965, with subsequent editions in 1971 and 1976. It should be noted that most professionals who adhere to these ideas and methods prefer the term "psychoeducational" rather than "psychoanalytic." Psychoeducational reflects the educational slant, focusing on intervention within the educational setting rather than removal from the educational setting for therapy. It also differentiates these ideas from the more pure psychoanalytic concepts.

> Psychoeducational is somewhat difficult to define, but is generally thought to mean a focus on affective and cognitive factors in behavior. One can identify persons who describe the psychoeducational approach (e.g., Carl Fenichel, Nicholas J. Long, William C. Morse, Ruth G. Newman. . .) much more easily than one can describe the major features of the approach itself. Nevertheless, it seems clear from the discourse of psychoeducational proponents that (a) the psychodynamic concepts of instincts, drives, and needs are taken into account but (b) intervention is focused on the cognitive and affective problems of children, and (c) it is assumed that by resolving the affective and cognitive problems of children, i.e., by helping the child gain insight into his needs and motivations, his problem behavior will be changed. (Kauffman, 1977, pp. 187–188)

Many of the approaches that evolved from psychoanalytic concepts that remain popular today incorporate concepts from humanistic psychology. Humanistic psychology is more subjective, socially oriented, and holistic than psychoanalysis while being less fatalistic and sexist. In the educational field, those who follow the concepts of humanistic psychology advocate more freedom in education. They believe that education should be more in the hands of the students and less determined by authorities. Among the humanists, well-known psychologists such as Maslow, Allport, Combs, and Rogers can be included as well as special educators such as Knoblock, Dennison, and Grossman. Generally speaking, humanists in special education have called for more freedom and openness in education with a stress on self-determination and self-evaluation. According to Knoblock (1973), humanists recognize "the growth potential residing in each person as he moves toward his goal of self-realization. . . [since humanism] attempts to impose less and explore more" (Knoblock, 1973, p. 359).

Knoblock (1973) has described an open-education program based on humanistic principles designed for emotionally disturbed children. The educational environment is set up to provide freedom and flexibility in which the children are provided the opportunity to "act out their feelings" and the teacher can react and assist the children to work through and gain an understanding of their true feelings. Knoblock points out that the teacher in an open classroom does not act as an authoritarian figure who makes all of the decisions. The children are permitted to make some decisions, and, therefore, they are able to exert a degree of control over their environment. This type of approach is expected to assist each child in overcoming any feelings of inadequacy or a negative self-concept by providing for constructive ego development.

As mentioned earlier, humanistic education concepts have been integrated into many psychodynamic/psychoeducational approaches; or, vice versa, psychoeducational concepts have been integrated into humanistic approaches. Knoblock (1973) has described how the two approaches (open education/humanistic and psychodynamic/psychoeducational) interrelate.

> Open education for troubled children is, in my opinion, a logical extension of the psychoeducational model. The tenets of this model apply to open education, and, in fact, by creating an open environment we may be enhancing the opportunity to implement approaches commonly thought of as psychoeducational. For example, both models advocate the integration of affect and content in classrooms. Both rely on acknowledging and responding to the feelings and behaviors of children. . . . Both believe that often learning will take place only if it is put in the context of relationships and only if the learner feels good enough about himself as a learner and person. (pp. 362–363)

A radical departure from the psychoanalytic concepts as well as subjective interpretation of and permissiveness toward inappropriate behaviors occurred during the early 1960s. Special educators began applying the techniques and methods of behavioral psychology. The behavioral model follows an empirical, scientific emphasis. From this viewpoint, it is believed that many maladaptive (disturbed, disordered) behaviors are learned and that maladaptive behavior (learned or not) can be most effectively dealt with by clearly specifying the problem behavior and controlling the child's environment—more specifically, the antecedents and consequences that have the potential to influence the behavior(s).

Although noted in 1913 by Watson (respondent conditioning) and in the 1930s by Skinner (operant conditioning), behaviorism was considered too radical for use with public school children until the late 1950s and early 1960s when, among others, Haring and Phillips (1962) and Whelan and Haring (1966) began showing the effects of structure and contingency control in the modification of the behaviors of emotionally disturbed public school children. Haring, Whelan, and others introduced many special educators to the ideas and concepts of behaviorism. Hewett (1967, 1968) also worked within the behavioral framework in setting up his now famous projects and studies on the "engineered classroom." Much of this early work in special education was done with mildly and moderately disturbed children. While some psychologists were applying behavioral techniques with seriously disturbed individuals in settings such as psychiatric hospitals, special educators were working primarily with the mildly and moderately disturbed. During the late 1960s and ealry 1970s, however, special educators increasingly applied what they read in the literature regarding the effects of behavioral techniques on the severely maladaptive and bizarre behaviors of children to children labeled severely disturbed or psychotic. They were particularly influenced by the work of Lovass and his associates (Lovaas, 1966, 1967; Lovaas & Koegel, 1973) and Hewett (1968) regarding how behavioral principles could be utilized to teach speech, language, reading, and self-help skills to these children. Lovass and Hewett did most of their research at the University of California at Los Angeles.

In addition to behaviorism, the ecological approach gained widespread popularity in the late 1960s and early 1970s. In the ecological approach the locus of the disturbance is perceived as not in the child but in the interaction of the child and environment (Rhodes, 1970). Thus the intervention centers on the environmental influences of the family, community, and school, in addition to the child. Project Re-Ed (Hobbs, 1965, 1966) is one of the most widely recognized applied projects that was developed in accordance with the ecological viewpoint. It focuses on all aspects of the child and the environment—the changing of the social system that includes the child, home, school, church, and community in ways that will promote better congruence and less discordance among elements of the social system. For example, in addition to the treatment the child receives, intervention occurs in the home and community to modify them in ways that will allow a healthier interaction and interface between the community, home, and child.

Another strategy that attracted many educators in the 1960s and early 1970s was the developmental approach. This approach is characterized by a change from simple activities, behaviors, and concepts to those of ever increasing complexity. It implies a classroom instructional sequence with hierarchical development. In the developmental approach for intervention the orientation is placed on normal behavior as a guide for learning. Deviation from the "normal standard" is considered to be a "lag" rather than abnormal or deviant.

Swanson and Reinert (1979) point out that the developmental approach includes two models: the "cognitive-interpersonal model" and "skill development." The cognitive-interpersonal model tends to rely heavily for direction on the work of theorists such as Piaget, Gagne, Kohlberg, Bloom, and Erickson. Emphasis in teaching focuses on the child as opposed to specific content and on cognitive, language, and affective processes that are applied across content areas. The skill-development approach is based on the writings of B. F. Skinner and the behavioral version of intervention. Those who advocate a skill-development approach typically argue that emotionally disturbed children need to develop specific skills that will enable them to compete effectively in school. The focus is on the child's observable performance in curricular content that has been task analyzed and sequenced in hierarchical steps.

Hewett (1967) has developed one of the most widely recognized developmental educational programs for disturbed children. His program includes a developmental sequence of seven educational goals. It incorporates behavior modification procedures to enable the children to reach the goals. As children progress in the program, they move up the following developmental sequence: (1) attention, (2) response, (3) order, (4) exploration, (5) social skills, (6) mastery, and (7) achievement. According to Hewett (1967), the developmental strategy

> hypothesizes that in order for successful living to occur, the child must pay attention, respond, follow directions, freely and accurately explore the environment, and function appropriately in relation to others. It further hypothesizes that the learning of these behaviors occurs during the normal course of development from infancy to school age, and failure to learn any or all of them may preclude the child's being ready for school. For such a child they constitute the "somethings" he must learn in the process of getting ready for school while he is actually there. (p. 42)

In the early 1970s William Rhodes directed a project at the University of Michigan to organize the scattered literature on behavior disorders, including information related to the approaches discussed above. Rhodes and his associates (1972a, 1972b, 1974) published a series of volumes under the general title *A Study of Child Variance* that summarized the various viewpoints and approaches that emerged in the twentieth century concerning the education of children with behavior disorders. The reader interested in obtaining additional information is referred to these volumes as well as a more recent publication entitled *Emotionally Disturbed and Deviant Children* by Rhodes and Paul (1978).

It should be evident from the discussion of intervention approaches that during the 1960s and 1970s there was a gradual shift from the medical model to more of a developmental/behavioral model (Wolfensberger 1977)—a model focusing on the programmatic needs of the handicapped rather than on causation, the previous focus.

This "model" shift influenced classification and labeling trends (see Hobbs, 1975). Earlier in the century labels flourished that were based on the bizarre symptoms that individuals display, for example, early infantile autism and childhood schizophrenia. In the later years labels or phrases such as "preacademic skills" and "basic skill development" began to appear that were based on the individual's functioning level and educational needs. As yet, however, there are no widely accepted ways of defining or classifying children according to educational needs. Sontag, Smith, and Sailor (1977) suggest that we classify children according to the type of instruction needed—general special education (remedial academic instruction), severely handicapped education (basic skill development), and early education (divided into the areas of skill development and preacademic remediation). Haring, Nietupski, and Hamre-Nietupski (1976) suggest that we define the needs of children according to the level of resources needed to produce acceptable educational progress. Kauffman (1977) proposed a definition of children with emotional or behavioral disorders based on educational needs (see Chapter 1). Finally, the work of Herbert Quay (1972) and his colleagues must be mentioned as an empirically based way of defining and classifying the behavioral disorders of children according to the behaviors they display (see Chapter 1).

Along with changes in labeling practices, there was an increased emphasis on the environmental factors involved in treatment, as reflected in the milieu therapy and behavioral and ecological approaches that have become popular in special education. Largely as a result of the emphasis on the interaction of the individual and his environment, the term "emotionally disturbed," which tends to infer a poorly functioning subconscious or "inner self," has been replaced with a more functional label, "behaviorally disordered." This terminology has gained more acceptance among those concerned with the mildly disturbed than among those concerned with the more seriously emotionally disturbed. In other words, professionals often use the term "behaviorally disordered" to refer to children who exhibit mild "behavior problems" while reserving the term "emotionally disturbed" for those who exhibit serious emotional difficulties.

Also, partly as a result of the emphasis on environmental influences, the setting in which treatment is provided received considerable attention during the 1960s and 1970s. Findings consistently indicated that placement in environments segregated from "normal" individuals did not foster positive gains in the behavior of those placed in such environments (Wolfensberger, 1969).* Based on these and other findings, there was and

---

*While much of the work of Wolfensberger and others was done with children labeled as being severely mentally retarded, the implications of their findings and philosophy is applicable when discussing the emotionally disturbed or behaviorally disordered.

is a move toward normalization—placement of the individual into a situation that is as much as possible like the situation he would be in if he were not considered to be disturbed or behaviorally disordered.

Consistent with the normalization principle, several movements gained momentum during the same period. "Mainstreaming," for one, focuses on getting the mildly disturbed integrated into regular education programs with the support necessary to maintain the child in that situation. "Deinstitutionalization" focuses on getting the seriously disturbed as well as retarded out of institutions and back into the public schools and integrated into regular education where ever possible. The deinstitutionalization movement includes providing for the needs of all children in the community setting with a family structure either with natural or foster parents or, if necessary, in a group home accomodation.

When reviewing historical landmarks and events, it soon becomes obvious that there has been a gradual progression over the years from providing segregated to mainstreamed arrangements. In the early 1900s we noted that many children, especially those considered to be severely disturbed, were nearly always treated (although not always educated) in hospital and/or residential settings such as state mental health institutions. Those identified as being more mildly disturbed were, for the most part, enrolled in special schools or special classes. In some cases these children also received the services of community health or child guidance clinics during nonschool hours. Beginning with the 1960s there was a tremendous swing toward more normalized and mainstreamed arrangements, and currently mildly disturbed children are being integrated into regular classes and the seriously disturbed are being placed in special classes in the public schools and in some cases within regular school classes and activities. (Roseville, a Minnesota school district, for example, has integrated seriously disturbed children into most regular school activities.) With the progression in school programs toward more integrated or mainstreamed arrangements, models for providing assistance to children in mainstreamed settings who display maladaptive behavior have been implemented. The itinerant teacher, resource room, crisis teacher, and consulting teacher are among the most popular. Accompanying the changing emphasis in school programs has been a swing within the mental health field toward small community-based mental health outpatient or residential centers rather than large, state-supported hospitals and institutions.

Along with these movements, the principle "zero reject" gained popularity. "Zero reject" noted the need for the education of *all* individuals regardless of handicap, potential, or life expectancy. The concept is based on the philosophy that all individuals can profit from education. Because of this and because of our democratic principles and emphasis on equality, the philosophy gradually evolved that everyone has a right to a "free and appropriate education." Zero reject has had particular significance for the more seriously disturbed since it implies that no child regardless of the seriousness of his difficulties should be denied an educational program designed to meet his/her needs.

In the 1960s also educators and others called for the extension of free public education to include early childhood education and adult education. They felt that many children should begin education as early as possible and should continue to receive educational services beyond adolescence to gain their maximum potential.

The movements to extend public education had a strong influence on legislation. Public Law 94-142—the Education for All Handicapped Children Act—passed by the U.S. Congress in 1975, was a milestone in providing education for the handicapped. It mandated free and appropriate education of all individuals in the least restrictive environment. Its purpose is:

> To assure that all handicapped children have available to them . . . a free, appropriate public education which emphasizes special education and related services to meet their unique needs, . . . to assist states and localities to provide for the education of all handicapped children, and to assess and assure the effectiveness of efforts to educate handicapped children. (Pelosi & Hocutt, 1977, p. 3)

It was through this law that the ideas and concepts that gained popularity in the 1960s and 1970s began to be implemented.

No review of the twentieth century would be complete without citing court decisions that had considerable impact on educational opportunities for all exceptional children, including the emotionally disturbed. While there has been a great deal of litigation at both the state and national levels on the behalf of the handicapped, one court decision in particular has had a widespread impact on school programs. The 1971 *Pennsylvania Association for Retarded Children v. Commonwealth of Pennsylvania* court decision acknowledged the right of all children including the severely/profoundly handicapped to a free public education.

While the above events have influenced the lives of all handicapped children in a variety of ways, they have had special meaning for the severely/profoundly emotionally and behaviorally disordered. They generated a great deal of interest in the education problems of the severely/profoundly handicapped since both the court decision and legislation put an emphasis on the rights of *all* children to a free appropriate public education.

Finally, it should be mentioned that parents became increasingly involved in the 1960s and 1970s as participants in educational programming for their children. Parent involvement in the education of their children is not a new phenomenon; what is of landmark importance in the history of parent involvement in school programs is the active parental movement on behalf of education for the handicapped. Parent influence—mainly through strong, organized parent groups—has been felt in court actions, legislation, and additional funding for professional resources. With the passage of P.L. 94-142, the rights of parents as participants in educational decision making and programming for their children was certified.

While all exceptional children, including the seriously emotionally disturbed have benefited, it should be noted that the history of special education shows that parents of emotionally disturbed children have not, generally speaking, been as involved in organizing strong parent groups and in litigation and legislation as the parents of many other handicapped children, for example, those classified as being mentally retarded or learning disabled. One reason may be that, in the past at least, parents of emotionally disturbed children were often identified as being responsible for the maladaptive behaviors that their children exhibited. They became the "scapegoat." As Deno (1978) stated:

> This may be one of the reasons that associations of parents of emotionally disturbed children are more conspicuous by their absence than their political strength in most areas of the country, and that where such associations are found their membership is very small in relation to the number of children who are estimated to be disturbed but unserved. (p. 34)

The 1900s can be viewed as a time of considerable change. During this period new philosophies (e.g., developmental/behavioral/normalization) emerged, and legislation was enacted to implement the strategies inherent in the philosophies. (A summary of these is found in Table 2-1.) Many of the gains made resulted not only from study and research but also through the struggle and perseverance of strong child advocacy groups composed of parents and professionals who fought for the rights of the handicapped including the behaviorally disordered. In fact, advocacy is probably the "key" or most powerful reason for many of the changes, especially in the 1960s and 1970s. We now must look to the future for further refinements, modifications, and changes using the knowledge and experiences gained in the past to help guide the way as we move ahead.

Table 2-1
Historical Landmarks in the 1900s

Landmark Statements or Concerns

1909	Ellen Key, the Swedish sociologist, forecast the 1900s as the *Century of the Child*
1908	Clifford Beers wrote *A Mind That Found Itself* about the agonies of mental illness
1920	Thomas Haines advocated public school involvement with all children including those who exhibit severe forms of maladaptive behavior
1971	*Pennsylvania Association for Retarded Citizens* v. *Commonwealth of Pennsylvania*—all children have the right to a public education
1975	P.L. 94-142—Education for All Handicapped Children Act—mandated educational services for all children regardless of severity or type of handicap

Evaluation

1905	Alfred Binet developed an intelligence test to discriminate between the disturbed and retarded
1921	Herman Rorschach devised an inkblot test designed to measure emotional and personality variables
1962	E.M. Bower and N.M. Lambert developed a screening instrument to detect emotional disturbance for use in the public schools

Organizational Structures

1909	National Committee for Mental Hygiene founded by Clifford Beers, Adolph Meyer, and William James
1912	U.S. Children's Bureau created by Congress
1922	Council for Exceptional Children founded
1964	Council for Children with Behavioral Disorders
1965	National Society for Autistic Children
1974	American Association for the Education of the Severely and Profoundly Handicapped—in 1979 name modified to the Association for the Severely Handicapped

Development of Facilities and Placement Options

1909	William Healy established the Juvenile Psychopathic Institute in Chicago to study psychological and sociological factors of juvenile delinquency
1911	Arnold Gesell founded the Clinic for Child Development at Yale

1914	First teacher-training program for educating the handicapped at the University of Michigan
1931	First psychiatric hospital opened in the United States, Bradley Home, Rhode Island
1934	L. Bender organized children's program at Bellevue Psychiatric Hospital in New York
1943	Sonja Shankman Orthogenic Residential School at University of Chicago founded
1946	School programs for emotionally disturbed established in New York City—"600" schools
1950s	Pioneer House for deliquents (the emotionally disturbed) established in Detroit
1953	First day school program for children labeled seriously disturbed in New York
1960s and 1970s	Establishment of programs based on concepts such as normalization, mainstreaming, zero reject, deinstitutionalization, and community living

Classification/Categorization

1930s	Movement toward more labels based on symptoms
1933	H.W. Potter described the condition "childhood schizophrenia"
1935	Leo Kanner initially described the condition "early infantile autism"
1949	B. Rank and his associates advocated a return to indefinite labeling and proposed the generic term "atypical child"
1952	M.S. Mahler delineated another subgroup with the condition symbiotic infantile psychosis
1975	N. Hobbs published the results of a project investigating classification practices in the books *Issues in the Classification of Children* and *The Futures of Children*
late 1970s to present	Movement away from educationally irrelevant labels (emotional disturbance, mental retardation, learning disabilities) to more educationally useful groupings by functioning level and/or programming needs

Treatment Approaches and Strategies

1900–1910	Freud's contributions to the literature describing the psycho-analytical treatment approach gained widespread popularity
1913	John B. Watson wrote a paper "Psychology as a Behaviorist Views It" setting forth the behavioral position but not readily accepted due to the "radicalness" of the position

1920s	Movement toward mental hygiene and child guidance clinics in the public schools; philosophical views included working with mild as well as severe cases and interdisciplinary collaboration
1930s	B.F. Skinner initially presented operant conditioning procedural considerations
1947	V. Axline proposed a play-therapy approach to treatment based on psychoanalytic approach
Mid 1900s	A variety of ideas related to treatment of emotional disturbed children proposed (e.g., Bettleheim—milieu therapy; Redl and Wineman—life-space interviewing; Morse—crisis teacher)
1950s–1960s	Special educators began researching and using behavior modification principles in the education of exceptional children (e.g., Haring & Phillips, 1962; Hewett, 1968; Whelans & Haring, 1966)
1960	P.H. Berkowitz and E.P. Rothman published their classic book *The Disturbed Child: Recognition and Psychotherapy in the Classroom* describing classification and educational procedures
1965	N.J. Long, W.C. Morse, and R.G. Newman edited a book, *Conflict in the Classroom,* that synthesizes current ideas and thought about educating children in conflict
1965	W.C. Rhodes popularized the ecological approach, and N. Hobbs implemented Project Re-Ed
1967	F.M. Hewett popularized the developmental approach
late 1960s–early 1970s	Much research regarding behavior principles with seriously disturbed children (e.g., Lovaas, 1966, 1967; Lovaas & Koegel, 1973)
1973	P. Knoblock popularized a humanistic/open-education approach to treatment
early 1970s	Rhodes and his associates at the University of Michigan did a conceptual project in emotional disturbance to clarify, among other things, the models and methods of intervention—*A Study of Child Variance* (3 volumes) the result of the project
after 1960s	Gradual shift away from (1) the medical to a developmental/behavioral model and (2) segregated to mainstreamed programs

REFERENCES

Adler, A. *Social interest, a challenge to mankind.* New York: Capricorn, 1964.
Axline, V. *Play therapy.* Boston: Houghton Mifflin, 1947.

Baker, E.M., & Stullken, E.H. American research studies concerning the "behavior" type of exceptional child. *Journal of Exceptional Children,* 1938, *4,* 36–45.

Beers, C.W. *A mind that found itself: An autobiography.* New York: Longmans, Green, 1908.

Bender, L. Childhood schizophrenia—Its recognition, description, and treatment. *American Journal of Orthopsychiatry,* 1956, *26,* 499–506.

Bergman, P., & Escalona, S. Unusual sensitivities in very young children. *Psychoanalytic Study of the Child,* 1949, *3–4,* 333–352.

Berkowitz, P.H. Pearl H. Berkowitz. In J.M. Kauffman & C.D. Lewis (Eds.), *Teaching children with behavior disorders: Personal perspectives.* Columbus, OH: Merrill, 1974.

Berkowitz, P.H., & Rothman, E.P. *The disturbed child: Recognition and psychoeducational therapy in the classroom.* New York: New York University Press, 1960.

Berkowitz, P.H., & Rothman, E.P. (Eds.). *Public education for disturbed children in New York City.* Springfield, IL: Thomas, 1967.

Bettelheim, B. *Love is not enough.* New York: Macmillan, 1950.

Bettelheim, B., & Sylvester, E.A. A therapeutic milieu. *American Journal of Orthopsychiatry,* 1948, *18,* 191–206.

Blatt, B. Toward an understanding of people with special needs. In J.M. Kauffman & J.S. Payne (Eds.), *Mental retardation: Introduction and personal perspectives.* Columbus, OH: Merrill, 1975.

Bower, E.M., & Lambert, N.M. *A process for in-school screening of children with emotional handicaps.* Princeton, NJ: Educational Testing Service, 1962.

Brigham, A. Schools in lunatic asylums. *American Journal of Insanity,* 1845, *1,* 326–340.

Burke, D. Countertheoretical interventions in emotional disturbance. In W.C. Rhodes & M.L. Tracy (Eds.), *A study of child variance* Vol. 2, *Interventions).* Ann Arbor: University of Michigan, 1972.

De Sanctis, S. *Neuropsichiatria infantile.* Rome: Stock, 1925.

Descuret, J.B.F. *Medecine de passions.* Paris: Bechet et Labe, 1841.

Despert, J.L. Schizophrenia in children. *Psychiatric Quarterly,* 1938, *12,* 366–371.

Despert, J.L. *Schizophrenia in children.* New York: Brunner/Mazel, 1968.

DuPont, H. *Educating emotionally disturbed children.* New York: Holt, Rinehart & Winston, 1974.

Emminghaus, H. *Die psychischen Storungen des Kindesalters.* Tubingen, Ger.: Laupp, 1887.

Gardner, W.I. *Children with learning and behavior problems.* Boston: Allyn & Bacon, 1974.

Haines, T.H. State laws relating to special classes and schools for mentally handicapped children in the public schools. *Mental Hygiene,* 1925, *9,* 545–551.

Hamburger, A. *Vorlesungen uber die Psychopathologie des Kindesalters.* Berlin: Springer, 1926.

Haring, N.G., Nietupski, J., & Harme-Nietupski, S. *Guidelines for effective intervention with the severely handicapped: Toward independent functioning.* Unpublished manuscript, University of Washington, 1976.

Haring, N.G., & Phillips, E.L. *Educating emotionally disturbed children.* New York: McGraw-Hill, 1962.

Henry, N.B. (Ed.). *The education of exceptional children.* Forty-ninth yearbook of the National Society of Education, Part II. Chicago: University of Chicago Press, 1950.

Hewett, F.M. Educational engineering with emotionally disturbed children. *Exceptional Children,* 1967, *33,* 459–470.

Hewett, F.M. *The emotionally disturbed child in the classroom.* Boston: Allyn & Bacon, 1968.

Hewett, F.M. Frank M. Hewett. In J.M. Kauffman & C.D. Lewis (Eds.), *Teaching children with behavior disorders: Personal perspectives.* Columbus, OH: Merrill, 1974.

Hewett, F.M. *Education of exceptional learners.* Boston: Allyn & Bacon, 1977.

Hobbs, N. How the Re-ED plan developed. In N.J. Long, W.C. Morse, & R.G. Newman (Eds.). *Conflict in the classroom.* Belmont, CA: Wadsworth, 1965.

Hobbs, N. Helping the disturbed child: Psychological and ecological strategies. *American Psychologist,* 1966, 21, 1105–1115.

Hobbs, N. (Ed.). *Issues in the classification of children* (Vols. I, II). San Francisco: Jossey-Bass, 1975.

Ireland, S.S. *The mental affections of children.* New York: Blakiston, 1898.

Itard, J.M.G. *The wild boy of Aveyron.* Trans., G. Humphrey & M. Humphrey. New York: Appleton-Century-Crofts, 1962.

Kanner, L. Autistic disturbances of affective contact. *Nervous Child,* 1943, *2,* 217–250.

Kanner, L. Child psychiatry: Retrospect and prospect. *American Journal of Psychiatry,* 1960, *117,* 15–22.

Kanner, L. Emotionally disturbed children: A historical review. Child Development, 1962, *33,* 97–102.

Kanner. L. *Child psychiatry* (4th ed.). Springfield, IL: Thomas, 1972.

Kauffman, J.M. *Characteristics of children's behavior disorders.* Columbus, OH: Merrill, 1977.

Kazdin, A.E. *Behavior modification in applied settings.* Homewood, IL: Dorsey, 1975.

Key, E. *The century of the child.* New York: Putnam, 1909.

Kirk, S.A. *Educating exceptional children.* Boston: Houghton Mifflin, 1974.

Kirk, S.A., & Gallagher, J.J. *Educating exceptional children.* Boston: Houghton Mifflin, 1974.

Knoblock, P. Open education for emotionally disturbed children. *Exceptional Children,* 1973, *39,* 355–365.

Lewis, C.D. Introduction: Landmarks. In J.M. Kauffman & C.D. Lewis (Eds.), *Teaching children with behavior disorders: Personal perspectives.* Columbus, OH: Merrill, 1974.

Lilly, M.S. Special education: A tempest in a teapot. *Exceptional Children,* 1970, *37,* 43–49.

Long, N.J., Morse, W.C., & Newman, R.G. (Eds.). *Conflict in the classroom* (3rd ed.), Belmont, CA: Wadsworth, 1976. (1st ed., 1965).

Lovaas, O.I., & Kogel, R.L. Behavior therapy with autistic children. In C.E. J.K. Wing (Ed.), *Early childhood autism: Clinical, educational, and social aspects.* Elmsford, NY: Pergamon, 1966.

Lovaas, O.I. A behavior therapy approach to the treatment of childhood schizophrenia. In J.P. Hill (Ed.), *Minnesota symposia on child psychology.* Minneapolis: University of Minnesota Press, 1967.

Lovaas, O.I., & Kogel, R.L. Behavior therapy with autistic children. In C.E. Thoresen (Ed.), *Behavior modification in education.* Chicago: University of Chicago Press, 1973.

Lutz, J. *Uber die Schizophrenic in Kindersalter.* Zurich: Fussli, 1937.

Mahler, M.S. On child psychosis and schizophrenia. *Psychoanalytic Study of the Child,* 1952, *7,* 286–305.

Manheimer, M. *Les troubles mentaux de l'enfance.* Paris: Societe d' Editions Scientifiques, 1899.

Maudsley, H. *The pathology of the mind.* New York: Appleton, 1880.

McDowell, F., & Sontag, E. The severely profoundly handicapped as catalysts for change. In E. Sontag (Ed.), *Educational programming for the severely and profoundly handicapped.* Reston, VA: Council for Exceptional Children, 1977, pp. 3–5.

Moreau De Tours, P. *La folie chez les enfants.* Paris: Baillere, 1888.

Morse, W.C. The education of socially maladjusted and emotionally disturbed children. In W.M. Cruickshank & G.O. Johnson (Eds.), *Education of exceptional children and youth* (2nd ed.). Englewood Cliffs, NJ: Prentice-Hall, 1967.

Mosak, H., & Dreikurs, R. Adlerian psychotherapy. In R. Corsini (Ed.), *Current psychotherapies.* Itasca, IL: Peacock, 1973.

Parkinson, J. Observations on the excessive indulgence of children, particularly intended to show its injurious effects on their health, and the difficulties it occasions in their treatment during sickness. In R. Hunter & I. Macalpine (Eds.), *Three hundred years of psychiatry, 1835 – 1860.* London: Oxford University Press, 1963. (Originally London: Symonds et al., 1807)

Pelosi, J., & Hocutt, A. *The education for all handicapped children act: Issues and implications.* Chapel Hill: Frank Porter Graham Child Development Center, University of North Carolina, 1977.

Potter, H.W. Schizophrenia in children. *American Journal of Psychiatry,* 1933, *89,* 1253–1270.

Quay, H.C. Patterns of aggression, withdrawal and immaturity. In H.C. Quay & S.J. Werry (Eds.), *Psychopathological disorders of childhood.* New York: Wiley, 1972.

Rank, B. Adaptation of the psychoanalytic techniques for the treatment of young children with atypical development. *American Journal of Orthopsychiatry,* 1949, *19,* 130–139.

Redl, F., & Wineman, D. *Children who hate.* New York: Free Press, 1951.

Redl, F., & Wineman, D. *Controls from within.* New York: Free Press, 1952.

Reinert, H.R. *Children in conflict.* St. Louis: Mosby, 1976.

Reynolds, M.C., & Birch, J.W. *Teaching exceptional children in all America's schools.* Reston, VA: Council for Exceptional Children, 1977.

Rhodes, W.C. A community participation analysis of emotional disturbance. *Exceptional Children*, 1970, *37*, 309–314.

Rhodes, W.C., & Paul, J.L. *Emotionally disturbed and deviant children: New views and approaches.* Englewood Cliffs, NJ: Prentice-Hall, 1978.

Rhodes, W.C., & Head, S. (Eds.). *A study of child variance* (Vol. 3: *Service delivery systems*). Ann Arbor: University of Michigan, 1974.

Rhodes, W.C., & Tracy, M.L. (Eds.). *A study of child variance* (Vol. 1: *Theories*). Ann Arbor: University of Michigan, 1972. (a)

Rhodes, W.C., & Tracy, M.L. (Eds.). *A study of child variance* (Vol. 2: *Interventions*). Ann Arbor: University of Michigan, 1972. (b)

Robinson, F.J., & Vitale, L.J. Children with circumscribed interest patterns. *American Journal of Orthopsychiatry*, 1954, *24*, 755–766.

Rothman, E.P. Esther P. Rothman. In J.M. Kauffman & C.D. Lewis (Eds.), *Teaching children with behavior disorders: Personal perspectives.* Columbus, OH: Merrill, 1974.

Skinner, B.F. *Science and human behavior.* New York: Free Press, 1953.

Sontag, E., Smith, J., & Sailor, W. The severely and profoundly handicapped: Who are they? Where are they? *Journal of Special Education*, 1977, *11*, 1.

Ssucharewa, G. Uber den Verlauf der Schizophrenien in Kindesalter. *Zeitschrift fur d ges Neurol*, 1932.

Swanson, H.L., & Reinert, H.R. *Teaching strategies for children in conflict.* St. Louis: Mosby, 1979.

Szurek, S. Psychotic episodes and psychic maldevelopment. *American Journal of Orthopsychiatry*, 1956, *26*, 519–543.

Watson, J.B. Psychology as the behaviorist views it. *Psychological Review*, 1913, *20*, 158–177.

Whelan, R.J., & Haring, N.G. Modification and maintenance of behavior through systematic application of consequences. *Exceptional Children*, 1966, *32*, 281–289.

Wing, J. Kanner's syndrome. In L. Wing (Ed.), *Early childhood autism* (2nd ed.), Elmsford, NY: Pergamon, 1976.

Wolfensberger, W. The origin and nature of our institutional models. In R.B. Kugel & W. Wolfensberger (Eds.), *Changing patterns in residential services for the mentally retarded.* Washington, DC: President's Committee on Mental Retardation, 1969.

Ziehen, T. *Die Geisteskrankheiten des Kindesalters.* Berlin: Reuther & Reinhard, 1926.

SELECTED READINGS FOR FURTHER STUDY

Bender, L. Childhood schizophrenia—Its recognition, description, and treatment. *American Journal of Orthopsychiatry*, 1956, *26*, 499–506.

Berkowitz, P.H., & Rothman, E.P. (Eds.). *Public education for disturbed children in New York City.* Springfield, IL: Thomas, 1967.

Henry, N.B. (Ed.). *The education of exceptional children*. Forty-ninth yearbook of the National Society of Education, Part II. Chicago: University of Chicago Press, 1950.

Hobbs, N. (Ed.). *Issues in the classification of children* (Vols. I, II). San Francisco: Jossey-Bass, 1975.

Hunter, R., & Macalpine, I. (Eds.), *Three hundred years of psychiatry, 1835–1860*. London: Oxford University Press, 1963.

Kanner, L. Child psychiatry: Retrospect and prospect. *American Journal of Psychiatry*, 1960, 117, 15–22.

Kanner, L. Emotionally disturbed children: A historical review. *Child Development*, 1962, *33*, 97–102.

Kauffman, J.M. Nineteenth-century views of children's behavior disorders: Historical contributions and continuing issues. *Journal of Special Education*, 1976, *10*, 335–349.

Kazdin, A.E. *Behavior modification in applied settings*. Homewood, IL: Dorsey, 1975.

Lewis, C.D. Introduction: Landmarks. In J.M. Kauffman & C.D. Lewis (Eds.), *Teaching children with behavior disorders: Personal perspectives*. Columbus, OH: Merrill, 1974.

Wolfensberger, W. The origin and nature of our institutional models. In R.B. Kugel & W. Wolfensberger (Eds.), *Changing patterns in residential services for the mentally retarded*. Washington, DC: President's Committee on Mental Retardation, 1969.

3
Current Trends in Special Education

The education of children labeled emotionally disturbed, as well as special education in general, is undergoing a rapid transition as traditional assumptions regarding the kinds of services provided exceptional students and the environments in which those services are offered are being questioned. Because of the rapid changes occurring, it is becoming increasingly difficult to maintain a clear focus in regard to exactly where the field of special education is headed and why. Therefore, it is becoming difficult to maintain an integrated, organized perspective of the trends and movements. If we should lose perspective of where special education is going and why, the resulting confusion could cause a disintegration of the cohesiveness of the field and subsequent progress.

The purpose of this chapter is to present, from one viewpoint, an interpretation and rationale regarding a few of the major trends in special education. Since many have the potential for considerable impact on the futures of children, it is imperative that we consider those that have the greatest consequences for the seriously emotionally disturbed and that we understand these trends and the rationale(s) behind them. In the authors' opinion there are five trends in particular to analyze and interpret in relation to the education of these children:

1 Placement of exceptional children in normal settings
2 Direct and functional methods of identifying programming needs
3 Individualization of instruction within a consistent, organized process of instruction
4 Education as a primary treatment approach
5 Increasing concern for quality programming.

PLACEMENT IN NORMAL SETTINGS

How can an individual be expected to learn to live in a "normal" community setting with "normal" people if he is placed in an "abnormal" setting with a group of "abnormal" people? In education circles questions such as this are increasing in frequency. As pointed out by Brown (1978), the end result of six autistic children being placed in a segregated class-room with a special teacher is six autistic children and one autistic teacher.

In other words, people learn from people. If a "normal" child were to be placed in a special school or class with all "disturbed" children, he/she would probably, over a period of time, begin to display deviant or maladaptive behaviors. Logic would dictate that any child or anyone placed in an abnormal environment has a reduced chance of learning "normal" behaviors. If we accept the idea that it is difficult to learn "normal" behaviors in an environment where many abnormal behaviors are being displayed, we might conclude that a child who is "disturbed" has very little chance of learning more "normal" behaviors, if the only models available are children who display a variety of deviant behaviors. In short, anyone—"normal" or "handicapped"—reared in such an environment has a reduced chance of learning to display more "normal" behaviors.

This is not to imply that the only thing needed to change or "cure" children who display maladaptive behaviors is to place them in as normal an environment as feasible. This obviously would be an oversimplification. Placing such children in as normal an environment as possible, however, enhances the probability that they will learn to display a growing number of more "normal" behaviors. Conversely, placing such children in an abnormal environment, where nearly everyone displays deviant behaviors, reduces the probability of them learning to display more "normal" behaviors.

The arguments regarding the placement of labeled children in normal settings apply when discussing children who exhibit severe as well as mild exceptional characteristics that influence learning. Russo and Koegel (1977) have argued that segregated special classes for children who have traditionally been classified as severely disturbed (autistic, in this case) may not be justified:

[S]uch classes . . . present a potential problem, in that in most cases they are composed solely of autistic children. Thus, such classes may provide merely another form of exclusion. By placing every autistic child in a classroom made up entirely of autistic children, we may deprive those children of several possible benefits, including the influence of appropriate role models and the exposure to a "nonautistic" curriculum taught in regular classrooms. (p. 580)

Since special class placement of children who exhibit severe learning handicaps may not be appropriate, Russo and Koegel (1977) conducted an experimental study to investigate the feasibility of integrating a child labeled autistic into a normal public school classroom. They summarized the results of their study as follows:

> The results showed (1) that during treatment by a therapist in the classroom, the child's appropriate verbal and social behaviors increased, and autistic mannerisms decreased; and (2) training teachers in behavioral techniques was apparently sufficient to maintain the child's appropriate school behaviors throughout kindergarten and the first grade. (p. 579).

The feasibility of integrating seriously disturbed children into regular school activities whenever possible is further supported by the Roseville, Minnesota, special project. According to Deno (1978), elementary-age children labeled as being seriously disturbed have been successfully mainstreamed into many regular classroom activities. In this project teachers are given support in terms of special management assistants who stay with designated children throughout the day, consultation help, and in-service education support. "The fact that they could be maintained beneficially and without undue disruption to others in the regular settings seems a significant advancement for such disturbed children" (Deno, 1978, p. 180).

Not everyone agrees that children should be placed in as normal an environment as possible. There are individuals who argue in support of segregation, even for children who exhibit learning characteristics that only mildly influence learning. For example, Becker (1978) empirically studied differences among groups of children with various disability labels and found that children who have been given various labels by psychologists and educators have different characteristics. He used his findings to support segregation and differential programming according to disability labels. His argument is that since children given different categorical labels were found to exhibit different characteristics, they should be provided different, segregated educational programs. Such arguments, however, are not likely to slow the trend toward integration (generic grouping) or placement of exceptional individuals including the "emotionally disturbed" in normal settings. Becker's conclusions in support of segregation can be questioned for the following reason.

It has long been recognized that differences in learning characteristics can be found in all individuals regardless of their being assigned labels. Males have different learning characteristics than females, but should one or both be given a disability label and segregated because one group is not the same as the other on certain variables? The same argument could be supported for body type, interests, attitudes, race, and socioeconomic status. The mere identification of differences is not sufficient to warrant segregated programming. That is, while differences exist among individuals and groups in society, it does not necessarily follow that we should segregate according to these differences. Many professionals now believe that it is possible, given the necessary resources, to individualize instruction within the "regular" classroom to meet the unique needs of *all* children, including those traditionally labeled emotionally disturbed.

One of the problems in our society is intolerance of people who may be perceived as "different." We must learn to live with, work with and understand those who are "different" from ourselves, and this cannot come about if we continue to use our discoveries that people are different as justification for categorizing and segregating people from each other. To reach the objective of people living and working together, we need to begin in the schools when children are young. "Prejudice against those from whom one is different can be addressed and reduced only if opportunities for contact and interaction are available on an ongoing basis" (Lilly, 1979, p. 47). This idea is not a new phenomenon but has been approached on the basis of sex and race. Now it is the turn of children who have been given disability labels.

As clearly noted by Hamre-Nietupski, Branston, Gruenwald, and Brown (1979):

> When severely handicapped and nonhandicapped students attend the same schools from the time they are very young, the chances of learning tolerance, understanding and acceptance of differences among people are enhanced substantially. It is experience with human differences that *prevents* fear and *promotes* understanding. (p. 8)

In closing this section it should be noted that the authors are addressing the question of normalized placement and not classroom arrangements and groupings within a normalized placement. It is recognized that individual differences may require various classroom arrangements or groupings. The governing principles for any grouping made should apply, however, for *all* children (Hobbs, 1975). If grouping occurs, it "should be based upon those specific program-relevant variables empirically related to the child's learning or behavior characteristics" (Gardner, 1977, p. 70). The reader is referred to Pasanella and Volkner (1977) for some ways of grouping children within regular classrooms to facilitate individualized assessment and planning.

DIRECT AND FUNCTIONAL METHODS FOR IDENTIFICATION OF PROGRAMMING NEEDS

In the past the procedures employed to determine the programming needs of handicapped children involved a diagnostic/labeling process similar to that used in identifying physiological problems in the medical field. The mystique of the diagnostic/labeling procedure in education is being broken down and replaced with more direct and functional methods for identification of appropriate programming needs. As pointed out by Gallagher (1979):

> There seems to be a growing tendency in special education to dispense with the extraordinary battery of tests that many school psychologists or diagnosticians felt to be important in the past. The reason for a reduced emphasis on the tests is that while such instruments may provide useful background information, they really do not help significantly in the planning for educational treatment—the direct and immediate concern of the teacher. One day after the elaborate psychodiagnostic information is provided to the teacher . . . teachers are really on their own in terms of designing and planning what is to be done with the youngster. (p. 42)

In other words, the major problem is that traditional psychodiagnostic evaluations *do not* provide the type of information teachers need. This is especially true when the diagnosticians focus, as they traditionally have, on uncovering the causes and disabilities underlying the child's inability to perform in order to assign a label to the child. This kind of focus does not produce relevant information that teachers can use in their daily instruction.

> Ultimately, the types of information that will be useful to the teacher in curriculum decision making include knowledge of the skills required for mastery of a subject matter, knowledge of how to sequence those skills, and knowledge of which skills a student has and has not mastered in that subject-matter domain. (Samuels, 1979, p. 58)

Some of the better known criticisms of the diagnostic/labeling procedure are reviewed briefly to provide a perspective from which the present trends in the identification of programming needs can be analyzed. Initially, the diagnostic/labeling procedure includes a period of data gathering by a team of professionals. The data gathered are then organized and analyzed according to standardized norms. Once all of the data are analyzed, a decision is made regarding the underlying disability and what label (e.g., MR—mentally retarded; ED—emotionally disturbed; LD—learning disabled) the child should be given. Based primarily on the label given, the child's chronological age, and the severity of the problem, an educational placement decision is made. Once the child is placed, the classroom teacher generally observes, through testing and direct observation, the child's behavior in various curricular areas, develops an individualized educational program, and implements the program.

There are several reasons why this procedure is losing favor among professional educators. The analysis of the data gathered in terms of standardized norms to determine the child's disability and the label that he should be given typically requires a considerable energy expenditure and provides little return in regard to enhancing a child's progress. Unfortunately, as mentioned earlier, the label assigned generally communicates or provides little information that is useful for educational programming. That is, we cannot determine the child's reading level, arithmetic skills, length of attention span, or whether he exhibits biting and/or hitting behaviors on the basis of the label alone. In addition, we cannot glean from the label information regarding consequences that may be effective in reinforcing or punishing behaviors of the child, what types of antecedent stimuli might elicit positive responses, or any other knowledge of the child that is necessary to program appropriately for his needs. Kanfer and Saslow (1969) and Zigler and Phillips (1961) rightly point out that little information is given about treatment, which should be the major advantage of engaging in diagnosis and classification. We do, however, by means of the label, provide an expectation by others of the child to exhibit inappropriate behavior; this can be detrimental to the potential progress of the child through the frequently noted "self-fulfilling prophecy" phenomenon. Beez (1968), Foster, Ysseldyke, and Reese (1975), and Haskett (1968) have provided data to support the self-fulfilling prophecy phenomenon. Although there has been much criticism of some of the research related to the self-fulfilling prophecy on methodological grounds, little research is available to show that such a phenomenon does not occur.

In summary, it has not been demonstrated that the traditional diagnostic/labeling procedure can contribute to positive changes in the behaviors of children; quite to the contrary, it has in many cases been shown to be detrimental. Simches (1970) asserts:

> We must develop identification systems which provide an understanding of the child so that programs can be built around the child's skills. We cannot continue to use taxonomy of labels that have a tendency to homogenize children into meaningless diagnostic label categories based primarily on psychometrics, medical findings, or psychiatric examinations. (p. 10)

The procedure that is replacing the traditional diagnostic/labeling model involves a straightforward "direct-assessment and intervention" strategy. This strategy also has been referred to as the "behavioral" or "task analytical model." It involves the assessment of a child's behaviors (e.g., academic, social, emotional, physical) in the natural setting in which the child typically interacts. This usually is done by a team of professionals from various disciplines. Although the use of norm-referenced tests are not excluded when needed for various purposes, the assessment

Table 3-1
A Comparison of Two Models of Evaluation*

	Diagnostic/Labeling (Psychoeducational)	Direct Assessment (Behavioral, Task Analytical)
The basic assumption is . . .	if a student fails at a task, it is because the student has something wrong with his cognitive or perceptual abilities	if a student fails at a task, it is because he has not mastered an essential subtask of that task.
The source of failure . . .	resides within the student	resides within the environment
Evaluation begins with . . .	the student	the task on which the student is failing
The tests used . . .	try to measure cognitive or perceptual abilities	try to measure student behavior
The most frequently used tests are . . .	norm-referenced tests based on logically developed theories of learning	criterion-referenced tests based on empirically validated sequences of tasks
The conclusions drawn include . . .	the student's cognitive or perceptual strengths and weaknesses	what the student can or cannot do
Treatment is directed at . . .	changing the student's cognitive or perceptual abilities	changing the student's task-related behavior.
Instruction involves . . .	presentations that allow for weaknesses while taking advantage of strengths	presentations that are directly related to a sequence of tasks
Instructional treatments are identified by . . .	making predictions from tests of student ability	monitoring the student's progress in several treatments

*Adapted from Howell, Kaplan, and O'Connell (1979, pp. 7–8). Reprinted by permission.

is not, generally speaking, norm-referenced but is based on the individual functioning of the child in various curricular areas (criterion-referenced). Once the assessment is completed, the team's analysis of the child's behavior is used to build a program based on the child's needs (considering his functioning level, chronological age, and the requirements of the environment he is and will likely be living in). The program is then implemented in the child's natural environment or in an environment as close to the natural as possible.

No attempt is made in the direct-assessment and intervention strategy to label the child as having some problem or disability; the focus is on determining the level at which he is functioning in various curricular areas (e.g., social, emotional, cognitive). The child's present repertoire of behaviors is then compared with those behaviors needed to function in various natural environments or environments as close to the natural as possible, and an educational program is designed and implemented.

The direct-assessment and intervention model is gaining favor among professionals. The primary reason is that the procedures (i.e., direct assessment of observable behaviors and intervention based on the observed behaviors) inherent in the model lead to positive changes in children's behaviors. Obviously, child change is the most important criterion in evaluating the effectiveness of any educational procedure.

An advantage of the model is its focus on individual characteristics and needs rather than normative comparisons and disability groupings. When disability groups based on normative comparisons are used, the traditional approach to treatment is to separate the children given the disability label from the "normal" so they can be treated differently (since they are considered to be different). Segregated placement and treatment has been found frequently to result in exposure to lowered expectations and an abnormal peer group (e.g., all MR children, all LD, all EDs) that can be detrimental to positive child gains. Numerous individuals have repeatedly outlined the detrimental effect of segregating children with handicaps into unnatural settings (Brown, 1978; Gardner, 1977).

The direct-assessment and intervention procedure facilitates maintenance in the natural setting by avoiding labeling and subsequent segregation associated with it. The support and programming (intervention) provided is designed to meet the individual needs of each child within as normal an environmental setting as possible. Table 3–1 compares the diagnostic/labeling model and the direct-assessment model.*

The authors here do not mean to imply that no classification and

---

*The reader is referred to Howell, Kaplan and O'Connell (1979) for detailed information about the direct assessment (or behavioral or task-analysis) approach and for further comparisons of the approach with the diagnostic/labeling (or psychodiagnostic) approach.

labeling systems are needed for any reason. Classification may be important to research into causes of individuals exhibiting exceptional behaviors that could lead to preventive measures and medical interventions based on etiology. The primary responsibility of the educator, however, is in the teaching/learning/education of an individual. As has been repeatedly indicated in the literature, changing behavior through learning involves the same process for all organisms (see the following section) regardless of cause or etiology of the disorder.

INDIVIDUALIZATION WITHIN A SINGLE TREATMENT APPROACH (OR PROCESS OF INSTRUCTION)

The field of special education has traditionally accepted the idea that children designated as handicapped must be approached and treated in a unique and different way than other children. This belief in the necessity of differential treatment has led to segregated (different, unique) educational programs for labeled children. Fortunately, the concept of differential treatment for the "handicapped" is now waning. Gardner (1977) has stated that "there are no unique strategies for use with exceptional children which differ in kind from those used with normal children" (p. 74). Stephens (1977) also alluded to this same point: "instructional procedures need not differ as a function of the differences in diagnosis" (p. 5). Deno (1978), too stated, "Children with problems do not need qualitatively different teaching approaches. They need learning management conditions that permit a teacher to apply in a more controlled way the same kinds of instructional skills that the teacher should be using with all children" (p. 14).

Before proceeding further, it should be stressed that the authors are not suggesting that all children are the same in learning characteristics and that individualization of instruction is not necessary. It is recognized that basically *all* children are unique individuals in terms of variables such as age, sex, maturational level, background experience, IQ, and learning styles. What is being emphasized is that *all children are unique, not just those labeled handicapped*. These differences among children dictate that each child be evaluated in terms of *his* unique learning characteristics and that an individualized educational plan be devised in terms of the objectives to be reached and variables such as type, level, and sequencing of curricular materials or type and strength of positive and aversive consequences. While the uniqueness of each child requires individualized educational planning, the basic overall process of education is not different, however, for some children. It is the *same* for all children.

The belief in differential treatment for the "handicapped" has persisted despite repeated demonstration by empirical research (see Stuart, 1970) that the behavior of all living organisms, regardless of any assigned label, is best modified or changed from an environmental perspective through the same overall process—contingent manipulation of antecedent and consequent stimuli. Stimuli that precede and influence a response are generally referred to as "antecedents." Stimuli that follow and influence a response are generally referred to as "consequences." Stimuli (antecedent or consequent) may include any aspect of the environment, such as scheduling, curricular materials, recreational items, social praise, method of presentation, physical arrangement of the setting, or a warm, accepting environment versus a cool, more "matter-of-fact" environment. The appropriate manipulation or control of antecedents and consequences will result in "learning" or behavior change for all individuals. A schematic of the learning process components and their relationship to each other is presented in Figure 3-1.

Differentiation occurs not in the overall *process* but in the objectives of the program and the particular selection of antecedents and consequences used to facilitate learning or progress toward the objectives. This differentiation or individualization should occur for *all* children, not just a few (e.g., those given a disability label). All children are different in the behavior(s) they exhibit, which may be influenced by aspects such as cognitive abilities, brain damage, motor control, neurological integration, experience repertoires, and basic temperaments, whether they are labeled handicapped or normal.

During organized educational programming (environmental engineering) individual differences may result in different objectives and in the differential selection of antecedent and consequent stimuli that correspond with the characteristics of the child. Stimuli differences may involve type, level, and sequencing of curricular materials or type and strength of positive and aversive consequences. In short, individual differences do influence the objectives and stimuli selection but not a change in the *overall treatment or educational process*. Regardless of the objectives of the program or which type of stimuli leads to learning for the individual, the basic overall educational process is the *same*. In the process of learning or behavior change, all organisms are influenced by the manipulation of antecedent and/or consequent stimuli.

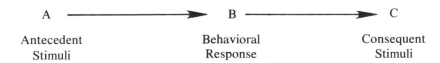

Fig. 3-1.   Schematic of Learning Process Components

EDUCATION AS TREATMENT

In the past, questions of whether schools should be in the "treatment business" and whether teachers can serve as therapists without exceeding their professional competence were asked more frequently in relation to services for emotionally disturbed children than for any other handicapped children. . . .

The questions arose mainly out of the fact that the word "treatment" had come to connote medical intervention rather than the more general definition of the handling or management of a person, substance, or process. Throughout the last two decades . . . evidence has been mounting in favor of well-directed reeducation to improve the behavioral and social adjustment of children. This educational model (as opposed to the "medical" model) approach has brought educators into the mainstream of society's treatment systems. (Deno, 1978, p. 11)

In the past education and treatment were often considered separate functions. Thus, many children were (and still are in some cases) sent to treatment sessions (i.e., child guidance clinic, psychiatrist's office) a few hours a week and then sent to the classroom for education at other times. Today the dichotomy between education and treatment is being recognized as inappropriate.

The inappropriateness of the dichotomy becomes apparent if the following is accepted. Education is the process of changing or developing behaviors that enable individuals to function independently in, adapt to, contribute to, and enjoy the environments in which they spend their lives to the greatest extent possible. Treatment for individuals labeled handicapped also is the process of changing or developing behaviors that enable individuals to function independently in, adapt to, contribute to, and enjoy the environments in which they spend their lives to the greatest extent possible. Thus, education is a treatment for dealing with handicapping conditions.

It is beginning to be recognized that not only is education a treatment, but it is one of the most effective treatments, based on the environmental engineering approach (Cruickshank, Bentzen, Ratzebury, & Tannhauser, 1961; Haring & Phillips, 1962; Hewett, 1967), that is currently assisting handicapped individuals to live a happy and productive life. Some other treatments (e.g., psychodynamic therapy) have not been found to be as effective (see Stuart, 1970). Empirical data suggest that an effective treatment for bringing about behavior change is education or environmental engineering. Because of this and other events "education has come to play an increasingly prominent role in the treatment of children's disorders" (Kauffman, 1977, p. 43). Society has begun to seek out education to coordinate and carry out the treatment process (environmental structuring or engineering) required to change the behaviors of individuals traditionally labeled handicapped. It should be noted that educators cannot take the credit for developing the environmental engineering treatment approach. The approach is based on behavioral theory developed by the hard work of many experimental psychologists. Educators are merely beginning to *apply* systematically in classrooms the techniques developed; thus, the application of behavioral theory is becoming known as "educational treatment."

Although education plays an important role in the treatment of behavior disorders, it should not be forgotten that brain damage, disease, genetic factors, basic temperament, biochemical irregularities, and malnutrition can and probably do have an influence on how the child is likely to behave (Kauffman, 1977).

Education most certainly is not the only effective treatment. Biomedical as well as other treatments are often necessary and effective. Surgery and drugs, for example, can sometimes alleviate the symptoms of a handicapping condition.

> Yet, even when evidence suggesting possible physiological involvement surfaces in medical tests that probe for within-child causes or etiology, the implications of the evidence for educational instruction have not been established. The bridge between medical evidence and the instructional procedures required to ameliorate learning problems has not yet been constructed. So far, most of the instructional methods which have been found to be effective . . . can be applied without reference to the physiological origin of a learning or behavior problem. Whatever value there may be in knowing the medical etiology of a child's problem, it usually has only meager bearing on the choice of instructional method for the child. Unfortunately, too many educators invest distressing and unjustified amounts of child time and service resources in looking for within-child explanations. (Deno, 1978, p. 2)

This does not in any way negate the importance of teachers working, as any concerned citizen would, to alleviate malnutrition and poor medical care for all children. But the teachers' primary area of expertise is in the teaching-learning process, which is an important and worthwhile treatment, whereas teachers, generally, neither have the knowledge or expertise to deal with treatments involving medication, surgery, or other medical therapies.

QUALITY PROGRAMMING

In part at least, the questions addressed in the previous sections of this chapter have recently become issues in special education because of the concern by many parents and educators for accountability. Accountability has, in the last few years, become a password in education. Subjectivism in educating the handicapped shifted to more objective questions focusing on quantitative accountability: How many children are being served or not served? How many hours per day is service being provided? How many certified teachers are available? Quantitative accountability was a major step in the evolution of special education.

On the heels of the quantitative accountability movement, demands for *qualitative* accountability (i.e., demonstrating changes in children's behavior and hence the quality of services provided) are gaining impetus. The questions in regard to servicing are beginning to change. It is assumed that all children must receive educational services (quantitative accountability), but now the questions include, Are the children receiving appropriate services? Are the children making positive gains in academic, social and other areas as a result of the programming received? In other words, data on "child change" is becoming increasingly important. Questions about changes in children's behaviors (qualitative accountability) are increasing in frequency and will soon be as prevalent as questions about how many children are being served (quantitative accountability). This shift, although a positive step in the field, is causing many educators to step back, evaluate, and in many cases reconstruct the services now being offered. Unlike quantitative accountability, in which educators can eventually feel the job is done—i.e., all children are receiving services by trained or certified teachers—*qualitative accountability* is never ending. In short, quality programming for children is a rapidly growing and ever expanding goal. (Table 3-2 is included to provide a synopsis of the trends discussed in this chapter.)

CONCLUSION

A growing number of professionals are beginning to question the wisdom of trying to change or "fix" problem behaviors (those that lead to the label handicapped) in isolated, specially designed settings such as special classrooms, clinics, and institutions. Holland (1978) pointed out that if the very theory on which behavior therapy is based is correct, then the solution to making lasting changes in behaviors cannot rest in the specially arranged contingencies in the special setting. Unfortunately, the special

Table 3–2
Trends in Special Education

Trend	Some Advocates	Impact
Normalization	Wolfensburger (1969) Reynolds and associates (1972, 1978) Hobbs (1975) Brown (1978) Lilly (1979)	Children remaining in community setting Mainstreaming
Direct and functional methods for identification of programming needs	Gallagher (1979) Haring (1977) Ysseldyke & Salvia (1974)	Changes in labeling procedures Direct assessment of programming needs in various curricular domains Intervention based on assessment
Individualization within single treatment approach	Gardner (1977) Stephens (1977) Deno (1978)	Increasing acceptance of a single learning schematic Individualization within the schematic for every child
Education as treatment	Stuart (1970) Deno (1978) Kauffman (1977)	Acceptance of the teaching/learning process as an effective treatment for children who display maladaptive behaviors
Quality programming	Martin (1975) Haring (1977)	Accountability changing from quantitative concerns (child change data will supplement number served in evaluative data)

educator or psychologist often misses the point. He/she attempts a technical fix in the clinic or special classroom for a problem such as extremely aggressive behavior or the failure of the child to interact with others. But outside the clinic all of those conditions prevail that maintain the behavior in the first place, and the behavior gradually readjusts to these conditions when the child is no longer required to function in the special setting.

Based on our current knowledge of how behaviors are acquired and maintained, this is exactly what we would expect (Haring, 1977). Behavior adapts to the contingencies operating in the environment: "the Experimental Analysis of Behavior, tells us that behavior adapts to contingencies—any contingency—not just those arranged by the psychologist" (Holland, 1978, p. 164).

Because of the need to establish conditions in all settings, not just isolated settings, that foster healthy or appropriate behaviors, a large number of people must become more aware and knowledgeable in regard to establishing and maintaining healthy environments. These people include parents, siblings, friends, policemen, janitors, bus drivers, insurance salesmen, secretaries, and grocery store clerks. According to Kazdin (1975), "a large reservoir of potential personnel which could be employed for treatment and rehabilitation purposes, namely, nonprofessionals . . . has not been utilized" (p. 9).

As the present trends progress, there is also a growing recognition that all children, not just children designated handicapped, have individual differences that influence learning. Every individual is different from another in behaviors or learning characteristics. It is ineffective to group children on the basis of a few characteristics and expect them all to learn. All individuals should receive "special attention" that focuses on meeting individual needs rather than a generic disability. Rather than focus on problems or disabilities, a negative approach, educators must focus on the strengths and needs of each child with whom they are to facilitate learning or behavior change. Thus, in the future for generic maximal educational benefit to all the concept that *Every Child Is a Special Child* will need to be accepted and practiced. Getting children back into more normal settings without labels will hopefully provide impetus to all involved individuals to begin looking at all children in regard to their individual strengths and needs rather than only labeled children, as is presently the case in many situations. Shane (1979) rightly asserts that educators in the 1980s will have an opportunity to make education more special and personalized for all children—not just for the handicapped. When all children are viewed individually the concept of *Every Child Is a Special Child* can begin to become a reality.

REFERENCES

Becker, L.D. Learning characteristics of educationally handicapped and retarded children. *Exceptional Children,* 1978, *44,* 502–511.
Beez, W.V. Influence of biased psychological reports on teacher behavior and pupil performance. *Proceedings of the 76th Annual Convention of the American Psychological Association,* 1968, pp. 605–606.
Brown, L. *Criterion of ultimate functioning.* Presented at the annual spring lec-

ture series in Special Education, University of Northern Iowa, Cedar Falls, April 1978.

Brown, L. A rationale for comprehensive longitudinal interactions between severely handicapped students and nonhandicapped students and other citizens. *AAESPH Review,* 1979, *4,* 3–14.

Cruickshank, W.M., Bentzen, F., Ratzebury, F., & Tannhauser, M.A. *A teaching method for brain-injured and hyperactive children.* Syracuse, NY: Syracuse University Press, 1961.

Deno, E. *Educating children with emotional, learning, and behavior problems.* Minneapolis: Leadership Training Institute/Special Education, University of Minnesota, 1978.

Foster, G.G., Ysseldyke, J.E., & Reese, J.H. "I wouldn't have seen it if I hadn't believed it." *Exceptional Children,* 1975, *41,* 469–473.

Gallagher, J.J. The interdisciplinary sharing of knowledge. *Journal of Special Education,* 1979, *13,* 41–43.

Gardner, W.I. *Learning and behavior characteristics of exceptional children and youth.* Boston: Allyn & Bacon, 1977.

Hamre-Nietupski, S., Branston, M.B., Gruenewald, C., & Brown, L. Curricular strategies for developing comprehensive longitudinal interactions between severely handicapped students and nonhandicapped individuals in school and nonschool environments. In L. Brown, S. Hamre-Nietupski, S. Lyon, et al (Eds.), *Curricular strategies for developing comprehensive longitudinal interactions between severely handicapped students and others and for developing acquisition and performance of skills in the presence of naturally occurring cues and correction procedures* (Vol. VIII, Part 1). Madison, WI: Madison Metropolitan School District, 1979.

Haring, N.G. Welcome address of the second annual AAESPH conference. N. G. Haring & L.J. Brown (Eds.), *Teaching the severely handicapped* (Vol. 2). New York: Grune & Stratton, 1977.

Haring, N.G., & Phillips, E.L. *Educating emotionally disturbed children.* New York: McGraw-Hill, 1962.

Haskett, M.S. *An investigation of the relationship between teacher expectancy and pupil achievement in the special education class.* Unpublished dissertation, University of Wisconsin, 1968.

Hewett, F.M. Educational engineering with emotionally disturbed children. *Exceptional Children,* 1967, *33,* 459–471.

Hobbs, N. *The futures of children.* San Francisco: Jossey-Bass, 1975.

Holland, J.G. Behaviorism: Part of the problem or part of the solution? *Journal of Applied Behavior Analysis,* 1978, *11,* 163–174.

Howell, K.W., Kaplan, J.S., & O'Connell, C.Y. *Evaluating exceptional children.* Columbus, OH: Merrill, 1979.

Kanfer, F.H., & Saslow, G. Behavioral diagnosis. In C.M. Franks (Ed.), *Behavior therapy: Appraisal and status.* New York: McGraw-Hill, 1969.

Kauffman, J.M. *Characteristics of children's behavior disorders.* Columbus, OH: Merrill, 1977.

Kazdin, A.E. *Behavior modification in applied settings.* Homewood, IL: Dorsey, 1975.

Lilly, M.S. *Children with exceptional needs.* New York: Holt, Rinehart & Winston, 1979.

Martin, E. The federal commitment to education of the severely and profoundly retarded. In *Educating the 24 Hour Retarded Child,* Arlington, Texas: NARC, 1975.

Pasanella, A., & Volkner, C. *Coming back . . . or never leaving.* Columbus, OH: Merrill, 1977.

Reynolds, M.C., & Barlow, B. Categories and variables in special education. *Exceptional children,* 1972, *38,* 357–366.

Reynolds, M.C., & Birch, J.W. *Teaching exceptional children in all America's schools.* Reston, VA: Council for Exceptional Children, 1977.

Russo, D.C., & Koegel, R.L. A method for integrating the autistic child into a normal public-school classroom. *Journal of Applied Behavior Analysis,* 1977, *10,* 579–590.

Samuels, J.S. An outside view of neuropsychological testing. *Journal of Special Education,* 1979, *13,* 57–60.

Shane, H. Forecast for the 80's. *Today's Education,* 1979, *68,* 62–65.

Simches, R.F. The inside-outsiders. *Exceptional Children,* 1970, *37,* 5–15.

Stephens, T.M. *Teaching skills to children with learning and behavior disorders.* Columbus, OH: Merrill, 1977.

Stuart, R.B. *Trick or treatment: How and when psychotherapy fails.* Champaign, IL: Research Press, 1970.

Ysseldyke, J.E., & Salvia, J. Diagnostic prescriptive teaching: Two models. *Exceptional children,* 1974, *41,* 181–186.

Wolfensberger, W. The origin and nature of our institutional models. In R. B. Kugel & W. Wolfensberger (Eds.), *Changing patterns in residential services for the mentally retarded.* Washington, DC: President's Committee on Mental Retardation, 1969.

Zigler, E., & Phillips, L. Psychiatric diagnosis and symptomatology. *Journal of Abnormal Social Psychology,* 1961, *63,* 69–75.

SELECTED READINGS FOR FURTHER STUDY

Brown, L. A rationale for comprehensive longitudinal interactions between severely handicapped students and nonhandicapped students and other citizens. *AAESPH* Review, 1979, *4,* 3–14.

Deno, E. *Educating children with emotional, learning, and behavior problems.* Minneapolis: Leadership Training Institute/Special Education, University of Minnesota, 1978.

Gallagher, J.J. The interdisciplinary sharing of knowledge. *Journal of Special Education,* 1979, *13,* 41–43.

Haring, N.G. Welcome address of the second annual AAESPH conference. In N.G. Haring & L.J. Brown (Eds.), *Teaching the severely handicapped* (Vol. 2). New York: Grune & Stratton, 1977.

Holland, J.G. Behaviorism: Part of the problems or part of the solution? *Journal of Applied Behavior Analysis,* 1978, *11,* 164–174.

Lilly, M.S. *Children with exceptional needs.* New York: Holt, Rinehart & Winston, 1979.

Reynolds, M.C., & Barlow, B. Categories and variables in special education. *Exceptional Children,* 1972, *38,* 357–366.

PART II

The educational training needs of children who exhibit severe forms of maladaptive behavior are the concern of Part II. Chapter 4 examines programming in general, while each of the four other chapters in Part II focus on a specific curricular area.

More specifically, Chapter 5 considers some of the most common factors that should be taken into account when teaching children who display severe forms of maladaptive behavior. Chapter 6 provides information regarding teaching considerations and procedures for developing basic language skills. Then Chapter 7 discusses procedures that have proven successful in changing social, emotional, and attitudinal behaviors. In Chapter 8 the focus is on teaching for self-control, and Chapter 9 details procedures for reducing severe forms of maladaptive behavior.

The four specific training areas addressed in Chapters 6 through 9 were selected for two reasons. One, they are of paramount importance in facilitating and enhancing the adaptability of any child to classroom environments. Self-control and attitudinal, emotional, and social development as well as the development of language and the absence of severe maladaptive behaviors are critical to the functioning of all children. Second, many of the children about whom this volume is concerned require extensive training in these areas.

4
General Considerations in Programming

The process of learning—involving assessment, determining objectives, and designing programs as well as ongoing monitoring and evaluation—is the same for students labeled seriously disturbed as it is for other students. Educating some students, especially those who display very serious behavioral maladjustments, however, does require that the teacher be able to recognize, monitor, and systematically modify certain critical variables or difficulties.

Some of these critical variables or difficulties are disruptive behavior, self-stimulation, lack of motivation, and stimulus overselectivity. Also included is the difficulty many of these children have learning in a large group and the fact that any gains that are made tend not to generalize and maintain. These difficulties tend to impede the education process.

The purpose of this chapter is to provide an overview of the most common variables that tend to interfere with the education of children who exhibit severe maladaptive behavior. In addition, a few critical teaching procedures teachers need to be proficient in using to facilitate the academic and social progress of these children are reviewed.

Most of the information contained in this chapter was adapted directly from the following sources: G. Dunlap, R. Koegel, and A. Egel, "Autistic Children in the School," *Exceptional Children,* 1979, *45,* 552–558; and A. Rincover, R. Koegel, and D. Russo, "Some Recent Behavioral Research on the Education of Autistic Children," *Education and Treatment of Children,* 1978, *1,* 31–45. All information is reprinted with permission.

DISRUPTIVE BEHAVIORS

Disruptive behaviors such as tantrums and aggression toward self, other people, and objects generally cause major disturbances and, as such, must be promptly eliminated if the child is going to remain in school. Fortunately, researchers have established a relatively thorough understanding of the variables known to control even the most extreme of these behaviors (Carr, 1977) and have developed a number of effective treatment techniques. For example, the availability of time-out (Bostow & Baily, 1969; Solnick, Rincover, & Peterson, 1977), restitutional over-correction (Foxx & Azrin, 1972), paced instructions (Plummer, Baer & LeBlanc, 1977), extinction and the use of aversives (Lovaas & Simmons, 1969), and reinforcement for nonresponding (Repp & Deitz, 1974) illustrate the wide variety of options. The importance of knowing how to select the *right procedures* for the *right child* and situation should be stressed. The reader is referred to Chapter 8 for more details related to these procedures.

SELF-STIMULATION

Self-stimulation has posed one of the most pervasive and resistant obstacles to effective treatment. A number of studies have shown its interference and incompatibility with learning and performance of appropriate behaviors (Koegel & Covert, 1972; Koegel, Firestone, Kramme, & Dunlap, 1974; Lovaas, Litrownik, & Mann, 1971; Risley, 1968). Thus, elimination of self-stimulatory behaviors is highly recommended as one of the first steps in treatment.

Attempts to reduce these behaviors have included the use of reinforcement for nonresponding (Deitz & Repp, 1973; Mulhern & Baumeister, 1969), contingent electric shock (Lovaas, Schaeffer & Simmons, 1965; Risley, 1968), a quick slap on the hand (Foxx & Azrin, 1973; Koegel & Covert, 1972), brief contingent restraint (Koegel et al., 1974), positive practice overcorrection (Epstein, Doke, Sajwaj, et al, 1974; Foxx & Azrin, 1973; Wells, Forehand, Hickey, & Green, 1977), and sensory extinction (Rincover, 1978 a). Exactly how some of these procedures are employed is outlined in Chapter 8.

MOTIVATION

A major difficulty encountered in the classroom treatment of disturbed children is the problem of motivation. Left to themselves, these children show little, if any, motivation to learn new appropriate behaviors. In the past most treatment programs attempted to overcome this problem by selecting powerful primary reinforcers, such as food (Lovaas, Berberich, Perloff, & Schaeffer, 1966; Risley & Wolf, 1967); and pain reduction (Lovaas, Schaeffer, & Simmons, 1965). Serious problems, however, often arise in the use of these primary reinforcers. Such reinforcers are "artificial" in the sense that they do not occur contingently in the natural environment (Ferster, 1967). As a result, children seem to discriminate between training and posttraining settings, on the basis of these reinforcers, and responding eventually extinguishes in extratherapy environments (Koegel & Rincover, 1977; Lovaas, Koegel, Simmons, & Long, 1973). The behaviors developed with primary reinforcers are generally limited to those environments where such reinforcers are consistently available. In addition, reinforcers such as food have high satiation characteristics; after a relatively short period of time responding becomes inconsistent and the children are very difficult to teach.

At least some children labeled seriously disturbed appear highly motivated to perform certain behaviors. In particular, they may persistently engage in stereotyped, repetitive behavior, such as rhythmic rocking, finger flapping, and spinning objects in their environment (Foxx & Azrin, 1973; Koegel & Covert, 1972; Lovaas, Litrownik, & Mann, 1971; Rimland, 1964). In general, these self-stimulatory behaviors appear to provide no external consequences. Rather, they appear to be maintained primarily by the sensory stimulation that they produce (Rincover, 1978 b).

Since some of these children spend so much time engaged in self-stimulatory behavior, the implication may be that sensory stimulation is an extremely powerful reinforcer for these children. Furthermore, a substantial amount of data has accumulated that demonstrates such a functional relationship between operant behavior and its sensory consequences. These studies are generally considered to evidence an operation described as "sensory reinforcement," which refers to the unconditioned properties of sensory events to increase the probability of behaviors that they follow (Kish, 1966).

Two approaches have been identified in which sensory reinforcement might be manipulated in an attempt to teach such children. First, researchers have attempted to identify and use sensory events as (external) reinforcers to teach these children. For example, teachers of four autistic children were asked what kind of sensory stimulation was preferred by each child. When these stimuli (strobe light, music, and the like) were briefly presented contingent on correct responses, the children were able to learn simple language skills. Subsequently, the researchers investigated how powerful these externalized sensory stimuli were in maintaining behavior by providing five seconds of each type of sensory stimulation contingent on five bar presses (FR5). The results showed, first, that the reinforcing effects of these sensory stimuli were idiosyncratic to specific children. For example, one child preferred the music and another child preferred a strobe light. In addition, it was found that these sensory reinforcers produced a relatively high rate of responding that proved quite durable over time, although response rates varied to a great extent across sessions. Finally, it was discovered that the children did eventually satiate on their initially preferred sensory event; however, only a small change in that sensory event (e.g., changing the frequency of the strobe) resulted in a renewed high rate of responding that was equally durable over time (Rincover, Newsom, Lovaas, & Koegel, 1977).

This study illustrated that some sensory events occurring in the child's natural environment can have a reinforcing effect. These reinforcers also were found to have very low satiation characteristics, which may yield more favorable results in treatment than edible reinforcers (Rincover & Berry, 1977).

A second approach to using sensory reinforcers lies in the direct manipulation of self-stimulatory behavior. For example, research in the area of sensory deprivation shows that under various conditions of sensory restriction organisms will respond to obtain alternate sources of stimulation (Zubeck, 1969). Therefore, Newsom (1974) conducted a study to investigate the effects of restricting certain types of sensory stimulation in autistic children by restraining their most persistent self-stimulatory behavior. Significantly, he found that when one such behavior was suppressed, another self-stimulatory behavior immediately increased. Koegel, Firestone, Kramme, and Dunlap (1974) then set out to determine the effects of suppressing all of a child's self-stimulatory behavior. Initially, in an attempt to "prime" an adaptive behavior to replace self-stimulation, each child was first trained to play appropriately with a variety of toys. After pretraining with toys, with no restrictions yet on self-stimulatory behavior, the children spent most of their time engaged in self-stimulation and showed little interest in the toys. When self-stimulation was subsequently suppressed, appropriate play rose to a high level without external reinforcement (cf. Epstein, Doke, Sajwaj, et al, 1974). An important problem still remained, as discussed by Koegel and associates (1974), in the continued dependence of appropriate play on the suppression of self-stimulation: when the children were returned to baseline conditions (no suppression), self-stimulation immediately increased to base level and appropriate play decreased or dropped out entirely.

Further research is obviously needed to investigate the extent of behavior change that can be produced by restricting self-stimulation in addition to procedures for maintaining changes in these nontarget behaviors. One such study investigated the amount of adaptive behavior change that can be programmed and maintained by eliminating self-stimulatory behavior through "sensory extinction," a procedure that may produce a durable suppression of self-stimulation (Rincover, 1978a). Self-stimulatory behavior was eliminated in two children when a certain sensory consequence to that behavior was masked or removed. For example, a child who initially would spin or twirl objects (e.g., a plate) on a hard surface immediately ceased to engage in that self-stimulatory behavior when the auditory feedback was removed by carpeting the table. In an attempt to program maintenance, the child was subsequently taught to play with toys producing his preferred kind of sensory stimulation (Rincover, Cook, Peoples, & Packard, 1979). The results showed that: (1) the child engaged in spontaneous appropriate play—however, he played only with the toy producing auditory feedback; and (2) with no carpeting on the table, self-stimulation was maintained at or near zero frequency. A second child participated in the "sensory extinction" procedure, with similar results. Child 2 engaged in stereotyped, repetitive finger flapping, which was extinguished by masking the proprioceptive feedback with a vibrator (placed on the back of his hand). The maintenance results for Child 2 were similar to those of Child 1, with the following exception: this child played only with the toys producing kinesthetic stimulation.

STIMULUS OVERSELECTIVITY

As mentioned in Chapter 1, overselectivity has received and will likely continue to receive considerable attention. It concerns the tendency of some seriously disturbed children, particularly those labeled as being autistic, to respond to only a restricted portion of complex stimuli in their environment (Lovaas, Schreibman, Koegel, & Rehm, 1971). The ramifications of overselective responding have been discussed in relation to much of the children's development, including language acquisition (Lovaas et al., 1973), social behavior (Schreibman & Lovaas, 1973), generalization of responding across environments (Rincover & Koegel, 1975), and ability to use extra stimuli to guide learning (Koegel & Rincover, 1976).

Consider the effect that overselectivity has had on the development and refinement of prompting techniques. Prompts typically are extra stimuli that teachers employ in conjunction with instructions to guide children to the completion of correct responses (e.g., pointing to an E in an E versus F discrimination, when the instruction "Touch E" is presented). Overselectivity research has shown that while some children may respond correctly with the prompt present, they have difficulty in transferring their responding to the (verbal) instruction as the prompt is withdrawn. While this has been found repeatedly to be the case with extra stimulus prompts, Schreibman (1975) and Rincover (1978b) have developed prompting procedures that work around the selective responding problem. Their strategies, which are very applicable in school environments, rely on within-stimulus prompts that exaggerate the distinctive features of the target stimuli (e.g., thickening the bottom bar of the *E* in the *E* versus *F* discrimination). Thus, the child is not required to respond to extra stimuli, and overselectivity does not present a learning problem.

Other strategies for overcoming the problem of overselectivity per se are also under examination (Koegel & Schreibman, 1977; Schreibman, Koegel, & Craig, 1977), but at the moment the within-stimulus prompt approaches appear to be the most useful. An awareness of the phenomenon may, in itself, assist teachers in understanding and dealing with the problem.

GENERALIZATION AND MAINTENANCE OF GAINS

Many studies have shown that gains made by children in clinic or school settings do not automatically transfer to other environments (e.g., Stokes & Baer, 1977). In 1975 Rincover and Koegel related the failure of generalization in some children labeled seriously disturbed (autistic in this case) to overselectivity; that is, analyses showed that many children responded in clinic sessions to idiosyncratic and often irrelevant stimuli (e.g., mannerisms of the therapist) that were not necessarily present in extraclinic situations. In order to overcome this problem, it appears to be necessary to identify the stimulus that the children selectively respond to and ensure that it is one that is present in extratherapy environments.

In a later study Koegel and Rincover (1977) showed that generalization problems had an additional dimension. Performance of treatment gains in extraclinic settings typically failed to maintain for more than a few trials, giving the impression that the child had not generalized. In this case, however, the children had discriminated between settings in terms of differential reward schedules and merely ceased responding in one environment. To overcome this problem, the researchers disguised the distinction between the environments by (1) thinning the reinforcement schedule in the clinic and (2) providing occasional rewards in the extraclinic setting. The combination of these two procedures produced durable performance in both settings. These results highlight the influence teachers can exert beyond the classroom.

LEARNING IN A LARGE GROUP

One problem that immediately surfaces in a classroom setting is that behaviors acquired in a one-to-one situation often do not generalize to a larger group setting (Bijou, 1972; Koegel & Rincover, 1974; Peterson, Cox, and Bijou, 1972). In one classroom study (Koegel & Rincover, 1974) eight seriously disturbed children were individually taught a number of basic classroom skills, such as attending to the teacher, verbal and non-verbal imitation, and simple receptive language skills. Then, their performance of the same skills was measured in larger group sizes. The data showed that performance of behaviors learned in one-to-one sessions was greatly reduced in a classroom-sized group of eight children with one teacher. Furthermore, performance was significantly reduced in a group of only two children. In conjunction with these results, additional weekly observations of these children in a group of eight, during which time the teacher attempted to train new behavior, indicated that no new learning occurred.

In the second phase of this experiment procedures for gradually increasing the group size were introduced in an attempt to program generalization from 1:1 to 8:1. Initially children participated in 1:1 sessions in which the schedule of reinforcement was thinned from CRF (continuous reinforcement) to FR2 (a reinforcer after two correct responses). Then, when each child performed two responses for only one reinforcer, two children were brought together with one teacher and two teacher aides, and the aides alternately reinforced one child on one trial and the second child on the next. The teacher aides initially prompted the children to respond when no response occurred, and the prompt was faded on subsequent trials. When these two children were responding correctly on at least 80 percent of the trials, with no prompts, the schedule of reinforcement was again gradually thinned to FR4 (a reinforcer after four correct responses). At that point the two children were brought together with two other children who had participated in similar training, to form a group of four. These fading procedures continued until the final group size of eight children was achieved, where each child would reliably and accurately respond to questions and instructions for infrequent rewards. Furthermore, it is significant that when these basic attention and imitation skills generalized to the group of eight, via this fading procedure, each child then acquired new skills in the classroom of eight children with one teacher, such as telling time, reading first-grade books, printing letters of the alphabet, and solving arithmetic problems.

It should be noted here that there is some evidence that at least some children labeled seriously disturbed can function in groups larger than eight when the teacher is trained to deal with the unique behavior of the children. For example, Russo and Koegel (1977) demonstrated that a child classified as being autistic could be integrated into a normal public school classroom with one teacher and 20 to 30 "normal" children. These researchers had a behavioral specialist work with the child in the regular classroom; afterward they trained the child's regular teachers to foster

and maintain the gains made by the specialist. This was apparently sufficient to maintain the child within the regular classroom with her peers
throughout kindergarten and the first grade (see Chapter 11 for more information).

CRITICAL PROCEDURES FOR TEACHING

√ Five procedures have been described that appear to help a person
teach children labeled seriously disturbed (Koegel, Russo, & Rincover,
1977). The procedures can be summarized as follows: First, the teachers
must know how to present instructions correctly. Instructions should be
clear, consistent, and to the point, not obscured among a barrage of verbi-
age. A teacher should also know how to present reinforcers effectively. A
reinforcer can be described as any stimulus that the child will work to
obtain. A reinforcer should be given immediately after a correct response
and only after correct responses, so that the child will soon associate the
correct response with reward.

The third procedure a teacher should know is how to shape a new
behavior by rewarding successive approximations (Skinner, 1953). There
are some behaviors that are best taught by breaking them down into
small, graduated steps. For example, to teach a child to imitate the word
"mama," a teacher may first give the child a reward every time he/she
says "m" (which may be a very frequent sound in his repertoire). Then,
when the child is saying "m" consistently, one can reward the child only
when he says "ma." After the child has learned this, he may be rewarded
only when he says "mama."

A teacher should also know how to prompt or guide the child to respond correctly and how to fade out that prompt or guidance so that the
child is responding on his own (Koegel & Rincover, 1976; Rincover,
1978a; Schreibman, 1975). If the child is echolalic and the teacher says,
"What color is this?" the child may simply echo the question. In this case
the teacher might prompt a correct response by saying the question very
softly and then immediately modeling the correct response, for example,
"red," in a loud voice. In this way the child may not repeat the question,
yet will repeat the correct answer. On subsequent trials the teacher would
fade and eventually remove the prompt. For example, the loudness of the
question could be gradually increased, and the loudness of the model
("red") decreased, until the child is consistently answering "red" to the
question "What color is this?"

Numerous procedures can be used to prompt a child and to fade the
prompt subsequently. Consequently, it is often difficult to decide which
prompt to use and how to remove it. Furthermore, it is easy to err when

using such procedures; for example, certain prompts may not facilitate correct responding for a given child or the child may selectively respond to the prompt and learn nothing about the instruction. A teacher should exercise great care when using prompting procedures, and we refer the reader to more detailed discussions of these issues in Koegel and Rincover (1976), Koegel and Schreibman (1977), Newsom and Simon (1977), Rincover (1978b), Rincover and Koegel (1975), and Schreibman (1975).

A final procedure that a teacher should know is how to present discrete trials. This simply means that between the end of one trial (e.g., the reinforcer) and the beginning of the next (e.g., the next instruction) there should be a time interval in which no on-task responding is required. A consistent series of discrete trials minimizes distracting and confusing information, thereby helping the child to learn as quickly as possible.

There are obviously other procedures that teachers should be aware of, such as defining, measuring, and charting behaviors. These procedures are covered thoroughly in numerous textbooks in psychology and special education and therefore are not discussed here. The reader who might desire or need information about these and other procedures is referred to Sulzer-Azaroff and Mayer (1977) and Martin and Pear (1978).

REFERENCES

Bijou, S.W. The technology of teaching handicapped children. In S.W. Bijou & E. Rebes-Inesta (Eds.), *Behavior modification: Issues and extensions.* New York: Academic Press, 1972.

Bostow, D.E., & Bailey, J.B. Modification of severe disruptive and aggressive behavior using brief timeout and reinforcement procedures. *Journal of Applied Behavior Analysis,* 1969, *2,* 31–38.

Carr, E.G. The motivation of self-injurious behavior: A review of some hypotheses. *Psychological Bulletin,* 1977, *84,* 800–816.

Deitz, S.M., & Repp. A. C. Decreasing classroom misbehavior through the use of DRL schedules of reinforcement. *Journal of Applied Behavior Analysis,* 1973, *7,* 385–390.

Dunlap, G., Koegel, R., & Egel. A. Autistic children in the school. *Exceptional Children,* 1979, *45,* 552–558.

Epstein, L.H., Doke, L.A., Sajwaj, T.E., et al. Generality and side effects of overcorrection. *Journal of Applied Behavior Analysis,* 1974, *7,* 385–390.

Ferster, C.B. Arbitrary and natural reinforcement. *Psychological Record,* 1967, *17,* 341–347.

Foxx, R.M., & Azrin, N.H. Restitution: A method of eliminating aggressive-disruptive behavior of retarded and brain-damaged patients. *Behaviour Reserach and Therapy,* 1972, *10,* 15–27.

Foxx, R.M., & Azrin, N. The elimination of autistic self-stimulatory behavior by overcorrection. *Journal of Applied Behavior Analysis,* 1973, *6,* 1–14.

Kish, G.B. Studies of sensory reinforcement. In W.K. Honig (Ed.), *Operant behavior: Areas of research and application*. New York: Appleton-Century-Crofts, 1966.

Koegel, R.L., & Covert, A. The relationship of self-stimulation to learning in autistic children. *Journal of Applied Behavior Analysis*, 1972, *5*, 381–387.

Koegel, R.L., Firestone, P.B., Kramme, K.W., & Dunlap, G. Increasing spontaneous play by suppressing self-stimulation in autistic children. *Journal of Applied Behavior Analysis*, 1974, *7*, 521–528.

Koegel, R.L., & Rincover, A. Treatment of psychotic children in a classroom environment: I. Learning in a large group. *Journal of Applied Behavior Analysis*, 1974, *7*, 45–49.

Koegel, R.L., & Rincover, A. Some detrimental effects of using extra stimuli to guide learning in normal and autistic children. *Journal of Abnormal Child Psychology*, 1976, *4*, 59–71.

Koegel, R.L., & Rincover, A. Research on the difference between generalization and maintenance in extra-therapy responding. *Journal of Applied Behavior Analysis*, 1977, *10*, 1–12.

Koegel, R.L., Russo, D.C., & Rincover, A. Assessing and training teachers in the generalized use of behavior modification with autistic children. *Journal of Applied Behavior Analysis*, 1977, *10*, 197–205.

Koegel, R.L., & Schreibman, L. Teaching autistic children to respond to simultaneous multiple cues. *Journal of Experimental Child Psychology*, 1977, *24*, 299–311.

Lovaas, O.I., Berberich, J.P., Perloff, B.F., & Schaeffer, B. Acquisiton of imitative speech in schizophrenic children. *Science*, 1966, *151*, 705–707.

Lovaas, O.I., Koegel, R.L., Simmons, J.Q., & Long, J.S. Some generalization and follow-up measures on autistic children in behavior therapy. *Journal of Applied Behavior Analysis*, 1973, *6*, 131–166.

Lovaas, O.I., Litrownik, A., & Mann, R. Response latencies to auditory stimuli in autistic children engaged in self-stimulatory behavior. *Behaviour Research and Therapy*, 1971, *9*, 39–49.

Lovaas, O.I., Schaeffer, B., & Simmons, J.Q. Building social behavior in autistic children by use of electric shock. *Journal of Experimental Research and Personality*, 1965, *1*, 99–109.

Lovaas, O.I., Schreibman, L., Koegel, R.L., & Rehm, R. Selective responding by autistic children to multiple sensory input. *Journal of Abnormal Psychology*, 1971, *77*, 211–222.

Lovaas, O.I., & Simmons, J. Q. Manipulation of self-destruction in three retarded children. *Journal of Applied Behavior Analysis*, 1969, *2*, 143–157.

Martin, G., & Pear, J. *Behavior modification: What it is and how to do it*. Englewood Cliffs, NJ: Prentice-Hall, 1978.

Mulhern, T., & Baumeister, A.A. An experimental attempt to reduce stereotype by reinforcement procedures. *American Journal of Mental Deficiency*, 1969, *74*, 69–74.

Newsom, C.D. *The role of sensory reinforcement in self-stimulatory behavior*. Unpublished doctoral dissertation, University of California at Los Angeles, 1974.

Newsom, C.D., & Simon, K.M. A simultaneous discrimination procedure for the measurement of vision in nonverbal children. *Journal of Applied Behavior Analysis*, 1977, *10*, 633–644.

Peterson, R.F., Cox, M.A., & Bijou, S.W. Training children to work productively in classroom groups. *Exceptional Children*, 1972, *37*, 491–500.

Plummer, S., Baer, D.M., & LeBlanc, J.M. Functional considerations in the use of procedural timeout and effective alternative. *Journal of Applied Behavior Analysis*, 1977, *10*, 689–706.

Repp, A.C., & Deitz, S.M. Reducing aggressive and self-injurious behavior of institutionalized retarded children through reinforcement of other behaviors. *Journal of Applied Behavior Analysis*, 1974, *7*, 313–326.

Rimland, B. *Infantile autism*. New York: Appleton-Century-Crofts, 1964.

Rincover, A. Sensory extinction: A procedure for eliminating self-stimulatory behavior in autistic children. *Journal of Abnormal Child Psychology*, 1978a, *6*, 299–310.

Rincover, A. Variables affecting stimulus-fading and discriminative responding in psychotic children. *Journal of Abnormal Psychology*, 1978b, *87*, 541–553.

Rincover, A., & Berry, K. *Comparing sensory and edible reinforcers in the treatment of autistic children*. New York: Association for the Advancement of Behavior Therapy, New York, 1977.

Rincover, A., Cook, R., Peoples, A., & Packard, D. Using sensory extinction and sensory reinforcement principles for programming multiple treatment gains in autistic children. *Journal of Applied Behavior Analysis*, 1979, *12*, 221–233.

Rincover, A., & Koegel, R.L. Setting generality and stimulus control in autistic children. *Journal of Applied Behavior Analysis*, 1975, *8*, 235–246.

Rincover, A., Koegel, R., & Russo, D. Some recent behavioral research on the education of autistic children. *Education and Treatment of Children*, 1978, *1*, 31–45.

Rincover, A., Newsom, D.C., Lovaas, O.I., & Koegel, R.L. Some motivational properties of sensory stimulation in psychotic children. *Journal of Experimental Child Psychology*, 1977, *24*, 312–323.

Risley, T.R. The effects and side effects of punishing the autistic behaviors of a deviant child. *Journal of Applied Behavior Analysis*, 1968, *1*, 21–34.

Risley, T.R., & Wolf, M.M. Establishing functional speech in echolalic children. *Behaviour Research and Therapy*, 1967, *5*, 73–88.

Russo, D., & Koegel, R. A method for integrating an autistic child into a normal public school classroom. *Journal of Applied Behavior Analysis*, 1977, *10*, 579–590.

Schreibman, L. Effects of within-stimulus and extra-stimulus prompting on discrimination learning in autistic children. *Journal of Applied Behavior Analysis*, 1975, *8*, 91–112

Schreibman, L., Koegel, R.L., & Craig, M.S. Reducing stimulus overselectivity in autistic children. *Journal of Abnormal Child Psychology*, 1977, *5*, 425–436.

Schreibman, L., & Lovaas, O.I. Overselective response to social stimuli by autistic children. *Journal of Abnormal Child Psychology*, 1973, *1*, 152–168.

Skinner, B.F. *Science and human behavior*. New York: Free Press, 1953.

Solnick, J.V., Rincover, A., & Peterson, C.R. Determinants of the reinforcing and punishing effects of time-out. *Journal of Applied Behavior Analysis*, 1977, *10*, 415–424.

Stokes, T.F., & Baer, D.M. An implicit technology of generalization. *Journal of Applied Behavior Analysis,* 1977, *10,* 349–368.

Sulzer-Azaroff, B., & Mayer, G. *Applying behavior analysis procedures with children and youth.* New York: Holt, Rinehart & Winston, 1977.

Wells, K.C., Forehand, R., Hickey, K., & Green, K.D. Effects of a procedure derived from the overcorrection principle on manipulated and nonmanipulated behaviors. *Journal of Applied Behavior Analysis,* 1977, *10,* 679–688.

Zubek, J.P. *Sensory deprivation: Fifteen years of research.* New York: Appleton-Century-Crofts, 1969.

SELECTED READINGS FOR FURTHER STUDY

Carr, E.G. The motivation of self-injurious behavior: A review of some hypotheses. *Psychological Bulletin,* 1977, *84,* 800–816.

Dunlap, G., Koegel, R., and Egel, A. Autistic children in the school. *Exceptional Children,* 1979, *45,* 552–558.

Ferster, C.B. Arbitrary and natural reinforcement. *Psychological Record,* 1967, *17,* 341–347.

Koegel, R.L., & Covert, A. The relationship of self-stimulation to learning in autistic children. *Journal of Applied Behavior Analysis,* 1972, *5,*381–387.

Koegel, R.L., Russo, D.C., & Rincover, A. Assessing and training teachers in the generalized use of behavior modification with autistic children. *Journal of Applied Behavior Analysis,* 1977, *10,* 197–205.

Rincover, A. Sensory extinction: A procedure for the treatment of self-stimulation in autistic and retarded children. *Journal of Abnormal Child Psychology,* 1978a, *6,* 299–310.

Rincover, A. Variables affecting stimulus-fading and discriminative responding in psychotic children. *Journal of Abnormal Psychology,* 1978b, *87,* 541–553.

Rincover, A., Koegel, R., & Russo, D. Some recent behavioral research on the education of autistic children. *Education and Treatment of Children,* 1978, *1,* 31–45.

Risley, T.R. The effects and side effects of punishing the autistic behaviors of a deviant child. *Journal of Applied Behavior Analysis,* 1968, *1,* 21–34.

Stokes, T.F., & Baer, D.M. An implicit technology of generalization. *Journal of Applied Behavior Analysis,* 1977, *10,* 349–368.

5
Teaching Language to the Nonverbal Child

A severe delay in language development, and as a consequence the inability to communicate effectively, is a common characteristic of children who exhibit severe forms of maladaptive behavior. Unfortunately, without extensive training, many of these children are unable to communicate their basic needs and feelings. They cannot express their pain, joys, and satisfactions or understand what others try to communicate to them.

Not long ago many educators and psychologists rationalized that the language problems of these children were beyond help. It has only been within the past several decades that serious attention has been given to developing intervention strategies to enhance the language development of children given labels such as seriously disturbed, retarded, psychotic, autistic, or handicapped. Fortunately, research (e.g., Lovaas, Berberick, Perloff, & Schaeffer, 1966) has demonstrated that many of these interventions can successfully change the language behaviors of these children. Children who could not communicate in the past are now being helped to learn speech and language systems that can be used to communicate effectively with teachers, parents, classmates, and friends.

The importance of learning language is enhanced when we consider that the ability to communicate is basic to the very quality of human life as well as the success of the education process. It permits an otherwise isolated individual to interact with others. Since language is critical to the basic potential of the children to profit from a wide array of informal and formal educational experiences, this chapter is extensive. The chapter is divided into seven sections:

1 Language
2 Normal language acquisition

LANGUAGE

Before discussing how language develops and how it can be taught, we should define basic terminology often used in discussions of language development.

Language, Speech, and Communication

First, the terms language, speech, and communication should be clarified. *Language* "is a set of rules and principles by which symbolic representations and meanings are correlated" (Schiefelbush, Ruder, & Bricker, 1976, p. 272). It is the symbolic representation of information. In short, it is a symbol system, and the symbols can be verbal or nonverbal.

Speech is the oral, vocal response mode by which spoken language becomes overt behavior. "Speech involves the use of systemized vocalizations or articulations usually to express words or verbal symbols" (Berry, 1976, p. 8). Speech can be divided into at least three major components: (1) articulation—the formation of sounds; (2) rhythm—the timing of sounds and words in the production of verbalizations; and (3) voice—production of sounds by means of vocal-fold vibrations with modification by the resonators.

Rieke (1978) explains clearly that *communication* "is the giving and receiving of information, signals, or messages. It is an exchange between people, but is *not* limited to oral or written words. It may be accomplished by gesturing, talking, or writing" (p. 119). A child can possess adequate language and speech but not be an effective communicator. He may not listen to the teacher and, consequently, not comprehend instructions, or perhaps he never asks questions or talks with his peers. He has a problem communicating (giving and receiving information) although his language and speech development is adequate. On the other hand, a child can, at least minimally, communicate with others and not possess either adequate speech or a formal language system. Eye movements, arm movements and/or smiles, for example, often communicate a message.

Structural Levels of Language

Language is composed of four structural levels—phonology, morphology, syntax, and semantics.

Phonology deals with the production of speech sounds. At this level, the focus is on the articulation of sounds. A phoneme is the smallest indivisible unit of sound. Phonemes correlate with changes of meaning in words as in *t*op and *p*op. A morpheme (smallest indivisible unit of meaning) is made up of one or more phonemes. The morpheme *I* is made up of a single phoneme, whereas the morpheme *my* is made up of two separate sounds (Cohen, Gross, & Haring, 1976; Lahey, 1973).

Morphology is the linguistic system of meaning units in language. A morpheme is the smallest indivisible unit of meaning. According to Lahey (1973), morphemes include words such as *graph* that cannot be broken down into smaller units. Meaningful units that cannot stand alone such as prefixes (e.g., poly) and suffixes (e.g., the plural morpheme *s)* are included also.

Syntax is the specification of the patterns in which linguistic forms, such as words and phrases, are arranged (Cohen, Gross, & Haring, 1976). In other words, syntax refers to the grammar system of language—the way words are put together to form sentences. "A car pushes Billy" has a different meaning from "Billy pushes a car."

Semantics refers to "the specification of the meanings of linguistic forms and syntactic patterns in relation to objects, events, processes, attributes, and relationships in human experience" (Carroll, 1967, p. 43). It is the system of *meaning* in language. It is probably the least understood aspect of language. Children with semantic language problems may have little vocabulary understanding and usage and may have difficulty relating a string of words to a meaningful association (Lerner, 1976).

Receptive and Expressive Functions

The skills of receiving and understanding information are termed "decoding" or "receptive functions." Typically, in the educational process, we receive information primarily through the auditory and visual channels. We also, of course, receive information through the touch, taste, and smell channels. The reception of a message by the receiver can only be ascertained by observing what the receiver does (e.g., points, speaks) as a consequence of a message being sent or provided. For example, if we ask a child to touch his nose, the only way to determine if he actually received the message is to observe what he does. If he touches his nose, we assume that he received the message and that he has a receptive vocabulary and understanding of the phrase "touch your nose." If he does not touch his nose, we have no way of knowing whether or not he actually received and understood the message. He might have received the message but chose because of motivational reasons not to respond, or he may not have responded because of physiological impairment in regard to such things as the muscle strength and coordination needed to touch his nose. There are numerous reasons why he may not have responded. The point being made is that "the reception of the message can only be ascertained by observing some consequent act (performance) on the part of the receiver" (Gray & Ryan, 1973, p. 2).

In regard to receptive functions, the function of understanding the meaning of language has begun to receive considerable attention. More specifically, the importance of cognitive structure development as described by Piaget is being recognized as a critical factor (Furth, 1970). Understanding (semantic ability) language is presently assumed by some language specialists (Miller, 1977; Miller & Yoder, 1972a) to involve not only the past and present experiences of the child, but also his cognitive abilities on the figurative level, making present of a concrete reality (e.g., imitation, play) and making the operative level a stage of more abstract knowledge and understanding (e.g., time, space, causality).

The skills of producing or expressing information are termed "encoding" or "expressive functions." In the educational process we express information primarily thorugh speaking and writing. Speaking and writing behaviors are directly observable. Although speaking and writing, as vehicles for expressive communication, are desired whenever possible, we should not overlook the role of eye movements, hand and arm movements, smiles, and a wide variety of gestures as vehicles for the expression of messages.

In regard to the acquisition of these two sets of skills, receptive and productive (expressive), there is controversy concerning which skills come first. The traditional thesis is that reception (comprehension) precedes production (Fraser, Bellugi, & Brown, 1963; Ingram, 1974; McCarthy, 1954; Miller, 1977; Shipley, Smith and Gleitman, 1969). Some educators have postulated that production may precede comprehension (Guess, Sailor, & Baer, 1974); others consider it not to be a matter of importance (Gray & Ryan, 1973). Several research studies tend to indicate that reception and expression may be functionally independent in the early stages of language development (Guess & Baer, 1973) while at later stages the interrelationship is still unclear (Bloom, 1974).

In regard to *teaching* expressive and receptive language skills to the handicapped, until more research is conducted, it appears most appropriate to follow the recommendations of Guess, Sailor, and Baer (1977) that we should "train both modalities simultaneously or in rapid succession, but do not necessarily expect that the development of one through training, will automatically enhance the development of the other, without direct training" (p. 363).

NORMAL LANGUAGE ACQUISITION

Several of the most generally accepted steps that occur in normal language development are reviewed here to provide basic guidelines about the steps normal children progress through in language acquisition. Knowledge of such information can provide a perspective from which to consider a child's level and rate of progress in language development. It is not intended to provide a sequence for language teaching programs to follow unalterably since it has not been empirically shown that we *must* teach language in the exact same sequence that it normally develops (Guess, Sailor, & Baer, 1977). It is logical, if not empirically verified, however, to consider at least in what sequence children normally acquire language when trying to determine the best sequence for teaching language. There is little disagreement on this point. Care in interpretation must be exercised in considering the progression of a child along normal developmental steps since children often vary in the specific development sequence and the age at which they acquire a particular skill (Bricker, Ruder, & Vincent, 1976).

Prelinguistic Stage of Development

The first level in the acquisition of language is the prelinguistic stage of language development. Generally, this level occurs during the first year of life (Bensburg, 1965; Bricker, Ruder, & Vincent, 1976), prior to the production of a child's first word. Included in the prelinguistic stage are initial communicative vocal and motor responses, cooing and initial vocal exploration, babbling, and basic receptive skills. In addition, nonlinguistic motor and cognitive abilities are developed that are considered by some (e.g., Piaget, 1970) to be prerequisite to the more advanced language acquisition stages.

INITIAL COMMUNICATIVE VOCAL AND MOTOR RESPONSES

At birth a child can produce vocalizations by means of crying (Bensburg, 1965). Within the first months of life the infant begins to develop communicational patterns with which he interacts with is parents or caretakers. Vocally, by varying the tonal qualities of the crying response, the child communicates his desire for such things as food, dry diaper, or attention to pain or irritation (Bateson, 1971; Bensburg, 1965; Menyuk, 1974; Rieke, 1978). Communication by means of motor responses also begins during this period. Responses such as smiles, eye contact, and reaching have been noted as being used by infants in the first months of life (Lewis & Freedke, 1972).

COOING AND INITIAL VOCAL EXPLORATION

Cooing, making low, soft dovelike sounds, is initially engaged in by the infant approximately in the second or third month of life (Bensburg, 1965). It is during this cooing stage that the child begins to exert some control (other than simply varying tonal qualities of random utterances) over the sounds that he vocally produces. In addition to the cooing response, initial vocal exploration of sounds are produced in approximately the second and third months. During initial vocal exploration the infant produces varied and unpredictable noises and sounds. Some of the sounds produced during this exploratory period are so unusual that imitation of the sounds would be difficult for an adult (Bricker, Ruder, & Vincent, 1976).

BABBLING

During the third to fourth month of life the infant begins to make sounds that approximate the language strings of other individuals in his environment and begins to emit the sounds repeatedly (Bricker, Ruder, & Vincent, 1976). This is referred to as "babbling," the production of strings of sounds. (Strings of sounds refers to several sounds grouped together in a sequence without taking a breath.) The babbling sequence continues, increasing in complexity until approximately 12 to 15 months. During the babbling stage several advances occur. A major one is the introduction of prosadic features into the infant's vocalizations (Menyuk, 1974). Prosadic components of language include such features as pitch, noise quality, location, and loudness. Once prosadic features are brought under control, at approximately eight to nine months (Nakazima, 1962), the recognition of the segmental aspects of the infant's vocalizations develop (Menyuk, 1974). The recognition of separate segments (individual sound units, syllables) in the language string is another major step. Other advances that develop during the babbling period include an increase in the frequency and length of the vocalizations and changes in the content of the segments vocalized (Irwin, 1957; Nakazima, 1962).

BASIC RECEPTIVE SKILLS

As for receptive skills, three basic aspects can be differentiated for the sake of clarity of the following discussion. The first is the recognition of the semantic intent of the language of others through intonational features of the speech. For example, the infant at approximately two to five months responds differentially to the language of others based on such features as the familiarity of the voice, anger, and the sex of the speaker (Kaplan & Kaplan, 1970). Differences between statements and questions, based on intonational features, are recognized by the infant at approximately five to eight months (Kagan & Lewis, 1965). The second aspect of recognizing semantic intent involves several advances. Infants begin to respond differentially to speech and nonspeech sounds at approximately six months (Kagan & Lewis, 1965). The child also begins to respond differentially to words. As the child has repeated experiences with a particular word in conjunction with an object or environmental event, the meaning of the word begins to develop (Bensburg, 1965). The third aspect is the child's recognition of his own potential control over the environment by means of vocalization. The child, of course, controls his environment to some degree before the babbling period. In early infancy the child's differential cry incorporates varied tonal qualities that have the effect of controlling the environment. Thus, the cry for attention has different tonal qualities than the cry for hunger or anger (Menyuk, 1974). The refinement of the recognition of the infant's ability to manipulate the environment continues to occur in the babbling phase, demonstrated by the infant's utterances that approximate different word meanings in attempts to control the enviornment (Bricker, Ruder, & Vincent, 1976). With the onset of the heightened recognition of the child of the enviornmental control that can be exerted, the motivational element necessary for rapid language acquisition is heightened.

OTHER PREREQUISITE SKILL DEVELOPMENT

Areas such as sensory-motor development and concept acquisition are prerequisite to and interrelated with linguistic development (Bricker & Bricker, 1974; Bricker, Ruder, & Vincent, 1976; Piaget & Inhelder, 1969; Premack, 1970; Sinclair de Zwart, 1973). The following list includes several of the major prerequisite skills that normally develop concurrently with the prelinguistic stage. The prerequisites are stated in terms of what most children are able to demonstrate prior to using language symbols for communication purposes.

1 Children can recognize themselves as separate from objects and other physical stimuli in their environment before they can manipulate symbols (words) (Piaget & Inhelder, 1969).
2 An individual's interaction with an environmental referent (object) is important to the ability to label the referent (Bloom, 1970). In respect to this, children are capable of manipulating objects in a relevant manner prior to manipulating language symbols (Piaget & Inhelder, 1969).
3 Children can recognize that a language symbol (word) represents an environmental referent (object) (Premack, 1970).
4 Children can discriminate between different language symbols as well as between different environmental referents (Premack, 1970).
5 Children can recognize the difference between various language symbol arrangements (differences in language symbol arrangement may result in semantic differences) (Premack, 1970).
6 Children can imitate the actions of others. Bricker, Ruder, and Vincent (1976) point out the importance of the acquisition of imitation skills, typically acquired early in the prelinguistic stage.
7 The development of complex motor control of the articulators is acquired by the child before word production results (Bricker, Ruder & Vincent, 1976).

Table 5–1 summarizes the stages of normal language acquisition.

Table 5-1
Normal Language Acquisition

Approximate Age Range	Level	Description
Prelinguistic Stages (0–12/15 mos.)		
0–1 mo.	Initial communicative motor and vocal responses	Develops communicative patterns by variations of tonal qualities (e.g., crying) and motor responses (e.g., smiles)
2–3 mos.	Cooing and initial vocal exploration	Low soft dovelike sounds, exerting some control over sounds, producing varied unpredictable noises and sounds
3/4 mos.–12/15 mos.	Babbling	Makes sounds that approximate language strings, prosadic features brought under the control of the child, increased frequency and length of vocalizations
0–12/15 mos.	Basic receptive skills	Recognition by the child of semantic intent of others through intonational features of speech, of speech and nonspeech sounds and particular words, and of his control over the environment by vocalizations
0–12/15 mos.	Other prerequisite skill development	Areas such as sensory motor development and concept acquisition that are prerequisite to and interrelated with linguistic development also occur

Table 5-1 *(continued)*
Normal Language Acquisition

Approximate Age Range	Level	Description
Linguistic Stages (12/15 mos.–adult)		
12–15 mos.	Initial verbalization	Child utters his first word—can consistently use the word with a specific object or situation
15 mos.–2½/3 yrs.	Syntactic development	Initial production of two word utterances, develops a basic linguistic organizational system, telegraphic speech (18 mos.), sentences (25 mos.)
2½/3 yrs.–6/7 yrs. and on through adulthood	Complex linguistic structures	Expansion and refinement of syntactic development level
12/15 mos.–adult	Continued receptive skill development	Receptive skills expand as the linguistic stages progress—both quantitative and qualitative increase

Linguistic Stages of Development

The linguistic stages of development, which denote the period in which the child uses language symbols for communication purposes begin approximately at 12 to 15 months and continue to develop until adult speech is achieved (Bricker, Ruder & Vincent, 1976).

INITIAL VERBALIZATIONS

The first stage of linguistic development centers around the child's utterance of his first word, which is generally from 12 to 15 months of age. Although the production of sounds that approximate the pronunciation of words are emitted during the babbling period, such utterances are not considered words "until the child uses them consistently in the presence of a specific object or situation" (Bricker, Ruder, & Vincent, 1976, p. 305). Any utterance that is used by the child to designate a particular object, situation, or class of objects would be considered a word.

The developmental process of the initial word acquisition and the development of subsequent words is not clearly recognized or generally accepted (Bricker, Ruder, & Vincent, 1976; Reese & Lipsitt, 1970). The controversy stems from the hypothesized sequence of the development of the initial and subsequent word utterances. Some authorities argue that production of the first word occurs prior to comprehension (Nakazima, 1970) while others contend that comprehension precedes production (Berry, 1969; Bullowa, Jones, & Bever, 1964; Fraser, Bellugi, & Brown, 1963; Winitz, 1973). It has also been suggested that comprehension occurs between the time that production is moving from an inaccurate to an accurate utterance (Greenfield, 1969). Murai (1963–1964), however, suggests that the techniques of fostering language acquisition used by the mother or caretaker may determine the sequence of development involved in initial word utterances. This would cause the discrepancies noted among language specialists.

SYNTACTIC DEVELOPMENT

The onset of syntactic development comes with the child's production of two-word utterances (Bricker, Ruder & Vincent, 1976). A child develops a basic linguistic organizational system according to rules for word sequencing (Bricker, Ruder, & Vincent, 1976). The child's utterances, considered to be learned by imitation (Skinner, 1957), were previously evaluated by contrasting them to the adult language pattern; however, more recently it has been suggested that children develop their own language patterns, based on semantic intent, referred to as generative rules (Chomsky, 1965; Lenneberg, 1967). Thus, the normal language acquisition sequence is still unclear in regard to the role of imitation versus generative properties of syntactic language development (Cohen, Gross, & Haring, 1976; Guess & Baer, 1973).

When the child is approximately 18 months old, he generally produces a limited number of words to convey a message. This frequently is referred to as "telegraphic speech" (Bricker, Ruder, & Vincent, 1976; Brown & Bellugi, 1964; Ruder, Bricker, & Ruder, 1975). During this phase content words are used, for example, "more drink," without prepositions or articles (Bricker, Ruder, & Vincent, 1976). The use of sentences generally starts at about 25 months of age (Bensburg, 1965). Sentences are categorized in developmental stages based on the mean length of the utterance (Bloom, 1972; Bowerman, 1973; Brown, 1973). This first stage of two-word sentences typically involves the agent–action function (e.g., boy sleeps) or the action-object function (e.g., push truck), and the later stage of three-word sentences typically involves the agent–action–object function (e.g., baby push truck) (Bricker, Ruder, & Vincent, 1976).

COMPLEX LINGUISTIC STRUCTURES

The complex linguistic structure phase of linguistic development is basically an expansion and refinement of the syntactic development level. At this stage of development basically the same function of agent–action–object relationships persist but incorporate refinements that lead toward the acquisition of adult linguistic structural form (Ruder & Smith, 1974). Refinement in the areas of structural distinctions, modifying words, morphological inflections, tense, and morphological transformational rules are incorporated into the child's language repertoire. By the time the child enters the first grade most of the "adult" transformations have been incorporated (Menyuk, 1974).

CONTINUED RECEPTIVE SKILL DEVELOPMENT

As the linguistic stages progress, the receptive skill development in language continues to expand. Although there is some controversy regarding the sequence of onset of the production and comprehension aspects of words (Guess, Sailor, & Baer, 1974), most of the literature affirms that linguistic understanding precedes production (Berry,1969; Fraser, Bellugi, & Brown, 1963; Winitz, 1973).

Although it is widely held that comprehension precedes production, the specific temporal relationship between the production and comprehension aspects of linguistic development are still unclear (Menyuk, 1974). The literature in language development, however, does provide a few comparisons:

1 The infant probably comprehends many words and phrases emitted by an adult prior to the production of his first word (Bricker, Ruder & Vincent, 1976).
2 When the child is in the stage of producing one-syllable utterances, he appears to have the ability to understand two-syllable utterances (Menyuk, 1974).
3 Although a child may use one phonological sequence for several words, he appears to encounter no difficulty in identifying particular words within the set (Erwin-Tripp, 1966).
4 At approximately 15 to 18 months the ability of the child to understand more complex verbal utterances appears to increase (Bricker, Ruder, & Vincent, 1976). This seems to occur just prior to the onset of "telegraphic speech," which emerges at about 18 months.
5 When the child begins to produce two-word "strings," he generally not only comprehends, but also is able to use correctly such semantic relations as possession, reoccurrence, location, and negation (Bloom, 1970, 1972; Bowerman, 1973; Brown, 1973).

6   At a later stage, when more complex sentences are beginning to develop, the child does not begin to listen to another's speech, as it relates to his own verbalizations, until approximately 2½ to 3 years of
age (Yeni-Komshian, Chase, & Mobley, 1967). Prior to this time the
child's perception of another individual's speech is that of an independent speech stimulus that does not disrupt the child's ongoing speech
behavior.

In addition to the correlation of receptive skills to produce abilities
noted above, Menyuk (1974) suggests another apsect of receptive skill
development that should be considered. In receptive skill development
there appear to be both quantitative and qualitative differences in the
comparison of receptive skills to production. Not only does the child understand more words than he produces, but also he can perceive different
distinctions of utterances than those he uses (Menyuk, 1974).

Various aspects of receptive skills develop as the productive skills of
the child increase. In order to get a clear picture of the receptive development process, more research is needed since these processes in normal
children have received little attention (Friedlander, 1970).

CONSIDERATIONS FOR TEACHING LANGUAGE

In the development of a language system there are several basic considerations that can have an impact on the overall progress of a handicapped child. The following are a compilation of a few of the more poign-
ant considerations singled out by authors and researchers in the field of
language development.

The Communication System to Use

*Use a communication system that will be least restrictive yet within
the ability level of the handicapped individual.* If the language system
developed is restricted to use with the teacher and/or parents, the child is
deprived of input that can be offered by others. The child is also restricted
in expressing his ideas, needs, and desires to other individuals. In essence, with a restricted communication system we would be depriving the
handicapped child of learning experiences that he so desperately needs.

Verbal language is the most common and widely used and understood vehicle for communication and has, at the present time, the potential for providing more specific information than other language systems
(e.g., sign language). Through the oral production of words the handicapped individual is provided the means to communicate with a wide au-
dience.

In regard to the use of verbalizations as a focus of language development for the handicapped, the specific abilities of the individual must be examined. In order to use verbalizations efficiently as a communication system, the individual must have at least the auditory skills to receive the speech sounds, the intellectual ability to understand the system (encoding and decoding), and the oral/motor mechanism necessary to produce the sounds. If these are not present, either another language system (e.g., sign language) must be developed or verbalizations may only be employed in a restricted manner. An example of a situation in which restricted verbalizations may be used is a handicapped individual with the auditory skills and intellectual ability to develop verbal communication skills but not the oral/motor mechanism necessary to produce them. In such a case verbalizations may be employed for receptive language while some type of symbol system involving fingers, hands and/or head nodding, and the like could be used for expression.

The abilities of the child, especially his auditory ability, should be evaluated early in life (Linde & Kopp, 1973) to determine what steps will be necessary to develop a communication system. In addition, steps can be taken to help overcome any deficiencies and/or prevent further deterioration. If deficiencies are not detected and overcome or compensated for, the child may lose his chance for valuable early stimulation and learning experiences. Early detection is of particular importance to children with a severe language delay due to the relatively high incidence of multiple handicapping conditions and their need for maximally effective learning experiences.

While early detection of deficiencies in abilities necessary for developing verbalizations is of paramount importance, precautions should be taken against underestimating the handicapped child's potential (especially intellectual) for developing and using verbalization skills (Mueller, 1975). Testing the abilities of a very young child presents numerous problems (Cronbach, 1960). It is, therefore, important not to make an irreversible decision early in a child's life that he/she cannot develop verbal language (receptive and/or expressive). An irrevocable decision made early in a child's life is entirely inappropriate. Such a decision can work to make a misdiagnosis a reality. A decision that a child will not be able to develop verbal language skills can result in a lack of the stimulation necessary to develop language, which, in time, causes lack of verbal development.

Similarly, it is important not to *overemphasize* the use of gestures as the only means of communication if the potential for oral verbalization is present (Mueller, 1975). If the child's needs are met by means of gestural communication, the incentive to develop expressive verbalizations may be reduced. The child's gestural communication attempts should be ignored if he has the basic expressive verbalization skills yet rarely uses them. In this way if the child wants his needs met he is forced to communicate orally.

A word of caution is in order. Although it is important to limit a child's reliance on gestural communication once verbalizations are possible, *beginning communication* can and should focus on gestural comunication (Linde & Kopp, 1973). Gestures require a lower degree of motor development and are easier to use. Reinforcement of gestures, such as pointing or nodding, is important in developing an initial interchange of ideas (communication) with children with a language delay. Gestures, of course, are quite appropriately used in the communication process throughout life; however, after verbal language is possible, gestures should not be relied upon as the sole or primary means of communication. Gestures should be thought of as an augmentative mode of communication, *not* as a substitute mode of communication.

In even the most severely handicapped the early focus of an educational program should lead toward the development of oral language, if at all possible, as the vehicle for communication. Only in rare cases should the communication emphasis be shifted away from verbal communication toward nonverbal. The individual abilities of the child should be used to determine the degree to which other communication modes should be relied on. Be careful not to underestimate potential or to engage a child in a communication system that is unproductive in regard to the population with whom he will be required to communicate throughout his life. Reality, of course, dictates that some children be provided with a nonverbal symbol system, if they are to become communicators. A few of the most prominent nonverbal symbol systems are reviewed later in this chapter.

The selection of a symbol system (verbal versus nonverbal) to be stressed and developed in a handicapped child is a very complex task. To make matters worse, the best system for a child may change as the child grows and develops additional abilities. The selection process, therefore, is not a one-time decision; it is a continual process (Vanderheiden & Harris-Vanderheiden, 1976). Nor is it a decision that the teacher should make alone; it is an important decision that can be best made by an interdisciplinary team.

Early Stimulation

Properly presented, early stimulation is a major factor in the subsequent development of language. Many children with a severe language delay have been deprived of "normal" environmental stimulation and interactions (Bensburg, 1965). This has occurred, in part at least, because these children are, due to their handicapping condition(s), often slow to develop expressive skills and may not respond or they may emit bizarre gestures or facial expressions. These bizarre responses or lack of responses are often interpreted as total lack of understanding on the part of the child, and, thus, the adult may stop providing the stimulation needed to build a solid foundation for language development. Due to the lack of adequate environmental stimulation, compounded with poor intellectual ability, the prognosis for the development of language, under such circumstances, has in the past been poor. To avoid this problem, educational programs for children with language delays should include planned environmental stimulation, both in repetition and exposure to a broad range of experiences.

As with so many other aspects of educating children who exhibit severe forms of maladaptive behavior, providing early environmental stimulation is a complex matter. Just as the lack of environmental stimulation may be extremely detrimental to language development, the excessive bombardment with sensory stimuli may be equally as devasting to the language development process (Bensburg, 1965; Linde & Kopp, 1973; Mueller, 1975). Often it is difficult for the handicapped individual to organize his perceptions of an experience to determine the relevant from irrelevant stimuli (Linde & Kopp, 1973; Mueller, 1975). To make matters worse, the degree of stimulation that should be presented may depend on the unique characteristics of each child. While a high degree of sensory stimulation might enhance the progress of some low-activity children, it could impair the progress of already highly aroused children (Crosby, 1972).

In order to avoid unnecessary verbal (auditory) stimuli bombardment yet provide a strong base for language development, several considerations should be kept in mind. Appropriate verbal (auditory) stimulation is important to the subsequent development of language. Keep verbalizations very simple and consistently use the same words to label objects and activities so specific words become connected to particular things in the child's environment. Limit the number of words used; speak slowly and clearly (Bensburg, 1965). Initially avoid the use of pronouns when talking to the young handicapped child. Such labels as "this," "that," "there," and "those," not being item specific, may lead to confusion (Linde and Kopp, 1973). Also avoid using "baby talk" with the child. The baby-talk labels must be unlearned and the generally used term for the item or activity learned. Such a procedure is required since the use of baby talk by an older individual is typically not socially accepted.

Other aspects that should be noted regarding the early presentation of verbalizations to a handicapped child include storytelling and the use of mechanical productions of verbalizations. In storytelling the vocabulary complexity and the visual representations included to enhance understanding should be analyzed in terms of the needs of the individual child. In regard to vocabulary complexity, telling a story about a cow, for example, is of little conceptual use if the child has never seen a cow or has no idea what it might be (Mueller, 1975). The vocabulary complexity of a story may be confusing to a young handicapped child who has not had the opportunity to conceptualize many of the words or sentence structures being used. The length of the story should also be considered in terms of the handicapped child's attention span. If the child becomes frustrated, a tendency for the child to develop avoidance mechanisms toward listening to stories could result.

Frequent and clear pictures, free from complexity, may offset the impact of the problem of vocabulary complexity to some degree so that stories previously considered unapplicable may be acceptable due to the visual explanations of the words made available in the story.

The use of mechanically produced verbalizations, such as the television, radio, and tape recorder, should also be carefully evaluated in regard to the child's needs. Until the handicapped child recognizes the importance of language and has some degree of success in decoding verbalizations, mechanical verbal productions have questionable value. Generally, such sounds tend to fade into the background for the young handicapped child (Mueller, 1975) since although the machine may provide a good presentation of speech, it does not provide the personal interaction element that allows for the interchange of ideas and the use of tangible cues to enhance understanding of the verbalizations presented. In short, mechanical productions do not allow for two-sided exchanges. The child is not reinforced for his attempts at interaction with such items. In addition to the lack of personal feedback, the control of vocabulary complexity with television and radio is usually lacking. The bombardment with complex verbalizations may cause confusion, frustration, loss of interest, or possible withdrawal (Mueller, 1975). For these reasons, the use of mechanical verbalization producers must be closely evaluated in regard to their applicability for providing early language stimulation for the handicapped child.

In addition to early experiences with language, other experiences are thought to be necessary for later language development. Sensorimotor as well as language experiences are said to be essential to the development of certain cognitive schemes, which, in turn, are thought to be necessary for language development.

There is increasing support for the notion that the emergence of language in the child cannot be attributed singly to the presence of certain innate linguistic factors, but that language is the logical outgrowth of the child's development of certain cognitive skills. That is, the process of acquiring language is seen as more than just the acquisition of words and their subsequent use in various combinations. Rather, the child is said to acquire language as a result of various interactions with his or her environment, and these interactions are thought to precede and directly influence the acquisition of language. . . . The cognitive theorist specifically bases his views on those of Piaget concerning the development of the sensorimotor stages of intelligence and the subsequent emergence of language at about the age of 18 months. That language appears at this time is said to result from the necessity for the prior formation of certain cognitive schemas. (Graham, 1976, p. 374)

The establishment of cognitive schemes "involves a set of structures progressively constructed by continuous interaction between the subject and the external world" (Piaget, 1970, p. 703).

Some prerequisite behaviors could influence later language and communication development. Robinson (1976) has identified three Piagetian-based sensorimotor behaviors that she feels are particularly important in regard to language development: means–ends development, causality concepts, and object permanence.

Means–ends development is "the repetition of responses that result in the continuation of an event" (Robinson, 1976, p. 6). According to Robinson, if the infant engages on numerous occasions in gross motor movements such as flailing of arms and legs and this results in movement of a toy such as a mobile suspended above his crib, he begins to learn that he has the power to interact with and control the physical environment around him.

The *causality concept* can probably be best explained by an example. When an adult stops playfully bouncing an infant on his lap and the infant wiggles, the adult sometimes interprets the wiggle as meaning the baby wants to be bounced some more. With this development we have the beginning of a gesture system, one that is extremely dependent upon context but is an important part of the development of communication, for it marks the point at which the child begins to use a response to make something happen that he cannot produce himself (Robinson, 1976, p. 6).

Object permanence is the recognition that an object still exists after all sensory contact with the object has terminated. Robinson (1976) stated:

Object permanence is assumed to be a necessary requisite for the development of representational communication where reference is made to an absent object, person, or event. With whatever communication system is used, spoken words, hand gestures, signs, plastic chips, or pictures, the individual parts of that system are used to represent an object or event that exists or did exist at one time. Presumably when a person uses one of the various communication systems for representation, he can do so because an object or event exists for him independent of his sensory contact with it. We have not yet encountered any children who demonstrate communication in the sense of making a request for absent objects, people, or events who do not also demonstrate object permanence. (p. 9)

A word of caution needs to be inserted here. While the development of prelinguistic cognitive schemes appears to be necessary for language acquisition, there is evidence that cognitive advances by themselves are not sufficient to explain the development of language (Cromer, 1974). Language should be taught directly to nonverbal language-delayed children. Procedures and activities for teaching language are presented later in this chapter.

Well-planned and well-organized early intervention programs may serve a preventive function in addition to a corrective function (Bricker & Bricker, 1974). Early stimulation patterns and early sensory and perceptual training may prevent at least some aspects of the language delays often seen in older developmentally delayed individuals (Graham, 1976).

The Choice of Language Forms and Functions

When choosing the language forms and functions to be presented in a language development program, several factors should be taken into account. The content presented in the program should be related to what the handicapped child is familiar with and can use to help him communicate with others each day (Bensburg, 1965). If a child is taught the word "ball" because it is a relatively simple task (in the hierarchy of pronouncing words) but the child does not have a ball generally accessible in his environment, the word is of little use. In such cases the ability to use the word may be lost since the child does not have the opportunity to use it and thus the natural reinforcement available in the environment is not provided (Schiefelbusch, Ruder, & Bricker, 1976). If natural reinforcement is not available to maintain the response, the response may be lost (Bricker & Bricker, 1974; Ferster, 1972). On the other hand, when the child discovers the power of language for manipulating his environment, the consequences of language usage become reinforcing in themselves (Graham, 1976).

To enhance the utility of the content chosen, the handicapped child should be given an opportunity to talk with someone listening to him and to listen to someone else talking to him (Bensburg, 1965). For utility of what is learned in language development activities the child must be given an opportunity to use his new skills and encouragement to do so. These opportunities should be provided in various settings by making others (such as parents, therapists, doctors, and other teachers) aware of the importance of taking time to listen to and talk with the handicapped child.

When selecting the content of a language training program, it is important that the children know the functional use of the objects that are part of the lesson. If a child does not know the functional use of an object, do not expect him to understand its receptive label (Bricker, Ruder, & Vincent, 1976). Knowing what an object does is prerequisite to an understanding of the label assigned. An individual cannot be expected to understand the label "reliquary," if he does not know that it is a small box to hold a relic. If the functional use of an object is not known, the label can be memorized; the understanding and appropriate use of the label, however, may not be acquired.

If a child cannot discriminate an object from other environmental stimuli, he cannot be expected to produce its verbal label (Bricker, Ruder, & Vincent, 1976). Thus the ability to discriminate the objects and the other stimuli in a proposed lesson must be a consideration when setting up a program. Before a child can accurately label a cow as a "cow," he must first be able to recognize the difference(s) of the cow from other animals such as a horse, cat, and dog. He should not, for example, label a cow, horse, cat, and dog as "dog."

PROCEDURES FOR TEACHING LANGUAGE

Teaching language to nonlanguage or language-delayed handicapped children is a complex process. The procedures described here are made up of components frequently employed by researchers and language specialists (e.g., Guess, Sailor, & Baer, 1974; Hartung & Hartung, 1973; Risley & Wolf, 1974). These components have consistently been shown to be effective in developing language in handicapped children (Bricker & Bricker, 1970; Lovaas, 1968; Risely & Wolf, 1974).

The procedures are primarily based on imitation and differential reinforcement. Graham (1976) pointed out that there is controversy surrounding this method:

> The use of imitation, in particular, has received a great deal of criticism as being a departure from the way in which the normal child acquires language. This criticism has been generated in a long-standing debate between linguists and pscholinguists, on the one hand, and behaviorists, on the other hand (Jakobovits & Miron, 1967). Behaviorists hold that the acquisition of language can be explained by principles of learning theory (Skinner, 1957), while statements in the psycholinguistic literature hold that processes such as imitation cannot possibly explain the emerging linguistic sophistication evidenced

by the child as he becomes a language user (Brown & Bellugi, 1964; Ervin, 1964; Miller, 1967).

More recently, the view has been expressed that, while imitation may not be a necessary element in normal language acquisition, the techniques of imitation and differential reinforcement together can be very successfully applied in establishing some form of verbal behavior in the individual who has not acquired language in the normal manner (Bricker, 1972; Bricker & Bricker, 1974; Gray & Ryan, 1973), and that perhaps the inherent differences between a language acquisition model and a language intervention model should be acknowledged (Gray & Ryan, 1973; Risley, Hart, & Doke, 1972; Ruder, 1972). (Graham, 1976, pp. 390–391)

This argument, of course, stems from the issue surrounding developmental versus remedial or nondevelopmental approaches to teaching language. The reader is referred to Guess, Sailor and Baer (1977) for a brief review of this issue.

Teaching language to the handicapped can be conveniently divided into nine steps. The first several steps can be considered prerequisites that are necessary before actually teaching language.

Arranging the Environment

Prior to beginning any educational program, pertinent environmental conditions must be arranged so they are conducive to the goals of the program (objectives that the learner is expected to achieve). A wide variety of variables should be considered at this point. Concerns with lighting, comfort of the child, positioning of both the child and the teacher to facilitate maximal performance and interaction, as well as ventilation and a generally pleasant attractive situation free from clutter and distracting stimuli will improve the probability of success. Materials should be readily accessible to enable the teacher to efficiently present the necessary antecedent and consequent events without interruptions in the session. The environment should be evaluated and needed modifications done prior to introducing the child to the session activities.

Eliminating Disruptive Behaviors

Behaviors that interfere with the learning process must be eliminated or brought under stimulus control before new responses can be efficiently added to the child's repertoire (Hartung & Hartung, 1973; Risley & Wolf, 1974). Programs for language development fail most often because teachers, at the beginning of the program, do not establish behavior control (Schiefelbusch, Ruder, & Bricker, 1976).

Various approaches can be employed to reduce or eliminate disruptive behavior. Counterconditioning, the process of reinforcing a behavior that is incompatible to the disruptive behavior, constitutes a positive approach to eliminating disruptive behavior. Often times, however, a more direct focus on the undesirable behavior is required. Time-out from positive reinforcement, contingent upon the undesirable behavior, has been effectively employed (Risley & Wolf, 1967; Turner, 1970). For severely disruptive behaviors such as tantrums and self-destructive behavior punishment in the form of spanking or shouting at the child has been used (Lovaas, Berberich, Perloff, & Schaeffer, 1966). If all other methods have been tried and failed, the use of electric shock as a punisher has been effective (Risley, 1968). Although empirical research has found that such methods as spanking and shock have been effective in reducing undesirable behavior, these approaches are generally not viable options for classroom use due to the ethical, moral and legal issues involved. Whatever method is used, it must be recognized that there is no one universal reinforcer or punisher that works for all children at all times. Thus, it may be necessary to try various approaches before finding the one that is effective in changing the rate, duration, and/or intensity of the behavior. For a comprehensive discussion of the various approaches for eliminating disruptive behavior, see Chapter 8.

Establishing Attending Behavior

Once the environment is arranged and any disruptive behavior is eliminated, the next step is to bring the attention of the child under stimulus control (Schiefelbusch, Ruder, & Bricker, 1976). Until the attention of the child is focused on the task, learning cannot occur.

The first major procedure for actually teaching language is imitation, and imitation is contingent upon the attention and eye contact of the child. "The child who does not attend adequately to outside cues is incapable of modifying his behavior accordingly and will hardly establish an imitative repertoire leading to the effective use of language" (Hartung & Hartung, 1973, p. 73).

Attending behavior can be brought under the stimulus control of the teacher as can other behaviors. Typically the use of consequent stimuli, such as reinforcers for shaping and maintaining attending behavior, are employed. The environment, for example, might be arranged so that reinforcement is only available when the child attends. When the child does not attend, a time-out from positive reinforcement situation results. This approach has been found to be effective in shaping attending behavior (Blake & Moss, 1967).

For developing stimulus control, considerable stress is also put on the antecedent stimuli used to elicit the attending behavior. Using antecedent stimuli that the child currently tends to focus his attention on and shaping attention to the teacher's eyes or task while fading the initially used antecedent has been successful (Risley, 1968; Risley & Wolf, 1967). The initially used antecedent stimulus should be one whose properties are reinforcing for the child. Examples of such stimuli are a brightly colored favorite toy or an item that emits an interesting sound. Another approach focusing on the antecedent stimuli to develop initial attention involves a loud noise or manual guidance to elicit attending behavior, gradually fading the noise or guidance.

Developing Motor Imitation Skills

Although the function of imitation as a part of the normal developmental sequence of language is a point of controversy (Chomsky, 1965), imitation is one of the most powerful training tools available for language intervention (Bricker & Bricker, 1974). In most behaviorally oriented language development programs the importance of the imitation process as a prerequisite skill for teaching language to handicapped children is acknowledged. The question that most typically arises is whether to train motor imitation prior to verbal imitation or to begin directly with the verbal.

Programs for teaching language to handicapped children have utilized both methods effectively. Some programs begin with verbal imitation (Lovaas, 1968; Raymore & McLean, 1972; Risley & Wolf, 1967) while others begin with motor imitation (Baer, Peterson, & Sherman, 1967; Bricker & Bricker, 1970; Hartung & Hartung, 1973; Kent, Klein, Falk, & Guenther, 1972).

Motor imitation has been included as a step in language training for several reasons: First, many severely behaviorally handicapped children have little if any imitative skills. When first trying to develop imitative skills, it is much easier to train motor imitation than verbal since physical guidance can be applied to begin motor imitation whereas the physical guidance of tongue and lips to culminate in the desired sound(s) is much more difficult (Bricker & Bricker, 1970). This physical guidance can be systematically faded to achieve the desired imitative response(s) (Guess, Sailor, & Baer, 1974).

Second, investigators working with severely handicapped children have noted that there appears to be, in this process, a development of an imitative skill that is generalized to other motor responses. Each successive attempt to produce imitation of a new response is more quickly acquired by the child (Baer, Peterson, & Sherman, 1967). Once established, the imitative response seems to involve a generalized imitative response

(Gewirtz & Stingle, 1968). Although motor imitation does not appear directly to generalize to vocal imitation (Garcia, Baer, & Firestone, 1971), the imitation skills developed with motor movements can provide a strong base from which to develop verbal imitation.

Motor imitation also may provide a preventive measure for inaccurate articulation. When the speech error patterns of children were examined, the most common errors involved a change in the place of articulation (Bricker, 1967). These places of articulation involve visually observable changes in the placement of the articulators (Bricker & Bricker, 1974). Thus, if motor imitation of the articulators is paired with verbal imitation, fewer articulation errors may result.

There are two criteria for imitation to occur: (1) the action of the child must be similar to and happen after the example is provided by the model, and (2) the child must differentially respond to the imitative stimulus (Metz, 1965). Prior to the actual development of the imitative response, the child's current imitative repertoire should be assessed (Peterson, 1968) in order to establish where to begin to strengthen the imitative response.

One way to begin for a child with no apparent imitation skill is to provide verbal and visual cues for imitation and then physically guide the child through the action before reinforcing (Bricker & Bricker, 1970). For example, say, "Amy, touch your nose": touch your (teacher) nose, physically move the child's hand to her nose, then reinforce. As the strength of the response increases, gradually fade the physical prompt, shaping the behavior until it can be successfully performed by the child when given only verbal and visual cues.

Once a motor response can be consistently imitated by the child on command, begin teaching another imitative motor response. Initially only develop one response at a time until the child becomes proficient in imitative skills.

Simple gross motor movements should be trained first, gradually moving to more complex and finer motor movements (Bricker & Bricker, 1974). In order to enhance the subsequent transfer to vocal or verbal imitations, the teaching of fine motor movements, such as facial, lip, and tongue movements, is important.

In summary, the process of developing motor imitation involves basically the use of shaping, prompting, and fading and then chaining techniques (Guess, Sailor, & Baer, 1974). ✓

Teaching Receptive Language

Once motor imitation has been achieved, comprehension generally has a more formal role in the language training program (Bricker, Ruder,

& Vincent, 1967; Kent, 1974). In regard to sequencing, functional use of objects appears to be a precursor to the comprehension of an object's name (Bricker & Bricker, 1974). At this stage children are taught to use objects that will later be verbally introduced. For example, they are taught such things as to drink from a cup, push a toy truck, and open a door.

Once the use of an object is comprehended by the child, the next step in receptive skill training is the comprehension of the object's name or label. Although some programs advocate the training of comprehension of labels prior to the verbal imitation stage (Kent, 1974), other programs (Bricker, Ruder, & Vincent, 1976) recommend that such training be done simultaneously with or immediately after verbal imitation training. In comprehension of labels, body parts and common objects generally precede action words. Comprehension of single-word elements should precede word combinations.

Comprehension of labels is taught by getting the child to imitate a model's motor response of pointing at the appropriate object when its label is stated by the teacher. The model is gradually faded until the child can point to the appropriate object when presented the verbal label.

Teaching receptive language should be integrated throughout the process of teaching language. It is not a totally separate, "one-shot" procedure.

Developing Verbal Imitation Skills

Verbal imitation is the next step involved in the development of language skills. "Verbal imitation ranges from imitation of a single sound such as /a/ to the production of a sequence of several words" (Bricker, Ruder, & Vincent, 1976, p. 310). It is considered to be a "necessary condition" (Peterson, 1968) for the development of speech and is an important component in procedures designed to teach speech and language to nonvocal children (Guess, Sailor, & Baer, 1974).

Verbal imitation should begin when motor imitation is consistently carried out on command (Hartung & Hartung, 1973). Before the teacher attempts to teach imitation of words (e.g., ball), some imitation of sounds (e.g., *b*) should be established since the imitation of sounds is easier than the imitation of words (Garcia, Baer, & Firestone, 1971).

As previously noted, the incorporation on fine motor facial, mouth, and tongue movements into the motor imitation repertoire generally makes the transition to vocal imitation quite smooth (Sloane, Johnston, & Harris, 1968). Along with the focus of fine motor movements of the tongue and lips is the integration of vocal imitation. Generalize the motor imitation skills by chaining together the motor imitation with the vocal imitation until the motor imitation can be faded out and reliable vocal imitation results (Baer, Peterson, & Sherman, 1967; Hartung & Hartung, 1973).

If the child is totally nonvocal and it is difficult to get him to emit any sound(s), a technique that could be used involves shaping vocalizations by reinforcing lip movements that often result in a spontaneous moan (Sherman, 1965). If a spontaneous vocalization does not result, several techniques such as blowing activities or clearing the throat paired with lip movements can result in vocal sounds (Pronovost, Wakstein, & Wakstein, 1966). If there are still no vocal sounds, have the child imitate mouth movements and push in on his abdomen (Schell, Stark, & Giddan, 1967). Once a vocal sound is achieved, it should be shaped into a desired vocalization. There are other ways to do this. For example, after the child finishes eating and burps, the teacher could reinforce this sound and gradually shape it into a meaningful speech sound. After a sound is elicited, it should be brought under stimulus control through verbal imitation procedures.

Shaping procedures for developing verbal imitation generally progress through the following steps (Hartung & Hartung, 1973):

1. Reinforcement applied for all vocalizations and for visually fixating on teacher's mouth and/or eyes.
2. Reinforcement applied if vocalizations emitted within a specified time after the teacher's sound.
3. Reinforcement applied for being within a designated time interval after teacher makes sound and if the sound resembles the sound of the teacher.
4. Reinforcement applied for imitative vocalizations (child's sound closely matches teacher's sound).

As for which sounds or words should be taught first, begin with whatever is easiest and most useful to the child. Usually vowels are easier than consonants (Bricker, Ruder, & Vincent, 1976). If the child has any sounds he emits spontaneously, these could serve as a starting point to begin bringing vocalizations under stimulus control. Use sounds that production can be aided by the use of physical prompts and also sounds that have a distinct visual component that can aid the child in his imitation efforts (Lovaas, Berberich, Perloff, & Schaeffer, 1966). Once a basic repertoire of sounds is developed, use these sounds in the imitative production of words. For example, if the child has mastered the sounds of *a, b,* and *l,* the word "ball" could be used for imitation purposes.

Several investigators who have had experience working with nonverbal children have observed that after a child acquires the skill to imitate one word, there might be a considerable lapse of time before a second word can be imitated (Hartung & Hartung, 1973). This lapse could be two months or longer for some children, even when consistent training is provided (Hartung, 1970). Once two to three words are imitatively established in a child's repertoire, however, a general imitative response seems to develop that facilitates the future imitation of new words.

At this point, in some children, "a compulsive parroting of what they hear" (Risley & Wolf, 1974, p. 151) begins to occur. The child does not communicate but does mimic what was said (usually both words and phrases) a moment earlier (echolalia) or mimics what has been said a hour or even several days or weeks earlier (delayed echolalia) (Premack & Premack, 1974). This phenomenon of echolalia has been repeatedly documented when training language skills in nonverbal children (Hartung, 1970; Hewett, 1965; Risley & Wolf, 1967) and adults (Isaacs, Thomas, & Goldiamond, 1960).

It is theorized that echolalia is the initial expression of a silent language repertoire that the nonverbal child acquires through his experiences with other individuals but never uses. If this is so, it would account for the spontaneous imitation and good pronounciation of words that is usually characteristic in echolalia (Hartung & Hartung, 1973).

Although children who exhibit the echolalia response are in a sense imitating, the imitation response is sporatic and generally cannot be consistently evoked (Risley & Wolf, 1974). Therefore, before the child can move on to develop naming skills, the echolalic response must be shifted to imitative control. This can be done through systematic reinforcement so the responses occur more promptly and reliably.

Although we have already discussed imitation training, it might be helpful to review it here as it relates to echolalia. Risley and Wolf (1974) present a clear explanation:

> Imitation training involves reinforcing a response made by the child only when it immediately follows the same response made by the therapist. The child's response may already have existed in his echolalic repertoire or it may have been shaped into a high probability response. The therapist can shift the response to imitative control by reinforcing it when it occurs after the presentation of an identical modeled stimulus or *prompt*. In this manner larger units of previously randomly occuring behavior can be brought under imitative control. Once a child accurately imitates most words, phrases, and sentences, then any topography of verbal behavior (i.e., any word, phrase, or sentence) can be produced when desired by presenting the child with the prompt to be imitated.

Echolalia, then, is of significance to the therapist, for, since the echolalic child already has verbal responses, the arduous task of shaping them is unnecessary. Once the child's responses are brought under imitative control, so that, for example, he says, "that's a cow" when the therapist has just said "that's a cow," the only remaining step is to shift the control of his response to the appropriate stimuli, so that, for example, he says "that's a cow" to a picture of a cow. This shift to naming is made by fading out the imitative prompt in gradual steps. . . . In this manner the responses acquire their appropriate "meanings" (p. 151).

Caution should be taken in this process since with the increase of consistent and prompted imitative responding there is also often an increase in delayed echolalia (Risley & Wolf, 1974). Along with the imitative responses an additional response that the child might have heard an hour or even a day before may be added. For example, the teacher says, "My name is Mary" and the child says, "My name is Mary. Don't touch that, it will break and we will have to throw it away." Do not reinforce the child when delayed echolalia accompanies the immediate imitative response. The delayed echolalia must be extinguished prior to moving on to a higher skill.

In summary, if echolalia does appear in a child who is developing language, the process of establishing language skills is generally much easier since the echolalia eliminates the need to shape the initial production of each word. Once the echolalia is brought under imitative control, you can move to the naming procedure.

Developing Nonimitative Verbalizations

For the purpose of this discussion the process of developing nonimitative verbalizations will be divided into three basic levels: (1) the naming of pictures and objects, (2) answering questions, and (3) establishing requests and questions.

In all three of these levels the receptive and expressive skills of the child are developed. In the research reviewed here the sequence of development, however, may vary. Although it is usually assumed that receptive training should precede expressive training, there is no agreement among researchers that this is necessarily true.

NAMING

Naming "involves the emission of the appropriate response in the presence of some stimulus object" (Risley & Wolf, 1974, p. 162). To accomplish this, there is a shift of stimulus control from the verbal prompt (imitation) to appropriate objects and pictures (naming) (Hartung & Hartung, 1973). Teaching the naming of objects should be begun once imitation reliably occurs (Guess, Sailor, & Baer, 1974) and a short latency period between the prompt and the response develops (Risley & Wolf, 1974).

In the naming process generally nouns are presented before verbs (Bricker, Ruder, & Vincent, 1976), and in some programs there is an almost immediate move to prepositions and pronouns (Lovaas, 1968). Generally, one naming word is presented initially. Once this is consistently and correctly used, another new word is introduced. This sequence is followed until the child develops a repertoire of vocabulary words. Once several words are mastered by the child, the development of other new words are more quickly established (Risley & Wolf, 1974).

The procedure used in the transition from imitation to naming is relatively consistent in the behaviorally oriented language research. The steps detailed here are the ones employed by Risley and Wolf (1974); they are very similar to the procedures used by others (e.g., Hartung, 1970; Lovaas, 1968; Sloane, Johnston & Harris, 1968).

1. The attention of the child should be shifted from the teacher to the object or picture to be named. If this cannot be done easily on command, one way to do so is to hold the reinforcer behind the picture or object. As the attention of the child more consistently focuses on the object or picture with reinforcement contingent upon it, the prompt (holding reinforcer behind the object) can be faded.

2. The teacher holds up an object and says, "What is this?" When the child attends to the object, the teacher verbally prompts with the object's name. The teacher then reinforces the child for imitating the verbal prompt.

3. After several trials the teacher holds up the object and asks the question, "What is this?" The verbal prompt is delayed for several seconds in an effort to get the child to respond without the prompt. If this does not occur, providing only a partial verbal prompt (usually the beginning sounds of the word) is attempted. The idea is to provide only as much prompt as is needed. Fading the prompt can be done in several ways: (1) by omitting parts of the sounds of the word, leaving off more and more as the child gains proficiency, (2) by giving the prompt in a quieter and quieter voice until the prompt is no longer necessary, and (3) by providing a greater time lapse between the question and presentation of object and the verbal prompt.

4. If at any time during the procedure the child imitates the question, a time-out procedure is programmed. This entails the object being withdrawn and the teacher looking away from the child. When the child is quiet for a few seconds, the teacher resumes the procedure.

Although, procedurally, most programs transfer from verbal imitation to naming objects and pictures as has been outlined, there are some unique procedures that do not strictly adhere to this model. The Bricker approach (Bricker, Ruder, & Vincent, 1976) focuses on comprehension of objects prior to naming them. Before the child is requested to name an object, he is taught to point to and functionally use it; in other programs such comprehension activities occur after the actual naming process (Guess, Sailor, Keogh, & Baer, 1976). In another approach broader concept formations are built in during the naming development process. Lovaas (1968) has the child respond to various objects in a set with the same label such as using various kinds of balls or chairs as the stimulus is presented (e.g., a small red chair, a large red chair, a small rocking chair). As in other areas of the language development process, the transition from verbal imitation to nonimitative verbalizations is basically a shift of stimulus control, accomplished through shaping, prompting, and fading techniques.

ANSWERING QUESTIONS

The process of answering questions is a natural outgrowth of the naming process. Teaching the naming of objects and other things involves the presentation of a question, an object or picture, and the fading of a verbal prompt (the teacher naming the object or picture). This is done to elicit a labeling response from the child. Essentially, the answering of questions involves the same process as naming with the exception of the object or picture. In answering questions a question is presented with a verbal prompt (the teacher providing the answer for imitation) that is gradually faded. There is a stimulus control shift from the verbal prompt to the verbal question in learning question answering.

Answering questions is typically begun after the transition from imitation to naming has occurred. The naming of an object or picture is considered learned only after the child can consistently label the object or picture on different occasions and in various situations with only intermittent reinforcement (Risley & Wolf, 1974). Once a repertoire of labels are established, then answering of questions can begin.

A basic procedure for establishing question-answering behavior has been suggested in the literature (Hartung & Hartung, 1973), one that incorporates many of the same steps employed when establishing the naming response. In this procedure the child imitates both the question and the answer. Gradually, more time elapses between the teacher's presentation of the question and the answer. Again, as in the naming procedure, the anticipatory gesture of the child may cause him to give the response (answer) before prompting (the teacher providing the answer for imitation). "Thus, by lengthening the interval between question and answer, the clinician is establishing proper stimulus control of new responses" (Hartung & Hartung, 1973, p. 83).

In other words, it is hoped by lengthening the time between the teacher's presentation of the question and answer, the child will say the answer before the teacher does. Sometimes, even after the child learns to say the answer without it being provided for imitation, he will continue to imitate the question. If the child continues to imitate the question, the question is said very quietly with the hope that the child will not repeat (imitate) the question and will say the answer without it being provided for imitation. In short, gradually the question should be faded from imitation by saying it more quietly and quickly and the answer is emphasized by inflection and loudness (Risley & Wolf, 1974). If this procedure is not successful, the child's imitation of the question is extinguished by ignoring or punishing it and the child is reinforced for saying the answer without it having to be provided for imitation. When ignoring or punishing the child's imitation of the question, it is essential to be extremely careful. You do not want to extinguish all imitative responses (the child's generalized imitative behavior).

This procedure is first used to establish simple one-word answers to a question. For example, "What is your name? Bill." Once a repertoire of single-word answers are established, the same procedure is used to establish a repertoire of answers to questions that involve phrases and sentences (Hartung & Hartung, 1973; Risley and Wolf, 1974).

In regard to the progression of the responses presented, programs tend to vary. An example of one comprehensive approach to the development of phrases and sentences is the sequence recommended by Bricker, Ruder, and Vincent (1976). The initial development involves two-word phrases commonly using the verb-object phrase (e.g., "What did you do? Push truck"). Once established the next step involves three-word phrases, frequently using the subject-verb-object grouping (e.g., "Who ate the cookie? Mary ate cookie"). At this point the inclusion of modified nouns (including colors, shapes and sizes), adjectives and noun phrases, noun modification through the use of prepositions, verb modification, expansion using modified nouns and verbs, pronoun use, prepositions using interrogatives, and modification of prepositions using negation are presented and established consecutively (Bricker, Ruder, & Vincent, 1976).

In this sequence the basic establishment of phrases and sentences, when necessary, occurs through initial imitation with a shift to the stimulus control of a direct verbal question.

ESTABLISHING REQUESTS AND QUESTIONS

Once naming and answering is consistently a part of the child's repertoire, the establishment of requests and questions can begin. As in the previous two levels, this involves a stimulus control shift from imitation to the appropriate circumstance(s) (environmental stimulus or stimuli).

The shift required to establish requests and questions, however, is more difficult for the child to discriminate since in "naming" the stimulus control was a particular object or picture plus a verbal question directed toward the child; in "answering a question" there was a specific verbal question directed toward the child, while in "establishing requests or questions" the stimulus control shift involves moving from imitation to focusing on a condition in the environment that is not specifically directed at the child although it is, initially at least, brought to his attention.

The change required in establishing requests and questions, being somewhat a similar problem to the previous one (a shift of stimulus control), entails a similar procedure to accomplish the objective. Initially, the child must be taught to imitate the request or question until the child consistently responds to the verbal prompt (Hartung & Hartung, 1973; Risley & Wolf, 1974). At this point the stimulus control shift to the appropriate circumstance(s) should be done. Often once establishing of requests and questions is begun, the shift comes about without specific training (Risley & Wolf, 1974). Generally, this is due to the natural reinforcers that are paired with the emission of the phrases, sentences, or questions. In essence the child may recognize the functional use of the verbalizations. For example, by emitting the verbalization (request or question) the child may gain control over the environment such as the response to "Cookie, please," "Open the door," and "May I swing?" When teaching requests and questions, be sure to draw upon the vocabulary repertoire the child already has established for more efficient development.

If the spontaneous use of requests and questions does not occur, they should be shaped by gradually fading the prompt by giving only the first one or two words (e.g., "Open the . . . ," "I want . . .") (Hartung & Hartung, 1973; Risley & Wolf, 1974).

In regard to the establishment of request verbalizations, Sloane, Johnston, and Harris (1968) developed an effective approach for severely retarded children. The children were taught to label food items (a strong reinforcer for the particular children they were working with). Following this, the children were taught requests for these food items. Once requests for food items were established, they were generalized to nonfood items.

Developing Functional Speech

Functional speech involves the process of the child using an oral language system to manipulate conditions within the immediate environment. Once a child has a repertoire of requests or questions, he can begin using his speech functionally. He can begin to recognize or, if necessary, be shown that his verbal responses can have an impact on his immediate environment (Hartung & Hartung, 1973). It is at this point that the natural reinforcers available in the environment begin to influence speech development (Risley & Wolf, 1974; Schell, Stark & Giddan, 1967; Schiefelbusch, Ruder, & Bricker, 1976).

The establishment of functional speech requires again a stimulus control shift from the teacher directing the child's attention to various items or conditions in the environment to the child focusing on the circumstances in the environment independently in order to receive the natural reinforcers that are available. When this shift is made, the child can start using language that is spontaneous and situationally appropriate. The realization by the child of the power of language to manipulate the environment results in the consequent stimulus of language taking on reinforcing properties (Marshall & Hegrenes, 1972). Thus, once functional speech is discovered by the child, the motivational elements of language development no longer need to be constantly programmed by the teacher in contrived ways.

The development of functional speech in a child may occur spontaneously as a result of the child learning about the reinforcers operating in the environment during the phase of developing request and questions. With more severely/profoundly handicapped individuals, however, the process of developing functional speech will most likely require systematic programming before naturally occurring reinforcers take over to facilitate and maintain further speech development. The process typically employed by language specialists (Hartung & Hartung, 1973; Risley & Wolf, 1974) is a shaping procedure using prompts and gradually fading the prompts.

1. The teacher provides a verbal model expressing a desire of the child. For example, the child may point to the water fountain to be lifted up in order to get a drink. The teacher may put his hands around the child's waist and say, "Life me up, please." If the child imitates the sentence, the teacher lifts him for a drink. If the child does not imitate, the teacher should repeat the sentence to be imitated. (Generally, the child will imitate the teacher's words due to the reinforcement history for imitative responses evident in the prior language development steps.)

2. The verbal prompt is gradually faded by saying fewer and fewer of the words until only the physical prompt of the teacher is needed to evoke the phrase. The physical prompt is then faded. In the case of lifting the child to the water fountain, the teacher may only need to put his or her hands on the child's waist (without providing the verbal prompt). The next step might be for the teacher to be only in close proximity to the water fountain. In this sequence one should be sure to consider deprivation and satiation principles that influence the de-

sire for the natural reinforcer so the motivational element is still operating.

3. The gradual fading in of the question "What do you want?" is done simultaneously with the second step, the fading of the verbal imitation and physical prompts. If the child imitates the question, present the question in a softer voice with a louder partial verbal prompt. This fading process should continue until the environmental elements—the water fountain and the question—result in the child emitting the request, "Life me up, please."

In the procedure of developing functional speech, the desires, likes, and dislikes of the child should be considered in the selection of the activities or environmental conditions to be focused on. Hartung and Hartung (1973) found that teaching a child to reduce or eliminate a condition that annoyed him was effective in developing functional speech. In this case a hand was placed on the head of a child who found this condition adversive. The child was taught to say "Stop it" to get the hand removed from his head. Schell, Stark, and Goddan (1967) used different types of foods; the child was required to say the foods that he wanted or did not want to receive.

The development of functional language should be based on the particular language needs of the child being taught (Lloyd & Cox, 1972). The vocabulary that is useful for one child may be nonfunctional for another. The needs of a child in an institution as to vocabulary that is relevant may not be functional for a child living with his family or in a group home. Differences in the types of relationships the child has with other people and objects in the environment will influence the functional language needs of each child (Graham, 1976).

Teaching Generalization

When acquired behavior occurs in situations other than the training setting within the child's natural environment or is extended or carried over into such situations, the child has generalized the learned behavior (Guess, Sailor, Keogh, & Baer, 1976; Risley & Wolf, 1973; Schiefelbusch, Ruder, & Bricker, 1976). The process involved in generalization is basically also one of shifting stimulus control of a response from one stimulus to several different stimuli (McLean, 1970). The major purpose of this shift is to "increase the use of a newly taught skill with persons different from the language trainer, and in environments different from the student's training area" (Guess, Sailor, Keogh, & Baer, 1976, p. 311).

Once a child develops some basic speech skills, he/she will often spontaneously generalize outside of the training environment (Hartung & Hartung, 1973). Imitation often spontaneously generalizes since the act of speech frequently becomes a conditional reinforcer due to the systematic application of reinforcement whenever imitation occurs (pairing process) and it can be maintained by intermittent social reinforcement (Baer, Peterson, & Sherman, 1967). Also, self-initiated or functional speech tends to generalize spontaneously because of the consequent natural reinforcers that operate in the environment (Hartung & Hartung, 1973).

In some cases, however, generalization does not spontaneously occur, and thus it needs to be built into the child's behavioral repertoire systematically. The following techniques and considerations can be used to enhance the generalization of speech:

1. Use words relevant to the child's daily life in various settings and situations (Hartung & Hartung, 1973). By using words that symbolize items and activities that are generic to various settings, experiences, and individuals, generalization is more likely to occur since the opportunity to use the words in different situations is available.
2. The child's learning program should take place in as normal or natural an environment as possible. This will eliminate the need to generalize skills learned in an unnatural environment to a more natural environment.
3. If it is necessary to separate the child from the ongoing classroom activities for short individual training sessions (to eliminate distractions for example), gradually introduce other individuals into the training situation (Risley & Wolf, 1973; Strait, 1968). The transition of speaking only to the teacher to speaking to other individuals is more easily accomplished if others are brought into the training setting since the only variable that will have changed for the child is the increase of people. Of course, a change in all variables should eventually occur, including having the child apply the new skills in many different settings and with many different people.
4. Train parents, parent surrogates, and other individuals who have daily contact with the child to use therapeutic procedures (Risley & Wolf, 1974; Schiefelbusch, Ruder, & Bricker, 1976). Train them to respond selectively (reinforce appropriate speech based on the child's current and emerging speech repertoire) in order to get the maximal practice and transfer of the speech that is being developed in the training situation. In this way the effects of the language development program can be integrated with the ongoing events of the natural environment (Schiefelbusch, Ruder, & Bricker, 1976).
5. Use social reinforcers, which may initially be paired with the more tangible reinforcers in the training setting, so that a smooth transfer to various settings can more easily occur (Hartung & Hartung, 1973). Social reinforcement can be easily used by many individuals in various settings.

6. After a language training session use the words worked on during the session in diffcrent situations (Risley & Wolf, 1974). After the language session and you—the teacher—are walking down the hall with the child, going out on the playground, returning with the child to the classroom, or just beginning another activity, talk with the child while he and you both use the new word(s) or language skill(s). The child thus learns the appropriate language use not only is supposed to occur during the training session, but also pervades all aspects of the natural environment. In short, be sure that language usage by the child is reinforced in a wide variety of settings (Hartung & Hartung, 1973).

7. If possible, periodically conduct the language training session in the child's home (Risley & Wolf, 1974). By focusing the language training session in the child's natural environment, the transition to using language in the natural environment outside of the formal language session is easier. The child need only generalize the circumstances for emitting language rather than having to generalize both the circumstances and the location.

8. Introduce more individuals into the language development process outside of the training setting by distributing a current list of the child's language repertoire to individuals who frequently interact with the child (Tramontana & Stimbert, 1970). In this way a variety of individuals can use, prompt, and reinforce the language repertoire of the child in a variety of situations, thus promoting generalization of the child's language repertoire.

9. In addition to prompting generalization of the language skills across individuals and settings, also build in opportunities to use the language symbols and skills in a variety of functions and experiences (Schiefelbusch, Ruder, & Bricker, 1976). Using diffeient items in a class of objects as well as using items in various activities promotes more extensive transfer of words into wider usage for communication.

Generalization of language does not necessarily occur only after functional speech is achieved. Generalizations should be programmed into the language development sequence as the different skills are established (Bricker, Ruder, & Vincent, 1976; Guess, Sailor, Keogh, & Baer, 1976; Schiefelbusch, Ruder, & Bricker, 1976). By building in generalization at the early stages, transfer of more complex skills comes about more easily as a result of the child's earlier experiences with generalization. In other words, early generalization experiences increase the probability of more spontaneous transfer of new skills as the child's repertoire of language increases. As the child learns to gain some control over his environment through functional speech, he can also gain through generalization

Table 5-2
Procedures for Developing Language Skills

Prerequisite Skills	Arrange the environment
	Eliminate disruptive behavior
	Establish attending behavior
Intervention Steps	Develop motor imitation
	Teach receptive language
	Develop verbal imitation
	Develop nonimitative verbalizations
	Develop functional speech
	Teach generalization

an expansion of his functional speech to different people and settings, thus gaining more control over his immediate environment (Guess, Sailor, & Baer, 1974). In short, through the development of generalization skills there often results an increase in the use of language by the child as well as transfer of skills to various individuals, settings, activities, functions, and experiences.

The nine procedures detailed here to aid in developing language skills are summarized in Table 5-2.

DEVELOPING COMMUNICATION: SAMPLE ACTIVITIES

When developing communication, the teacher will have to organize specific activities into an educational program tailored for the particular child(ren). Before deciding on which activities to include, however, it is necessary to evaluate the unique characteristics and functioning level of the child(ren) in order to specify appropriate objectives. Parents and professionals (doctor, psychologist, psychiatrist, speech therapist, and the like) who are working with each child should be asked to furnish data regarding the child's functioning level as well as information about any handicapping characteristic(s) (e.g., hearing impairment) that might be relevant to the design of an educational program. In addition, the teacher has available numerous developmental scales that can be employed to determine further the functioning level of the pupils. The developmental pinpoints compiled by Cohen, Gross, and Haring (1976) would also be valuable guidelines for assessment.

Precise measurement (as done in behavior modification projects) of a child's responses during task or activities is essential. For example, a frequency count of the number of verbalizations (precisely defined) a child makes during a five- to ten-day baseline period (before any specially designed program is implemented) should provide information about the extent to which the response is occurring. This will assist in more precisely pinpointing where to start teaching and can also be used to determine whether or not the particular teaching strategy, when implemented, actually is changing the frequency of verbalization.

In this section the authors have outlined some activities that are relevant to the education of the handicapped. They are merely a sample of different types of activities pertinent to communication.* For convenience they have been grouped into four categories

1. Development of simple responses
2. Readiness activities for communication in the form of oral speech
3. Gross motor imitation activities prerequisite for verbal imitation
4. Finer motor imitation activities

and subdivided as to objective and relevant activities.

Development of Simple Responses

1. *Objective:* To develop simple responses to sounds.
   Activity: 1. Stand behind the child.
                 2. Make a sound with a squeaky toy, rattle, drum, bell, etc.
                 3. Observe to see if the child stops movement, smiles, blinks, squeals, and/or turns toward the sound source. Two adults (e.g., teacher and aide) should be available, if possible, so one adult can observe the child's reaction when the sound is made and provide immediate reinforcement.
                 4. If the child makes a response, reinforce him (with juice, hug).
                 5. If the child does not respond, it may be necessary to prompt the response physically (e.g., place hand on head and stop movements) and gradually fade the prompt.
2. *Objective:* To develop attending response to command: "Look at me." (This is a prerequisite for teaching many other language concepts as well as teaching receptive vocabulary for phrase "Look at me.")
   Activity: 1. Sit in front of child.

---

*The activities presented were developed from Johnson and Werner (1975), Kent (1974), and Myers, Sinco, and Stalma (1973). See these sources for additional ideas.

2. Position your face on same visual plane and in close proximity to child's face.
3. Say, "Look at me."
4. If the child looks at your face, reinforce him. In the beginning stages it is sometimes necessary to hold the reinforcer in close proximity to your face (simultaneously with giving the command), which will hopefully encourage the child to look at you.
5. If the child will not look at you, you may have to repeat the command with the reinforcer held in front of your face with one hand as you take your other hand and move the child's head in the desired direction.
6. Gradually fade your physical assistance.
7. Reinforce appropriate responses. At first it may be necessary to reinforce for not resisting when you turn his head, then for turning his head slightly in desired direction, and so on through numerous stages as you shape the "looking response" by gradually requiring more and more behavior of the child before delivering the reward.

3. *Objective:* To develop the "stop" response to the word *no* (receptive vocabulary for word *no*).

   Activity:
   1. Pinpoint an inappropriate response the child frequently exhibits. (Be sure it is a behavior the child can be physically made to stop. Examples include head banging, hitting self, grabbing food.)
   2. Everytime the behavior occurs say "No" and simultaneously stop the behavior. Repeat "No" firmly several times as you stop the behavior.
   3. If the child does not stop the behavior, it may be necessary to pair a stimulus that is known to be aversive to the child with the word *no* (example, slap wrist simultaneously with saying "No").
   4. Be sure to reinforce the child for behaviors incompatible with the inappropriate behaviors.

4. *Objective:* To have the child look at objects (prerequisite for teaching many other language concepts as well as teaching receptive vocabulary for phrase "Look at ————").

   Activity:
   1. Select a brightly colored object with which the child is familiar.
   2. Place the object in front of the child.

3. Point to the object and say, "Look at [this]" (name of object).
4 If the child does not respond, move the object closer to his face.
5. If necessary, use physical assistance to turn the child's head toward the object.
6. It may be necessary to use a small dish containing edibles that you know the child likes.
7. Place the dish of edibles close to the child's face and say, "Look!" (In the beginning you should tip the dish slightly toward the child's face.)
8. Reinforce the child for looking into the dish with one of the edibles.
9. The teacher can then place the dish on the table and point to it saying, "Look at the dish."
10. After the child looks fairly consistently at one dish on the table, the teacher can place two dishes spaced apart on the table and ask the child to look at one of them and then the other randomly.
11. The teacher should begin substituting objects for the dishes of edibles.

Readiness Activities for Communcication in the Form of Oral Speech

5. *Objective:* To develop tongue extension. (As with any activity, this one can be contraindicated for some children, for example, those with tongue-thrust problems.)

Activity:
1. Sit directly in front of the child.
2. Position yourself in close proximity to his face on the same visual plane.
3. Put a small amount of food (e.g., pudding) on the end of a tongue depressor.
4. Let the child taste the food by placing a small amount in his mouth with the tongue depressor.
5. Place the tongue depressor with food just outside the mouth.
6. Praise and stroke the child if he sticks his tongue out of his mouth to reach the food (which should be the reinforcer itself).

6. *Objective:*   To develop tongue and jaw muscles essential for speech.

   Activity: 1. Sit directly in front of the child on the same visual plane.
                  2. Place peanut butter (any sticky substance the child likes) on the left or right cheek inside the child's mouth. You can accomplish this by putting peanut butter on the end of a tongue depressor and spread on inside of the cheek.
                  3. If necessary, assist the child in removing the peanut butter with his tongue by using the tongue depressor to manipulate his tongue. You can assist the child by touching, with the tongue depressor, the tongue on the side that is opposite from the direction that you want the tongue to go.
                  4. Gradually fade your assistance of touching the tongue with the tongue depressor as the child begins to move his tongue.

Gross Motor Imitation Activities Prerequisite for Verbal Imitation

7. *Objective:*   To develop imitation of very simple gestures.
   Activity: 1. Gesture (wave) and say "Bye, bye" whenever leaving the child.
                  2. Take the child's hand and wave bye, bye while saying the words when someone else is leaving and modeling the response
                  3. Gradually fade your physical assistance.
                  4. At first reinforce any movement of the hand and gradually require the movement to be closer to the actual response before delivering the reinforcer.

8. *Objective:*   To have the child imitate a variety of nonverbal behaviors.
   Activity: 1. Sit facing the child in close proximity to his face.
                  2. Say, "Look at me."
                  3. Immediately after the child looks, perform a motor task such as grasping, lifting, and dropping a block in a can.
                  4. Put the block directly in front of the child.
                  5. If the child puts his hand on the block, reinforce him (however, wait a few seconds and see if he

will perform the entire response before reinforcing).

6. Require the child to lift the block before reinforcing.
7. Require the child to drop the block in the can before reinforcing.
8. If the child does not even touch the block, repeat your instructions, "Look at me," and repeat the task.
9. Then place the child's hand on the block and assist him to grasp the block, lift it, and drop it in the can.
10. Fade physical assistance beginning with the dropping responses and gradually fade assistance for lifting and then grasping.
11. Provide reinforcement for each step completed and gradually increase the criteria for reinforcement.

Kent (1974) made the following suggestions about motor imitation:

1. Tasks such as simple object manipulation appear to be the easiest to imitate; for example, pushing a car. Clapping hands, extending both arms out to the front, touching body parts, and so forth are a little more difficult than simple object manipulation.
2. Movements that are visible are easier to imitate than movements that are not readily visible; and it is easier to imitate an action involving both arms and both feet than one that involves just one limb.

Finer Motor Imitation Activities

After the child learns to imitate gross movements fairly consistently, he should be required to imitate finer movements that can aid the development of the muscle coordination necessary for oral speech such as rounding lips, opening and closing mouth, moving tongue side to side, in and out, up and down, and blowing on objects (kleenex, match) with lips rounded (Johnson & Werner, 1975). Then the following activities can be introduced.

9. *Objective:* To have the child imitate sounds.
   Activity: 1. Sit directly across from the child on same visual plane.
   2. Select a sound that you have heard the child make repeatedly (example, "bah-bah").

          3.   Say, "Billy, say 'bah-bah.'"

          4.   Reinforce him at first for any sound he makes.

          5.   Gradually require the sound to be closer to the one you make.

          6.   Require the child to imitate sounds that can be combined into simple words.

10. *Objective:* To have the child imitate simple words.

     Activity: 1.   Sit directly in front of the child and on the same visual plane.

          2.   Select two sounds that the child can make, such as $k + eee$.

          3.   Say, "Mary, say, 'key,'" as you hold up a key.

          4.   Reinforce. For example, give her the key and praise her for any approximations of the word "key."

          5.   Gradually require closer and closer approximations until she imitates "key."

11. *Objective:* To have the child point to objects named.

     Activity: 1.   Sit directly in front of the child and on the same visual plane.

          2.   Select two objects the child is familiar with and knows the functional use of.

          3.   Say, "Billy, show me the 'keys' or 'ball.'"

          4.   Have someone model the response (pointing to the correct item) for the child to imitate if necessary.

          5.   Gradually fade the model.

          6.   Reinforce the child for any approximations and gradually require the exact correct response within a specified time after your command.

12. *Objective:* To have the child name objects.

     Activity: 1.   Select objects the child is familiar with and knows the functional use of, such as, key, ball, baby.

          2.   Sit across from the child on the same visual plane.

          3.   Hold object or picture of object close to face.

          4.   Say, "What is this?"

          5.   If the child does not respond, say, "What is this?" and have model say "key" or "ball" or "baby."

          6.   Reinforce the model's correct response and child's response if he imitates the model's response.

          7.   Gradually fade the model's response.

13. *Objective:* To have the child perform actions named (e.g., push car).

Activity: 1. Select actions that the child has engaged in, for example, push car, throw ball, take off coat.
2. Say, "Susie, push the car."
3. Have someone else (classroom aide or peer) model the correct response. Reinforce the model.
4. Repeat, "Susie, push the car."
5. Reinforce the child for the correct response.
6. If he does not respond correctly, you may have to prompt him physically and gradually fade the prompt.

14. *Objective:* To have the child ask simple questions.
Activity: 1. Select a reinforcer that you know the child particularly likes that he has learned to say (e.g., candy).
2. Sit directly across from the child and someone else (aide or peer) who can model the response.
3. Hold the reinforcer close to your face and have the model say, "Can I have candy?"
4. Reinforce the model's response and the child's response, also, if he imitates the model.
5. Gradually fade the asking of questions by the model.

A Note of Caution

The author's intent in this section was not to present a comprehensive list of activities for fostering language development. A teacher can evolve many others that will serve to achieve the objectives set for the particular child(ren).

A note of caution is in order. One should not look upon the activities as providing information about what to teach after the child can perform a particular response or reach a particular objective. For example, you should not try to have the child reach objective 14 after he/she can perform the response indicated in objective 13. The gap between the responses may be too wide. You should refer to the developmental pinpoints and various developmental scales to get an idea of the sequence to follow. For example, after a child learns to point to various objects named, the next step is to determine what to *teach next* (the next objective). The next step is *not* to select an activity. Remember that the sequence is generally "fine-focused" (very small steps) for the severely behaviorally handicapped child. After you determine what to teach next, there are many excellent sources of activities (Finnie, 1975; Johnson & Werner, 1975; Kent, 1974; Linde & Kopp, 1973; Myers, Sinco, & Stalma, 1973) that can be referred to for information about activities.

PROGRAMS TO ENHANCE LANGUAGE DEVELOPMENT

Since the middle of the 1960s a growing number of professionals have focused their attention on ways to foster language acquisition in nonverbal and severely language-delayed children. Many of the programs and approaches have evolved from contributions of linquistics, psycholinquistics, and/or behaviorism. Some have been based on a particular theoretical framework and research findings; others, on trial-and-error experiences of personnel working directly with severely language-delayed children. A representative sample of these programs are reviewed here.

Lovaas (1968) reported on a language program based on operant conditioning procedures. It was developed for psychotic children and stresses the establishment of expressive vocal behavior and the production of speech. The program begins with verbal imitation training and progresses through a logical sequence including object labeling, prepositions, and spontaneous speech. Contingent delivery of reinforcers for correct responses is emphasized. In Lovaas's research primary reinforcers were delivered in the early stages of training but a shift was gradually made to social and secondary reinforcers. This research demonstrated that at least some nonverbal, psychotic children can learn to imitate speech, label objects, and express simple needs.

Tawney and Hipsher (1972) developed a programmed instructional package designed to teach functional language skills to nonverbal and speech-deficient children.

> The program, called *Systematic Language Instruction* (SLI) emphasizes behavioral prerequisites to language production such as attending, motor skills, and receptive processes. The program is especially suited to low-functioning children who may need to learn behaviors such as sitting quietly or watching what the teacher does before training begins. (Schiefelbush, Ruder, & Bricker, 1976, p. 279)

The program can be used for small-group instruction. It is based on operant conditioning techniques. The child progresses through a carefully defined sequence. For each step in the sequence a target response is specified. Any prerequisites necessary to enter each step are explained. A pretest–posttest procedure is outlined for each step.

Gray & Ryan (1973) present a teaching strategy to promote language acquisition based on a behavioral interpretation of language. The program is designed to teach nonlanguage children how to talk. The focus is on oral, expressive language. Gray & Ryan define language as "the ability of a speaker in a novel environment to generate a syntactically correct and situationally appropriate sentence that he has not just previously heard" (p. 1). The procedures that the teacher should follow are presented in detail. Also included are philosophical and speculative discussions about the nature and the development of language. Data and findings of eight years of work with the teaching strategy are presented to support its validity.

Kent (1974) published a highly structured program for language acquisition designed to teach language to low-functioning retardates. The content is carefully sequenced, and all procedures are explained in detail. A variety of tasks, sequenced according to difficulty, are presented.

The program, which focuses on receptive as well as expressive language development, is organized into three sections: preverbal, verbal-receptive, and verbal-expressive. Attending behaviors and motor imitation are emphasized during preverbal training. Receptive and expressive language skills are stressed in the verbal sections. The purpose of the verbal-receptive section is to teach a limited receptive vocabulary. During the beginning phase of training the child is required to respond differentially by pointing to or finding various objects, body parts, and room parts. The purpose of the verbal-expressive section is to teach a simple expressive vocabulary. The child is initially required to name body parts, objects, and room parts taught during the verbal-receptive phase.

Guess, Sailor, and Baer (1974, 1977) and Guess, Sailor, Keogh, and Baer (1976) describe a training program for use with nonverbal, seriously speech-deficient children. The program is designed to produce generalized functional language usage by children in their everyday living environments. There is pretraining assessment and evaluation of the child's existing language repertoire and then the child is taught, if necessary, to imitate vocal sounds and simple words. The program is organized across four dimensions of language functions: reference, control, self-extended control, and integration.

Reference refers to the basic function of language, which is, of course, to symbolize. The child is taught productive (expressive) labels for things and actions of importance to him and is taught to respond correctly to receptive stimuli by pointing to the objects labeled by the teacher or by answering yes or no.

Control refers to the power of labels in controlling the environment. The child is taught request forms of language (productive skills) such as "I want [thing]" and to acknowledge another's questions (receptive skills) about his wishes by responding, for example, "Yes" or "No" or "You want [thing]."

The self-extended control dimension teaches how to extend referents (labels for things, actions, etc.). This is done by teaching the child to request instructions when he does not know. The child is taught to ask questions such as "What is that?" in response to unknown things and "What are you doing?" in response to unknown actions.

Integration refers to putting together reference, control, and self-extended control in such a manner that previously taught skills are integrated with currently taught skills to maximize appropriate interaction with the environment. This includes teaching children to discriminate when to seek appropriate information via question asking and when to respond with appropriate referents (labels) when the information already exists in their repertoire.

A second function of integration is dialogue which, conceptually, provides a teaching framework requiring the child to chain together all or some of the previously learned skills, so that they can carry on a simple but appropriate conversation centered around a functional activity or theme (Guess, Sailor, Keogh, & Baer, 1976, p. 308).

The content of the total language program is divided into six areas of emphasis: persons and things, action with persons and things, possession, color, size, and relation. The program is taught in a step-by-step fashion. Each step follows a similar format: For each there are specific training goals and rationale, designation of the stimulus materials needed, instructions regarding the procedures to be followed, and recommendations for extending (generalizing) training to the child's home or other settings.

The program also measures and teaches, if necessary, reception (receptive understanding) after expressive (productive) speech. Guess and his associates (1976) explain the rationale of their design:

The training of productive skills first in the program, followed by receptive training (if necessary) of the same skill is not intended to minimize the importance of receptive training, but to emphasize the productive nature of the program, which, by design, has the purpose of bringing the children rapidly into the speaking community (as contrasted to the mute but instruction-following community)'' (p. 308)

Bricker, Ruder, and Vincent (1976) set forth a language training regimen developed mainly by Bricker and Bricker (1970, 1974) and based on over ten years of research with language-deficient children (Bricker & Bricker, 1974; Ruder & Smith, 1974). This functional language program integrates linguistic and psycholinguistic theory and operant conditioning procedures and is based on normal language acquisition. All training stimuli (e.g., words) selected are useful to the children in their daily activities.

The development of prerequisite skills before actually teaching language is stressed. The overall emphasis is on the development of certain prerequisite cognitive strategies based on Piagetian theory. Also stressed are the importance of (1) teaching the child to imitate gross and fine motor movements before introducing imitation of sounds and (2) teaching an object's functional use before asking the child to understand the receptive label for the object.

Part I involves training of initial agent–action–object construction. The focus is on use of linguistic structures expressing agent – action – object semantic relations. As Bricker and his colleagues (1976) point out, however, the child who speaks in three-word strings, such as the agent–action–object form "Boy push car" is not speaking adult-style speech. Part II involves training in modifications of the agent–action–object structures (e.g., function words and modifiers such as articles, adjectives, and adverbs). The purpose is to teach the linguistic   and semantic functions necessary for the child's speech to be similiar to adult speech.

For additional information regarding the language intervention programs reviewed above as well as numerous other language programs, see Fristoe (1975, 1976). She published the results of a national survey of language-intervention programs designed for use with language-deficient children. She listed 229 programs and provided information on 187. Of these, 31 are described in journals and/or commercially published books; 66 are distributed privately as experimental editions; 39 are published in kit form; and 51 were in the process of preparation at the time of her survey (Graham, 1976).

ALTERNATIVES TO SPEECH AS A VEHICLE FOR COMMUNICATION

Communication also occurs in nonspeech ways, and very early in life children learn to communicate using these means—wiggles, smiles, nods of the head, flailing of arms and legs, and the like. For example, as already noted, when an adult stops playfully bouncing an infant on his lap and the infant wiggles, the adult sometimes interprets the wiggle as meaning the baby wants to be bounced some more. Thus, the infant has effectively communicated the message, "I want to be bounced some more" (Robinson, 1976). Of course, nonspeech ways of communicating are not used exclusively in infancy and childhood. Everyone uses various gestures to communicate throughout life. For example, an individual with his "thumb out" on the side of a highway is communicating a message.

There is a growing interest in formalized nonspeech language systems. Some handicapped children lack the physiological capacity to develop the more normal oral language system. With these children it becomes imperative to develop some type of nonspeech language system, and numerous techniques have been designed to assist such children. Four of the most successful will be briefly examined in this section: the use of plastic symbols, the Bliss symbols, American Sign Language (ASL), and communication aids such as language boards. For a more thorough review and discussion, see Vanderheiden and Harris-Vanderheiden (1976) and Vanderheiden and Grilley (1975).

Plastic Symbols

Carrier (1973, 1976) and Hollis and Carrier (1975) furnish a succinct description of the Non-Speech Language Initiation Program (NON-SLIP), a training program to teach communication behavior to the severely/ profoundly handicapped. Its objective is to teach children a strategy for learning language as opposed to teaching a circumscribed set of "functional" communication responses. What is interesting about the program is that communication is taught in a nonspeech mode.

Rather than spoken words, the symbols for various morphemes to be taught are geometric forms of different shapes cut from 3-inch squares of masonite. Each form is marked on its face with colored tape to indicate the grammatical class of the linguistic constituent it is to represent (noun, verb, article, plural marked, etc.). The shape of the form (triangle, square, etc.) indicates the specific morpheme to be represented. (Hollis & Carrier, 1975, p. 409)

The child is required to arrange the appropriate symbols on a plywood tray (similar to the tray of a chalkboard) in a left-to-right sequence as if he were writing sentences. For correct responses he receives positive reinforcement.

It should be noted that if communication could be established through a nonspeech response mode, later it might assist more natural oral speech development. "It seems reasonable to hypothesize that mastery of a comprehensive set of concepts (nonspeech language) should make it much easier to learn the more functional response mode such as speech" (Hollis & Carrier, 1975, p. 410). In fact, the term *initiation* is included in the title of the program to stress that the program should not be used as a total language training program but as a way of getting children started in the process of learning linguistic communication skills.

Bliss Symbols

The use of Bliss symbols as a symbol system for communication has gained popularity in recent years. Developed by Charles Bliss while he was in China about 1942, the symbols are patterned after Chinese writing, and were designed as a universal language-system of communication called "semantography." This system was not used with children until Shirley McNaughton, a teacher in Canada, started using the symbols with cerebral palsied children in the early 1970s, as an alternative to traditional orthography (written words) for language board use. Since then, this system has been used as a method of communication with many nonverbal severely handicapped children.

Vanderheiden and Harris-Vanderheiden (1976) describe the symbols as follows:

> Bliss symbols are both ideographic and pictographic. By ideographic, it is meant that a Bliss symbol represents an idea or a concept that may be expressed by the child. Pictographic implies that the symbol is also "picturelike." Consider the following examples:

| want | like | happy | sad |

> The above samples all have one similar component, the heart, and all have similar meanings: They have to do with emotion of some sort. The heart symbol, then, is representative of the concept emotion and consistent throughout the system wherever an emotion is expressed.
>
> From the next set of examples, it is seen that Bliss symbols are also pictographic:

| man | lady | father | mother |

> Blis symbols often visually resemble the concept or ideas that they are portraying. It is important to note that the Bliss symbols always appear with a word describing the basic meaning of the symbol printed directly beneath them. Thus, the system can be used with total strangers, and there is no need to "learn" the system to be able to communicate with someone who uses Bliss symbols. (p. 636)

Sign Language

Kotkin and Simpson (1976) investigated the use of "sign language coupled with the spoken word to facilitate the development of receptive and expressive language for the nonverbal child" (p. 75). In addition, they presented guidelines for the use of sign language and procedures to accomplish the following goals by means of sign language—(1) development of receptive vocabulary, (2) development of expressive language, (3) development of sentence structure and length, and (4) use of sign language as a primary means of communication.

Other professionals (e.g., Moores, 1974) have also stressed the value of sign language being taught to selected handicapped individuals. Some professionals have adapted oral language acquisition programs to sign language. For example, Snell (1974) adapted Kent's (1974) language-acquisition program for the severely retarded to sign language.

Communication Aids

In addition to step-by-step programs and procedures that have been developed for teaching communication, numerous aids are available for assisting in the communication process. Robinault (1973) described a large number of them, including the conversation board. A chart(s) composed of useful pictures, letters, words, signs, or numbers is covered with clear plastic and mounted securely on a desk or plywood board. "The student uses his fingers or clenches a small dowel stick to point to letters, words, or numbers on the chart that he wishes to use. If he has no hand use, he may direct his eyes to words" (Robinault, 1973, p. 141).

Wendt, Sprague, and Marquis (1975) describe a communication device called the Auto-Com. This device permits a student to slide a specially devised hand unit equipped with a magnet across a letter board. If the student pauses at a particular letter, a switch under the letter closes and a signal is sent to an electric typewriter and a printed symbol is typed. It can also record messages on a television screen or a tape printout. The Auto-Com is a portable device that can be attached to a wheelchair. It can be used both as a lap tray and as a communication board.

Wendt, Sprague, and Marquis (1975) are impressed with the device's potential.

> The Auto-Com has opened up a new area for persons who lack expressive language skills; although it cannot be used by everyone. Its effectiveness and ultimate functional use will depend on the individual's unique combination of physical and intellectual abilities . . . . The Auto-Com facilitates communication for the child who can understand the symbol system and has the motor skill to use and operate the device (p. 42).

There is a growing interest in alternative symbol systems and communication aids that can assist the handicapped to better communicate with those around them. This interest should lead to a better understanding of the communication process as well as enhance the educational potential of many handicapped children.

Communication aids should be considered as supplementary channels that increase communication—not substitute channels of communication. "They are not meant to replace the existing communication abilities of the child in much the same manner as writing and gesturing are additional means of communication for the speaking child" (Vanderheiden & Harris-Vanderheiden, 1976, p. 610).

The use of communication aids has not been found to decrease the development of speech in those children capable of developing speech. In fact, such aids can actually assist speech development (McNaughton & Kates, 1974; Vanderheiden & Harris-Vanderheiden, 1976; Victor, 1974).

REFERENCES

Baer, D.M., Peterson, R.F., & Sherman, J.A. The development of imitation by reinforcing behavioral similarity to a model. *Journal of Experimental Analysis of Behavior,* 1967, *10,* 405–416.

Bateson, M.C. *The interpersonal context of infant vocalization.* Quarterly Progress Report, No. 100, 170–176. Cambridge, MA: Research Laboratory of Electronics, Massachusetts Institute of Technology, January 15, 1971.

Bensburg, G.J. *Teaching the mentally retarded.* Atlanta: Southern Regional Educational Board, 1965.

Berry, M.F. *Language disorders of children: The bases and diagnoses.* New York: Appleton-Century-Crofts, 1969.

Berry, P. *Language and communication in the mentally handicapped.* Baltimore: University Park Press, 1976.

Blake, P., & Moss, T. The development of socialization skills in an electively mute child. *Behaviour Research and Therapy,* 1967, *5,* 349–356.

Bloom, L. *Language development: Form and function in emerging grammars.* Cambridge, MA: MIT Press, 1970.

Bloom, L. Semantic features in language development. In R.L. Schiefelbusch (Ed.), *Language of the mentally retarded.* Baltimore: University Park Press, 1972.

Bloom, L. Talking, understanding, and thinking. In R.L. Schiefelbusch & L. Lloyd (Eds.), *Language perspectives: Acquisition, retardation, and intervention.* Baltimore: University Park Press, 1974.

Bowerman, M. *Learning to talk: A cross-linguistic comparison of early syntactic developments, with special reference to Finnish.* London: Cambridge University Press, 1973.

Bricker, D.D., Ruder, K.F., & Vincent, L. An intervention strategy for language-deficient children. In N.G. Haring & R.L. Schiefelbusch (Eds.), *Training special children.* New York: McGraw-Hill, 1976.

Bricker, W.A. Errors in the echoic behavior of preschool children. *Journal of Speech and Hearing Research,* 1967, *10,* 67–76.

Bricker, W.A. A systematic approach to language training. In R.L. Schiefelbusch (Ed.), *Language of the mentally retarded.* Baltimore: University Park Press, 1972.

Bricker, W.A., & Bricker, D.D. A program of language training for the severely language handicapped child. *Exceptional Children,* 1970, *37,* 101–111.

Bricker, W.A., & Bricker, D.D. An early language training strategy. In R.L. Schiefelbusch & L. Lloyd (Eds.), *Language perspectives: Acquisition, retardation, and intervention.* Baltimore: University Park Press, 1974.

Brown, R.W. *A first language: The early stages.* Cambridge: Harvard University Press, 1973.

Brown, R.W., & Bellugi, U. Three processes in the child's acquisition of syntax. *Harvard Educational Review,* 1964, *34,* 133–151.

Bullowa, M., Jones, L.G., & Bever, T.G. The development from vocal to verbal behavior in children. *Monographs of the Society for Research in Child Development,* 1964, *29*(1, Whole No. 92), 9–34.

Carrier, J.K. Application of functional analysis and a non-speed response mode to teaching language. Parsons Kansas Research Center Report No. 7. Parsons: Parsons State Hospital and Training Center, 1973.

Carrier, J.K. Application of nonspeech language system with the severely language handicapped. In L. Lloyd (Ed.) *Communication Assessment and Intervention Strategies,* Baltimore: University Park Press, 1976.

Carroll, J.B. Psycholinguistics in the study of mental retardation. In R.L. Schiefelbusch, R.H. Copeland, & J.O. Smith (Eds.), *Language and mental retardation.* New York: Holt, Rinehart, & Winston, 1967.

Chapman, R., & Miller, J. *Word order in early two- and three-word utterances: Does production precede comprehension?* Paper presented to Stanford Child Language Research Forum, Stanford, California, 1973.

Chomsky, N.A. *Aspects of the theory of syntax.* Cambridge, MA: MIT Press, 1965.

Cohen, M.A., Gross, P.J., & Haring, N.G. Developmental pinpoints. In N.G. Haring & L.J. Brown (Eds.), *Teaching the severely handicapped.* New York: Grune & Stratton, 1976.

Cromer, R.F. The development of language and cognition: The cognition hypothesis. In B. Foss (Ed.), *New perspectives in child development.* Harmondsworth, Eng.: Penguin, 1974.

Cronbach, L.L. *Essentials of psychological testing.* New York: Harper & Row, 1960.

Crosby, K. Attention and distractibility in mentally retarded and intellectually average children. *American Journal of Mental Deficiency,* 1972, *77,* 46–53.

Ervin, S.M. Imitation and structural change in children's language. In E.H. Lenneberg (Ed.), *New directions in the study of language.* Cambridge, MA: MIT Press, 1964.

Ervin-Tripp, S. Language development. In L.W. Hoffman & M.L. Hoffman (Eds.), *Review of child development.* New York: Russell Sage Foundation, 1966.

Ferster, C.B. Clinical reinforcement. *Seminars in Psychiatry,* 1972, *4,* 101–111.

Finnie, N.R. *Handling the young cerebral palsied child at home.* New York: Dutton, 1974.

Fraser, C., Bellugi, U., & Brown, R. Control of grammar in imitation, comprehension, and production. *Journal of Verbal Learning and Verbal Behavior,* 1963, *2,* 121–135.

Friedlander, B.L. Receptive language development in infancy: Issues and problems. *Merrill-Palmer Quarterly,* 1970, *16,* 7–51.

Fristoe, M. *Language intervention systems for the retarded: A catalog of original structured language programs in use in the U.S.* Montgomery: State of Alabama Department of Education, 1975.

Fristoe, M. Language intervention systems: Programs published in kit form. In L. Lloyd (Ed.) *Communication Assessment and Intervention Strategies,* Baltimore: University Park Press, 1976.

Furth, H. On language and knowing in Piaget's developmental theory. *Human Development,* 1970, *13,* 241–257.

Garcia, E.E., Baer, D.M., & Firestone, I. The development of generalized imitation within experimentally determined boundaries. *Journal of Applied Behavior Analysis,* 1971, *4,* 101–112.

Gewirtz, J.L., & Stingle, K.G. Learning of generalized imitation as the basis for identification. *Psychological Review,* 1968, *75,* 374–397.

Graham, L.W. Language programming and intervention. In L.L. Lloyd (Ed.), *Communication assessment and intervention strategies.* Baltimore: University Park Press, 1976.

Gray, B., & Ryan, B. *A language program for the non-language child.* Champaign, IL: Research Press, 1973.

Greenfield, P.M. *Who is "dada"? Some aspects of the semantic and phonological development of a child's first word.* Unpublished paper, Research and Development Center in Early Childhood Education, Syracuse University, 1969.

Guess, D., & Baer, D. Some experimental analyses of linguistic development of institutionalized retarded children. In B.B. Lahey (Ed.), *The modification of language behavior,* Springfield, IL: Thomas, 1973.

Guess, D., Sailor, W., & Baer, D. To teach language to retarded children. In R.L. Schiefelbusch & L. Lloyd (Eds.), *Language perspectives: Acquisition, retardation, and intervention.* Baltimore: University Park Press, 1974.

Guess, D., Sailor, W., & Baer, D. A behavioral-remedial approach to language training for the severely handicapped. In E. Sontag, J. Smith, & N. Certo (Eds.), *Educational programming for the severely and profoundly handicapped.* Reston, VA: Council for Exceptional Children, 1977.

Guess, D., Sailor, W., Keogh, W. & Baer, D. Language development programs for severely handicapped children. In N.G. Haring & L.J. Brown (Eds.), *Teaching the severely handicapped.* New York: Grune & Stratton, 1976.

Hartung, J.R. A review of procedures to increase verbal imitation skills and functional speech in autistic children. *Journal of Speech and Hearing Disorders,* 1970, *35,* 204–217.

Hartung, S.M. & Hartung, J.R. Establishing verbal imitation skills and functional speech in autistic children. In B.B. Lahey (Ed.), *The modification of language behavior.* Springfield, IL: Thomas, 1973.

Hewett, F. Teaching speech in an autistic child through operant conditioning. *American Journal of Orthopsychiatry,* 1965, *35,* 927–936.

Hollis, J., & Carrier, J. Research implications for communication deficiencies. *Exceptional Children,* 1975, *41,* 405–412.

Ingram, D. The relationship between comprehension and production. In R.L. Schiefelbusch & L. Lloyd (Eds.), *Language perspectives: Acquisition, retardation, and intervention.* Baltimore, University Park Press, 1974.

Irwin, O.C. Phonetoical descriptions of speech development in childhood. In *Kaisers Manual of Phonetics,* Amsterdam: North Holland Publishing, 1957.

Isaacs, W., Thomas J., & Goldiamond, I. Application of operant conditioning to reinstate verbal behavior in psychotics. *Journal of Speech and Hearing Disabilities,* 1960, *25,* 8–12.

Jakobovits, L.A., & Miron, M.S. (Eds.), *Readings in the psychology of language.* Englewood Cliffs, NJ: Prentice-Hall, 1967.

Johnson, V.M., & Werner, R.A. *A step-by-step learning guide for retarded infants and children.* Syracuse, NY: Syracuse University Press, 1975.

Kagan, J., & Lewis, M. Studies of attention. *Merrill-Palmer Quarterly on Behavior Development,* 1965, *4,* 95–127.

Kaplan, E.L., & Kaplan, G.A. The prelinguistic child. In J. Eliot (Ed.), *Human development and cognitive processes.* New York: Holt, Rinehart & Winston, 1970.

Kent, L.R. *Language acquisition program for the severely retarded.* Champaign, IL: Research Press, 1974.

Kent, L.R., Klein, D., Falk, A., & Guenther, H. A language acquisition program for the retarded. In J.E. McLean, D.E. Yoder, & R.L. Schiefelbusch (Eds.), *Language intervention with the retarded.* Baltimore: University Park Press, 1972.

Kotkin, R., & Simpson, S. A sign in the right direction: Language development for the non-verbal child. *AAESPH Review,* 1976, *1,* 75–81.

Lahey, B.B. *The modification of language behavior.* Springfield, IL: Thomas, 1973.

Lenneberg, E.H. Biological foundations of language. New York: Wiley, 1967.

Lerner, J.W. *Children with learning disabilities.* Boston: Houghton Mifflin, 1976.

Lewis, M., & Freedke, R. *Mother-infant dyad: The cradle of meaning.* Princeton, NJ: Educational Testing Service, 1972.

Linde, T., & Kopp, T. *Training retarded babies and preschoolers.* Springfield, IL: Thomas, 1973.

Lovaas, O.I. A program for the establishment of speech in psychotic children. In H. Sloane & B. MacAulay (Eds.), *Operant procedures in remedial speech and language training.* Boston: Houghton Mifflin, 1968.

Lovaas, O.I., Berberick, J., Perloff, B., & Schaeffer, B. Acquisition of imitative speech by schizophrenic children. *Science,* 1966, *151,* 705–707.

Lloyd, L.L., & Cox, B.P. Programming for the audiologic aspects of mental retardation. *Mental Retardation,* 1972, *10,* 22–26.

Marshall, N.R., & Hegrenes, J. The use of written language as a communication system for an autistic child. *Journal of Speech and Hearing Disorders,* 1972, *37,* 258–261.

McCarthy, D. Language development in children. In L. Carmichael (Ed.), *A manual of child psychology.* New York: Wiley, 1954.

McLean, J.E. Extending stimulus control of phoneme articulation by operant techniques. In F.L. Girardeau & J.E. Spradlin (Eds.), *A functional approach to speech and language.* ASHA Monograph No. 14, 1970, 24–47.

McNaughton, S., Kates, B. *Visual symbols: Communication system for the pre-reading physically handicapped child.* Paper presented at the American Association on Mental Deficiency Annual Meeting, Toronto, June, 1974.

Menyuk, P. Early development of receptive language: From babbling to words. In R.L. Schiefelbusch & L. Lloyd (Eds.), *Language perspectives: Acquisition, retardation, and intervention.* Baltimore: University Park Press, 1974.

Metz, J.R. Conditioning generalized imitation in autistic children. *Journal of Experimental Psychology,* 1965, *2,* 389–399.

Miller, G.A. Some preliminaries to psycholinguistics. In L.A. Jakobovits & M.S. Miron (Eds.), *Readings in the psychology of language.* Engelwood Cliffs, NJ: Prentice-Hall, 1967.

Miller, J. On specifying what to teach: The movement from structure, to structure and meaning, to structure and meaning and knowing. In E. Sontag, J. Smith, & N. Certo (Eds.), *Educational programming for the severely and profoundly handicapped.* Reston, VA: Council for Exceptional Children, 1977.

Miller, J., & Yoder, D. A syntax teaching program. In J. McLean, D. Yoder, & R. Schiefelbusch (Eds.), *Language intervention with the retarded.* Baltimore: University Park Press, 1972a.

Miller, J., & Yoder, D. On developing the content for a language teaching program. *Mental Retardation,* 1972b, *10,* 9–11.

Miller, J., & Yoder, D. An ontogenetic language teaching strategy for retarded children. In R.L. Schiefelbusch & L. Lloyd (Eds.), *Language perspectives: Acquisition, retardation, and intervention.* Baltimore: University Park Press, 1974.

Moores, D.F. Nonvocal systems of verbal behavior, In R.L. Schiefelbusch & L. Lloyd (Eds.), *Language perspectives: Acquisition, retardation, and intervention.* Baltimore: University Park Press, 1974.

Mueller, H. *Speech.* In N.R. Finnie (Ed.), *Handling the young cerebral palsied child at home.* New York: Dutton, 1975.

Murai, J.-I. The sounds of infants. *Studies of Phonology,* 1963–1964, *3,* 21–24.

Myers, D.G., Sinco, M.E., & Stalma, E.S. *The right-to-education child.* Springfield, IL: Thomas, 1973.

Nakazima, S. A comparative study of the speech developments of Japanese and American English in childhood. *Studies of Phonology,* 1962, *2,* 27–39.

Peterson, R.F. Some experiments on the organization of a class of imitative behaviors. *Journal of Applied Behavior Analysis,* 1968, *1,* 225–235.

Piaget, J. Piaget's theory. In P. Mussen (Ed.), *Carmichael's manual of child psychology.* New York: Wiley, 1970.

Piaget, J., & Inhelder, B. *The psychology of the child.* New York: Basic Books, 1969.

Premack, D. A functional analysis of language. *Journal of the Experimental Analysis of Behavior,* 1970, *14,* 107–125.

Premack, D. & Premack, A. Teaching visual language to apes and language-deficient persons. In R.L. Schiefelbusch & L. Lloyd (Eds.), *Language perspectives: Acquisition, retardation, and intervention.* Baltimore: University Park Press, 1974.

Pronovost, W., Wakstein, M.P., & Wakstein, J.J. A longitudinal study of the speech behavior and language comprehension of fourteen children diagnosed atypical or autistic. *Exceptional Children,* 1966, *33,* 19–26.

Raymore, S., & McLean, J.E. A clinical program for carry-over of articulation therapy with retarded children. In J.E. McLean, D.E. Yoder, & R.L. Schiefelbusch (Eds.), *Language intervention with the retarded.* Baltimore: University Park Press, 1972.

Reese, H.W., & Lipsitt, L.P. *Experimental child psychology.* New York: Academic Press, 1970.

Rieke, J. Communication in early childhood. In N. Haring (Ed.), *Behavior of Exceptional Children,* Columbus, OH: Merrill, 1978.

Risley, T. The effects and side effects of punishing the autistic behaviors of a deviant child. *Journal of Applied Behavior Analysis,* 1968, *1,* 21–35.

Risley, T., Hart, B., & Doke, L. Operant language development: The outline of a therpeutic technology. In R.L. Schiefelbusch (Ed.), *Language of the mentally retarded.* Baltimore: University Park Press, 1972.

Risley, T., & Wolf, M. Establishing functional speech in echolalic children. *Behaviour Research and Therapy,* 1967, *5,* 73–88.

Risley, T., & Wolf, M. Establishing functional speech in echolatic children. In O.I. Lovaas & B.D. Bucher (Eds.), *Perspectives in behavior modification with deviant children.* Englewood Cliffs, NJ: Prentice-Hall, 1974.

Robinault, I.P. *Functional aids for the multiply handicapped.* New York: Harper & Row, 1973.

Robinson, C.C. Application of Piagetian sensorimotor concepts to assessment and curriculum for severely handicapped children. *AAESPH Review,* 1976, *1,* 5–10.

Ruder, K.F. A psycholinguistic viewpoint of the language acquisition process. In R.L. Schiefelbusch (Ed.), *Language of the mentally retarded.* Baltimore: University Park Press, 1972.

Ruder, K.F., Bricker, W., & Ruder, C. Recent psycholinguistic research on the language acquisition process. In J. Gallagher (Ed.), *Review of research on exceptional children.* Washington, DC: Council on Exceptional Children, 1975.

Ruder, K.F., & Smith, M. Issues in language learning. In R.L. Schiefelbusch & L. Lloyd (Eds.), *Language perspectives: Acquisition, retardation, and intervention.* Baltimore: University Park Press, 1974.

Schell, R.F., Stark, J., & Giddan, J.J. Development of language behavior in an autistic child. *Journal of Speech and Hearing Disorders,* 1967, *32,* 51–61.

Schiefelbusch, R.L., Ruder, K.F., & Bricker, W.A. Training strategies for language-deficient children: An overview. In N.G. Haring & R. L. Schiefelbusch (Eds.), *Teaching special children.* New York: McGraw-Hill, 1976.

Sherman, J.A. Use of reinforcement and imitation to reinstate verbal behavior in mute psychotics. *Journal of Abnormal Psychology,* 1965, *70,* 155–164.

Shipley, E., Smith, C., & Gleitman, L. A study in the acquisition of language: Free responses to commands. *Language,* 1969, *45,* 322–342.

Sinclair de Zwart, H. Language acquisition and cognitive development. In T.E. Moore (Ed.), *Cognitive development and the development of language.* New York: Academic Press, 1973.

Skinner, B.F. *Verbal behavior.* New York: Appleton-Century-Crofts, 1957.

Sloane, H.N, Jr., Johnston, M.K., & Harris, F.R. Remedial procedures for teaching verbal behavior to speech deficient or defective young children. In H.N. Sloane, Jr., & B. MacAuley (Eds.), *Operant procedures in remedial speech and language training.* Boston: Houghton-Mifflin, 1968.

Slobin, D. Cognitive prerequisites for the development of grammar. In C. Ferguson & D. Slobin (Eds.), *Studies in child language development*. New York: Holt, Rinehart & Winston, 1973.

Snell, M. Sign language and total communication. In L. Kent (Ed.), *Language acquisition program for the severely retarded*. Champaign, IL: Research Press, 1974.

Strait, R. A child who was speechless in school and social life. *Journal of Speech and Hearing Disorders*, 1968, *23*, 253–254.

Stremel, K. Language training: A program for retarded children. *Mental Retardation*, 1972, *10*, 47–49.

Tawney, J., & Hipsher, L. *Systematic instruction for retarded children: The Illinois program*, (part II). Springfield: State of Illinois Office of the Superintendent of Public Instruction, 1972.

Tramontana, J., & Stimbert, V.E. Some techniques of behavior modification with an autistic child. *Psychological Reports*, 1970, *27*, 498.

Turner, R. A method of working with disturbed children. *American Journal of Nursing*, 1970, *70*, 2146–2151.

Vanderheiden, G., & Grilley, K. *Non-voral communication techniques and aides for the severely physically handicapped*. Baltimore: University Park Press, 1975.

Vanderheiden, G., & Harris-Vanderheiden, D. Communication techniques and aids for the non-vocal severely handicapped. In L.L. Lloyd (Ed.), *Communication assessment and intervention strategies*. Baltimore: University Park Press, 1976.

Victor, B. *Non-vocal communication system project 1964–73*. Iowa City: Campus Stores Publishers, University of Iowa, 1974.

Wendt, E., Sprague, M.J., & Marquis, J. Communication with speech. *Teaching Exceptional Children*, 1975, *8*, 39–42.

Winitz, H. Problem solving and the delaying of speech as strategies in teaching of language. *ASHA*, 1973, *15*, 583–386.

Yeni-Komshian, G., Chase, R.A., & Mobley, R.L. *Delayed auditory feedback studies in the speech of children between 2 and 3 years*. Annual Report. Johns Hopkins University Neurocommunications Laboratory. Baltimore: Johns Hopkins University School of Medicine, 1967.

SELECTED READINGS FOR FURTHER STUDY

Bloom, L. *Language development: Form and function in emerging grammars*. Cambridge, MA: MIT Press, 1970.

Bricker, D.D., Ruder, K.F., & Vincent, L. An intervention strategy for language-deficient children. In N.G. Haring & R.L. Schiefelbusch (Eds.), *Teaching special children*. New York: McGraw-Hill, 1976.

Bricker, W.A. Errors in the echoic behavior of preschool children. *Journal of Speech and Hearing Research*, 1967, *10*, 67–76.

Bricker, W.A. A systematic approach to language training. In R.L. Schiefelbusch (Ed.), *Language of the mentally retarded*. Baltimore: University Park Press, 1972.

Bricker, W.A., & Bricker, D.D. An early language training strategy. In R.L. Schiefelbusch & L. Lloyd (Eds.), *Language perspectives: Acquisition, retardation, and intervention*. Baltimore: University Park Press, 1974.

Bricker, W.A., & Bricker, D.D. A program of language training for the severely language handicapped child. *Exceptional Children*, 1970, *37*, 101–111.

Carrier, J.K. Application of functional analysis and a non-speed response mode to teaching language. Parsons Kansas Research Center Report No. 7. Parsons: Parsons State Hospital and Training Center, 1973.

Cohen, M.A., Gross, P.J., & Haring, N.G. Developmental pinpoints. In N.G. Haring, & L.J. Brown (Eds.), *Teaching the severely handicapped*. New York: Grune and Stratton, 1976.

Finnie, N.R. *Handling the young cerebral palsied child at home*. New York: Dutton, 1974.

Graham, L.W. Language programming and intervention. In L.L. Lloyd (Ed.), *Communication assessment and intervention strategies*. Baltimore: University Park Press, 1976.

Gray, B., & Ryan, B. *A language program for the non-language child*. Champaign, IL: Research Press, 1973.

Guess, D., & Baer, D. Some experimental analyses of linguistic development of institutionalized retarded children. In B.B. Lahey (Ed.), *The modification of language behavior*.

Guess, D., Sailor, W., & Baer, D. A behavioral-remedial approach to language training for the severely handicapped. In E. Sontag, J. Smith, & N. Certo (Eds.), *Educational programming for the severely and profoundly handicapped*. Reston, VA: Council for Exceptional Children, 1977.

Hartung, S.M. & Hartung, J.R. Establishing verbal imitation skills and functional speech in autistic children. In B.B. Lahey (Ed.), *The modification of language behavior*. Springfield, IL: C. Thomas, 1973.

Kent. L.R. *Language acquisition program for the severely retarded*. Champaign, IL: Research Press, 1974.

Lahey, B.B. *The modification of language behavior*. Springfield, IL: Thomas, 1973.

McLean, J.E. Extending stimulus control of phoneme articulation by operant techniques. In F.L. Girardeau & J.E. Spradlin (Eds.), *A functional approach to speech and language*. ASHA Monograph No. 14, 1970, 24–47.

Rieke, J. Communication in early childhood. In N. Haring (Ed.), *Behavior of Exceptional Children*, Columbus OH: Merrill, 1978.

Risley, T. & Wolf, M. Establishing functional speech in echolatic children. In O.I. Lovaas & B.D. Bucher (Eds.), *Perspectives in behavior modification with deviant children*. Englewood Cliffs, NJ: Prentice-Hall, 1974.

Schiefelbusch, R.L., Ruder, K.F., & Bricker, W.A. Training strategies for language-deficient children: An overview. In N.G. Haring & R.L. Schiefelbusch (Eds.), *Teaching special children*. New York: McGraw-Hill, 1976.

Snell, M. Sign language and total communication. In L. Kent (Ed.), *Language acquisition program for the severely retarded*. Champaign, IL: Research Press, 1974.

Stremel, K. Language training: A program for retarded children. *Mental Retardation*, 1972, *10*, 47–49.

6
Changing Attitudinal, Emotional, and Social Behaviors

While the schools generally have not implemented organized procedures for teaching attitudes, emotions, and sociability, the literature abounds with statements stressing the importance and need for such training (Beatty, 1969; Borich, 1971; Bradtke, Kirkpatrick, & Rosenblatt, 1972; Harbeck, 1970; Henderson, 1972; Homme, 1970; Ivey, 1969; Lazarus, 1973; Morris, 1972; Morse, 1971; Rogers, 1969, 1970; Schrag, 1972; Weinstein & Fantini, 1970; Winnett & Winkler, 1972). The recognition of the importance of systematically teaching such behaviors has been a concern of some psychologists and educators for many years (Prescott, 1938; Sandiford, 1936; Thorndike, 1906). In recent years this concern has intensified. As Strain, Cooke, and Appolloni (1976) have stated, "The belief that the American educational institution has been negligent in its attention to systematic methods and strategies for enhancing the social-emotional dimension of child development is now widely held" (p. 1). It also has been suggested that inadequate or unsystematic training in attitudes, emotions, and sociability may be a precipitating factor in the development of "emotional disturbance" (Schrag, 1972; Trower, Bryant, & Argyle, 1978).

Despite the consistency and strength of the expressed need in this area, little has been done to incorporate into the schools systematic training of atitudes, emotions, and sociability. One possible reason for this is the lack of empirically verified teaching procedures. In addition, the limited amount of research that has been done has not been pulled together to provide teachers with general guidelines for approaching the task. The authors purpose in this chapter is to organize the findings of empirical research in regard to some of the most common behaviorally based procedures that have been effectively used to develop or modify attitudes, emotions, and sociability.

DEFINING BEHAVIORS FOR EMPIRICAL VALIDATION

A mentalistic perspective of emotions, attitudes, and sociability has hindered the development of teaching procedures that can be empirically verified. Skinner (1953) rightly noted, "As long as we conceive of the problems of emotion as one of inner states, we are not likely to advance a practical technology" (p. 167). The same is true for the constructs of attitudes and sociability.

It was primarily the behavioral researchers who provided a means to bring the dimension of empirical validation to the study of attitudes, emotions, and sociability. Rather than viewing such constructs from a mentalistic perspective, behaviorists have examined these constructs in light of functional behavioral manifestations indicative of the constructs. For example, Strain, Cooke, and Apolloni (1976) in regard to the mentalistic constructs of "friendly," "humanitarianism," and "helpfulness" stated that "such behaviors as smiling, verbally complimenting, positively physically contacting and sharing would seem to be behavioral manifestations of the previously mentioned emotional states of children" (pp. 7–8). In other words, smiling, verbally complimenting, and positively physically contacting could be considered "friendly" behaviors, and sharing might be considered indicative of "humanitarianism" or "helpfulness."

As for the constructs of concern, what the authors actually are referring to are behaviors that are considered to be indicative of what many people think of as being "private events" (Ross, 1974). This approach is not intended to infer that such internal occurrences do not exist but simply that it is possible to place the focus on external indices that can be measured so that empirical validation of procedures for teaching in this area can be carried out (Ross, 1974; Strain, Cooke, & Apolloni, 1976; Trower, Bryant, & Argyle, 1978). In short, the behaviors associated with the "private events" are what actually constitute the area of concern. As Martin and Pear (1978) stated:

> Suppose Johnny's teacher, Ms. Smith, reports that he has a bad attitude toward school. What does Ms. Smith mean by this? Perhaps she means that Johnny frequently skips school, refuses to do his classwork when he does attend and swears at the teacher. Whatever she means when she talks about Johnny's "bad attitude," it is clearly his behavior with which she is really concerned. (p. 4)

What Martin and Pear observe is also true of emotions. When a bad temper is said to require modification, the temper may involve hitting others, breaking objects, swearing, or slamming a door. The concern of an individual being unsociable may involve not interacting with others, exhibiting few imitating behaviors, or frowning and withdrawing when approached by others. All of these behaviors of concern are observable and measurable and can be modified by means of behavioral programming.

Behaviors indicative of liking/warm, disliking/cold, or superiority/dominant, and inferiority/submissive focused toward individuals or things (including self) are usually labeled attitudinal behaviors (Foa, 1961; Lorr & McNair, 1965; Trower, Bryant, & Argyle, 1978). Behaviors indicative of subjective states within an individual not focused toward others (e.g., fear, happiness, anxiety) are considered emotional behaviors (Trower, Bryant, & Argyle, 1978). "Social behaviors may be defined as the behavior of two or more people with respect to one another or in concert with respect to a common environment" (Skinner, 1953, p. 297).

While it is feasible for discussion purposes to separate behaviors indicative of attitudes, emotions, and sociability into different categories, it should not be overlooked that many such behaviors are closely tied to one another and that any arbitrary categorizations or groupings are not likely to appear mutually exclusive. Only in a close analysis of the behaviors can one type be distinguished from another. Behaviors indicative of emotions are basically the same as attitudes; however, they are not directed toward a particular person or item. (Trower, Bryant, & Argyle, 1978). Thus, attitudinal behavior is characterized by distinct approach and avoidance behaviors toward a particular person or thing that are generally not exhibited with emotions. For example, an individual may exhibit undirected anger that would be considered an emotion; if the behaviors indicative of anger were directed toward a particular person or thing, however, it might be classified as an attitude. Similarly, sociability is closely linked with additudinal behaviors since approach or avoidance toward other persons is a key facor.

In the following section techniques that have implications for classroom use for modifying behaviors indicative of attitudes, emotions, and sociability will be considered.

TEACHING PROCEDURES

Attitudes

In a classroom it is not uncommon for the teacher to be called upon to teach an attitude about something. For example, many schools are currently being called upon to transmit a bad attitude toward cigarettes since they are considered to be a health hazard. This attitude is intended as a preventive measure to encourage children to avoid cigarettes and also to discourage their friends and relatives from smoking.

Before proceeding further, it should be noted that if in the teaching of

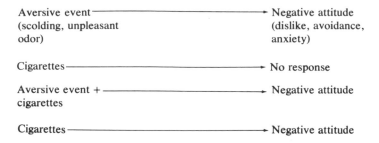

Fig. 6–1

attitudes a preventive rather than a remediative or corrective approach is used, the process is simplified. Teaching an attitude toward a neutral item is more efficient than teaching an attitude toward an item that has already acquired an attitude opposite from the one that you desire. If in teaching a bad attitude toward cigarettes it is determined that the students have already acquired a positive attitude toward cigarettes, the process of developing a bad attitude will need to be more intensive and the probability of success is decreased.

An effective method of developing a bad attitude or avoidance response toward cigarettes (or any other item) is to use an aversive conditioning procedure (Meichenbaum, 1977). Aversive conditioning follows the paradigm of classical or respondent conditioning developed by Pavlov (1927). In this procedure an aversive event is repeatedly presented with the item of concern (in this case cigarettes) until the target item gradually take on the properties (dislike, avoidance, bad attitude) of the aversive event. The paradigm for cigarettes appears in Figure 6–1.

The stronger the aversive stimuli used in the procedure, the more quickly and effectively the attitude toward the target item will change (Martin & Pear, 1978). The target item, as previously noted, should be one that is basically neutral. If the target item or event (e.g., cigarettes, playing with knives, fighting with others, smearing feces) is desirable to the person, the aversive event paired with it must be strong enough to counteract the desirability of the target item. While it is possible to teach a bad attitude toward an item or something that a child currently has a positive attitude toward, it is a difficult task.

Two procedures employing the same respondent conditioning paradigm can be used to teach children good or positive attitudes. The first procedure is referred to as "aversion relief" (Barlow, 1972) in which the *cessation of an aversive event* is paired with an item, idea or person the teacher wants the child to consider desirable (Kazdin, 1978). If the teacher should desire, for instance, to teach a positive attitude toward policemen, the paradigm would be as shown in Figure 6–2.

Removal of aversive ————————————→ Positive attitude
(stop nagging, cease scolding,   (liking, relaxation, relief,
elimination of unpleasant sound   approach)
or odor)

Policeman ——————————————→ No response

Removal of aversive + ———————→ Positive attitude
policeman

Policeman ———————————————→ Positive attitude

Fig. 6–2

Aversive Training and Aversion Relief

Maria, a 17-year-old female student labeled seriously disturbed, exhibited consistent unfearful or what might be considered bizarre approach behaviors toward flames of fire. She often stuck her fingers or face into the flames. Fortunately, an adult had been close by whenever a flame was present, and only minor redness or blistering had resulted. The potential hazards, however, were considerable. Maria was being taught to function more independently in the community, and it was recognized that she would be exposed to situations in which fire may be present, for example, cigarette lighter flames, gas stove flames. Therefore, the objective was to develop a fear of fire to be exhibited by Maria. Maria did exhibit intense fear behaviors (tenseness, crying) when loud siren blasts were presented. The teacher, Mr. T, arranged for the presentation of repeated simultaneous pairing of siren blasts with the presentation of flames of fire. After five sessions, with three pairings per session, when Maria was tested, it was found that the flame alone would elicit the fear behavior that was exhibited with the presentation of the siren. One week of daily aversive training resulted in fear behavior being exhibited in the presence of fire.

In combination with aversive training, aversion relief was also used to discourage Maria's approach behaviors toward fire. It was set up so that when the siren and flames were paired, the siren blast would stop as soon as Maria either looked or turned away from the fire. Thus the cessation of the aversive stimulus, the siren, was paired with a "nonflame" view so "nonflame" views would come to be a positive stimulus for Maria.

This training sequence with Maria was just an initial step toward "normalizing" Maria's emotions toward fire. It was carried out because of the hazardous nature of the behavior that she exhibited. Further training was planned to teach Maria to discriminate her fear behaviors toward fire since there will be some fire situations in which controlled or reasonable approach behaviors toward fire are appropriate, e.g., a campfire on a cold night. In other words, procedures were implemented to teach Maria when and how to approach a fire without fear when it was necessary to do so but at the same time to have a healthy fear of fire when it was appropriate to be fearful.

Fig. 6–3

Positive event ——————————————→ Positive attitude
(smiles, pleasant statements,   (liking, approach,
tokens)   smiles)

Books ——————————————————————→ No response

Positive event + ——————————————→ Positive attitude
books

Books ——————————————————————→ Positive attitude

Fig. 6–4

A second approach to teaching positive attitudes involves pairing a pleasant or desirable event with a neutral or disliked item that is considered desirable for the child to like or have a positive attitude toward (Gardner, 1977). In this procedure the item to be taught to be desirable is repeatedly paired with, and acquires the properties of, an item that is already desirable to the child. In school it is common to try to teach children to like books. Agan the classical or respondent conditioning paradigm would be as in Figure 6–4.

Attitudes, both positive and negative, can be systematically taught. It is not uncommon for teachers unconsciously to implement what has been detailed in the paradigms. With a conscious awareness in regard to atti-

---

Direct Respondent Conditioning

Carla, a young seriously disturbed multiply handicapped preschooler, exhibited behaviors indicative of an intense dislike of her new positioning wheelchair. As soon as it was brought into the room, Carla displayed behaviors indicative of anxiousness, which consisted of becoming tense and uncooperative. (This reaction appeared to be a generalization from her previous chair that she had outgrown and which apparently had become very uncomfortable and even painful for her to sit in.)

First the new chair was decorated in different colors and had different decals on it to differentiate it from the outgrown chair. Also, a respondent conditioning procedure was implemented so that whenever Carla was being placed in the chair, her favorite nursery rhyme music would be presented and she was allowed to play with her favorite toy, a Raggedy Ann doll. (Initially only the music was presented, and it appeared that the anxious behavior toward the chair was stronger and would overpower the relaxation and happy behavior elicited by the music. For this reason the combination of music and a favorite toy was used to provide sufficient strength to overcome the anxiousness.) The relaxation elicited by the music and toy quickly became paired (within three days) with the new positioning chair, and Carla began exhibiting happy, relaxed behaviors when the chair was presented without the additional music and toy stimuli.

It should be noted that it was assumed that the comfort resulting from relaxation in a properly fitted chair also influenced the rapid acquisition of the behavior change.

Fig. 6–5

tude change, however, the chance of potential success can be increased by monitoring and systematically implementing procedures to change and/or develop appropriate attitudes.

Teaching attitudes to children is an important aspect in the prevention of inappropriate behaviors even in environments in which behaviors cannot be monitored (e.g., neighborhood clubhouse, playground). The attitude a child has toward an item influences his behavior associated with it, both in private and public. If a child has a bad attitude toward smoking cigarettes, he is more likely to avoid smoking cigarettes and will be less likely to reinforce his peers for smoking.

In the conditioning procedures the items of concern (e.g., cigarettes, policemen) do not have to be available in the classroom to influence attitudes toward them. Representations of an item by pictures and slides, for example, have been successfully used (e.g., Feldman & MacCulloch, 1965). Also, the child(ren) can be asked to imagine or visualize the item of concern; thus, the teacher could ask the child, or class, to visualize smoking a cigarette, and an unpleasant odor could be presented simultaneously with the visualization. For the more seriously handicapped individual such procedures may not pertain since for such an approach to be used effectively, environmental awareness and good mental imagery that can be well controlled by the student is required.

Attitudes can be taught by procedures other than those based on respondent conditioning. If behaviors indicative of positive attitudes are reinforced, following an operant conditioning model, they will tend to occur more often (Sulzer-Azaroff & Mayer, 1977). In other words, if positive attitudinal behaviors toward school—such as attending school, participating in class activities, making positive statements about the teacher, other students, and assignments—are reinforced, they will tend to occur more often. Also, if the teacher models the attitude(s) desired, the child who needs a more positive or negative attitude will tend to imitate and express the attitude (Bandura, 1977). Peer modeling is another effective device for changing attitudes (Doland & Adelberg, 1967). These procedures which are summarized in Table 6–1, are discussed in more detail in the following sections. Although the discussions relate to changing behaviors indicative of emotions and sociability, many of the procedures are also applicable for changing attitudes.

Emotions

Behaviors indicative of emotional states can be systematically modified since they respond to environmental control (Franks, 1969; Goddenbaugh, 1931). Those indicative of or associated with emotions such as anger, fear, humanitarianism, and affection have been successfully modi-

Table 6–1
Teaching Procedures for Attitude Change

Technique	Procedure	Expected Results
Aversive conditioning	Aversive event is paired with item to be avoided	Avoidance response (or negative attitude toward the item)
Aversion relief	Cessation of an aversive event paired with item to be approached	Approach response (or positive attitude toward the item)
Direct positive respondent conditioning	Desirable event paired with an item to be approached	Approach response (or positive attitude toward the item)
Direct reinforcement	Reinforcer contigent on behavior indicative of a desired attitude	Increase in desired attitude
Direct punishment	Punisher contigent on behavior indicative of an undesirable attitude	Reduction of the behavior indicative of the bad attitude
Modeling and reinforcement	Model (teacher or peer) displays desired attitude and is reinforced	Exhibition of desired attitude by observer
Modeling and punishment	Punishment applied to model exhibiting undesirable attitude	Less exhibition of undesirable attitude by observer

fied (Anandam, Davis & Poppen, 1971; Lovaas, Schaeffer, & Simmons, 1965; Presbie & Coiteax, 1971).

One method of developing or increasing behaviors indicative of emotions is by a direct respondent conditioning procedure as described in the previous section when discussing attitude modification. This involves repeatedly pairing an event that elicits an emotion with a neutral event in order to cause the neutral event to elicit the emotion. Watson and Rayner's (1920) work with "Little Albert" was one of the first widely published accounts in which respondent or classical conditioning was used to teach an emotional reaction. In essence, what Watson and Rayner did was to teach "Little Albert" to fear a white rat he had not previously feared by pairing the rat with a loud noise. The paradigm illustrating this is shown in Figure 6–6.

Other procedures for modifying emotions include modeling or social imitation and direct reinforcement of behaviors indicative of the desired emotion. Social imitation or modeling involves putting a child in a situation with peers or other individuals who exhibit the behavior(s) indicative

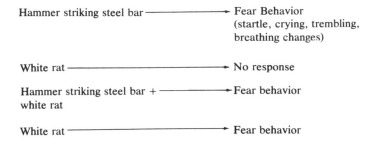

Fig. 6–6

of the emotion desired of the child. It has been found that children will generally imitate the behavior of their peers (Bandura, 1977). Humanitarianism or altruism can be fostered or decreased by having children view a generous or a stingy model (Byron, 1971; Presbie & Coiteax, 1971). Children who observe a generous model tend to exhibit more generous behavior, and children who observe a stingy model tend to exhibit more stingy, nonsharing behavior.

Social imitation is also an effective means to decrease an undesirable emotion such as fear. Fear reduction of an item has occurred as a result of a fearful child watching peers exhibit approach and play behaviors toward the feared object (Bandura, 1977). When children are put into a setting with a fearful child and the feared object, if the children approach and play with the feared object, the fearful child will tend gradually to exhibit approach behaviors toward the feared object. When social imitation is used, models can either physically be present in the classroom or symbolically displayed in films, slides, or pictures.

Direct reinforcement of behaviors has been effective in modifying behaviors indicative of various emotions. Affection indicated by smiling behaviors directed toward others can be increased by the use of positive reinforcement contingently applied (Brackbill, 1958; Hopkins, 1968; Zelazo, 1971). An eight-year-old boy was taught to smile at a high rate by providing candy for each smile (Hopkins, 1968). Eventually the candy was replaced by social reinforcement. This teaching of affectional behavior through direct reinforcement has been repeatedly found to be effective with a variety of children (Zelazo, 1971). Conversely, the withholding of the reinforcer(s) that previously followed a behavior indicative of an emotion that should be decreased has been found to be effective also. Reducing emotions such as anger, as indicated by temper tantrums, by withholding the reinforcer(s) that previously followed the tantrums is known as "extinction." Williams (1959) found that when adult attention, often a positive consequence of temper tantrums, is withheld when such anger is exhibited, the emotion of anger decreases.

Extinction

James, a 14-year-old student, exhibited behaviors indicative of rage and anger whenever he found his classroom assignment to be difficult. Careful evaluations show that James was capable of completing the assignments with minimal effort. Peer and teacher attention appeared to maintain the youth's rage and anger behaviors of tearing up his worksheet, lying on the floor, flailing his arms and legs, and hitting his head.

Mr. S, the classroom teacher, talked with the other students one day when James was absent about his problem behaviors. All decided that they wanted to help James. The conclusion drawn was to pretend that James was not even in the classroom when he exhibited the problem behavior and to tell James how good he was doing when he worked on or completed his assignment at his desk. Within five days the rage/anger behaviors dropped to a zero rate with only one reoccurrence of short duration the following week. Subsequently, the students and teacher gradually "leaned" the reinforcement schedule so less attention was needed to maintain James' on-task behavior.

In this case Mr. S, with the help of his class, was able to modify rage/anger behaviors by applying extinction procedures.

Fig. 6–7

Another effective means of modifying emotions is "direct conditioning" (Jones, 1924a). Direct conditioning involves determining an event that produces a strong positive emotion that is incompatible with the emotion that one desires to decrease (e.g., fear, anger, anxiety). Have the child engage in the event that produces a strong positive emotion that is incompatible with that which is to be decreased; gradually introduce the event that evokes the undesirable emotion. The effectiveness of this technique was reported by Jones as early as 1924. When a hungry child was being fed, which elicited a pleasant satisfying positive reaction, an event that elicited fear was gradually introduced into the setting, beginning far enough away so that it did not interfere with the process of eating. The feared object was gradually moved closer to the child during the eating process until the feared object was within the child's touch but the positive reaction to eating was still maintained. Considerable caution must be exercised in the use of this procedure. With both a desirable and an undesirable emotion being elicited, it is possible that the undesirable may be conditioned over the desirable one. In the previous example, a fear reaction could have become attached to food. This direct conditioning procedure is very similiar in nature to the widely used technique of "systematic desensitization," in which increasingly stronger anxiety-evoking situations (often imagined) are brought forth when an individual is relaxed in order to reduce an anxiety reaction (Kazdin, 1978). Martin and Pear (1978) outlined what therapists do when employing desensitization. There are many implications for how teachers could proceed when attempting to reduce fear, anxiety, or related emotional reactions. The following discussion is an adaptation of what Martin and Pear detailed.

Systematic desensitization first involves teaching the fearful child to induce deep-muscle relaxation.* Generally speaking, the child should be taught alternately to tense and then relax a set of muscles so that the muscles are more deeply relaxed following the tensing than before. The child should eventually learn how to relax deeply. After deep-muscle relaxation training the teacher should then assist the child in determining all of the stimuli or situations that elicit a particular inappropriate fear or anxiety reaction. The object is to help the child identify not only the stimulus, situation, or item that elicits the most intense anxiety, but also related stimuli that elicit lesser degrees of anxiety. The anxiety-eliciting stimuli or situations are then arranged in a hierarchy, with those that elicit the least anxiety at the bottom and those that elicit the most anxiety at the

---

Systematic Desensitization

Diane, a 10-year-old student labeled schizophrenic as a result of numerous earlier failure experiences and bizarre behavior episodes in a classroom setting, exhibited intense fear, withdrawal, and anxiety whenever she was placed in a desk and given assignments resembling academic or preacademic tasks. When given a worksheet. Diane would sit, make no response, masturbate, or make heavy dark scribble lines over the entire paper.

In the classroom the positive stimuli that Diane responded to the strongest was quiet instrumental music. This music tended to result in smiling, relaxed behavior.

A hierarchy of steps was designed to move Diane from simple floor activities involving gross movement to sitting in her seat doing fine motor pencil-and-paper activities. Instrumental music was played at each step. The progression was as follows: With instrumental music playing Diane was to sit on the floor and build structures with blocks, then move to puzzles, to using crayons and large pieces of newsprint paper, then move to standing at counter, standing at table, sitting at table, to sitting at desk. Gradually both the activity and setting was changed to accommodate movement more closely toward the objective of having Diane sitting relaxed and calm at her desk working on pencil-and-paper activities. On one step, moving from standing at the counter to sitting at the table, the music was not strong enough to result in relaxation rather than anxiety. Thus the steps were restructured moving back to standing at the counter and adding intermediate steps of sitting at the counter, standing at the table, and then to sitting at the table.

This procedure took a month and a half to accomplish the objective. A minimum of two sessions occurred each school day.

Fig. 6–8

---

*Because of its popularity more detailed information is presented about desensitization than is presented about some of the other procedures or techniques. For additional information, see Martin and Pear (1978), Kazdin (1978), Agras (1972), Mahoney (1974), Meichenbaum (1977), and Hatzenbuehler and Schroeder (1978).

top. For example, if a child has a fear of heights, the hierarchy could be looking out a sixth-floor window of the school building as the most feared situation, through a series of steps to looking out over the classroom while standing on a small step stool as minimally anxiety producing.

After the teacher has taught the child how to induce self-relaxation and to construct a hierarchy of anxiety-eliciting stimuli, training begins. First the child is instructed to relax; then he is instructed to imagine clearly the first scene in the hierarchy. If the child experiences any anxiety while visualizing the scene, he signals this to the teacher. If no anxiety has been signaled, the teacher, after about 7 to 10 seconds, signals the child to relax and to stop imagining the scene. After two successes of imagining a scene (with a 15 to 30 second period of relaxation after each presentation), the teacher then instructs the child to imagine clearly the

Table 6–2
Teaching Procedures for Modifying Emotional Behavior

Technique	Procedure	Expected Results
Direct respondent conditioning	Repeatedly pair an event that elicits an emotional reaction with a neutral stimulus	Neutral event will acquire the power to elicit the same emotional reaction evoked by the stimulus it is paired with
Social imitation or modeling	Place child in a situation to observe peers or others exhibiting a desired emotion	Child will tend to imitate the emotion
Direct reinforcement	Reinforcer contingent on the exhibition of a desired emotion	Increase in the desired emotion
Direct conditioning	Presentation of an event or stimulus that evokes a strong emotion that is incompatible with the undesired emotion	Decrease in the undesired emotion
Systematic desensitization (modification of direct conditioning)	Increasingly stronger anxiety-evoking situations (often imagined) are presented when an individual is relaxed in order to reduce an anxiety reaction	Reduction of undesirable fear behaviors

next scene in the hierarchy. At the first indication of anxiety the teacher immediately instructs the child to cease imagining the scene. After the child is again completely relaxed, the teacher instructs him to imagine the previous scene. If no anxiety is experienced with that scene, the next scene in the hierarchy is attempted again. In this manner of alternately imagining scenes and then relaxing without imagining them, the child gradually proceeds through the least anxiety-eliciting scenes to the most anxiety-eliciting scenes. At each step relaxation counteracts the anxiety brought on by that scene.

It should be pointed out that in addition to using each procedure discussed separately, some procedures have been successfully used in combination. For example, modeling in combination with "direct conditioning" has been found to hasten the modification of the emotion desired (Jones, 1924b). Table 6–2 summarizes the procedures discussed for modifying emotional behavior.

Sociability

Through the years social behaviors have been a major concern of the classroom teacher. While the concern has been expressed, many teachers, being unaware of effective procedures to enhance social skills, have not made a conscious effort to teach these skills in a systematic way. There are several procedures nevertheless, that have been successfully used.

One of the most effective procedures to influence social behaviors is the contingent application of positive reinforcement (Strain, Cooke, & Apolloni, 1978). In the classroom situation the use of teacher attention to modify social behavior has repeatedly been successful. The procedure involves providing positive teacher attention to children who exhibit "isolated" or little interaction behavior when they come into social contact with other children (Strain, Cooke, & Apolloni, 1978). The applicable paradigm (Figure 6–9) is a basic operant conditioning one.

Depending on the needs of the child, prompting the behavior and/or shaping it may be necessary to get the behavior to occur so that the positive reinforcement can be applied. Another successful approach makes use of peer attention as a positive reinforcer (Wahler, 1967). In this approach peers are taught to provide reinforcement involving positive attention contingent on the social approach, interaction, or social initiation behavior of an isolate (child who exhibits withdrawn behavior). The pri-

Social contact ——————————————————→ positive teacher
by an isolate   attention

Fig. 6–9

Direct Reinforcement

Chad, a four-year-old seriously handicapped student, had minimal skills in basic functioning areas, communication, and environmental awareness. During a sensory-awareness training session Chad exhibited spontaneous smiling and giggling behavior. (This was the first apparently controlled vocalization made by Chad in the classroom setting other than crying.) This was immediately responded to by considerable positive social attention that apparently acted as a reinforcer since the incidence of smiling/giggling behavior subsequently increased.

With the increase in this behavior, Chad "appeared happier," decreased his crying behavior, and seemed to become more aware of his environment (e.g., focused his attention for increasing periods of time to designated stimuli). Also, Chad, who had previously received little attention from others except for planned programming work, began to be presented with more spontaneous opportunities to interact with individuals other than classroom personnel since others began to recognize him as "such a pleasant, happy little fellow." Apparently, people tend to "like" and interact with children who smile and giggle and appear to be happy.

Fig. 6–10

mary difficulty in using peer attention as a reinforcer is the problem involved in maintaining control over the peer attention being applied (Wahler, 1967), although when systematically applied it has been found to be effective with many children.

Negative reinforcement has also been successfully used to increase social approach behaviors (Lovaas, Schaeffer, & Simmons, 1965). The removal of an aversive event is made contingent upon approach behaviors toward others. Social approach behaviors increase since they become associated with the removal of an aversive or unpleasant event. For example, Lovaas and associates (1965) presented shock when withdrawal or avoidance behaviors were exhibited and "relief from shock" when social approach behaviors were exhibited. The negative reinforcement was effective in increasing social and affectional (hugs) behavior.

The most common and popular procedure for dealing with building social behaviors is modeling, which also can be referred to as "observational learning" or "social imitation." It is one of the most effective means of modifying social behavior since many social behaviors are assumed to be naturally acquired by means of modeling (Bandura, 1977). Modeling involves having a situation in which a model or models display social behaviors that are viewed by an "isolate" or "withdrawn" child whose behavior is to be modified. For example, social approach behaviors may be modeled in front of a child in order to encourage social approach or interaction behaviors. This procedure has worked exceedingly well in enhancing social behaviors in socially mildly deficient children in a classroom setting. Modeling, however, has not been as successful with severely withdrawn children (O'Connor, 1969, 1972).

Although modeling was not very effective with severely withdrawn children, a procedure combining modeling and operant conditioning has proved to be more successful. This procedure called "imitation training" was developed by Bandura, Grusec, and Menlove (1967). It has been effective in developing the social behaviors of severely socially withdrawn children. In imitation training the model's desirable social behavior is reinforced, thus increasing the chances of the isolated child matching the model's behavior. Table 6–3 briefly outlines the procedures that have been successful in increasing social behaviors.

Other considerations in teaching social behaviors involve the environmental arrangement. The environmental arrangement of a classroom can itself considerably influence the behavior of a child. For example, the degree of integration or segregation of pupils by such variables as sex, race, intelligence, or behavior in the seating arrangement can influence

Table 6–3
Teaching Procedures for Increasing Social Behaviors

Technique	Procedure	Expected Results
Direct positive reinforcement	Positive reinforcer contingent on a desirable social behavior	Increase in the reinforced social behavior
Peer positive reinforcement (modification of direct reinforcement)	Have peers positively reinforce appropriate social behaviors	Increase in reinforced social behaviors
Negative reinforcement	Removal of an aversive event contingent on positive social behavior	Increase in the positive social behavior reinforced
Modeling	Model exhibits positive social behavior that is observed	Increase in observer's positive social behavior
Imitation training	Social behavior modeled by a peer is positively reinforced	Increase in the appropriate social behavior of the observer
Environmental arrangement	Increase cooperative group activities, decrease amount of nonsocial-type play equipment, increase amount of social toys, pair isolated child with a favorite toy	Increase in social behavior

---

Social Imitation/Modeling

In a preschool class for children labeled seriously disturbed, one teacher, Ms R, became concerned about the students' obvious lack of concern for each other. Whenever any one child fell down, was hurt by another, or simply did not feel well, the child's classmates failed to display any behavior(s) that might indicate they were upset or concerned.

Ms. R decided to demonstrate to all of the children how concerned she was whenever anyone fell down, was hurt, or was in a distressful situation. She would stop her activity to comfort or help verbally the distressed child. She made a special effort to do this in such a way that all the children in the classroom could observe her assisting and comforting the child.

Within the week the preschoolers began to attend to and provide help and comfort to peers who experienced a distressing occurrence. While initially comforting behavior began to be exhibited at an extremely high rate (even providing comfort for sneezing), it leveled off to an appropriate rate within the second week.

In this way Ms. R was successful in teaching preschool handicapped children to exhibit "caring" behaviors by using social imitation/modeling.

Fig. 6–11

the development of attitudes and social relationships between and among such groups.

Social interaction of normal and withdrawn or isolated children has been increased by arranging groups for a cooperative task (Altman, 1971; Kinney, 1953; Stendler, Damrin, & Haines, 1951). In addition, social interaction has been enhanced by decreasing the amount of independent-type play equipment available (Johnson, 1935), having available more toys that foster social play and/or less toys that encourage independent play (such as clay and sandbox) (Parten, 1933; Quilitch & Risley, 1973). An ordinary doll house was found to be one of the most social toys by Quilitch and Risley (1973). Training in the use of toys that foster interaction has also been found to enhance the subsequent social interactions of children (Allen, Turner, & Everett, 1970; Buell, Stoddard, Harris, & Baer, 1968; Johnston, Kelly, Harris, & Wolf, 1966). Also pairing a withdrawn child with a highly valued item (e.g., in a classroom with a favorite toy or candy) tends to increase the reinforcing value of the child; therefore social interaction with that child by his peers tends to increase (Kirby & Toler, 1970). Depending on the behaviors that you wish to develop in the students, the environmental arrangement should be analyzed and modified, if necessary, to facilitate the acquisition of the desired behavior.

CONCLUSION

A basic understanding of respondent and operant conditioning should be a prerequisite for implementing the procedures discussed in this chapter. In addition, the reader should be aware that there are many variables that can influence whether or not a procedure is successfully implemented. For example, unprogrammed events sometimes occur in the environment that tend to counteract the desired influence of the procedure being implemented. When a positive event is paired with an item or results in a behavior and an aversive event also occurs. the strength of the positive and aversive events will compete with each other. Whichever is strongest will likely influence the child's perception of the item or performance of the behavior. For example, the library teacher may pair smiles and positive teacher attention with reading books in order to get a child to develop a positive attitude toward books. On the other hand, the child may also receive aversive input paired with books if he is a bad reader and goes to a special class or group for reading where his peers ridicule him, the special reading teacher scolds him for poor reading, and he experiences failure whenever he picks up a book and attempts to read. If the aversive input is stronger than the positive, the child will learn to dislike rather than like books. Thus when teaching an attitude or emotion the environment must be analyzed for competing events that could weaken or negate the influence of the procedure to be used, and these events must be controlled to the highest degree possible if appropriate learning is to have an opportunity to occur.

The selection of the stimuli to elicit or reinforce a response is another factor or variable that can influence the effectiveness of a procedure. While the procedures described have proven to influence successfully behaviors indicative of attitudes, emotions, and sociability, there have been cases in which such procedures have been unsuccessful (Kazdin, 1978). This tends to confirm the complexity of environmental stimuli impinging on an individual in regard to influencing his behavior. This, of course, is true of all procedures. For example, the presentation of a smiling face to one child may elicit approach behaviors while for another child it may elicit avoidance. This does not necessarily indicate, however, that the principles of behavior change inherent in the procedure are not applicable, since the problem may be in the selection of the stimulus to elicit the behavior. What is desirable or aversive to one child is not necessarily desirable or aversive to another. Watson and Rayner (1920) conditioned or taught fear behavior in a child by presenting a loud noise with a white rat. Others, using the same procedure (respondent conditioning) and stimuli (loud noise and white rat), though, did not successfully condition fear (Bregman, 1934; English, 1929). It may be that these unsuccessful investigators did not pair two stimuli wherein one produced fear and the other was neutral to the particular individuals with whom they worked. The problem could have been that the loud noise did not originally elicit fear in the individuals; therefore, pairing it with the white rat (the supposedly neutral stimulus) did not cause the white rat eventually to elicit fear.

No one behavior may be considered exclusive to one of the three categories. Sharing behavior, for example, can be perceived as an emotional behavior of altruism or caring, an attitudinal behavior of liking or positiveness, and/or a social behavior of appropriate interpersonal interaction.

Although modification of social, emotional, and attitudinal behaviors have been discussed separately, the procedures are not mutually exclusive in regard to each category. While a procedure has been empirically tested and verified with one type of behavior (e.g., indicative of a certain attitude) does not necessarily confirm its ineffectiveness in being used to modify another type of behavior (e.g., indicative of an emotion).

REFERENCES

Agras, W.S. *Behavior modification: Principles and clinical applications.* Boston: Little, Brown, 1972.

Allen, K.E., Turner, K.D. & Everett, P.M. A behavior modification classroom for head start children with problem behaviors. *Exceptional Children,* 1970, 37, 119–127.

Anandam, K., Davis, M., & Poppen W.A. Feelings . . . to fear or to free? *Elementary School Guidance and Counseling,* 1971, 5, 181–189.

Bandura, A. *Social learning theory.* Englewood Cliffs, NJ: Prentice-Hall, 1977.

Bandura, A. Grusec, J.E. Menlove, F.L. Vicarious extinction of avoidance behavior. Journal of *Personality and Social Psychology,* 1967, 5, 16–23.

Barlow, D.H. Aversive procedures. In W.S. Agras (Ed.), *Behavior modification: Principles and clinical applications,* Boston: Little, Brown, 1972.

Beatty, W.H. Emotions: The missing link in education. *Theory into Practice,* 1969, 8, 86–92.

Borich, G.D. Accountability in the affective domain. *Journal of Research and Development in Education,* 1971, 5, 87–96.

Brackbill, Y. Extinction of the smiling response in infants as a function of reinforcement schedule. *Child Development,* 1958, 29, 115–124.

Bradtke, L.M., Kirkpatrick, W.J., & Rosenblatt, K.P. Intensive play: A technique for building affective behaviors in profoundly mentally retarded young children. *Education and Training of the Mentally Retarded,* 1972, 7, 8–13.

Bregman, E.O. An attempt to modify the emotional attitudes of infants by the conditioned response technique. *The Pedagogical Seminary and Journal of Genetic Psychology,* 1934, 45, 169–198.

Buell, J., Stoddard, P., Harris, F.R. & Baer, D.M. Collateral social development accompanying reinforcement of outdoor play in a preschool child. *Journal of Applied Behavior Analysis,* 1968, 1, 167–173.

Byron, J.H. Model affect in children's altruism. *Child Development,* 1971, 42, 2061–2065.

Doland, D.J., & Adelberg, K. The learning of sharing behavior. *Child Development*, 1967, *38*, 695–700.

English, H.G. Three cases of the "conditioned fear response." *Journal of Abnormal and Social Psychology*, 1929, *24*, 221–225.

Feldman, M.P., & MacCulloch, M.J. The application of anticipation avoidance learning to the treatment of homosexualiity. I. Theory, technique and preliminary results. *Behavior Research and Therapy*, 1965, *2*, 165–183.

Foa, U.G. Convergences in the analysis of the structure of interpersonal behavior. *Psychological Review*, 1961, *68*, 341–353.

Franks, C.M. *Behavior therapy: Appraisal and status.* New York: McGraw-Hill, 1969.

Gardner, W.I. *Learning and behavior characteristics of exceptional children and youth.* Boston: Allyn & Bacon, 1977.

Goddenbaugh, F. *Anger in young children.* Minneapolis: University of Minnesota Press, 1931.

Harbeck, M.B. Instructional objectives in the affective domain. *Educational Technology*, 1970, *10*, 49–52.

Hatzenbuehler, L.C., & Schroeder, H.E. Desensitization procedures in the treatment of childhood disorders. *Psychological Bulletin*, 1978, *85*, 831–844.

Henderson, L.A. A review of the literature on affective education. *Contemporary Education*, 1972, *44*, 92–99.

Homme, L.E. Contingency contracting with parents. In *Proceedings: Early childhood intervention research conference.* Institute III: Exceptional Children and Adults. Tampa: University of South Florida, 1970.

Hopkins, B.L. Effects of candy and social reinforcement, instructions and reinforcement schedule leaning to the modification and maintenance of smiling. *Journal of Applied Behavior Analysis*, 1968, *1*, 121–129.

Ivey, A.E. The intentional individual: A process-outcome view of behavioral psychology. *Counseling Psychologist*, 1969, *1*, 56–60.

Johnston, M.K., Kelley, C.S., Harris, F.R. & Wolf, M.M. An application of reinforcement principles to development of motor skills of a young child. *Child Development*, 1966, 37, 379–387.

Jones, M.C. A laboratory study of fear: The case of Peter. *Pedagogical Seminary and Journal of Genetic Psychology*, 1924a, *31*, 308–315.

Jones, M.C. The elimination of children's fears. *Journal of Experimental Psychology*, 1924b, *7*, 382–390.

Kazdin, A.E. *History of behavior modification.* Baltimore: University Park Press, 1978.

Lazarus, A.A. On assertive behavior: A brief note. *Behavior Therapy*, 1973, *4*, 697–699.

Lorr, M. & McNair, D.M. Expansion of the interpersonal behavior circle. *Journal of Personality and Social Psychology*, 1965, *2*, 813–830.

Lovaas, O.I., Schaeffer, B., & Simmons, J.Q. Building social behavior in autistic children by use of electric shock. *Journal of Experimental Research in Personality*, 1965, *1*, 99–104.

Mahoney, M.J. *Cognition and behavior modification.* Cambridge, MA: Ballinger, 1974.

Martin, G. & Pear, J. *Behavior modification: What it is and how to do it.* Englewood Cliffs, NJ: Prentice-Hall, 1978.

Meichenbaum, D. *Cognitive-behavior modification.* New York: Plenum Press, 1977.

Morris, J.E. School accountability and the affective domain. *School and Society,* 1972, *100,* 228–230.

Morse, W.C. Special pupils in regular classes: Problems of accommodation. In M.C. Reynolds & M.D. Davis (Eds.), *Exceptional children in regular classrooms.* Washington, DC: U.S. Office of Education, 1971.

O'Connor, R.D. Modification of social withdrawal through symbolic modeling. *Journal of Applied Behavior Analysis,* 1969, 1, 15–22.

O'Connor, R.D. Relative efficacy of modeling, shaping, and the combined procedures for modification of social withdrawal. *Journal of Abnormal Psychology,* 1972, 79, 327–334.

Pavlov, I.P. *Conditioned reflexes: An investigation of the physiological activity of the cereberal cortex.* (G.V. Anrep, Ed. & Trans.). London: Oxford University Press, 1927.

Presbie, R.J., & Coiteax, P.F. Training to be generous or stingy: Imitation of sharing behavior as a function of model generosity and vicarious reinforcement. *Child Development,* 1971, *42,* 1033–1038.

Prescott, D.A. *Emotion and the educative process.* Washington, DC: American Council on Education, 1938.

Rogers, C.R. *Freedom to learn.* Columbus, OH: Merrill, 1969.

Rogers, C.R. *On encounter groups.* New York: Harper & Row, 1970.

Ross, A.O. *Psychological disorders of children.* New York: McGraw-Hill, 1974.

Sandiford, P. *Educational psychology: An objective study.* New York: Longmans, Green, 1936.

Schrag, F. Learning what one feels and enlarging the range of one's feelings. *Educational Theory,* 1972, *22,* 382–394.

Skinner, B.F. *Science and human behavior.* New York: Free Press, 1953.

Strain, P.S., Cooke, T.P., & Apolloni, T. *Teaching exceptional children.* New York: Academic Press, 1976.

Sulzer-Azaroff, B. & Mayer, G.R. *Applying behavior-analysis procedures with children and youth.* New York: Holt, Rinehart, & Winston, 1977.

Thorndike, E. *The principles of teaching.* New York: Seller, 1906.

Trower, P., Bryant, B., & Argyle, M. *Social skills and mental health.* Pittsburgh, PA: University of Pittsburgh Press, 1978.

Wahler, R.G. Child-child interactions in free field settings: Some experimental analyses. *Journal of Experimental Child Psychology,* 1967, 5, 278–293.

Watson, J.B., & Rayner, R. Conditioned emotional reactions. *Journal of Experimental Psychology,* 1920, *3,* 1–14.

Weinstein, G., & Fantini, M.D. *Toward humanistic education: A curriculum of affect.* New York: Praeger, 1970.

Williams, C.D. The elimination of tantrum behavior by extinction procedures. *Journal of Abnormal and Social Psychology,* 1959, *59,* 269.

Winnett, R.A., & Winkler, R.C. Current behavior modification in the classroom:

Be still, be quiet, be docile. *Journal of Applied Behavior Analysis*, 1972, *5*, 499–504.

Zelazo, P. Smiling to social stimuli. *Developmental Psychology*, 1971, *4*, 32–45.

SELECTED READINGS FOR FURTHER STUDY

Agras, W.S. *Behavior modification: Principles and clinical applications*. Boston: Little, Brown, 1972.

Bandura, A. *Social Learning theory*. Englewood Cliffs, NJ: Prentice-Hall, 1977.

Mahoney, M.J. *Cognition and behavior modification*. Cambridge, MA: Ballinger, 1974.

Meichenbaum, D. *Cognitive-behavior modification*. New York: Plenum Press, 1977.

Strain, P.S., Cooke, T.P., & Apolloni, T. *Teaching exceptional children*. New York: Academic Press, 1976.

Lewis Polsgrove, Ph.D.

Indiana University
Bloomington, Indiana

7

Self-control: Methods for Child Training

Behavioral scientists have long been interested in applying operant technology to develop ideal social and educational environments (Skinner, 1953, 1968; Staats, 1959, 1975a, 1975b). A generation of applied studies have employed external reinforcement systems to manage effectively children's social and academic behavior (Hanley, 1971; Kazdin & Bootzin, 1972; O'Leary & Drabman, 1971). To date, a variety of studies have demonstrated the success of these systems for managing children's behavior in public schools (Hewett, 1967; O'Leary & Becker, 1967) and in the home (Patterson, 1973), as well as in institutional settings (Haring & Phillips, 1962; Phillips, 1971). Because of their success some writers have advocated their wholesale use (Skinner, 1968; Staats, 1973).

The unlimited use of behavioral technology for managing children's behavior raises some important issues, however. First, it creates a risk that children may become overly dependent on them and not develop necessary skills for maintaining behavior or for dealing with novel or unstructured situations. Second, the effects of these systems rarely generalize across settings or over time (O'Leary & Drabman, 1971). The use of behavioral technology to manipulate children into conforming to often unwarranted institutional goals, moreover, is ethically questionable (Rogers, 1956; Rogers & Skinner, 1956; Winnett & Winkler, 1972).

These issues of generalization training and freedom versus control have influenced researchers and practitioners to develop techniques for

---

This chapter is a reprint of an article by Lewis Polsgrove that appeared in *Behavioral Disorders*, 1979, *4*, 116–130. Reprinted with permission.

teaching children behavioral self-control. This emerging technology has particularly important implications for deinstitutionalization as well as for mainstreaming exceptional children into regular classroom environments. The intent of this chapter is to familiarize teacher trainers and practitioners with some of the major concepts of self-control literature, to discuss methods by which children acquire self-regulatory behavior, and to describe and assess the methods currently available for training children in self-control. Present techniques for training children in self-control are based on a number of laboratory and analog studies that have been adequately described elsewhere (Aronfreed, 1968; Bandura, 1969, 1971; Masters & Mokros, 1974). This chapter will thus review available applied studies and evaluate the utility of self-control training techniques in field settings.

PERSPECTIVE ON SELF-CONTROL

Persons choose to delay immediate gratifications presumably because of anticipation of the ultimate benefits that they may receive by such decision making (Thoresen, 1973; Thoresen & Mahoney, 1974). This assumption has led most writers on the subject to agree that the "ultimate source of control" lies in the external environment (Kanfer & Karoly, 1972; Skinner, 1953; Thoresen & Mahoney, 1974). Explanations of the self-control process thus are concerned with methods that individuals use to maintain their behavior in the absence of immediate external control. Most individuals have some capacity for self-control; one may be able to pass up an extra helping of parfait or the thirtieth cigarette of the day. But a long-term behavioral self-control program may require a number of complex cognitive skills—the ability for self-observation and for interpreting complex internal and external stimuli as well as the capacity for planning, selecting, and maintaining appropriate behavior (Goldfried & Merbaum, 1973).

While the traditional operant behaviorism has emphasized the role of environmental variables in controlling behavior (Skinner, 1953), a number of behaviorists (e.g., Bandura, 1969; Mahoney, 1974: Meichenbaum, 1975; Staats, 1975) recognize the interdependence of cognitive and external variables in determining behavior. These "cognitive behaviorists" assume covert behavior is influenced in the same manner as overt behavior, that is, by a combination of antecedent and consequent stimuli. Training persons in self-control, then, involves teaching them to manipulate internal and external discriminative and reinforcing stimuli to alter their behavior (Goldfried & Merbaum, 1973; Kanfer, 1976; Mahoney & Thoresen, 1974; Thoresen & Mahoney, 1974).

ACQUISITION OF SELF-CONTROL

Laboratory studies (Grusec, 1966; Liebert & Allen, 1967; Mischel & Liebert, 1966; Rosenhan, Frederick, & Burrowes, 1968) as well as applied research (Bolstad & Johnson, 1972; Felixbrod & O'Leary, 1973; Fredericksen & Fredericksen, 1975; Uhlman & Shook, 1976) have demonstrated that children can be taught self-controlling responses through contingently administered social and tangible reinforcement. Recent studies suggest that children may learn these responses through the use of didactic training methods as well, (Russell & Thoresen, 1976; Spivack, Platt, & Shure, 1976; Stark, 1976). Another important way children acquire self-controlling responses is through observational learning (Aronfreed, 1968; Bandura, 1969).

Aronfreed (1968) observed that children acquire internal sources of control as the result of direct training experiences provided by parents, teachers, or other significant persons. These agents teach children to control their behavior by rewarding appropriate behavior and punishing or withholding consequences for inappropriate behavior. According to Aronfreed (1968), positive or aversive stimuli present in a training situation become associated with certain physical, affective, and cognitive responses produced by the child. While external stimuli remain important sources of control, these "internal monitors" allow the child to evaluate his ongoing behavior and to anticipate its outcomes and maintain or alter it. With children who have adequate cognitive processing ability, agents can use verbal-symbolic methods rather than having to arrange training situations (Aronfreed, 1968).

Children also can learn to set behavioral performance standards, adopt patterns of self-evaluation and self-reinforcement, and exert verbal control over their behavior by observing and imitating social models (Bandura, Grusec, & Menlove, 1967; Bandura & Krupers, 1964; Bandura & Perloff, 1967; Goodwin & Mahoney, 1976; Luria, 1965; Meichenbaum & Goodman, 1971). Bandura (1969) considers the capacity for awareness, symbolic codification, memory storage, and response retrieval and activation as essential cognitive processes for the acquisition and subsequent performance of an observed behavioral sequence. He makes a sharp distinction, however, between acquisition of a behavioral sequence and its later performance. A child's acquisition in a modeled sequence also depends largely on characteristics of both the model and observer as well as consequences produced by the model's behaviors and the degree of attention that he has given to the model. Whether he reproduces a modeled sequence depends upon available reinforcement for these responses, his capacity to retain the behavioral sequence, his ability to reproduce the behavior, and the amount of motivation he has for imitating the behavior (Bandura, 1969, 1971).

SELF-MANAGEMENT METHODS

Accounts of how children acquire self-control are based largely on laboratory research and provide information that can be used for developing self-control training methods with children. The following discussion considers both *self-management methods,* which are primarily concerned with manipulating internal and external behavioral consequences to alter behavior, and *cognitive methods,* which emphasize manipulating covert antecedent events. These distinctions, however, are arbitrary—the procedures overlap considerably—and are made only for organization of the material to be presented.

Kanfer and Karoly (1972) and Kanfer (1975) view self-control as the final outcome of a three-stage self-regulatory process involving (1) self-monitoring, (2) self-evaluation, and (3) self-reinforcement. During the *self-monitoring* process the person may observe his behavior and, on the basis of this information, set behavioral standards. Next, the person may establish a contract with himself or another specifying the goals and contingencies that he must meet before allowing himself access to reinforcement. In the *self-evaluation* stage the person compares his performance against established standards. He may then alter or maintain his behavior through the use of *self-reinforcement* procedures. A number of studies have used self-monitoring, contracting, and self-evaluation and self-reinforcement for training children in self-control training programs. Studies related to these methods will be reviewed here.

Self-monitoring

Because behavior may become so thoroughly conditioned to certain stimulus conditions, persons who act inappropriately in a given situation may not be fully aware of the variables controlling their behavior. For example, children who have been frequently exposed to aggressive models or who have received social approval for aggressive behavior as a way of solving interpersonal conflicts may start fighting at the slightest provocation. To alter this pattern, a socialization agent may have them keep records of their aggressive acts to increase their behavioral awareness. Self-monitoring, thus, may be an important first step in "deautomatizing" a behavioral chain (Kanfer, 1975).

In training a child to monitor his behavior a trainer may first select and behaviorally define a target behavior. Next, he may have the child record examples of his behavior using a wrist counter, abacus, tally card, or stopwatch. The child also may maintain a graph, chart, or a journal of his behavior. Self-monitoring and recording provide visual feedback of the child's progress and lead to self-evaluation (Kanfer, 1975).

In several studies children were taught self-monitoring as part of a larger classroom program. Gottman and McFall (1972) discovered that disruptive adolescents contributed more to class discussions when asked to record instances in which they spoke out. Children in a comparison group, who recorded the number of times they felt like speaking out but failed to do so, decreased their class discussion behaviors. Bolstad and Johnson (1972) had elementary school students record the frequency of their unauthorized speech, out-of-seat behavior, and physical aggression; those who closely matched a classroom observer's frequency count received points that were redeemable for back-up reinforcers. This training was somewhat more effective in minimizing disruptive behavior than external reinforcement alone. Broden, Hall, and Mitts (1971) found that when a preadolescent girl recorded and reported her "study" and "nonstudy" behaviors weekly to a school counselor, classroom attention increased; self-recording, however, failed to maintain initial reductions of disruptive behavior in a second student. Glynn, Thomas, and Shee (1973) trained primary school children to monitor accurately their behavior and used these data as a basis for contingent self-reinforcement. Reiber, Schilmoeller, and LeBlanc (1976) taught five preschoolers to count their on-task behaviors during a listening class. Self-monitoring and showing the children a graph of their on-task behavior from preceeding days were effective in increasing their attending behavior.

Although some studies have shown that children tend to overestimate their desirable behaviors and to underestimate their undesirable behaviors, others reveal that accurate self-monitoring may not be essential for producing desirable changes in children's behavior. The effectiveness of self-monitoring in influencing behavior is unclear, however, for in most studies the contributions of experimenter expectancies, demand characteristics, and other variables were not isolated (McLaughlin, 1976). The results of recent studies indicate that when the effects of expectancies, observers, and sources of reinforcement are controlled, self-monitoring of social behavior may have limited utility as a "reactive" treatment (Cohen, 1977). Some evidence indicates, however, that associating behavioral self-recording directly to positive outcomes may improve its treatment effectiveness (Reith, Polsgrove, McLeskey, et al, 1978).

The available literature suggests that having children monitor their behavior produces mixed effects across situations, subjects, and behaviors. Kazdin (1974) concluded that (1) self-monitoring may be most effective when used early in a response chain, (2) having individuals record both target and incompatible behaviors simultaneously may increase its effectiveness, and (3) self-monitoring should be used continuously in the initial phases of a treatment program and faded to intermittent use in later stages. Self-monitoring may produce early behavioral changes that tend to dissipate over time unless supported with additional self-control procedures, such as contingency contracting, self-evaluation, or self-reinforcement (Kanfer, 1975; McLaughlin, 1976).

Contingency Contracting

Following a period of self-monitoring, individuals may set goals and specify the contingencies for reinforcing a particular set of their behavior. They may, in effect, contract with themselves or others to alter or maintain desirable behavior. Where self-arranged contracts have proven ineffective, externally controlled contracts may be necessary until an individual can assume the responsibility for controlling his behavior.

Contracts may vary from informal verbal agreements to formal, written documents. Formal, written contracts may be required when verbal contracts have failed to produce desirable behavioral outcomes. These contracts may contain several components:

1 The target behavior(s)
2 The performance criteria for the target behavior(s)
3 The payoff ratio between the target behavior(s) and the consequences
4 The time of delivery of payoffs
5 A bonus clause listing additional payoffs for near perfect performances
6 A penalty clause stating aversive consequences for failure to comply with the contract
7. The method for evaluating whether target behavior(s) meet selected criteria (Homme, et al., 1969; Kanfer, 1975; Stuart, 1971).

Contracts have proven useful for increasing responsibility taking in home chores (Dinoff & Rickard, 1969), for improving academic achievement (Cantrell, Cantrell, Huddleston, & Woolridge, 1969), for improving school attendance (Brooks, 1974; MacDonald, Gallimore, & MacDonald, 1970) as well as for reducing aggressive (Bristol, 1976) and delinquent behavior (Stuart, 1971; Tharp & Wetzel, 1969). In these studies the contract has been part of a treatment package: the specific effects of contracts in changing behavior was not investigated.

An important feature of contracts is that they may serve as a link between external and self-control programs. Homme and associates (1969) proposed a five-stage method for fading a child from trainer-controlled to student-controlled programs by use of contracts. In the first stage the trainer specifies the task to be performed, the criteria, the reinforcers, and the payoff ratio. Through negotiations with the trainer the child then gradually assumes responsibilities for these functions, until he can assume total responsibility for arranging all of these components.

No studies have been reported in which formal, written contracts were used systematically for developing children's self-control. A few researchers have studied modified forms of contracts as part of their studies. Felixbrod and O'Leary (1973), for example, demonstrated that students who selected their own goals and reward ratios were as academically productive as those whose goals and ratios were externally set; and they performed significantly better than a control group that received no opportunity to earn rewards.

More recently, Uhlman and Shook (1976) used Homme's (1969) model to train adolescent multiply handicapped students to manage their academic behavior. The teacher first specified weekly objectives, tasks, task schedules, and amounts of time that students could spend in free-time activities. Through negotiation with the teacher students gradually assumed total responsibility for directing their academic programs. The time students spent working, number of daily objectives met, and number of math problems completed increased sizably over baseline.

Brigham and Stoerzinger (1976) showed that children are highly motivated by selecting their own reinforcing events. In negotiating contracts children presumably have some control over establishing rules governing their behavior and may fulfill contracts in order to maintain freedom from external control (Brigham & Sherman, 1973, Kanfer, 1977; Kiesler, 1971). Thus, contracts may serve as discriminative stimuli for appropriate behavior in the absence of external controls. They may provide a method for shaping self-management skills by allowing children to select target behaviors, set goals, evaluate their behavior, and contingently administer self-reinforcement. These conclusions must be considered tenuous, however, as the data in this area are limited. Given the demonstrated success of contracts in managing a variety of children's behavior, it is surprising that this procedure has not been used more extensively for training children in self-control.

Self-evaluation and Self-reinforcement

Since the self-evaluation process involves a comparison of performance against established personal or normative standards, individuals may more readily evaluate their performances when behavioral data are available in the form of a graph or chart or when their goals are explicitly stated, as in a contract. Self-evaluation serves as a cue for determining the degree of allowable *self-reinforcement*. Thus, when persons evaluate their performance favorably, they may engage in positive covert and/or overt self-reinforcement; unfavorable evaluations may result in aversive self-administered consequences. In this way individuals alter or maintain their behavior independent of external controls.

Most research concerned with training children to control their behavior by using self-evaluation and self-reinforcement has involved an external training and feedback approach. Typically, trainers provide children opportunities to earn tokens for following classroom rules or meeting established behavioral standards. Their behavior is periodically evaluated by a teacher or observer to determine their eligibility for reinforcement. Those ratings that closely match those by trainers may become eligible for tokens or points. Thus, the children are taught to use their self-ratings for contingent self-reinforcement. Once acceptable patterns of self-evaluation and self-reinforcement are well established, the external control mechanisms are faded, giving the children full responsibility for managing their behavior.

In one study using this approach (Bolstad & Johnson, 1972) students in two self-evaluation/self-reinforcement groups showed less disruptive behavior than those assigned to a group that received only external reinforcement. These experimental groups emitted significantly less disruptive behavior than control groups. Fredericksen and Fredericksen (1975) also demonstrated that pre-adolescent special education students with self-management training could improve their task-oriented and prosocial behavior over that observed during teacher-controlled reinforcement periods. In a similar study by Turkewitz, O'Leary, and Ironsmith (1973) elementary school students' academic performances under self-management conditions were maintained at normal rates while their disruptive behavior dropped significantly below that observed during baseline.

The effects of self-evaluation and self-reinforcement also have been studied in clinic populations. Kaufman and O'Leary (1972) trained adolescents in a psychiatric hospital classroom to assess appropriately their compliance with teacher-imposed classroom rules. In an allied study, by Santogrossi, O'Leary, Romanczyk, and Kaufman (1973), similar subjects increased their disruptive behavior and became difficult to control even with a subsequent token program.

The studies reported here indicate that, under certain conditions, self-evaluation and self-reinforcement procedures can maintain academic behavior and minimize disruptive behavior. Although several investigators have reported the superiority of self-controlled over external-controlled programs, such conclusions must be regarded as tentative (McLaughlin, 1976). Almost all of the studies to date have exposed children to some type of self-management training before allowing them to control reinforcing events. In two studies in which students evaluated their behavior and scheduled their reinforcement without prior training (Klein & Gory, 1976; Santogrossi, O'Leary, Romanczyk, & Kaufman, 1973), control over the target behaviors was not established. Most studies also have failed to control for the presence of the teacher and observer as discriminative stimuli for appropriate behavior. Consequently, it is difficult to conclude whether the results obtained in these studies were the result of self-control or improved discrimination.

COGNITIVE METHODS

In current social learning theory cognitive stimuli—thoughts, feelings, and images—are considered links in a chain of external and internal events that may influence an individual's overt behavior (Mahoney, 1974; Meichenbaum, 1975). If, as is assumed, overt behavior is a function of covert behaviors, then the alteration of the covert behaviors may produce changes in overt behavior. This hypothesis has stimulated research interest in training problem children to manipulate instrumentally their cognitive behaviors as a means of self-control. Research in this area has begun only recently, but some promising new techniques have emerged. Although a considerable amount of overlap may exist between these strategies, three distinct procedures can be identified: self-instruction, problem solving, and modeling/rehearsal.

Self-instruction

The role of verbal behavior in influencing affective and overt behavior has received much recent attention in the behavioral literature (Bandura, 1969; Mahoney, 1974; Meichenbaum, 1975). A theoretical analysis of the relationship of affective experiences may be a combined effect of emotional arousal and the meaning that is attached to feelings, that is, whether persons experience "fear," "anger," or "apprehension" in a situation may be determined by the way they label their emotions (Schachter & Singer, 1962). Some evidence indicates that persons may alter feelings of elation or depression as a function of reading positively or negatively worded statements (Velten, 1968). Clinical studies also have successfully modified anxiety and depression by having clients use self-instructions (Flannery, 1972; Jackson, 1972; Meichenbaum & Cameron, 1974). In fact, some writers view therapy as a process in which persons are taught to talk appropriately to themselves to alter their behavioral responses (Goldfried & Goldfried, 1975; Homme, 1965; Kanfer & Phillips, 1970; Marston, 1965). This background underlies the interest in training children to use self-instructions for behavioral self-control.

Experimental studies indicate that children may be taught to control their behavior by using self-instructions. In a study by Hartig and Kanfer (1972), for example, children who were instructed to use verbal coping statements (e.g., "If I don't look at the toy, I'll be a good boy") showed a greater resistance to disobeying an adult's directions than those who merely recited nursery rhymes.

The use of self-instructions has been effective in increasing prosocial behaviors (O'Leary, 1968) as well as the ability to learn academic skills (Bem, 1976) and has been explored for training hyperactive and impulsive children to control their behavior (Meichenbaum & Cameron, 1974; Meichenbaum & Goodman, 1971; Palkes, Stewart, & Kahana, 1969).

Meichenbaum and Goodman (1969) taught impulsive children to improve their performances on complex motor tasks by using self-instructions. The children first watched a model perform a task while verbalizing self-instructions: the model asked questions about the task requirements, answered these questions by rehearsing and planning their solutions, used performance and error-correction statements, verbally managed feelings about failures, and provided self-reinforcing statements for adequate performance. Next, children performed the task while the model verbally directed them. The children then verbalized the instructions while performing the task. Finally, they were directed to instruct themselves covertly while doing the task. Compared to controls, children who were trained in these techniques showed significant improved performances on the Porteous Maze test, a standardized intelligence test, and a measure of cognitive control.

On the basis of this and other studies Meichenbaum and Cameron (1974) have outlined a strategy for teaching children self-management behaviors. They suggest that trainers initially select tasks that children can perform easily and introduce self-instruction as part of their natural activities. Children can be taught to break complex tasks down in small, sequential steps and to undertake a task stepwise. In working on a task trainers should model performance instructions as well as coping, relaxation, and reinforcing self-statements and then require children to imitate these as practice in performing a task. Children also may learn to manage their impulsive, aggressive, and emotional responses by being taught to identify internal and external stimuli that trigger these behaviors and to use these as cues for initiating self-instructional procedures.

At present the potential usefulness of self-instructional strategies for modifying children's academic and problem behavior remains unclear. The few studies that have been completed have been limited to carefully controlled experimental situations and to the use of relatively insignificant dependent variables. Some studies do indicate that self-instructional techniques may be useful in everyday classroom applications (Bommarito & Meichenbaum, 1975; Meichenbaum, 1975), but substantial corroborative evidence is unavailable. Further research is needed to determine the effectiveness of existing training procedures in natural settings to determine the effectiveness of this technique with a variety of academic and social target behaviors and with various child populations.

Problem Solving

Another way for developing self-control is to teach the children methods of effective problem solving (Mahoney, 1974; Spivack, Platt & Shure, 1976). This approach is not designed to teach children specific responses to specific problems. Instead, it gives them a general strategy for dealing with problem situations (D'Zurilla & Goldfried, 1973).

D'Zurilla and Goldfried (1973) have identified five phases of the problem-solving process that may be used to train children in self-control. In the *orientation phase* trainers may teach children to recognize problems as common events that should not be reacted to or ignored but that require action to resolve. In the *problem definition and formulation phase* children may be instructed in defining a problem, identifying its elements, and recognizing its origins as well as factors that prevent its resolution. Children then may be taught to *generate alternative solutions* to a problem in the third phase of the process; in this phase trainers may uncritically encourage children to produce as many diverse alternatives as possible to a problem (Mahoney, 1974). In the fourth, or *decision-making*, phase children may be instructed in methods for assessing alternatives in terms of their predicted outcomes. Finally, in the *verification phase* children may be taught the process of selecting and trying out the most desirable alternative in applied situations by observing its consequences and then comparing these outcomes against those predicted.

Only two studies investigating the effects of training children in problem solving have been reported to date. Spivack and Shure (1974) trained normal and disruptive preschoolers to generate alternative solutions to social problems. This instruction also was found to improve social functioning among disruptive children as well as normal children. These results suggest that training in problem solving may hold promise as an intervention as well as a prevention technique.

In a second study Russell and Thoresen (1976) used written materials and audiotapes of peers modeling the problem-solving process to teach institutionalized preadolescent aggressive children to deal with problem situations. The children gave somewhat more ($p < .10$) alternatives and consequences to simulated problems after this training than they produced beforehand. Anecdotal information from the institutional staff suggested that the children also generalized their newly acquired skills to applied situations.

Several basic studies (Spivack, Platt, & Shure, 1976) have indicated that deviant child populations may not be as adept as normal children at producing alternative solutions to social problems. The implications of these results are that training behaviorally disordered or impulsive children in interpersonal problem solving may be an important treatment technique for improving their self-control and adjustment. While preliminary field applications have produced some encouraging results, the data are too limited to evaluate the effectiveness of this approach for this purpose. There is a need to conduct further field studies on problem solving using direct behavioral measures to determine if this training will generalize across problem situations and if it will be maintained over time.

Modeling and Rehearsal

In training children in self-control through the use of social modeling and behavioral rehearsal a peer trainer might first model the desirable responses in a role-play problem situation or have the children observe these behaviors in vivo or on videotape. The children may then be required to imitate not only the appropriate verbal behaviors, but also all of the salient features of the response pattern—the voice inflections, gestures, and possibly even pauses. A trainer may then have the child reproduce the entire behavioral sequence with coaching and assistance. Finally, the child may be instructed to rehearse covertly the desirable behaviors.

Masters and Mokros (1974) have exhaustively reviewed the literature on children's self-reinforcement processes. The following are some of the highlights of their review that have implications for training children in self-control: (1) Children may more readily adopt externally imposed than modeled standards for self-reward: (2) Children tend to select the self-reinforcement standards of more lenient social models: (3) When a model's imposed standards conflict with his modeled standards for self-reinforcement, children tend to adopt the more lenient standards: (4) In general, children more readily adopt the self-reinforcement standards of competent, powerful models but not necessarily that of nurturant models: (5) Children tend to imitate self-regulatory behavior of models whose performances are closer to their competence levels rather than those who show superior performances: (6) A model's praise may increase a child's imitation of self-controlling behavior.

Experimenters have used modeling to reduce children's fear of animals (Bandura, Grusec, & Menlove, 1967; Bandura & Menlove, 1968; Ritter, 1968), to increase their social interactions (Ross, Ross, & Evans, 1971), to improve their task performance (Meichenbaum & Goodman, 1971), and to reduce their inappropriate classroom behavior (Csapo, 1972). Csapo (1972) demonstrated that having socially mature peers model appropriate behavior and award behaviorally disordered students tokens for imitating this behavior reduced the deviant behavior of these students, a reduction that was maintained for ten days after the treatment was withdrawn. Maintenance of behavior over time is a critical index of its value in promoting self-control.

Several studies have suggested that the effects of modeling for fostering children's self-control may be enhanced through the use of behavioral rehearsal procedures. In an early case study Gittelman (1965) used modeling and behavioral rehearsal techniques to reduce impulsive and aggressive behaviors in a preadolescent boy. After he identified situations that provoked the boy's anger, group members attempted to incite the boy's anger by acting out progressively more provocative scenarios (group members also modeled the boy's behavior in role-playing exercises). Reports indicated that this approach reduced aggression in the therapy group as well as in the school and home situations.

Goodwin and Mahoney (1975) applied a similar approach with three "hyperactive" boys. The boys played a "taunting" game in which one stood in an inner circle while the others attempted to provoke him into displaying aggressive behavior. The boys were shown videotaped models controlling their anger using self-instructions. By discussing and rehearsing these strategies the boys successfully reduced their aggressive and withdrawal behaviors in the therapy setting; the amount of disruptive behavior that they displayed in their regular school classroom also declined considerably during this time. Although the absence of a control group makes these findings tentative, they do suggest that a combination of modeling and rehearsal may be effective in developing children's self-control over their aggressive responses.

Modeling and rehearsal have also been used for training delinquent populations. Kifer, Lewis, Green, and Phillips (1974) used these techniques to teach predelinquent children and their parents to resolve conflicts. The experimenters presented the participants with written conflictual situations and had them identify and select outcomes to these situations. With instructional feedback provided by the training, the clients rehearsed these outcomes and negotiated settlements to the conflicts. Negotiations consisted of a statement of each person's position, identification of the issues, and tentative resolutions and outcomes. This training resulted in improved interpersonal negotiation skills between parents and their children, skills that transferred to home situations. Sarason and Ganzer (1973) trained delinquent youths in small groups in which they observed live models demonstrate appropriate behavior in scripted role plays. The plays involved conflicts familiar to the participants. After observing the models the youths discussed the content and outcome of the scenarios, imitated the model's behavior, and rehearsed their own version of the role play. Videotapes of their efforts were then reviewed and discussed. Sarason reported favorable results with this treatment package.

The results from laboratory research underscores the necessity for controlling agents—parents, teachers, and other authorities—to demonstrate appropriate self-regulatory behaviors themselves to foster the development of self-control in children. Studies also indicate that modeling is quite powerful in producing positive changes in children's behavior, and the addition of behavioral rehearsal may enhance its value for promoting children's self-control. As with other primarily cognitive approaches, however, field applications are very limited. The available field studies suffer from a lack of appropriate precision in data collection (Csapo, 1972), inadequate follow-up data (Csapo, 1972; Gittelman, 1965), unconvincing dependent measures (Gittelman, 1965), as well as a lack of appropriate control groups (Gittelman, 1965; Goodwin & Mahoney, 1975; Sarason & Ganzer, 1973). There is a need for applied studies that evaluate the contributions made by rehearsal procedures and that concentrate on the generalization and maintenance effects of this training using direct measures and appropriate comparison groups.

IMPLICATIONS AND EVALUATION OF SELF-CONTROL APPROACHES FOR TRAINING EXCEPTIONAL CHILDREN

The development of a technology of self-control stems from concerns relating to generalization and maintenance of training effects as well as those related to developing a "humanistic" approach to child guidance. The specific research issues related to self-control have been detailed elsewhere (Jeffery, 1974; Jones, Nelson, & Kazdin, 1977; Mahoney, 1972; McLaughlin, 1976) and will not be reiterated here. Instead, the results of field studies in self-management and cognitive approaches to self-control that have implications for training exceptional children will be summarized.

Self-management methods (self-monitoring, contracting, self-evaluation, and self-reinforcement) are probably the most well-researched self-control training procedures. Although the evidence is unclear, claims that self-management techniques rival external techniques in maintaining behavior are unfounded. In most studies history effects (Campbell & Stanley, 1963), sociocultural factors (Glynn, 1970), expectations and demand characteristics (Orne, 1969), and contributions of external reinforcement and discriminative stimuli have not been ruled out as competing hypotheses (Jones, Nelson, & Kazdin, 1977; McLaughlin, 1976). Studies, however, have yielded some valuable information concerning the use of these techniques.

In general, self-monitoring—the recording of one's behavior—appears to be an active intervention in its own right under conditions in which children are motivated to change or where external consequences maintain this behavior. This process appears to sensitize children to the frequency of their behavior and its controlling variables; thus practitioners can most effectively employ this technique by providing children with external reinforcement for maintaining self-monitoring accuracy and using the self-monitoring record to aid them in establishing and sequencing academic and social goals. This record also may be essential for shaping childrens' accurate self-evaluation and appropriate self-reinforcement.

Research indicates that a reliable procedure for training children in appropriate self-evaluation and self-reinforcement is first to establish these behaviors through external methods, such as contracts or token-reinforcement programs. Once the appropriate behaviors are established, external evaluations and control of reinforcement is gradually relinquished to the children through negotiation or fading procedures (Bolstad & Johnson, 1972; Drabman, Spitalnik, & O'Leary, 1973; Uhlman & Shook, 1976).

Although few researchers have evaluated cognitive approaches for training children in behavioral self-control, there is evidence accruing that these approaches may have considerable promise (Mahoney, 1974). The use of modeling and rehearsal for developing children's self-control appears to be particularly suited to applied situations. Trainers, first of all, would be well advised to model self-control for their students as well as to set reasonable standards for appropriate behavior and reinforce attainment of these by students (Bandura, 1969; Kanfer & Phillips, 1970; Masters & Mokros, 1974).

In cases involving interpersonal conflict teachers or peers could model appropriate methods of verbal and behavioral interaction (self-instructions, reinforcing self-statements, etc.) and have children rehearse these behaviors while receiving appropriate instructional feedback and reinforcement (Csapo, 1972). In the classroom teachers can also verbally model the steps for approaching and solving academic problems (Lovitt, 1976; Meichenbaum & Goodman, 1971) and require students to verbalize (rehearse) these steps prior to engaging in problem-solving activities. Thus, the procedure used by Meichenbaum and his associates (see Meichenbaum & Cameron, 1974) encompasses a highly useful combination of modeling, self-instruction, and rehearsal for both academic and social behaviors.

Problem solving as a self-control training technique differs from other methods in that the objective is to teach children a set of procedures that they can use across various situations. Available information (Spivack, Platt, & Shure, 1976) indicates that normal children may have more ability for interpersonal problem solving than deviant children. As an intervention technique teachers could be trained to teach deviant children that interpersonal, as well as intrapersonal, conflicts can be viewed as problems to be solved and that in many cases acting on problems is more effective than withdrawing from them or reacting to them emotionally. Teachers then could lead the children through a series of steps involving brainstorming alternative solutions and having them systematically try these out.

One of the most important issues currently facing researchers and practitioners alike is the generalization and maintenance of behavior (Stokes & Baer, 1977). Training children in behavioral self-control holds the promise that they may generalize appropriate behavior from one setting to another (i.e., from one classroom to another or from the school to the home setting) and that they may reduce their reliance on external control by maintaining appropriate behavior themselves (Cautela, 1969). Despite the growing literature related to teaching children self-control skills, the effects of this training across settings and over time has not been addressed adequately in the literature (McLaughlin, 1976). Clearly, future studies should evaluate the effectiveness of self-control training with children in terms of its generalization and maintenance effects (Karoly, 1977; Stokes & Baer, 1977).

REFERENCES

Aronfreed, J. *Conduct and conscience: Socialization of internalized control behavior.* New York: Academic Press, 1968.

Bandura, A. *Principles of behavior modification.* New York: Holt, Rinehart & Winston, 1969.

Bandura, A. *Psychological modeling: Conflicting theories.* Chicago: Aldine-Atherton, 1971.

Bandura, A., Grusec, J., & Menlove, F. L. Some social determinants of self-monitoring reinforcement systems. *Journal of Personality and Social Psychology,* 1967, *5*, 449–455.

Bandura, A., & Krupers, C. J. The transmission of patterns of self-reinforcement through modeling. *Journal of Abnormal and Social Psychology,* 1964, *69*, 1–9.

Bandura, A., & Menlove, F. L. Factors determining vicarious extinction of avoidance behavior through symbolic modeling. *Journal of Abnormal and Social Psychology,* 1968, *8*, 99–108.

Bandura, A. & Perloff, B. Relative efficacy of self-monitored and externally imposed reinforcement systems. *Journal of Personality and Social Psychology,* 1967, *7*, 111–116.

Bem, S. L. Verbal self-control: The estimate of effective self-instruction. *Journal of Experimental Psychology,* 1967, *74*, 485–491.

Bolstad, O. D., & Johnson, S. M. Self-regulation in the modification of disruptive classroom behavior. *Journal of Applied Behavior Analysis,* 1972, *5*, 443–454.

Bommarito, R., & Meichenbaum, D. *Enhancing reading comprehension by means of self-instructional training.* Unpublished manuscript, University of Waterloo, Ontario, 1975.

Brigham, T. A., & Sherman, J. A. Effects of choice and immediacy of reinforcement on single response and switching behavior of children. *Journal of the Experimental Analysis of Behavior,* 1973, *19*, 425–435.

Brigham, T. A., & Stoerzinger, A. An experimental analysis of children's preference for self-selected rewards. In T. A. Brigham, et al (Eds.), *Behavior analysis in education.* Dubuque, Ia: Kendall/Hunt, 1976.

Bristol, M. M. Control of physical aggression through school and home-based reinforcement. In J. D. Krumboltz & C. E. Thoresen (Eds.), *Counseling methods*. New York: Holt, Rinehart & Winston, 1976.

Broden, M., Hall, R. V., & Mitts, B. The effect of self-recording on the classroom behavior of two eighth-grade students. *Journal of Applied Behavior Analysis*, 1971, *4*, 191–199.

Brooks, B. D. Contingency contracts with truants. *Personnel and Guidance Journal*, 1974, *52*, 316–320.

Campbell, D. T., & Stanley, J. C. *Experimental and quasi-experimental designs for research on teaching*. Chicago: Rand McNally, 1966.

Cantrell, R. P., Cantrell, M. L., Huddleston, C. M., & Woolridge, R. L. Contingency contracting with school problems. *Journal of Applied Behavior Analysis*, 1969, *2*, 215–220.

Cautela, J. R. Behavior therapy and self-control: Techniques and implications. In C. Franks (Ed.), *Behavior therapy: Appraisal and status*. New York: McGraw-Hill, 1969.

Cohen, R. *The effects of self-monitoring on the academic and social behaviors of underachieving children*. Unpublished doctoral dissertation, Indiana University, 1977.

Csapo, M. Modeling and behavior control. *Teaching Exceptional Children*, 1972, *5*, 20–24.

Dinoff, M., & Rickard, H. C. Learning that privileges entail responsibility. In J. D. Krumboltz & C. E. Thoresen (Eds.), *Behavioral counseling: Cases and techniques*. New York: Holt, Rinehart & Winston, 1969.

Drabman, R. S., Spitalnik, R., & O'Leary, K. D. Teaching self-control to disruptive children. *Journal of Applied Behavior Analysis*, 1973, *6*, 10–16.

D'Zurilla, T. J., & Goldfried, M. R. Cognitive processes, problem-solving and effective behavior. In M. R. Goldfried & M. Merbaum (Eds.), *Behavior change through self-control*. New York: Holt, Rinehart & Winston, 1973.

Felixbrod, J. L., & O'Leary, K. D. Effects of reinforcement on children's academic behavior as a function of self-determined and externally imposed contingencies. *Journal of Applied Behavior Analysis*, 1973, *6*, 241–250.

Flannery, R. B. Use of covert conditioning in the behavior treatment of a drug-dependent college drop out. *Journal of Counseling Psychology*, 1972, *19*, 547–550.

Frederiksen, L. W., & Frederiksen, C. B. Teacher-determined and self-determined token reinforcement in a special education classroom. *Behavior Therapy*, 1975, *6*, 310–314.

Gershman, L. Eliminating a fire-setting compulsion through contingency management. In J. D. Krumboltz & C. E. Thoresen (Eds.), *Counseling methods*. New York: Holt, Rinehart & Winston, 1976.

Gittelman, M. Behavior rehearsal as a technique in child treatment. *Journal of Child Psychiatry*, 1965, *6*, 251–255.

Glynn, E. L. Classroom applications of self-determined reinforcement. *Journal of Applied Behavior Analysis*, 1970, *3*, 123–132.

Glynn, E. L., Thomas, J. D., & Shee, S. M. Behavioral self-control of on task behavior in an elementary classroom. *Journal of Applied Behavior Analysis*, 1973, *6*, 105–113.

Goldfried, M. R., & Goldfried, A. P. Cognitive change methods. In F. H. Kanfer & A. P. Goldstein (Eds.), *Helping people change: A textbook of methods.* Elmsford, NY: Pergamon, 1975.

Goldfried, M. R., & Merbaum, M. *Behavior change through self-control.* New York: Holt, Rinehart & Winston, 1973.

Goodwin, S. E., & Mahoney, M. J. Coping with aggression through cognitive modeling. In T. A. Brigham, R. Hawkins, J. W. Scott, & T. F. McLaughlin (Eds.), *Helping people change: A textbook of methods.* Elmsford, NY: Pergamon, 1975.

Gottman, J., & McFall, R. Self-monitoring effects in a program for potential high school dropouts. *Journal of Consulting and Clinical Psychology,* 1972, *39,* 273–281.

Grusec, J. Some antecedents of self-criticism. *Journal of Personality and Social Psychology,* 1966, *4,* 244–252.

Hanley, E. M. Review of research involving applied behavior in the classroom. *Review of Educational Research,* 1971, *40,* 597–625.

Haring, N. G., & Phillips, E. L. *Educating emotionally disturbed children.* New York: McGraw-Hill, 1962.

Hartig, M., & Kanfer, F. H. The role of verbal self-instructions in children's resistance to temptation. *Journal of Consulting and Clinical Psychology,* 1972, *31,* 127–136.

Hewitt, F. M. Educational engineering with E. D. children. *Exceptional Children,* 1967, *33,* 459–467.

Homme, L. Perspectives in psychology: XXIV. Control of coverants: The operants of the mind. *Psychological Record,* 1965, *15,* 501–511.

Homme, L., Csanyi, A. P., Gonzales, M. A., & Rechs, J. R. *How to use contingency contracting in the classroom.* Champaign, IL: Research Press, 1969.

Jackson, B. Treatment of depression by self-reinforcement. *Behavior Therapy,* 1972, *3,* 298–307.

Jeffrey, D. B. Self-Control: Methodological issues and research trends. In M. J. Mahoney & C. E. Thoresen (Eds.), *Self-control: Power to the person.* Monterey, CA: Brooks/Cole, 1974.

Jones, R. T., Nelson, R. E., & Kazdin, A. F. The role of external variables in self-reinforcement: A review. *Behavior Modification,* 1977, *1,* 147–175.

Kanfer, F. H. Self-management methods. In F. H. Kanfer & A. P. Goldstein (Eds.), *Helping people change: A textbook of methods.* Elmsford, NY: Pergamon, 1975.

Kanfer, F. H. *The many faces of self-control, or behavior modification changes its focus.* Paper presented at the Eighth International Banff Conference, Canada, March 1976.

Kanfer, F. H. Personal communication, March 22, 1977.

Kanfer, F. H., & Karoly, P. Self-control: A behavioristic excursion into the lion's den. *Behavior Therapy,* 1972, *3,* 398–416.

Kanfer, F. H. & Phillips, J. S. *Learning foundations of behavior therapy.* New York: Wiley, 1970.

Karoly, P. Behavioral self-management in children: Concepts, methods, issues and directions. In M. Hersen, R. M. Eisler, & P. M. Miller (Eds.), *Progress in behavior modification* Vol. 5. New York: Academic Press, 1977.

Kaufman, K. F. & O'Leary, K. D. Reward, cost and self-evaluation procedures for disruptive adolescents in a psychiatric hospital school. *Journal of Applied Behavior Analysis,* 1972, *5,* 293–309.

Kazdin, A. E. Reactive self-monitoring: The effects of response desirability, goal setting, and feedback. *Journal of Consulting and Clinical Psychology,* 1974, *42,* 704–716.

Kazdin, A. E., & Bootzin, R. R. The token economy: An evaluative review. *Journal of Applied Behavior Analysis,* 1972, *5,* 343–372.

Kiesler, C. A. *The psychology of commitment.* New York: Academic Press, 1971.

Kifer, R. E., Lewis, M. A., Green, D. R., & Phillips, E. L. Training pre-delinquent youth and parents to negotiate conflict situations. *Journal of Applied Behavior Analysis,* 1974, *7,* 357–364.

Klein, J. D., & Gory, E. L. The differential effects of noncontingent self-evaluation upon academic performance. In T. A. Brigham, R. Hawkins, J. W. Scott, & T. F. McLaughlin (Eds.), *Behavior analysis in education,* Dubuque, Ia: Kendall/Hunt, 1976.

Liebert, R. M. , & Allen, M. K. Effects of rule-structure and reward magnitude on the acquisition and adoption of self-reward criteria. *Psychological Reports,* 1967, *21,* 445–452.

Lovitt, T. C. Applied behavior analysis techniques and curriculum research: Implications for instruction. In N. G. Haring & R. L. Schiefelbusch (Eds.), *Teaching special children.* New York: McGraw-Hill, 1976.

Luria, A. R. Verbal regulation of behavior. In C. B. Stendler (Ed.), *Readings in child behavior and development.* New York: Harcourt Brace Jovanovich, 1965.

MacDonald W. S., Gallimore, R., & MacDonald, G. Contingency counseling by school personnel: An economical model of intervention. *Journal of Applied Behavior Analysis,* 1970, *3,* 175–182.

Mahoney, M. J. Research issues in self-management. *Behavior Therapy,* 1972, *3,* 45–63.

Mahoney, M. J. *Cognition and behavior modification.* Cambridge, MA: Ballinger, 1974.

Mahoney, M. J., & Thoresen, C. E. *Self-control: Power to the person.* Monterey, Ca: Brooks/Cole, 1974.

Marston, A. R. Self-reinforcement: The relevance of a concept on analogue research to psychotherapy. *Psychotherapy: Theory, Research and Practice,* 1965, *2,* 1–5.

Masters, J. C., & Mokros, J. R. Self-reinforcement processes in children. In H. Reese (Ed.), *Advances in child development and behavior* (Vol. 9). New York: Academic Press, 1974.

McLaughlin, T. F. Self-control in the classroom. *Review of Educational Research,* 1976, *46,* 631–663.

Meichenbaum, D. Toward a cognitive theory of self-control. In G. Schwartz & D. Shapiro (Eds.), *Consciousness and self-regulation: Advances in research.* New York: Plenum, 1975.

Meichenbaum, D., & Cameron, R. The clinical potential of modifying what clients say to themselves. In M. J. Mahoney & C. E. Thoresen (Eds.), *Self-control: Power to the person.* Monterey, Ca: Brooks/Cole, 1974.

Meichenbaum, D., & Goodman, J. Reflection-impulsivity and verbal control or motor behavior. *Child Development*, 1971, *40*, 785–797.

Meichenbaum, D., & Goodman, J. Training impulsive children to talk to themselves: A means for developing self-control. *Journal of Abnormal Psychology*, 1971, *77*, 115–126.

Mischel, W. *Personality and assessment*. New York: Wiley, 1968.

Mischel, W. Toward a cognitive social learning reconceptualization of personality. *Psychological Review*, 1973, *80*, 252–283.

Mischel, W., & Liebert, R. Effects of discrepancies between observed and imposed reward criteria on their acquisition and transmission. *Journal of Personality and Social Psychology*, 1966, *3*, 45–53.

O'Leary, K. D. The effects of self-instruction on immoral behavior. *Journal of Experimental Child Psychology*, 1968, *6*, 297–391.

O'Leary, K. D., & Becker, W. C. Behavior modification in an adjustment class: A token reinforcement program. *Exceptional Children*, 1967, *34*, 636–642.

O'Leary, K. D., & Drabman, R. Token reinforcement programs in the classroom: A review. *Psychological Bulletin*, 1971, *75*, 379–398.

Orne, M. T. Demand characteristics and the concept of quasi-controls. In R. Rosenthal & R. L. Rosnow (Eds.), *Artifact in behavioral research*. New York: Academic Press, 1969.

Palkes, H., Stewart, W., & Kahana, B. Porteus maze performance of hyperactive boys after training in self-directed verbal commands. *Child Development*, 1968, *39*, 817–826.

Patterson, G.R. Reprogramming the families of aggressive boys. In C.E. Thoresen (Ed.), *Behavior modification in education* (Vol. 15). Chicago: University of Chicago Press, 1973.

Phillips, E. L. Achievement place: Token reinforcement procedures in a home-style rehabilitation setting for pre-delinquent boys within a token economy. *Journal of Applied Behavior Analysis*, 1971, *4*, 45–59.

Reiber, J.L., Schilmoeller, G.L., & LeBlanc, J.M. The use of self-control to maintain attending of preschool children after self-counting procedures. In T.A. Brigham, R. Hawkins, J.W. Scott, & T.F. McLaughlin (Eds.), *Behavior analysis in education*. Dubuque, IA: Kendall/Hunt, 1976.

Reith, J., Polsgrove, L., McLeskey, J., et al. *The use of self-recording to increase the arithmetic performance of severely behaviorally disordered students*. Unpublished manuscript, Indiana University, Bloomington, Indiana, 1978.

Ritter, B. The group desensitization of children's snake phobias. *Behaviour Research and Therapy*, 1968, *6*, 1–6.

Rogers, C. Implications of prediction and control of human behavior. *Teacher's College Record*, 1956, *57*, 316–332.

Rogers, C.R., & Skinner, B.F. Some issues concerning the control of human behavior. *Science*, 1956, *124*, 1057–1066.

Rosenhan, D., Frederick, F., & Burrowes, A. Preaching and practicing: Effects of channel discrepancy on norm internalization. *Child Development*, 1968, *39*, 291–301.

Ross, D.M., Ross, S.A., & Evans, T.A. The modification of extreme social withdrawal by modeling with guided participation. *Journal of Behavior Therapy and Experimental Psychiatry*, 1971, *2*, 273–279.

Russell, M.L., & Thoresen, C.E. Teaching decision-making skills to children. In J.D. Krumboltz & C.E. Thoresen (Éds.), *Counseling methods*. New York: Holt, Rinehart, & Winston, 1976.

Santogrossi, D.A., O'Leary, K.D., Romanczyk, R.G., & Kaufman, K.F. Self-evaluation by adolescents in a psychiatric hospital school token program. *Journal of Applied Behavior Analysis*, 1973, *6*, 277–287.

Sarason, I.G., & Ganzer, V.J. Modeling and group discussion in the rehabilitation of juvenile delinquents. *Journal of Counseling Psychology*, 1973, *20*, 442–449.

Schacter, S., & Singer, J.E. Cognitive, social and psychological determinants of emotional states. *Psychological Review*, 1962, *69*, 379–399.

Skinner, B.F. *Science and human behavior*. New York: Free Press, 1953.

Skinner, B.F. *The technology of teaching*. New York: Appleton-Century-Crofts, 1968.

Spivack, G., Platt, J.J., & Shure, M.B. *The problem-solving approach to adjustment*. San Francisco: Jossey-Bass, 1976.

Spivack, G., & Shure, M. *Social adjustment of young children: A cognitive approach to solving real-life problems*. San Francisco: Jossey-Bass, 1974.

Staats, A.W. Behavior analysis and token reinforcement in educational behavior modification and curriculum research. In C.E. Thoresen (Ed.), *Behavior modification in education*. Chicago: University of Chicago Press, 1973.

Staats, A. W. *Social behaviorism*. Homewood, IL: Dorsey, 1975. (a)

Staats, A.W. *Complex human behavior*. Homewood, IL: Dorsey, 1975. (b)

Stark, J.A. An evaluation of semiprogrammed self-modification technique designed to improve self-control with groups of emotionally disturbed adolescents. In T.A. Brigham, R. Hawkins, J.W. Scott, & T.F. McLaughlin (Eds.), *Behavior analysis in education*. Dubuque, IA: Kendall/Hunt, 1976.

Stokes, T., & Bauer, D. An implicit technology of generalization. *Journal of Applied Behavior Analysis*, 1977, *10*, 349–367.

Stuart, R.B. Behavioral contracting within the females of delinquents. *Journal of Behavior Therapy and Experimental Psychiatry*, 1971, *2*, 1–11.

Stuart, R.B., & Lott, L.A., Jr. Behavioral contracting with delinquents: A cautionary note. *Journal of Behavior Therapy and Experimental Psychiatry*, 1972, *3*, 161–169.

Tharp, R.G., & Wetzel, R.J. *Behavior modification in the natural environment*. New York: Academic Press, 1969.

Thoresen, C.E. Behavioral humanism. In C.E. Thoresen (Ed.), *Behavior modification in education*. Chicago: University of Chicago Press, 1973.

Thoresen, C.E., & Mahoney, M.J. *Behavioral self-control*. New York: Holt, Rinehart & Winston, 1974.

Turkewitz, H., O'Leary, K.D., & Ironsmith, B. Generalization and maintenance of appropriate behavior through self-control. *Journal of Consulting and Clinical Psychology*, 1973, *43*, 577–583.

Uhlman, W.F., & Shook, G.L. A method of maintaining high rates of performance in an open classroom setting. In T.A. Brigham, R. Hawkins, J.W. Scott, & T.F. McLaughlin (Eds.), *Behavior analysis in education*. Dubuque, IA: Kendall/Hunt, 1976.

Velten, E. A laboratory task for induction of mood states. *Behaviour Research and Therapy,* 1968, *6,* 473–482.

Winett, R.A., & Winkler, R.C. Current behavior modification in the classroom: Be still, be quiet, be docile. *Journal of Applied Behavior Analysis,* 1972, *5,* 505–510.

SELECTED READINGS FOR FURTHER STUDY

Aronfreed, J. *Conduct and conscience: Socialization of internalized control behavior.* New York: Academic Press, 1968.

Bolstad, O.D., & Johnson, S.M. Self-regulation in the modification of disruptive classroom behvior. *Journal of Applied Behavior Analysis,* 1972, *5,* 443–454.

Drabman, R.S., Spitalnik, R., & O'Leary, K.D. Teaching self-control to disruptive children. *Journal of Applied Behavior Analysis,* 1973, *6,* 10–16.

Goldfried, M.R. and Goldfried, A.P. Cognitive change methods. In F.H. Kanfer & A.P. Goldstein (Eds.), *Helping people change: A textbook of methods.* Elmsford, NY: Pergamon Press, 1975.

Jones, R.T., Nelson, R.E., and Kazdin, A.F. The role of external variables in self-reinforcement: A review. *Behavior Modification,* 1977, *1,* 147–175.

Mahoney, M.J., & Thoresen, C.E. *Self-control: Power to the person.* Monterey, CA: Brooks/Cole, 1974.

McLaughlin, T.F. Self-control in the classroom. *Review of Educational Research,* 1976, *46,* 631–663.

Thoresen, C.E., & Mahoney, M.J. *Behavioral self-control.* New York: Holt, Rinehart & Winston, 1974.

8
Controlling Severe Maladaptive Behaviors

Published reports (Foxx & Azrin, 1973; Frankel, Moss, Schofield, & Simmons, 1976; Lovaas, Schaeffer, & Simmons, 1965; Repp & Dietz, 1974) have documented the existence of aggressive, self-injurious, and withdrawn/self-stimulatory behaviors. As a result of the impact of the "normalization principle" and recent legislation and litigation, many individuals who display such behaviors have been and/or will be placed in public school classrooms (Haring, 1977). Therefore, teachers urgently need methods to deal with severe forms of maladaptive behavior.

The important question for classroom teachers is, Can such behaviors be brought under control, and if so, how? Recent empirical research has repeatedly indicated that such behaviors can be controlled. Aggressive, self-injurious, and withdrawn/self-stimulatory behaviors have been brought under control by means of precise application of various applied behavior analysis procedures.

The purpose of this chapter is twofold—(1) to review and discuss the applied behavior analysis procedures that have been found to be effective in controlling severe forms of maladaptive behavior and (2) to outline several considerations that may influence the success with which severe forms of maladaptive behavior are controlled in a classroom setting.

This chapter is organized into three main sections. In section one the applied behavior analysis research related to procedures for controlling withdrawn/self-stimulatory, self-injurious, and aggressive behaviors is reviewed. In section two the procedures are examined, and section three

We would like to acknowledge Dr. Chuck Dedrick for his contribution to a prepublication draft of this chapter.

concludes the chapter with a discussion of several factors that should be considered when implementing applied behavior analysis procedures for controlling maladaptive behaviors in a classroom setting.

REVIEW OF PROCEDURES

Withdrawal and Self-stimulatory Behaviors

Some children display withdrawal and/or self-stimulatory behaviors. Withdrawal behavior involves *not* playing, talking, or interacting with others (Kauffman, 1977). Self-stimulatory behavior involves "repetitive, stereotyped behavior that has no apparent functional effects on the environment" (Foxx & Azrin, 1973, p. 1). Examples include head and body rocking, hand weaving, vocalizations, self and object mouthing, and object spinning.

Several applied behavior analysis procedures for increasing the social interactions of children displaying these behaviors have been found to be effective. In addition, various procedures have been applied successfully to decrease the occurrence of self-stimulatory behaviors.

Strain, Shores, and Timm (1977) investigated the effects of a socially active peer trying to get socially unresponsive children to play. The hypothesis was that "social stimuli may operate to set the occasion for social responding by the recipient of these events" (p. 298). A socially active peer was placed into a play situation with three withdrawn children. During the intervention phases the peer was instructed to try his best to get the other children to play. The results indicated that increased social initiations by the peer increased the positive social behaviors of the withdrawn subjects and also increased the number of self-initiated positive social behaviors that they exhibited. Previous studies (Strain & Timm, 1974; Strain, Shores & Kerr, 1976) done on the same population—handicapped preschoolers—also found the involvement of socially active peers with socially isolated or withdrawn subjects to be effective in increasing the positive social interaction behaviors of social isolates.

Burney, Russell, and Shores (1977) studied the effects of modeling procedures in combination with prompting and reinforcement on the positive social responses of two profoundly retarded, elementary-age children who resided in a community-based residential facility. The children possessed limited interactive responses. The procedure involved the trainer modeling positive social behaviors for the children. The social behaviors of the children were also prompted, and edible and social reinforcement was made contingent upon their social responses. Both children showed a significant increase in social responses. Generalization of the results, however, was limited.

Other researchers (Gibson, Lawrence, & Nelson, 1977; O'Connor, 1972) have also investigated modeling alone and in comparison or combination with other procedures. For the most part, they found that modeling with various populations is effective in fostering social interaction behaviors; however, its degree of effectiveness may be enhanced when combined with other procedures, such as providing verbal instructions and corrective feedback.

To increase independent play and social interactions of three severely retarded female adults who displayed withdrawn and "psychotic-like" behaviors, Wehman, Karan, and Rettie (1976) employed social reinforcement. Their study took place in a sheltered workshop during daily 25-minute activity sessions. The subjects were given a variety of play objects and were trained to interact with these objects by means of manual guidance, modeling, and verbal prompting. During the intervention phases they were socially reinforced for appropriate play. The results indicated that the use of play materials increased. There also was a decrease in psychoticlike behaviors and a slight increase in peer social interactions.

Various procedures have reduced self-stimulatory behavior. At the Georgia Retardation Center Repp, Dietz, and Speir (1974) studied the effects of differential reinforcement of other behavior (DRO) in combination with a mild form of punishment with adolescent and adult severely retarded individuals. The subjects were reinforced on a fixed-interval schedule when the inappropriate self-stimulatory behavior did not occur during the designated interval. When the inappropriate self-stimulatory type behavior did occur during the designated interval, the teacher said "No!" and no reinforcement was given. The investigators found that the application of DRO in combination with mild punishment was more effective in reducing self-stimulatory behavior than a mild form of punishment alone.

Murphy, Nunes, and Ruprecht (1977) studied the effects of verbal cueing and response cost upon the self-stimulatory behaviors of two profoundly retarded adults. The procedures were implemented in a public day school program. During classroom activities continual vibratory stimulation was provided (with a portable vibrator for one subject and a vibrator attached to a chair for the other). Contingent upon self-stimulatory behaviors (hyperventilation and hand mouthing), the subjects were given a verbal cue to stop, and the vibratory stimulation was stopped and not turned back on until self-stimulatory behaviors ceased. This procedure resulted in a reduction of self-stimulatory behavior to a near zero rate.

Punishment—the application of an aversive stimulus (or stimuli) contingent upon the target behavior—has proven to be effective in reducing a wide range of withdrawal/self-stimulatory behaviors. Punishment has been used with a variety of subjects and in a variety of settings. It has most often been used, however, with subjects classified as being severely disturbed or retarded who were residents of institutions or private residential schools. In most instances the procedure has been to apply a high-intensity aversive immediately following or contingent upon the self-stimulatory behavior(s).

In a study conducted in a university clinic Lovaas, Schaeffer, and Simmons (1965) enhanced the social behaviors and reduced the self-stimulatory behaviors of two five-year-old autistic children by using electric shock. Shock, by means of an electrical grid on the floor, was administered contingent upon pathological, withdrawn/self-stimulatory types of behavior. The shock was turned off or withheld whenever the children ceased to display withdrawn/self-stimulatory behaviors and approached the adults that were present. The subjects exhibited an increase in approach behaviors and a decrease in self-stimulatory behaviors in order to avoid shock. After the adults were associated with shock reduction and removal, the children showed an increase in affectionate and social interaction behaviors with the adults.

Baumeister and Forehand (1972), Lovaas and Simmons (1969), and Risley (1968) found electric shock to be effective in the almost complete suppression of self-stimulatory behavior(s). Bucher and Lovaas (1968) found that slapping the subject on the thigh suppressed self-stimulatory behaviors. Other aversive stimuli that have been effective in reducing self-stimulatory behaviors include shouting (Baumeister & Forehand, 1971), shouting and shaking (Risley, 1968), and shouting and slapping the subject's hand (Koegel & Covert, 1972). In general, when the degree of suppression is considered, punishment with a hight-intensity aversive has been very successful in reducing self-stimulatory behavior. It should be noted, though, that a few studies have reported less highly intense stimuli to be effective. For example, when Lamal (1976) sprayed Listerine on the hand contingent upon hand-sucking, it reduced the occurence.

Azrin and Foxx (1971) developed an overcorrection procedure and investigated (1973) its effectiveness in reducing self-stimulatory behaviors. Overcorrection involves two aspects, restitution and positive practice. In restitution there is the correction of the consequences of the behavior on the environment by the subject. Positive practice is a procedure in which the subject practices the appropriate or correct behavior. Generally, in regard to self-stimulatory behaviors, the positive component alone is used since in most cases the self-stimulatory behaviors have no effect on the environment to be corrected; however, restitution is used if appropriate.

Foxx and Azrin (1973) investigated the effect of overcorrection in comparison to the approaches of differential reinforcement of other behavior, noncontingent reinforcement, and physical punishment. The subjects were young, severely emotionally disturbed and retarded children who exhibited head-weaving, mouthing, and hand-clapping behaviors. The study took place in a day-care setting. The overcorrection procedure involved requiring the subjects to practice the correct forms of the relevant behaviors contingent upon the occurrence of self-stimulatory behaviors. For instance, in one example of headweaving the subject had to practice holding his head in sustained orientation (not moving) and to move only for functional reasons. Overcorrection was the only technique that completely suppressed the children's mouthing, head-weaving, and hand-clapping behaviors. Generalization of the procedure was effectively implemented in the home setting by the parents. (It should be noted that Kissel and Whitman (1977) examined unprogrammed generalization effects of the overcorrection procedure on self-stimulatory behaviors. They found that the generalization effects are not spontaneous over settings but need to be programmed into the procedure.)

Newman, Whorton, and Simpson (1977) observed the use of the overcorrection procedure in reducing self-stimulatory vocalizations in a group academic setting. The subject was an eight-year-old severely disturbed child.

> An adult applied his or her hand firmly to the subject's mouth in such a manner that noises could not be made and [held] it there consecutively for 30 seconds . . . at the end of the 30-second period the adult applying the treatment said, "Good being quiet" and then moved his or her hand from the child's mouth. In the event that the child was attemtping to make noises at the end of the 30-second period, the adult's hand remained over his mouth until he was quiet. (p. 160)

In addition, there was intermittent reinforcement for quiet on task behaviors throughout the day. This overcorrection procedure resulted in the reduction of self-stimulatory behaviors to a low rate, but complete suppression did not occur.

Other research supports the effectiveness of the overcorrection procedure in various situations and in dealing with various types of self-stimulatory behavior (Azrin, Kaplin, & Fox, 1973; Epstein, Doke, Sajwaj, et al, 1974; Ward, 1976; Webster & Azrin, 1973).

Another approach to reducing self-stimulation involves a focus on the environmental stimuli available during periods of self-stimulation. Guess and Rutherford (1967) provided objects that could be manipulated (e.g., teddy bear, volley ball) and sound-generating apparatus (e.g., play telephone that buzzed when dialed) to retardates (8 to 16 years of age) who exhibited self-stimulatory behaviors. When the manipulatable objects and sound-generating apparatus were available, self-stimulatory behaviors were reduced by approximately 50 percent. Other researchers have obtained similar results (Berkson & Mason, 1963; Davenport & Berkson, 1963; Kauffman & Levitt, 1965).

Self-injurious Behaviors

Those who exhibit self-injurious behavior endanger their physical well-being. Head banging, hitting, eye poking, chewing, and scratching, are manifestations of such behavior. Their continued and intense exhibitions can result in scars, abrasions, loss of sight and hearing, brain injury, and, in some cases, death (Bachman, 1972; Smolev, 1971).
Due to their potentially dangerous effects, continuous physical restraints rather than procedures to modify such behaviors have frequently been used. Researchers have, however, begun to find effective procedures for dealing with such behaviors. The following is an examination of some of the most frequently noted.

Self-injurious behaviors (SIBs) have been reduced through differential reinforcement of other behavior (DRO), which has been used both alone and in combination with other procedures. Repp and Deitz (1974) examined the effects of DRO plus a mild verbal reprimand versus a mild verbal reprimand alone. The subject was a ten-year-old severely retarded institutionalized female who scratched her face. The combination of DRO, in which M&M candies were provided on a fixed-interval schedule contingent upon an interval when SIB did not occur, plus a mild verbal reprimand ("No!") contingent upon SIB occurrence decreased the frequency of the SIB to a near zero rate whereas mild verbal punishment alone did not decrease the SIB.

Another approach for SIB reduction has been to make time-out contingent upon SIB. Lucero, Frieman, Spoering, and Fehrenbacker (1976) examined the effects of various time-out procedures on SIBs. The subjects were three profoundly retarded institutionalized female adolescents who exhibited various forms of head banging. The procedures used were carried out during the noon meal. Fifteen seconds of lost opportunity to receive (1) food (grasped arm), (2) attention (experimenter left the room), or (3) food and attention (experimenter picked up tray and turned away from subject) were made contingent upon SIB. A mild form of verbal punishment ("No!") was administered in conjunction with food removal. Praise and tactile stimulation was given when SIB did not occur. Withdrawal of food was the most effective in reducing the occurrence of head banging; withdrawal of food and attention, the next most effective; and removal of attention, the least effective. There appeared to be some generalization of SIB reduction to other meals, but there was no empirical verification. Other investigators (Ausman, Ball, & Alexander, 1974; Frankel, Moss, Schofield, & Simmons, 1976) have studied time-out in combination with other procedures such as DRO. They generally found time-out when combined with other procedures to be effective in reducing SIBs. In addition, Ausman and associates found the effects of time-out and DRO to generalize when training sessions were held in different locations and under different time periods and conditions.

Wolf, Risley, and Mees (1964) examined the effect of extinction in combination with mild punishment to reduce SIB of a behaviorally and physically handicapped preschooler. When SIB was exhibited at a hospital facility, the child was placed in an isolation room. When the SIB was exhibited in the isolation room, the door was closed. Parents were also trained to use this procedure when the child was at home. SIB was reduced by this procedure; however, more than four months was required to suppress it to a near zero rate.

Subjects who display SIB have generally been physically restrained. Schroeder, Peterson, Solomon, and Artley (1977) investigated the effects of a combination of physical restraint and reinforcement of relaxation, with and without EMG biofeedback signals. The subjects were two severely retarded male adolescents who were chronic head bangers. The investigation involved three conditions: (1) restraint for SIB and verbal reinforcement for relaxation, (2) restraint for SIB, verbal and edible reinforcement for relaxation, and EMG biofeedback, and (3) restraint for SIB, verbal and edible reinforcement for relaxation, and EMG biofeedback. The findings indicated that the combination of physical restraint and reinforcement was effective in reducing the occurrence of head banging, but the use of biofeedback with physical restraint and reinforcement was considerably more effective than physical restraint and reinforcement alone. The use of verbal and edible reinforcement for relaxation was more effective than verbal alone.

Food withdrawal has been used as a form of punishment for SIB. Myers and Deibert (1971) studied it as a means of reducing SIB. An 11-year-old retarded blind male who exhibited head-banging behavior was observed during meal time. When the child began to bang his head, the child was turned away from the table and his hands restrained for 15 seconds. If three SIBs occurred in one meal, the meal was delayed for two hours. The occurrence of SIBs during meals decreased rapidly to a near zero level. Generalization of training to other situations was programmed in until all SIB was eliminated.

In addition to withdrawal of food, other forms of punishment such as contingent electric shock or "odor pills" have been tried alone and in combination with other procedures. Young and Wincze (1974) examined the effects of reinforcing compatible and incompatible behaviors and contingent shock on SIBs. The subject was an institutionalized profoundly retarded female adult who exhibited head-banging behavior. The procedure involved several stages. The subject was first reinforced for a behavior compatible (eye contact) with head banging. The rationale was that if she had a clear means of earning reinforcement, she would not have to exhibit SIB. The compatible behavior increased in frequency; however, no decrease in SIB was observed. Next, reinforcement was provided for a behavior incompatible (sitting erect with hands lowered) with head banging. This also was ineffective. Finally, electric shock was made contingent upon SIB, and this proved to be very effective.

Corte, Wolf, and Locke (1971) investigated the effects of three procedures on SIB: elimination of social consequences, DRO, and contingent electric shock. The subjects were four profoundly retarded institutionalized adolescents who exhibited head banging, tongue and eye poking, finger chewing, hair pulling, and pulling skin off the face. Initially, two subjects were placed in a situation in which there was an elimination of all social consequences contingent upon SIB. There was no reduction in the frequency of SIB. Both subjects were then given candy on a fixed-interval schedule for no SIB and were placed in a short time-out situation when SIB occurred—still no decrease in the frequency of SIB for either subject. Both subjects were then deprived of lunch before the sessions and provided a spoonful of malt on a fixed-interval schedule contingent on no SIB. When DRO was combined with this deprivation condition, subject one's SIB rate rapidly declined to near zero, but the SIB rate of subject two did not decrease.

The final procedure attempted was to make electric shock contingent upon SIB for all four subjects of the study. Shock was administered (generally to the arm involved in the action) with an electric prod. Electric shock quickly eliminated the SIB of all four subjects. Generalization of the effects did not usually occur and required specific programming.

Contingent withdrawal of human contact and electric shock were used to decrease the head banging of a nine-year-old blind, psychotic institutionalized male (Tate & Baroff, 1966). The subject was restrained most of the day; however, he was taken for brief walks each day. When SIB was emitted during the walks, the experimenter's hand was removed from the subject's hand for three seconds. This procedure resulted in a considerable reduction of head hitting. Because of the damage risk involved to this child by head hitting, electric shock procedures were begun. Electric shock resulted in a near zero rate, and by the second day the child was able to be out of the restraints eight and a half hours. Subsequently, skills were developed, which were not possible prior to the elimination of SIB. Several other inappropriate behaviors were eliminated by the contingent presentation of the prod buzzing sound without the actual use of the shock itself. Lovaas and Simmons (1969) conducted a similar study and obtained similar results.

Tanner and Zeiler (1975) investigated the effects of an aversive odor as punishment for SIB. The subject, an institutionalized autistic female adult, engaged in self-slapping, particularly in the head area. First a capsule of aromatic ammonia was crushed and thrust under her nose contingent upon self-slapping. During the next phase a capsule was used contingent upon the subject brushing back her hair, which consistently preceded the slapping episodes. The findings indicated a rapid decline in self-slapping episodes during ammonia application for slapping. When ammonia was applied to the preceding behavior, the episodes immediately dropped to a zero rate. Subsequently, the ammonia capsules were carried by all staff and applied any time during the day contingent upon the subject brushing back her hair or slapping her face. It was noted that self-slapping behaviors occuring outside the experimental setting decreased considerably. Baumeister and Baumeister (1978) also studied the effects of aromatic ammonia as an aversive stimulus in a punishment procedure used to reduce SIBs in two young severely retarded children. They concluded that "aromatic ammonia inhalation appears to be an effective alternative for decelerating extremely maladaptive behaviors" (p. 71).

Prochaska, Smith, Marzilli, et al (1974) studied the generalizability possibilities of punishment by using a portable remote-control shock device. The subject, a nine-year-old profoundly retarded female, would strike her nose and chin with her fist. She lived at home with her parents and attended a day school. The shock device was attached to her upper arm under her clothing. Shock was made contingent upon SIB occurrence, and SIB was quickly brought to a zero rate. Generalization occurred to all situations such as stores, restaurants and recreational areas. It was hypothisized that the total environmental approach to shock for SIBs resulted in generalization where shock had not occurred. One side effect was that social interaction behaviors increased after the decline in SIBs.

One of the most recent approaches for dealing with SIB is overcorrection. Kelly and Drabman (1977) explored the effects of overcorrection in combination with DRO with a three-year-old visually handicapped male who exhibited a high rate of eye poking. Intensive practice in the "correct forms of the relevant behavior" was made contingent upon eye poking. When eye poking occurred, the child's arms were put down at his sides and then raised and lowered 12 times without touching his eyes. Noneye poking was verbally praised on a fixed-interval schedule. Eye poking was reduced to a near zero level. In addition, generalization of the effects occurred in a peer play situation with no further programming provided.

Azrin, Gottlieb, Hughart, and their associates (1975) as well as Measel and Alfiere (1976) examined the effects of overcorrection combined with other procedures such as DRO on the SIBs of adolescents and adults. For the most part their results were similar to those of Kelly and Drabman (1977), although one of the two subjects with whom Measel and Alfiere worked did not respond to overcorrection, DRO, or a combination of the two procedures.

Another relatively recent and unique approach for SIB control is "rage reduction." Saposnek and Watson (1974) applied this approach to a psychotic ten-year-old institutionalized male who displayed chronic head-slapping behavior. The experimenter would begin each session by holding the child in his lap. When head slapping began (along with kicking, screaming, and flailing) the experimenter would block the hand movement to the head and manually guide the child to his (the experimenter's) hand instead. This was continued until the child's body relaxed, and he was no longer hitting the experimenter's hand, kicking, screaming, or flailing. The results indicated a quick reduction of the SIB rate and after continued training the elimination of SIB.

Aggressive Behaviors

Generally there are two categories of aggressive behaviors: physical or verbal. Physical aggression includes biting, pinching, scratching, knocking over furniture, pushing, hair pulling, throwing items, grabbing, and spitting. Verbal aggression involves yelling, cursing, abusive language, and threats. Several procedures for controlling such behaviors are effective. Aggressive behaviors in older, larger individuals have received considerable attention due to the potential danger involved. For this reason several of the procedures noted have been specifically investigated with adolescents and adults.

Negative reinforcement (termination of experimenter-administered finger pressure on the inside upper bicep area of the subject's right arm) effectively decreased physically aggressive and other maladaptive behaviors of a severely retarded female adult in a day school setting (Mithang & Hanawalt, 1977). This was done by making the termination of finger pressure contingent on behaviors incompatible with maladaptive behaviors (e.g., hitting). The incompatible behaviors centered around paying attention to a prevocational task of collating a booklet. The negative reinforcement was effective in increasing on-task behaviors and decreasing aggressive behaviors. Physical prompts and verbal cues had been tried with the subject before the negative reinforcement procedure, but they did not work. Generalization of the approach by involving others in the administration of this form of negative reinforcement was found to be effective.

Another approach for controlling aggressive and other severe forms of maladaptive behavior is time-out. Hamilton, Stephens, and Allen (1967) investigated this procedure with adolescent and adult institutionalized severely retarded females who exhibited such behaviors as fighting and destruction of property. Time-out was made contingent upon the exhibition of aggressive and destructive behaviors. The subjects were confined to a chair in a time-out area for periods ranging from thirty minutes to two hours. The findings indicated that time-out did reduce to a very low rate the occurrence of aggressive and destructive behaviors.

The effect of time-out on the physically aggressive behaviors of two severely retarded children was also the subject of a study by Pendergrass (1972). Following physical aggression, the subject was removed from a classroom setting for two minutes. Not only were the aggressive behaviors reduced, but social interaction behaviors increased.

Frankel, Moss, Schofield, and Simmons (1976) investigated the effects of DRO and two time-out procedures. The study was conducted at a neuropsychiatric clinic with a six-year-old profoundly retarded girl who exhibited psychotic-like and aggressive behaviors (biting, pinching, and hair pulling). The time-out procedures implemented contingent upon aggressive behavior were (1) the child was placed in a chair facing away from other children in the room for two minutes and (2) the child was placed in a isolation booth for five minutes. Neither of these procedures were effective, which is, of course, contrary to what would have been expected after reading the results of the studies of Hamilton, Stephens, and Allen (1967) and Pendergrass, (1972) reviewed above. A DRO procedure was then instituted in which praise and candy were provided on a fixed-interval schedule when, during the interval, task-related correct responses and quiet appropriate responses were exhibited. When aggressive behaviors did occur, they were ignored. This differential reinforcement procedure resulted in a reduction of aggressive behaviors to a near zero rate. Other investigators (Bostow & Bailey, 1969; Repp & Dietz, 1974) have found DRO in combination with other procedures such as time-out and punishment to be effective in reducing aggressive behaviors.

Penniston (1975) examined the effects of token and social reinforcement, time-out, and response cost on the physical and verbal aggressive behaviors of 14 severely and profoundly retarded, institutionalized adolescent and adult males. Tokens and praise were given for appropriate behaviors. Initially, the tokens could be immediately traded for edibles and other back-up reinforcers. Later, when tokens were traded for back-up reinforcers less often, response cost (token withdrawal) and time-out (removal from the group to an isolated room for a five-minute period) were introduced. Physically and verbally aggressive behaviors were reduced to a near zero level.

Williams (1959) reported the use of extinction in eliminating aggressive verbal behavior (screaming and crying tantrums) in a 21-month-old behaviorally handicapped child living at home. At bedtime the child exhibited tantrum behavior if an adult attempted to leave his room before he was asleep. The procedure involved removal of adult attention (leaving the room) when tantrum behavior was exhibited. All tantrum behavior was eliminated by the tenth session.

Aversive stimuli such as shock have been employed to decelerate the occurence of aggressive and violent behaviors. To do so, an aversive stimulus (or stimuli) has been made contingent upon the behavior to be reduced or eliminated (punishment). Ludwig, Marx, Hill, and Browning (1969), applying faradic shock, found that shock was effective in reducing aggressive violent behaviors. Other researchers (e.g., Lovaas, Schaeffer & Simmons, 1965) in similar experiments have had the same results. Although such intense forms of punishment are effective, the plausibility of administering electric shock in public school classrooms is questionable.

Foxx and Azrin (1972) used a restitution procedure to reduce the aggressive behaviors of three institutionalized profoundly handicapped female adults. The general rationale was to "educate the offender to assume individual responsibility for the disruption caused by her misbehavior by requiring her to restore the disturbed situation to a greatly improved state" (p. 16). One subject threw furniture. She was required to restore the furniture to its proper position and straighten all other furniture in the area. She also had to apologize to the individuals whose furniture she threw or turned over. The frequency of throwing furniture was reduced to a zero or near zero rate. Prior to employing restitution procedures, punishment, time-out and social approval had been employed to reduce the aggressive behaviors, but these procedures were ineffective.

Webster and Azrin (1973) also examined overcorrection procedures in regard to their effect on the aggressive behaviors of eight institutionalized adult retardates. The behaviors exhibited included screaming threats and physical aggression (hitting, pinching, etc.) against peers and staff. The procedure contingent upon the aggressive behaviors was relaxation where a resident had to put on his/her sleeping clothes and stay in bed for two hours, with no smoking, eating, playing, and listening to the radio. With the implementation of the relaxation overcorrection procedure there was a significant reduction of the aggressive acts. In addition, staff reacted to the procedure positively and were more comfortable with it than other procedures in the presence of visitors on the wards.

In a study by Azrin and Powers (1975) the efficacy of four procedures on the disruptive behaviors of six emotionally disturbed male children was explored: (1) verbal cueing; (2) verbal cueing and response cost; (3) verbal cueing, response cost, and delayed positive practice; and (4) verbal

Table 8–1
Procedures for Modifying Severe Maladaptive Behavior

Procedure	Process	Comments
Extinction	Withholding reinforcement where it was previously applied	A long process; can be dangerous if used with some behaviors, for example, head banging
Differential reinforcement of other behaviors (DRO)	Reinforcement of a desirable behavior that is incompatible with the undesirable behavior to be reduced	Generally more effective when used in combination with other procedures; major advantage that it builds positive behaviors while decreasing undesirable ones
Time-out	Placement into a isolated, nonreinforcing situation contingent upon an undesirable behavior	More effective when used in combination with other procedures, generally not effective with withdrawal behaviors and when used with SIBs could be potentially dangerous
Punishment	Making an aversive consequence contingent upon an undesirable behavior	Most efficient and effective means of reducing severe forms of maladaptive behavior; however, ethical and moral considerations limit its usefulness
Overcorrection	Two-part process to be used in combination or individually: (1) restitution—restore the situation disturbed by an inappropriate behavior to an improved state; and (2) positive practice—practice exhibiting a positive behavior that is incompatible with the inappropriate behavior exhibited	In some cases immediate reduction of behavior and enduring results; also positive practice element fosters the development of appropriate behavior

cueing, response cost, and immediate positive practice. These procedures were carried out in a public school classroom. Verbal cueing (warnings, reminders) alone was found to be ineffective, but verbal cueing in combination with response cost (loss of recess) was effective in reducing disruptive behaviors by 60 percent. These procedures, however, in combination with positive practice (practice asking for permission to speak or be out of seat) reduced disruptive behaviors to a near zero rate. Applying the positive practice procedure immediately was more effective than delaying application.

In Table 8–1 the reader will find a brief summary and evaluation of the procedures discussed in this section for modifying severe maladaptive behavior.

EVALUATION OF PROCEDURES

It is apparent that researchers have begun to examine in depth the efficacy of various applied behavior analysis procedures in dealing with severe maladaptive behaviors. It is now time to evaluate these procedures.

While successful in a few cases (Lovaas & Simmons, 1969; Williams, 1959), extinction appears to be one of the least effective procedures when compared with others for dealing with severe maladaptive behaviors (Corte, Wolfer, & Locke, 1971). It is a difficult procedure to use appropriately with some forms of behavior (Repp & Deitz, 1974). For withdrawn and self-stimulatory behaviors it is generally the individual engaging in the behavior that controls the contingencies, so effective withdrawal of reinforcement is very difficult if not impossible. For SIBs and aggressive behaviors extinction may not be a viable alternative due to the potential danger of the behavior to the individual and others. Extinction often initially increases the behavior and is a long process (Lovaas & Simmons, 1969).

Much research has indicated that DRO is effective in reducing the occurrence of severe forms of maladaptive behavior (Mulher & Baumeister, 1969; Weiher & Harman, 1975). DRO, however, generally has been most effective when combined with other procedures, such as time-out or punishment (Ausman, Ball, & Alexander, 1974; Bostow & Bailey, 1969; Frankel, Moss, Schofield, & Simmons, 1976; Repp & Deitz, 1974). An advantage of DRO is that it reduces inappropriate behaviors by means of building appropriate ones into the individual's repetoire. As Hamilton, Stephens and Allen (1967) noted, it is important to maintain and build the behavior repetoire of the subject rather than focus only on reducing inappropriate behaviors.

Researchers have found time-out to be an effective procedure for reducing severe forms of maladaptive behaviors (Hamilton, Stephens, & Allen, 1967; Lucero, Frieman, Spoering, & Fehrenbacker, 1976; Pendergrass, 1972). As with DRO, however, time-out has been most successful when used in combination with other procedures (Ausman, Ball, & Alexander, 1974; Bostow & Bailey, 1969). It should be noted that research has not been conducted on the use of time-out with individuals who display withdrawn behaviors. If a researcher or teacher made time-out contingent upon the exhibition of withdrawn behaviors, the individual who wanted to be alone could exhibit withdrawn behaviors and he would be allowed to continue to do so by the nature of the time-out arrangement. The individual, thus, would be negatively reinforced for displaying withdrawn behaviors. In other words, whenever the individual displayed withdrawn behaviors, he/she would be reinforced by the reduction or avoidance of interaction with others, which might be exactly what the withdrawn individual desires. Also, it should be noted that the use of time-out with individuals exhibiting SIBs could be dangerous since the SIBs may continue during the time-out period.

Punishment procedures have proven to be the most efficient and effective means of reducing severe forms of maladaptive behavior (Baumeister & Forehand, 1972; Bucher & Lovaas, 1968; Lovaas, Schaeffer, & Simmons, 1965; Lovaas & Simmons, 1969; Ludwig, Marx, Hill, & Browning, 1969; Tanner & Zeiler, 1975; Yound & Wincze, 1974). Unfortunately, an intense aversive delivered immediately is often needed (Lovaas & Simmons, 1969). Electric shock has been the most successful aversive stimulus used in rapidly decreasing maladaptive behavior. Despite the facts that shock, while painful, (1) is not physiologically or psychologically detrimental to an individual, if properly administered (Lovaas, 1965), and (2) results in rapid reduction of severe behaviors that are potentially dangerous; emotional reactions to the words "electric shock" and thoughts of inhumane treatment, real or otherwise, have brought forth frequent denouncements of electric shock. As a result, although it has been found to be safe since the intensity can be well controlled, its use in most cases is likely not to be allowed in the public school setting. Other aversives, such as smelling aromatic ammonia and loud noises, have been used and found to be effective (Tanner & Zeiler, 1975). It is difficult, however, to monitor the intensity of these punishers, and if used excessively, they could cause physical damage to the individual (destruction of skin tissue and mucuous membranes and hearing impairment, respectively). With punishment, generalization is often poor and needs to be programmed into the procedure (Corte, Wolf, & Locke, 1971; Lovaas, Koegel, Simmons, & Long, 1973; Lovaas & Simmons, 1969). (In the other procedures reviewed in this chapter the generalization effect appears to be unclear and highly individualized in regard to the variables involved). Also consideration must be given to the prevention of potential side effects of punishment (such as avoidance) and the development of a repetoire of appropriate behaviors on which reinforcement can be focused.

Overcorrection, the final procedure to be considered, involves a highly integrated combination of procedures working together to decrease the frequency of behavior. Although research on this technique is relatively recent, the findings tend to indicate that in at least some cases overcorrection results in immediate reduction of behavior and enduring results (Kelly & Drabman, 1977; Measel & Alfiere, 1976). Also, in the positive practice element of the overcorrection procedure the individual is taught correct forms of the behavior. Thus, the focus is not only on decreasing inappropriate behavior, but also on fostering appropriate behavior. In addition, psychologists and teachers tend to feel more comfortable using this technique than traditional punishment (Webster & Azrin, 1973). More information regarding generalization (Kissel & Whitman, 1977) and application in public schools by the educational staff (Newman, Whorton, & Simpson, 1977) is needed in regard to overcorrection; just as it is needed with all the other procedures discussed.

When reviewing the various applied behavior analysis procedures for dealing with severe forms of maladaptive behavior, several things, fairly generic to all of the procedures, become apparent. First, individuals with similar problems respond differently to the same procedure. For example, Corte and associates (1971) worked with two profoundly retarded institutionalized adolescents using food withdrawal as a punisher to reduce maladaptive behavior. The technique was highly effective with one subject and ineffective with the other. Measel and Alfiere (1976) had similar results with two partially sighted retarded subjects when using reinforcement of incompatible behavior plus overcorrection. Strain and his associates (1974, 1976, 1977) found modeling to be effective in increasing the social interactions of withdrawn subjects, but modeling was more effective with some than others. It was postulated that this was because the subjects possibly differed along one or more dimensions: (1) in environmental awareness to the degree that the behavior of the peer to be modeled could be recognized and comprehended, (2) in their generalized imitative repetoire so behavior could be modeled, and (3) in their history of reinforcement with the consequences received by the model.

Another factor that becomes apparent is the importance of natural conditioning (Tanner & Zeiler, 1975) for the generalization and maintenance of behavior change beyond the training setting. Unless deliberately programmed in, many effective procedures do not have a strong generalization effect outside the training setting (Corte, Wolf, & Locke, 1971; Kissel & Whitman, 1977).

These findings are consistent with our current knowledge of how people learn. As Haring (1979) pointed out, anyone who is familiar with basic behavioral principles would not expect learned behavior(s) to generalize and maintain in settings that are not at least somewhat similar to the training setting. To alleviate this problem, it will be necessary to apply the basic principles in various settings under different conditions.

For example, Ausman, Ball, and Alexander (1974) reduced maladaptive behavior in a training setting but had to program for the behavior change in various locations, time periods, during different activities, and with different people in order for the effects to generalize. Corte, Wolf, and Locke (1971) and Tanner and Zeiler (1975) also had to program in an extension from the training setting to natural settings. Prochaska and associates (1974) programmed for generalization during the initial training procedures. They employed a remote-control unit to administer consequences of behavior in all the natural situations (home, school, bus, etc.) To reduce maladaptive behaviors across settings and found this approach to be effective. In regard to maintenance of behavior changes, Lovaas, Koegel, Simmons, and Long (1973) found that posttreatment gains (1) continued and improved when parents were trained in behavior therapy techniques and (2) dissipated when they were not trained. Thus, it appears that the durability of improvements will be largely a function of the posttreatment environment. Generalization and maintenance of results in reducing severe forms of maladaptive behaviors is extremely important since such behaviors can be detrimental to the individual (and/or others around him) in all settings.

A final aspect frequently noted in the research is the effectiveness of using a combination of various procedures versus one procedure in isolation. A positive approach (focusing on building appropriate behaviors) is frequently combined with an aversive one (focusing on decreasing inappropriate behaviors). DRO plus mild punishment has been more effective than mild punishment alone in reducing maladaptive behaviors (Repp & Deitz, 1974; Repp, Deitz, & Speir, 1974). DRO plus time-out also has proven highly effective (Ausman, Ball, & Alexander, 1974). Overcorrection is itself a complex combination approach (Foxx & Azrin, 1972; Kelly & Drabman, 1977; Measel & Alfiere, 1976). Schroeder and his associates (1977) found the combination of three procedures (physical restraint, reinforcement for relaxation and biofeedback) to be more effective than physical restraint and reinforcement alone. In short, combination procedures have frequently been shown to be more effective than one isolated procedure when dealing with severe forms of maladaptive behavior.

According to Smolev (1971), it is sometimes not necessary deliberately to use a combination approach while at other times it is.

> Sometimes, once the deviant behavior is removed, the individual begins to make contact with potentially reinforcing aspect of the environment that were always available, which automatically reinforce beneficial modes of behavior. Thus, widespread changes may result even though alternative behaviors were never deliberately established. . . . Often it is necessary deliberately to establish alternative behaviors, either because alternative desirable behaviors are not present in the child's repetoire, or because they have not previously

been reinforced sufficiently to have a high enough probability of occurring. . . . (p. 303)

IMPLEMENTATION IN CLASSROOMS

Consequences of Behavior

Determining potentially effective reinforcers and punishers that can
be used in a classroom setting with individuals who exhibit extreme forms
of maladaptive behavior is important to the success that teachers will
have in applying the procedures discussed in this chapter. While no universally effective reinforcers and punishers are likely to be found,
teachers need some ideas in regard to what might be effective. If an individual, classified as being psychotic or profoundly retarded, will only respond to very strong aversive stimuli such as electric shock (Baumeister
& Forehand, 1972; Lovaas & Simmons, 1969; Prochaska et al., 1974; Tate
& Baroff, 1966; Young & Wincze, 1974), aromatic ammonia (Tanner &
Zeiler, 1975), or reinforcing stimuli such as food (under deprivation conditions) (Corte, Wolf, and Locke, 1971), the teacher may be in trouble.
Ethical and legal considerations are likely to deem such stimuli inappro-
priate for use in public school classrooms.

Unfortunately, some individuals who exhibit severe maladaptive behaviors do not respond to conventional reinforcers and punishers. This is
why electric shock has been used or why some children have been placed
in a state of deprivation for food (to make food an effective reinforcer).
Applied behavior analysis research has demonstrated that we can change
the behavior of almost anyone if we have control of the environment,
mainly through effective reinforcers and punishers, but many teachers do
not have control (use) of some of the reinforcers and punishers that have
been shown to change the behaviors of psychotic and/or profoundly retarded individuals.

As these children are placed in the mainstream of education, we (society) must decide which reinforcers and punishers can properly be administered by teachers in public school classrooms. Presently, if teachers
use electric shock, for example, they are likely to suffer a barrage of dire
consequences (punishers) from parents, administrators, peers, and students. The justification of the treatment, in the past, has been that some
psychotic and profoundly retarded individuals do not respond to more
conventional type stimuli and the pain from shock is insignificant when
compared to the damage that the individual may do to himself when less
effective stimuli are used and the maladaptive behaviors continue to occur. Will this justification suffice if electric shock is used in public school

classrooms? If teachers can not use highly intense stimuli such as electric shock, what type of punishers (and reinforcers) can they use and will these be effective?

Of course, it is possible that systematic and long-term application of learning theory and appropriate curricular content by qualified teachers, as well as normalization experiences, will reduce the severity of many maladaptive behaviors that we see today and thus the need for extreme punishers and reinforcers will be unnecessary. Also procedures such as overcorrection (Epstein et al., 1974; Foxx & Azrin, 1973; Webster & Azrin, 1973) and differential reinforcement of other behavior (Mulher & Baumeister, 1969; Weiher & Harmann, 1975) are receiving increased attention, and in the application of these procedures less intense types of reinforcers and punishers are being used. It should be noted that differential reinforcement of other behavior and overcorrection are ineffective in some cases (Measel & Alfiere, 1976; Young & Wincze, 1974). According to Foxx and Azrin (1973), some very severe forms of maladaptive behavior have been, to date, treated effectively *only* by severe pain shock.

Curriculum

Little research has been conducted to determine the effects of various curricular activities on the frequency of severe maladaptive behaviors. When reviewing research focused solely on consequent stimuli, it is not difficult to speculate that at least some of the behavior with which the researchers dealt could have been prevented in the first place. Let us take the study by Tanner and Zeiler (1975). It is possible that the behavior (slapping face) that these researchers changed would not have been occurring at such a high frequency if the subject of their study had been provided an opportunity and taught how to be involved in curricular activities. Unfortunately, the following quote from their study indicates the type of activities many autistic and/or profoundly retarded individuals engage in throughout the day. The researchers are describing the setting and indirectly the activities that their subject was engaged in when she displayed the inappropriate behavior.

> Observations were initially made in the day area where the unhelmeted subject occupied her usual chair in front of the television. However, at the request of the head nurse, we moved to an empty meeting room during baseline so that the subject's screaming and slapping would not disturb other patients. (Tanner & Zeiler, 1975, p. 54)

One must ask the question, How many "normal" individuals would display inappropriate behavior if their activities consisted of standing around in an empty meeting room or watching television all day every day from their usual chair?

From a research standpoint, it could be argued that curriculum being included in the study would have only been a confounding variable or would not have added anything in regard to investigating the effects of the particular consequent stimulus. The fact, however, that this environmental arrangement was what was provided for the individual on a daily basis, irrespective of the research being conducted, is what requires consideration and remediation.

Curricular activities play an important part in public school classrooms. They should be examined to determine what specific characteristics of curriculum most strongly influence the occurrence of maladaptive behaviors. For example, do maladaptive behaviors occur more frequently when an individual is engaged in group participation or independent work, in repetitive drill or active thinking, or work with immediate knowledge of results as opposed to delayed knowledge? When the classroom teacher is provided detailed information in regard to curriculum effects on severe forms of maladaptive behavior, he/she will be in a better position to control maladaptive behaviors.

Some research has been conducted that would tend to support the effect of curricular activities. Guess and Rutherford (1967) found that when subjects were engaged in the manipulation of objects and sound-generating apparatus, self-stimulatory behaviors were significantly reduced. Other researchers have obtained similar results (Berkson & Mason, 1963; Davenport & Berkson, 1963; Kauffman & Levitt, 1965). In light of these findings, more research is required to determine the characteristics or specific attributes of curricular materials and approaches that can be used to reduce severe forms of maladaptive behavior in classrooms.

Prevention

As public school education becomes a reality for the severely behaviorally handicapped, classroom teachers, particularly at the preschool level, will have an opportunity to help prevent maladaptive behaviors from developing in the first place.

To determine better preventive measures, the processes involved in the development of severe forms of maladaptive behavior require investigation. Based on theoretical models and research, professionals have begun to theorize in regard to the developmental process of severe forms of maladaptive behaviors. In regard to self-stimulatory behavior, Berkson (1967) and Lovaas (1967) relate it to a need inherent in organisms for a minimal level of stimulation.

Foxx and Azrin (1973) believe that autistic, inward-directed behaviors develop because they are reinforced by stimuli of a tactual, proprioceptive, and sensory nature. Such behaviors provide one of only a few ways autistic and retarded individuals can gain reinforcement due to their lack of making many outward-directed responses because of intellectual and emotional factors. These authors believe that a gross imbalance occurs in reinforcement for self-directed versus outward-directed behaviors.

Ferster (1961) explained the development of withdrawn behaviors as a result of a general deficiency of acquired reinforcers so impoverished behavioral development results. Frankel and Simmons (1976) provide a developmental analysis of self-injurious behaviors. When an unconditioned emotional respondent occurs that is intense enough to cause pain, it is likely to be reinforced by attention of persons nearby. After studying the development of self-injurious behavior, Lovaas, Freitag, Gold, and Kassorla (1965) concluded that such behavior is "a learned, operant or instrumental social behavior" (p. 67). Similarly, aggressive behaviors are thought to be learned operant or instrumental social behaviors.

Longitudinal observation studies will need to be conducted and careful records will need to be kept to verify the various ways in which maladaptive behaviors develop and gain response strength. Once we have a better grasp on such information, we can focus our attention on prevention methods. To enhance beneficial learning, it is the responsibility of educators to see that inappropriate behaviors are not learned only to be unlearned and subsequently replaced with appropriate behaviors. If teachers teach appropriate behaviors initially rather than inadvertently teach inappropriate behaviors, much learning time and effort can be conserved.

CONCLUSION

It is inhumane to allow an individual to continue to exhibit withdrawn, self-stimulatory, self-injurious, or aggressive behaviors. Such behaviors often result in pain and physical damage to the person exhibiting them and/or others. In addition, persons who display such behaviors are often deprived of environmental experiences and interactions required for growth.

Individuals who continue to exhibit self-stimulatory and withdrawal behaviors receive little (depending on the severity) input from the environment, thus learning is minimal. Also, muscular development may be inhibited if few physical movement activities are engaged in. Similarly, the continuous use of restraints on acting-out (SIB or aggressive) individuals as a solution is inhumane. Although restraints may reduce the exhibition of severe forms of maladaptive behavior, restraints block the opportunity of the individual's freedom to explore and can in some cases, cause physical degeneration (Geiger, Sindberg, & Barnes, 1974). For these and other reasons educators must develop a knowledge base and the skills necessary to deal with severe forms of maladaptive behavior.

REFERENCES

Ausman, J., Ball, T.S., & Alexander, D. Behavior therapy of pica with a profoundly retarded adolescent. *Mental Retardation,* 1974, *12,* 16–18.

Azrin, N.H., & Foxx, R.M. A rapid method of toilet training the institutionalized retarded. *Journal of Applied Behavior Analysis,* 1971, *4,* 89–99.

Azrin, N.H., Gottlieb, L., Hughart, L., et al. Eliminating self-injurious behavior by educative procedures. *Behaviour Research and Therapy,* 1975, *13,* 101–111.

Azrin, N.H., Kaplan, S.J., & Foxx, R.M. Autism reversal: Eliminating stereotyped self-stimulation of retarded individuals. *American Journal of Mental Deficiency,* 1973, *78,* 241–248.

Azrin, N.H., & Powers, M.A. Eliminating classroom disturbances of emotionally disturbed children by positive practice procedure. *Behavior Therapy,* 1975, *6,* 525–534.

Bachman, J.A. Self-injurious behavior: A behavioral analysis. *Journal of Abnormal Psychology,* 1972, *80,* 211–224.

Baumeister, A.A., & Baumeister A. Suppression of repetitive self-injurious behavior by contingent inhalation of aromatic ammonia. *Journal of Autism and Childhood Schizophrenia,* 1978, *8,* 71–77.

Baumeister, A.A. & Forehand, R. Effects of extinction of an instrumental response on stereotyped body rocking in severe retardates. *Psychological Record,* 1971, *21,* 235–240.

Baumeister, A.A., & Forehand, R. Effects of contingent shock and verbal command on body rocking of retardates. *Journal of Clinical Psychology,* 1972, *28,* 586–590.

Berkson, G. Abnormal stereotyped motor acts. In J. Zubin & H.F. Hunt (Eds.), *Comparative psychopathology—Animal and human.* New York: Grune & Stratton, 1967.

Berkson, G., & Mason, W.A. Stereotyped movements of mental defectives. III: Situation effects. *American Journal of Mental Deficiency,* 1963, *68,* 409–412.

Bostow, D.E., & Bailey, J.B. Modifications of severe disruptive and aggressive behavior using brief time-out and reinforcement procedures. *Journal of Applied Behavior Analysis,* 1969, *2,* 31–37.

Bucher, B., & Lovaas, O.I. Use of aversive stimulation in behavior modification. In M.R. Jones (Ed.), *Miami symposium on the prediction of behavior, 1967: Aversive stimulation.* Coral Gables, FA: University of Miami Press, 1968.

Burney, J., Russell, B., & Shores, R. Developing social responses in two profoundly retarded children. *AAESPH Review*, 1977, *2*, 53–60.

Corte, H.E., Wolf, M.M., & Locke, B.J. A comparison of procedures for eliminating self-injurious behavior of retarded adolescents. *Journal of Applied Behavior Analysis*, 1971, *4*, 201–213.

Davenport, R.K., & Berkson, G. Stereotyped movements of mental defectives.
II: Effects of novel objects. *American Journal of Mental Deficiency*, 1963,
67, 879–882.

Epstein, L.H., Doke, L.A., Sajwaj, T.E., et al. Generality and side effects of
overcorrection. *Journal of Applied Behavior Analysis*, 1974, *7*, 385–390.

Ferster, C.B. Positive reinforcement and behavioral deficits of autistic children.
Child Development, 1961, *32*, 437–456.

Foxx, R.M., & Azrin, N.H. Restitution: A method of eliminating aggressive-disruptive behavior of retarded and brain-damaged patients. *Behaviour Research and Therapy*, 1972, *10*, 15–27.

Foxx, R.M., & Azrin, N.H. The elimination of autistic self-stimulatory behavior
by overcorrection. *Journal of Applied Behavior Analysis*, 1973, *6*, 1–14.

Frankel, F., Moss, D., Schofield, S., & Simmons, J.Q. Case study: Use of differential reinforcement to suppress self-injurious and aggressive behavior. *Psychological Reports*, 1976, *39*, 843–849.

Frankel, F., & Simmons, J.Q. Self-injurious behavior in schizophrenic and
retarded children. *American Journal of Mental Deficiency*. 1976, *80*,
512–521.

Geiger, J.K., Sindberg, R.M., & Barnes, C.M. Head hitting in severely retarded
children. *American Journal of Nursing*, 1974, *74*, 1822–1825.

Gibson, F., Lawrence, P., & Nelson, R. Comparison of three training procedures
for teaching social responses to developmentally disabled adults. *American
Journal of Mental Deficiency*, 1977, *81*, 379–387.

Guess, D., & Rutherford, G. Experimental attempts to reduce stereotyping
among blind retardates. *American Journal of Mental Deficiency*, 1967, *71*,
984–986.

Hamilton, J., Stephens, L., & Allen, P. Controlling aggressive and destructive
behavior in severely retarded institutionalized residents. *American Journal
of Mental Deficiency*, 1967, *71*, 825–856.

Haring, N.G. Welcome address of the second annual AAESPH conference. In
N.G. Haring, & L.J. Brown, (Eds.), *Teaching the severely handicapped*.
New York: Grune & Stratton, 1977.

Kauffman, J.M. *Characteristics of children's behavior disorders*. Columbus, OH:
Merrill, 1977.

Kauffman, J.M., & Hallahan, D. Control of rough physical behavior using novel
contingencies and directive teaching. *Perceptual and Motor Skills*, 1973, *36*,
1225–1226.

Kaufman, M.E., & Levitt, H. A study of three stereotyped behaviors in institutionalized mental defectives. *American Journal of Mental Deficiency*, 1965,
69, 467–473.

Kelly, J.A., & Drabman, R.S. Generalizing response suppression of self-injurious
behavior through an overcorrection punishment procedure: A case study. *Behavior Therapy*, 1977, *8*, 468–472.

Kissel, R.C., & Whitman, T.L. An examination of the direct and generalized effects of a play-training and overcorrection procedure upon the self stimulatory behavior of a profoundly retarded boy. *AAESPH Review*, 1977, *2*, 131–146.

Keogel, R.L., & Covert, A. The relationship of self-stimulation to learning in autistic children. *Journal of Applied Behavior Analysis*, 1972, *5*, 381–387.

Koegel, R.L., Firestone, P.B., Kramme, K.W., & Dunlap, G. Increasing spontaneous play by suppressing self-stimulation in autistic children. *Journal of Applied Behavior Analysis*, 1974, *7*, 521–528.

Lamal, P.A. A simple technique for reducing self-stimulatory behavior of a retarded child. *Journal of Applied Behavior Analysis*, 1976, *9*, 140.

Lovaas, O.I. Behavior therapy approach to treatment of childhood schizophrenia. *Minnesota Symposium of Child Development*. Minneapolis: University of Minnesota Press, 1967.

Lovaas, O.I., Freitag, G., Gold, V.J., & Kassorla, I.C. Experimental studies in childhood schizophrenia: Analysis of self-destructive behavior. *Journal of Experimental Child Psychology*, 1965, *2*, 67–84.

Lovaas, O.I., Koegel, R., Simmons, J.Q., & Long, J.S. Some generalization and follow-up measures on autistic children in behavior therapy. *Journal of Applied Behavior Analysis*, 1973, *6*, 131–166.

Lovaas, O.I., Schaeffer, B., & Simmons, J.A. Experimental studies in childhood schizophrenia: Building social behaviors by use of electric shock. *Journal of Experimental Studies in Personality*, 1965, *1*, 99–109.

Lovaas, O.I., & Simmons, J.Q. Manipulation of self-destruction in three retarded children. *Journal of Applied Behavior Analysis*, 1969, *2*, 143–157.

Lucero, W.J., Frieman, J., Spoering, K., & Fehrenbacker, J. Comparison of three procedures in reducing self-injurious behavior, *American Journal of Mental Deficiency*, 1976, *80*, 548–553.

Ludwig, A.M., Marx, A.J., Hill, P.A., & Browning, R.M. The control of violent behavior through faradic shock. *Journal of Nervous Mental Disabilities*, 1969, *148*, 624–637.

Measel, C.J., & Alfiere, P.A. Treatment of self-injurious behavior by a combination of reinforcement for incompatible behavior and overcorrection. *American Journal of Mental Deficiency*, 1976, *81*, 147–153.

Mithang, D., & Hanawalt, D. Employing negative reinforcement to establish and transfer control of a severely retarded and aggressive nineteen-year-old girl. *AAESPH Review*, 1977, *2*, 37–49.

Morris, R.J., & Dolker, M. Developing cooperative play in socially withdrawn retarded children. *Mental Retardation*, 1974, *12*, 24–27.

Mulher, T., & Baumeister, A.A. An experimental attempt to reduce stereotypy by reinforcement procedures. *American Journal of Mental Deficiency*, 1969, *74*, 69–74.

Murphy, R., Nunes, D., & Ruprecht, M. Reduction of stereotyped behavior in profoundly retarded individuals. *American Journal of Mental Deficiency*, 1977, *82*, 238–245.

Myers, J., & Deibert, A. Reduction of self-abusive behavior in a blind child by using a feeding response. *Journal of Behavior Therapy and Experimental Psychiatry*, 1971, *2*, 141–144.

Newman, R., Whorton, D., & Simpson, R. The modification of self-stimulatory verbalizations in an autistic child through the use of overcorrection procedure. *AAESPH Review,* 1977, *2,* 157–163.

O'Connor, R.D., Relative efficacy of modeling, shaping, and the combined procedures for modification of social withdrawal. *Journal of Abnormal Psychology,* 1972, *79,* 327–334.

Pendergrass, V.E. Time-out from positive reinforcement following persistent, high-rate behavior in retardates. *Journal of Applied Behavior Analysis,* 1972, *5,* 85–91.

Peniston, E. Reducing problem behaviors in the severely and profoundly retarded. *Journal of Behavior Therapy and Experimental Psychiatry,* 1975, *6,* 295–299.

Prochaska, J., Smith, N., Marzilli, R., et al. Remote control of aversive stimulation in the treatment of head banging in a retarded child. *Journal of Behavior Therapy and Experimental Psychiatry,* 1974, *5,* 285–289.

Repp, A.C., & Deitz, S.M. Reducing aggressive and self-injurious behavior of institutionalized children through reinforcement of other behaviors. *Journal of Applied Behavior Analysis,* 1974, *7,* 313–325.

Repp, A.C., Deitz, S.M., & Speir, N.C. Reducing stereotypic responding of retarded persons by the differential reinforcement of other behavior. *American Journal of Mental Deficiency,* 1974, *79,* 279–284.

Risley, T.R. The effects and side effects of punishing the autistic behaviors of a deviant child. *Journal of Applied Behavior Analysis,* 1968, *1,* 21–34.

Saposnek, D.T., & Watson, L.S. The elimination of the self-destructive behavior of a psychotic child: A case study. *Behavior Therapy,* 1974, *5,* 79–89.

Schroeder, S.R., Peterson, C.R., Solomon, L.J., & Artley, J.J. EMG feedback and the contingent restraint of self-injurious behavior among the severely retarded: Two case illustrations. *Behavior Therapy,* 1977, *8,* 738–741.

Smolev, S.R. Use of operant techniques for the modification of self-injurious behavior. *American Journal of Mental Deficiency,* 1971, *76,* 295–305.

Strain, P.S., Shores, R.E., & Kerr, M.M. An experimental analysis of "spillover" effects on the social interaction of behaviorally handicapped preschool children. *Journal of Applied Behavior Analysis,* 1976, *9,* 31–40.

Strain, P.S., Shores, R.E., & Timm, M.A. Effects of peer social initiations on the behavior of withdrawn preschool children. *Journal of Applied Behavior Analysis,* 1977, *10,* 289–298.

Strain, P.S., & Timm, M.A. An experimental analysis of social interaction between a behaviorally disordered preschool child and her classroom peers. *Journal of Applied Behavior Analysis,* 1974, *7,* 583–590.

Tanner, B.A., & Zeiler, M. Punishment of self-injurious behavior using aromatic ammonia as the aversive stimulus. *Journal of Applied Behavior Analysis,* 1975, *8,* 53–57.

Tate, B.G., & Baroff, G.S. Aversive control of self-injurious behavior in a psychotic boy. *Behaviour Research and Therapy,* 1966, *4,* 281–287.

Ward, E.M. *Overcorrection: A component analysis of its effects on inappropriate and appropriate behavior among retarded children and adults.* Paper presented at Midwestern Association of Behavior Analysis, Chicago, May, 1976.

Webster, D.R., & Azrin, N.H. Required relaxation: A method of inhibiting agitative-disruptive behavior of retardates. *Behaviour Research and Therapy,* 1973, *11,* 67–78.

Wehman, P., Karan, O., & Rettie, C. Developing independent play in three severely retarded women. *Psychological Reports,* 1976, *39,* 995–998.

Weiher, R.G., & Harman, R.E. The use of omission training to reduce self-injurious behavior in a retarded child. *Behavior Therapy,* 1975, *6,* 261–268.

Whitman, T.L., Mercurio, J.R., & Caponigri, V. Development of social responses in two severely retarded children. *Journal of Applied Behavior Analysis,* 1970, *3,* 133–138.

Williams, C.D. The elimination of tantrum behavior by extinction procedures. *Journal of Abnormal and Social Psychology,* 1959, *59,* 269.

Wolf, M., Risley, T., & Mees, H. Application of operant conditioning procedures to the behavior problems of an autistic child. *Behaviour Research and Therapy,* 1964, *1,* 305–312.

Young, J.A., & Wincze, J.P. The effects of the reinforcement of compatible and incompatible alternative behaviors on the self-injurious and related behaviors of a profoundly retarded female adult, *Behavior Therapy,* 1974, *5,* 614–623.

SELECTED READINGS FOR FURTHER STUDY

Bachman, A.J. Self-injurious behavior: A behavioral analysis. *Journal of Abnormal Psychology,* 1972, *80,* 211–224.

Smolev, R.S. Use of operant techniques for the modification of self-injurious behavior. *American Journal of Mental Deficiency,* 1971, *76,* 295–305.

Strain, S.P. & Trimm, A.M. An experimental analysis of social interaction between a behaviorally disordered preschool child and her classroom peers. *Journal of Applied Behavior Analysis,* 1974, *7,* 583–590.

Sulzer, B. & Mayer G. *Applying Behavior-Analysis Procedures with Children and Youth.* New York: Holt, Rinehart & Winston, 1977.

PART III

The two chapters in Part III present empirical evidence related to the feasibility of educating within a classroom setting children labeled as being seriously disturbed. Both chapters provide strong supportive evidence for the educational programs and procedures advocated in this book. In Chapter 9 the researchers, Dennis Russo and Robert Koegel, studied the use of behavioral techniques to integrate an autistic child into a normal public school classroom with a single teacher and 20 or more normal children. In Chapter 10 the researchers, Andrew Meyers and Edward Craighead investigated educating within a classroom setting children who had been given various labels such as childhood schizophrenia, idiopathic psychomotor retardation, and autism. In both studies, the researchers employed extensive data collection procedures along with single-subject research designs.

Dennis C. Russo, Ph.D.

Children's Medical Center and
Harvard Medical School
Boston, Massachusetts

Robert L. Koegel, Ph.D.

University of California
Santa Barbara, California

9

A Method for Integrating an Autistic Child into a Normal Public School Classroom

In the past reviews of the literature on autism have discussed, as a central weakness in remediation of the disorder, the lack of available and effective classroom education programs and the almost total exclusion of the autistic child from public school programs (Brown, 1963; Lovaas & Koegel, 1973; Lovaas, Schreibman, & Koegel, 1974; Rutter, 1971). Recently, however, significant strides have been made toward providing effective educational opportunities for these children. Increased public awareness and interest in autism, legal actions filed on behalf of the autistic child and the right to an education, and recent research on the development of an educational technology specifically for teaching autistic children have resulted in many classrooms being established and new curricula devised.

The research on placing the autistic child in the "mainstream" of the educational environment has thus far fallen into two general categories: (1) the one-to-one teaching situation and (2) the formation of special education classes solely for groups of autistic children.

The one-to-one teaching situation, as documented in the literature, has been extremely productive in developing skills in autistic children. For example, programs for teaching conversational speech (Hewett, 1965; Lovaas, 1966; Risley & Wolf, 1967), generalized imitation (Lovaas, Freitas, Nelson, & Whalen, 1967; Metz, 1965), and appropriate play

This chapter is reprinted from an article by the same title that appeared in the *Journal of Applied Behavior Analysis*, 1977, *10*, 579–590. Reprinted with permission.

(Koegel, Firestone, Kramme, & Dunlap, 1974), as well as the control of inappropriate behaviors (Koegel & Covert, 1972; Wolf, Risley, & Mees, 1964) have been utilized for some time. Further, Koegel, Russo, and Rincover (1977) have developed procedures that are empirically effective in training teachers to work with autistic children in such one-to-one situations. While, undeniably, one-to-one therapy procedures are important in the remediation of problem behaviors and the teaching of new adaptive behaviors, the major problem with implementing such an approach in a public school system has been that of cost.

The second line of research, focusing on the development of special classes for autistic children, has attempted to increase the number of children with whom a given teacher can work. In recent years several investigators have suggested guidelines for such classes (Elgar, 1966; Halpern, 1970; Hamblin, Buckholdt, Ferritor, et al, 1971; Harper, 1969; Martin, England, Kaprowy, et al, 1968; Rabb & Hewett, 1967). Further, Koegel and Rincover (1974) reported systematic data showing that it is possible gradually to increase the size of such classes to at least eight children per teacher.

While such classes have been effective and are becoming more widely available, they still present a potential problem, in that in most cases they are composed solely of autistic children. Thus, such classes may provide merely another form of exclusion. By placing every autistic child in a classroom made up entirely of autistic children, we may deprive those children of several possible benefits, including the influence of appropriate role models and the exposure to a "nonautistic" curriculum taught in regular classrooms.

As a third alternative, the present study systematically investigated the feasibility of integrating an autistic child into a normal public-school classroom.

METHOD

Subject

A five-year-old girl, who had received a primary diagnosis of autism from an agency not associated with this study, served as the subject. She evidenced a relative lack of appropriate verbal behavior, rarely initiating verbal interactions with the teacher or the other children in her public school kindergarten class and generally failing to respond to the questions or commands of others. When she did engage in speech, it was generally out of context with her activity or characterized by pronoun reversal. For instance, when asking for a drink of water, she would say, "You want a drink of water."

The child's classroom behavior consisted of a small repertoire of generally inappropriate actions. She would often stand up in the middle of a work period and walk about the room twirling a large feather, a flower, or a handkerchief that she persistently carried with her. When she did interact with the teacher, she would ask, repetitively and without regard to classroom activities, to get either a drink of water or a tissue. If these requests were not met, a tantrum ensued, with screaming and physical withdrawal from the other people in the room.

In general, the child remained aloof, rarely interacting with anyone. Her behavioral repertoire consisted primarily of bizarre autistic mannerisms and stereotyped behaviors. She engaged in frequent repetitive finger manipulations in front of her eyes and rhythmic manipulations of the objects she carried. She would also frequently masturbate in class.

The baseline data reported below give a more empirical measurement of the child's pretreatment behavior.

Although the child's verbal and social behaviors were minimal, the fact that such behaviors were evidenced at all by an autistic child, suggested to us that she would show relatively good response to treatment. Nevertheless, because of her relative lack of appropriate behavior and relative abundance of inappropriate autistic mannerisms, school officials had made the decision that typifies the fate of autistic children: to exclude her from the school system. The child was, however, allowed to remain in school for the course of this investigation.

Settings

The entire investigation was conducted in the kindergarten and first-grade classrooms of an elementary school in Santa Barbara, California. In addition to the child and the therapist, present in both classrooms were an observer to record data, a teacher, a teacher's aide, and 20 to 30 normal children. The children attended school from 9:00 A.M. to 2:30 P.M., five days a week. Each classroom was equipped with tables and chairs, and a rug on which all of the children sat during story and discussion times. The rooms, each 9.1 by 9.1 m, contained toys, blocks, and other usual materials.

Design and Definitions

A multiple-baseline design across behaviors was employed to assess the effects of treatment by the therapist on the behavior of the child in each classroom. Implementation of the treatment program by the classroom teachers was instituted siimultaneously across behaviors. A brief reversal on social behavior was also instituted to assess the maintenance of treatment gains by the untrained kindergarten teacher.

Three target behaviors were selected on the basis of the following criteria: (1) that school officials demanded the behaviors be modified if the child was to remain in school and (2) that they were characteristic deficits of autistic children. The definitions and instructions used by the observers for recording target behaviors are listed below.

SOCIAL BEHAVIOR

Any response involving direct interaction with another person. The major criterion for including a response in this category was that the behavior would not be occurring if another person were not present. Examples of the behavior were saying hello to another student borrowing a toy from a child, sharing candy, and so forth. Social behavior was measured by frequency of occurrence during the session, with each instance recorded by a check on the data sheet.

SELF-STIMULATION

Any stereotyped movement, for example, rocking, repetitive finger movements, rhythmic manipulation of objects (feather, flower, handkerchief, etc.), and gazing at objects such as pencils or lights. Much of the child's self-stimulatory behavior was of a subtle nature, such as repetitive finger movements in the lap, and persistent, repetitive scratching and pulling of socks and other clothing. This behavior was measured by duration: every time an incidence of self-stimulation was observed, the observer started a stopwatch and allowed it to run until the offset of the behavior. Seconds of self-stimulation were kept cumulatively for each observation session and divided by the total session time to obtain the percentage of session time occupied by self-stimulatory behavior.

VERBAL RESPONSE TO COMMAND

Any appropriate verbal response to a verbal stimulus presented by the teacher or therapist. A verbal stimulus was any statement (e.g., "What color is this?") that required a verbal response from the child. This stimulus may have been directed to the child individually, or toward the entire class, requiring a group response. An appropriate verbal response was any verbal statement made within five seconds of the verbal stimulus that provided the type of response requested (e.g., the name of a color, "I don't know"), whether correct or incorrect. Each verbal stimulus, the response or lack of response, and whether or not the response was appropriate were recorded on the data sheet. This behavior was measured by the percentage of verbal stimuli responded to appropriately in each session.

Observation and Measurement

All observers had previous training in the general observation and recording of behavior and had successfully completed one under graduate course in the area of autism. Before observation in the classroom observers were taught the definitions and scoring procedures as well as the procedures for and the importance of unobtrusive observation. None of the observers was informed of the purpose of the study.

Measures were recorded in three 4-minute time samples per session, each separated by 9 minutes of no recording, giving a total measurement time of 12 minutes per session. Two measurement sessions were conducted each week throughout all conditions. Measurement sessions began at 9:30 A.M. All three target behaviors were recorded simultaneously during each session. Observers indicated each occurrence of social behavior, kept a cumulative record of self-stimulation of the stopwatch, and recorded each verbal stimulus and the child's response during each 4-minute sample.

EXPERIMENT I

The procedure for evaluating the child's behaviors, therapist treatment, and transfer of the program to the kindergarten teacher is presented below.

Baseline

Measurements were taken of the child's behavior in the kindergarten classroom with 20 to 30 other children present, before any intervention. The teacher was instructed to continue regular classroom activities. No attempt was made to manipulate reinforcement contingencies. At the start of this condition the therapist was introduced to the class as another teacher who would be visiting often in the future. During the class period the therapist sat next to the child in the last row of children, to habituate both the child and the rest of the class to his presence, but he interacted with neither the child nor her classmates.

Treatment by the Therapist

In order to dispense rewards easily and unobtrusively within the classroom, it was decided to employ a token economy (Kazdin & Bootzin, 1972; O'Leary & Drabman, 1971). The child received three one-hour pretraining sessions to establish tokens as reinforcers. These sessions were conducted after school during the third week of the baseline condition, in a small room (1.8 by 2.4 m) at the University of California, Santa Barbara. During the sessions the child was intermittently handed a white poker chip and prompted to exchange it for a food reward (one piece of candy, one potato chip, etc.) Token deliveries were not contingent on any specific behavior by the child. When she began to trade tokens for food without prompting, and saved at least three tokens for ten minutes the token program was implemented in the classroom during subsequent treatment conditions.

Treatment of social behavior in the classroom was begun in Week 4. Each occurrence of social behavior by the child during a session was followed by the presentation of a token and appropriate verbal feedback (e.g., "Good girl!") by the therapist. As in the previous condition, the therapist sat quietly next to the child and interacted with her only when social behaviors occurred. One-hour treatment sessions were carried out twice a week, beginning at 9:20 A.M., while the teacher continued to conduct the class according to her regular procedures. During the session the child saved tokens in a cellophane bag attached to her dress. After the session she was able to redeem her tokens at the "store," a small area at the rear of the classroom. After three weeks of treatment of social behavior by the therapist, the baseline condition was reinstated during Weeks 7 to 9, and treatment by the therapist was begun again in Week 10. This reversal was used to assess the effects of therapist treatment on social behavior.

Treatment of self-stimulation was begun in Week 10, concurrently with the second treatment of social behavior. During this condition each occurrence of self-stimulatory behavior was followed by the removal of tokens and an abrupt verbal statement, "No." The absence of self-stimulatory behavior for progressively longer intervals produced the contingent presentation of a token and the verbal statement, "Good sitting." In the early stages of treatment a prompting procedure was used to control self-stimulation. The therapist restrained the child from this behavior by placing his hands on the child's when she began to self-stimulate. The restraint was then faded gradually, and longer and longer periods (ultimately about 15 minutes) of no self-stimulatory behavior were shaped. The close physical proximity of the therapist, the use of a systematic shaping program, and the position of the child and therapist in the back of the room allowed the procedure to be conducted with a minimum of disruption to the class.

Beginning with Week 13, treatment was begun on verbal response to command. The therapist awarded the child a token every time she answered a question requiring a verbal response, whether the question was directed specifically toward her or toward the class as a whole, and regardless of whether the response was correct or incorrect. At first, the therapist prompted the child with the command, "Answer the question!" If she did not respond within 5 seconds she was prompted with the correct response and rewarded for repeating it. The prompt was then faded by increasing the interval between the teacher's verbal statement and the therapist's prompt. While initially the procedure required 15 to 20 seconds to produce a response, the necessity of waiting for a response or prompting it was a common occurrence among the other pupils in the class.

Training of the Teacher by the Therapist

The teacher was trained during Weeks 14 and 15, while regular morning measurement and treatment sessions by the therapist were continued. The teacher-training procedure included several components (general instruction, practice, and feedback) reported by Koegel, Russo, and Rincover (1977) as effective in training teachers in generalized behavior modification skills with autistic children. These components, demonstrated effective in one-to-one teaching situations, were adapted for use in the public school classroom in the present study. Training of the teacher involved four steps:

1 The teacher received general training in behavioral techniques. The following materials were used to acquaint the teacher with the behavioral approach, define terms, and present behavior-change strategies: *Teaching*/Discipline (Madsen & Madsen, 1970); *Parents Are Teachers* (Becker, 1971); and Volumes 1, 2, and 3 of the *Managing Behavior* series (Hall, 1971). Three one-hour sessions were required for the teacher and therapist to discuss the materials and review test questions.
2 The therapist discussed with the teacher the operational definitions and specific contingencies operative on the child. During two one-hour sessions the therapist and teacher discussed each of the definitions, the teacher was asked to describe examples of the child's behavior, and the therapist provided feedback and questions. At this time the teacher also received a complete explanation of the token economy.
3 With the therapist present, the teacher identified occurrences of the child's target behaviors. While an aide ran the class, the child was observed during three one-hour afternoon periods of free play and story time. When the teacher observed one of the target behaviors, she explained the behavior, how it fit the definition, and the applicable

token administration procedure. The therapist provided feedback and pointed out instances of target behaviors that the teacher had missed.

4 The teacher, under the therapist's supervision, began administering social reinforcement. During three additional afternoon periods the teacher provided verbal praise to the child for social behavior, quiet sitting, and verbal responding.

During Week 14, concurrent with the training of the teacher, the therapist began systematically to reduce the density of token reinforcement. From an initial rate of one token given for every occurrence of appropriate behavior, as defined, and the removal of one token for each instance of self-stimulation, the therapist began giving tokens on an intermittent basis. Social reinforcement (e.g., "Good girl") and saying "No" contingent on self-stimulation were continued at each occurrence of the target behaviors. As the fading of tokens continued, the therapist maintained behaviors by social reinforcement, while providing tokens for intervals of appropriate behavior (e.g., sitting quietly for 10 minutes, playing for several minutes with another child, responding appropriately to questions during a class activity).

During Week 15, under the therapist's direction, the teacher began to provide social reinforcement and tokens for appropriate behavior and to remove tokens contingent on self-stimulation. The child was moved to the front of the classroom to facilitate these interactions, with the therapist initially remaining close to her. The therapist was present at least four days each week during the fading of tokens and transfer of the program to the teacher (Weeks 14 and 15) to ensure a smooth transition. By putting the aide in charge of the class during parts of the school day, the teacher was able to spend more time with the child during the transfer. The therapist provided feedback to the teacher during each break in school activities.

Treatment by the Trained Kindergarten Teacher Without the Therapist's Assistance

Beginning with Week 16, the teacher totally took over treatment, carrying out the token program throughout the school day. The teacher was told to remain in close proximity to the child and to provide frequent, specific social feedback, with periodic tokens during breaks (about every 30 to 45 minutes). Instances of self-stimulation continued to be "consequated" by the immediate removal of tokens. On a sheet she kept with her, the teacher was asked to note why she had given tokens and the times at which they were administered. She reviewed this information with the therapist each day, either in person or by telephone. While maintaining control of the child's behavior with social feedback, the teacher increased the response requirement for tokens over a 14-day period by lengthening the time between token presentations. Eventually, the teacher was able to dispense tokens twice a day (once before lunch and once before the day ended) with a brief explanation to the child as to why she was receiving them. Verbal feedback, however, continued to be presented immediately after appropriate behaviors.

Observations during this condition were made twice each week on selected weeks, in the manner previously described. The therapist continued to visit the classroom at least twice a week during the first five weeks and once a week during the remaining five weeks.

Reliability

Over the course of the experiment, 135 reliability measures were obtained. At least two reliability sessions occurred in each condition for each of the three target behaviors. In each reliability session, observations were made independently by two observers during three four-minute blocks spaced nine minutes apart. Observers were said to be reliable if agreement on each behavior recorded within a given four-minute block was 80 percent or better. Reliability was calculated by dividing the lower number of units (occurrences or seconds) recorded for a particular behavior by the higher number of units recorded for the behavior, and multiplying the quotient by 100. Forty-four of the 45 measures for social behavior were above 80 percent (mean reliability $\rightleftarrows$ 89.2 percent per session; range $\rightleftarrows$ 67 percent to 100 percent). All of the reliability measures for self-stimulation were above 80 percent (mean $\rightleftarrows$ 92.1 percent; range $\rightleftarrows$ 85 percent to 99 percent), as were those for verbal response to command (mean $\rightleftarrows$ 93.2 percent; range $\rightleftarrows$ 83 percent to 100 percent.)

Results

Figure 9–1 shows the results of Experiment I across conditions for each of the three behaviors measured in the kindergarten classroom. The data reveal changes in the child's classroom behavior on all measures. First, consider the child's social behavior. During the three weeks of baseline she consistently emitted fewer than four social behaviors per session. When the therapist introduced token reinforcement in Week 4, the child's social behaviors immediately increased with a mean of 11.5 recorded during Week 6. Beginning with Week 7, a brief reversal (Baseline 2) was instituted to assess the reinforcing effects of the tokens. The child's rate of social behavior dropped to 5.5. per week in Week 7, and remained consistently below the treatment rate during the three weeks of this condition. In Week 10, when the therapist reinstituted token rein-

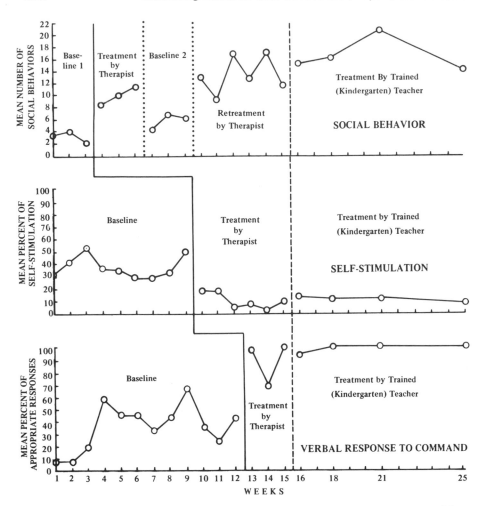

Fig. 9–1.   Social behavior, self-stimulation, and verbal response to command in the normal kindergarten classroom during baseline, treatment by the therapist, and treatment by the trained kindergarten teacher. All three behaviors were measured simultaneously.

forcement (Retreatment), the child's social behaviors again increased, reaching an average of 13 per session, and a high of 17.5 in Week 14. Measurements of the child's behavior in the Trained Teacher condition occurred in Weeks 16 to 25. Throughout the ten weeks of this condition the child's rate of social behavior remained as high as or higher than during treatment by the therapist.

The child's self-stimulatory behavior was measured during the same period. The occurrence of self-stimulation ranged from 27 percent to 54 percent during the nine weeks of baseline. It decreased to 19 percent during the first session of treatment by the therapist (Week 10) and continued to decrease to a low of 3 percent during Week 14. During the Treatment by the Trained Teacher condition the child's rate of self-stimulatory behavior was maintained at a level similar to that achieved during the Treatment by the Therapist condition (range $\rightleftarrows$ 8 percent to 14 percent).

The child's verbal response to command also showed systematic improvement. During baseline appropriate verbal responses showed great variability, ranging from 8 percent to 68 percent, with a mean of 35 percent appropriate responses per session. Beginning with the first session of treatment by the therapist, in Week 13, the child's percentage of appropriate verbal responses rose to 97 percent and ranged between 68 percent and 100 percent during the three weeks of treatment. A steady high rate of appropriate responses was maintained during the Treatment by the Trained Teacher condition. The child's rate of appropriate verbal responses was low during baseline, improved during treatment by the therapist, and reached a consistent level of 100 percent for the final eight weeks of treatment by the trained teacher.

EXPERIMENT II: FOLLOW-UP

On the kindergarten teacher's recommendation, the child was graduated at the end of the term to the first grade and a new teacher. During the first week of the new term, however, the school reported that the child's classroom behavior was again unmanageable and requested additional treatment for her. In order to ascertain whether the changes induced in the kindergarten classroom had, in fact, not been maintained after the summer vacation and the introduction of a new teacher and class, measures were again taken on the three target behaviors. Definitions of target behaviors, design of the investigation (with the exception of a reversal on social behavior), and recording and observation procedures were identical to those described previously.

Baseline in the First Grade

This condition was procedurally identical to the Baseline 1 condition in Experiment I. Measurements of the child's classroom behavior were begun during the second week of the first-grade term.

Retreatment by the Therapist

Retreatment of social behavior by the therapist was begun in Week 40 (as measured from the start of Experiment I). The procedures utilized were identical to those described in Experiment I, except for the fact that no token pretraining was given.

Treatment of self-stimulation, begun in Week 43, was conducted concurrently with treatment of social behavior. The procedures for treatment of self-stimulation were the same as those described in Experiment I.

A high, steady rate of appropriate verbal responses was observed between Weeks 37 and 46. Since this percentage was within the range of responses achieved during treatment of this behavior in Experiment I, no further treatment of verbal response to command was undertaken.

Training of the Teacher by the Therapist

The first-grade teacher was trained under the same procedure as the kindergarten teacher. During Week 46 she was trained to recognize the ,occurrences of the target behaviors in the classroom, to present and remove tokens, and to provide social feedback.

Treatment by the Trained First-Grade Teacher Without the Therapist's Assistance

Beginning in Week 47, the first-grade teacher took over treatment. Since treatment by the therapist in Experiment II involved reestablishing previously functional contingencies, the first-grade teacher took over on the final contingencies, using social reinforcement to provide immediate feedback to the child and dispensing tokens twice daily (before lunch and at the end of the school day). Otherwise, procedures were identical to those of Experiment I.

Reliability

At least two reliability sessions were held in each condition. Reliability, calculated as before, was over 80 percent for each category.

Results

Data on treatment during the child's first-grade year are presented in Figure 9–2. Baseline measures indicated that the child's social behaviors had decreased and her rate of self-stimulation had increased since treatment in kindergarten. Verbal response to command, however, had remained stable at previous treatment levels.

Retreatment by the therapist on social behavior and self-stimulation, using previously established contingencies, was sufficient to restore improved levels of the behaviors. Social behavior increased to over 12 re-

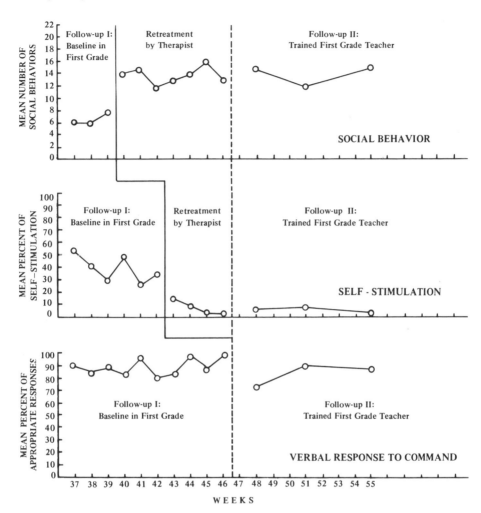

Fig. 9–2. Follow-up data in the normal first-grade classroom during baseline, retreatment by the therapist on social behavior and self-stimulation, and treatment by the trained first-grade teacher. All three behaviors were measured simultaneously.

sponses per session, and self-stimulation decreased to 3 percent by Week 46.

The child was monitored for ten weeks after the training of the first-grade teacher (Weeks 47 to 55). Her behaviors were maintained in the same range as during the Retreatment by the Therapist condition, with social behavior ranging between 12 and 16 responses per session and self-stimulation remaining below 10 percent.

DISCUSSION

The present results may be summarized as follows: First, the child showed considerable improvement in classroom performance for each of three behaviors treated. Her final performance on each of these behaviors was more than adequate, as judged by school officials, to ensure her continuation in the public schools. Second, training the kindergarten teacher in behavior modification techniques seemed sufficient to enable her to maintain all of the treatment behaviors over a ten-week formal measurement period, which was the remainder of the academic year. The concreteness of the token procedure, coupled with the increased response requirement for obtaining a token, appeared to provide a means for maintaining strong behavioral control without constant teacher attention. Third, recurrence of problems with two of the target behaviors at the onset of the first-grade year was rapidly remediated by the therapist and maintained after the training of the first-grade teacher. No further problems were reported by the school through the remainder of that year, nor during the child's second- and third-grade years when she had different teachers.

It may be important to note that the behavior change induced by the therapist was maintained after the training of the teachers. The brief return to baseline in Experiment I and the lack of maintenance of two target behaviors that necessitated retreatment in the first-grade classroom lend additional support to the notion that training facilitated maintenance. The introduction of the therapist in a one-to-one situation within the broader context of the classroom allowed for intensive treatment to bring the child's autistic behaviors under control. After such control was established and the teacher was trained, the child's behavior was maintained with little disruption to the classroom routine.

One study has shed some light on the importance of the development of maintenance environments to the long-term success of behavior modification with autistic children. Lovaas, Koegel, Simmons, and Long (1973) provided extensive follow-up data that show that when autistic children are discharged from a behavior modification treatment program, their continued improvement is to a large extent a function of the post-treatment environment. Children who were discharged to state hospitals regressed. Children who were discharged to their parents' care (after the parents received some training in basic principles of behavior modification) continued to improve. The present results imply that training classroom teachers contributed to the maintenance of treatment behaviors. This is particularly true because two of the three behaviors deteriorated when the child entered first grade with a new teacher. It is also possible, however, that the thin partial-reinforcement schedule used during the fi-

Table 9–1

Characteristics and placements of four additional autistic children placed in normal classrooms. Procedures used were similar to those described in the study.

Child	Pre-treatment	Age at Placement	Verbal Behavior at Placement	Placement	Curriculum Level	Duration of Placement
1	1 yr	5 yr	Some conversational speech (3- to 5-yr level)	Kindergarten	Same	1 yr
2	2 yr	10 yr	Able to express simple one sentence demands— e.g., "I want candy," or "I want bathroom."	Fifth grade	First-second Grade	1 yr
3	2 yr	6 yr	Some conversational speech (3- to 5-yr level)	Kindergarten	Same	1 yr
4	2 yr	6 yr	Able to express simple one-sentence deamnds— e.g., "I want outside," or "I want candy."	Kindergarten	Same	1 yr

nal stages of treatment may have contributed to the maintenance results (cf. Koegel & Rincover, 1977). Research on variables contributing to treatment durability is still in its infancy, and continued research in this area will undoubtedly prove very important.

Generality of Results

Autistic children have previously been excluded from public school programs or in some cases are given only the option of a "special" autism class. The significance of this study lies in its suggestion that school teachers can easily learn to teach at least some autistic children in regular classrooms. Although much research is still necessary, we expect that a fairly large number of autistic children may be able to benefit from the treatment described here.

Using the procedures outlined in the present paper, four additional autistic children have been placed in normal public school classes. Table 9-1 describes the characteristics and placements of these children. All were fairly advanced, in that they had some minimal social and verbal behavior at the time of their placements. In each case the abilities of the particular child were matched to those of the class, and deficits remediated with one-to-one training in the classroom before the program was transferred to the teacher. Each of the four children was given extensive pretreatment, using the procedures described by Koegel and Rincover (1974) and Rincover and Koegel (1977), before placement was attemtped. Therefore, this study suggests that, in addition to higher-level autistic children, some lower-level autistic children trained in a class composed solely of autistic children, might upon "graduation" (achievement of a minimal appropriate behavioral repertoire) be placed in a normal classroom among children who provide more appropriate role models. A study of the conditions and child characteristics resulting in successful placements may prove to be both interesting and beneficial for the future education of autistic children.

REFERENCES

Becker, W.C. *Parents are teachers*. Champaign, IL: Research Press, 1971.
Brown, J.L. Follow-up of children with atypical development (infantile psychosis). *American Journal of Orthopsychiatry, 1963, 33*, 855–861.
Elgar, S. The autistic child. *The Slow Learning Child, 1966, 13*, 91–102.
Hall, R.V. *Managing behavior*, (Vols. 1, 2, 3). Lawrence KA: H. & H. Publishing, 1971.
Halpern, W.I. The schooling of autistic children: Preliminary findings. *American Journal of Orthopsychiatry, 1970, 40*, 665–671.

Hamblin, R.L., Buckholdt, D., Ferritor, D., et al, *The humanization process.* New York: Wiley, 1971.

Harper, J. Establishment of an educational programme for a group of autistic children. *The Slow Learning Child,* 1969, *16,* 3–14.

Hewett, F.M. Teaching speech to an autistic child through operant conditioning. *American Journal of Orthopsychiatry,* 1965, *35,* 927–936.

Kazdin, A.E., Bootzin, R.R. The token economy: an evaluative review. *Journal of Applied Behavior Analysis,* 1972, *5,* 343–372.

Koegel, R.L., Covert, A. The relationship of self-stimulation to learning in autistic children. *Journal of Applied Behavior Analysis,* 1972, *5,* 381–387.

Koegel, R.L., Firestone, P.B., Kramme, K.W., & Dunlap, G. Increasing spontaneous play by suppressing self-stimulation in autistic children. *Journal of Applied Behavior Analysis,* 1974, *7,* 521–528.

Koegel, R.L., & Rincover, A. Treatment of psychotic children in a classroom environment: I. Learning in a large group. *Journal of Applied Behavior Analysis,* 1974, *7,* 49–59.

Koegel, R.L. Rincover, A. Research on the difference between generalization and maintenance in extra-therapy responding. *Journal of Applied Behavior Analysis,* 1977, *10,* 1–12.

Koegel, R.L., Russo, D.C., & Rincover, A. Assessing and training teachers in the generalized use of behavior modification with autistic children. *Journal of Applied Behavior Analysis,* 1977, *10,* 197–205.

Lovaas, O.I. A program for the establishment of speech in autistic children. In J. Wing (Ed), *Early childhood autism.* Elmsford, NY: Pergamon, 1966.

Lovaas, O.I., Freitas, L., Nelson, K., & Whalen, K. The establishment of imitation and its use for the development of complex behavior in schizophrenic children. *Behaviour Research and Therapy,* 1967, *5,* 171–181.

Lovaas, O.I., & Koegel, R.L. *Behavior modification in education, NSSE yearbook.* Chicago: University of Chicago Press, 1973.

Lovaas, O.I., Koegel, R.L., Simmons, J.Q., & Long, J.S. Some generalization and follow-up results on autistic children. *Journal of Applied Behavior Analysis,* 1973, *6,* 131–164.

Lovaas, O.I., Schreibman, L., & Koegel, R.L. A behavior modification approach to the treatment of autistic children. *Journal of Autism and Childhood Schizophrenia,* 1974, *4,* 111–129.

Madsen, C.H., Jr., & Madsen, C.K. *Teaching/discipline.* Boston: Allyn & Bacon, 1970.

Martin, G.L., England, G., Kaprowy, E., et al. Operant conditioning of kindergarten class behavior in autistic children. *Behaviour Research and Therapy,* 1968, *6,* 281–294.

Metz, J.R. Conditioning generalized imitation in autistic children. *Journal of Experimental Child Psychology,* 1965, *2,* 389–399.

O'Leary, K.D., & Drabman, R. Token reinforcement programs in the classroom: A review. *Psychological Bulletin,* 1971, *75,* 379–398.

Rabb, E., Hewett, F.M. Development of appropriate classroom behaviors in a severely disturbed group of institutionalized children with a behavior modification model. *American Journal of Orthopsychiatry,* 1967, *37,* 313–314.

Rincover, A., & Koegel, R.L. Classroom treatment of autistic children: II. Individualized instruction in a group. *Journal of Abnormal Child Psychology,* 1977, *5,* 113–126.

Risley, T.R., & Wolf, M.M. Establishing functional speech in echololic children. *Behaviour Research and Therapy,* 1967, *5,* 73–88.

Rutter, M. The description and classification of infantile autism. In D.W. Churchill, G.D. Alpern, & M.K. DeMycr (Eds), *Infantile autism.* Springfield, IL: Thomas, 1971.

Wolf, M.M., Risley, T., & Mees, H. Application of operant conditioning procedures to the behavior problems of an autistic child. *Behaviour Research and Therapy,* 1964, *1,* 305–312.

Andrew W. Meyers, Ph.D.

Memphis State University
Memphis, Tennessee

W. Edward Craighead, Ph.D.

Pennsylvania State University
University Park, Pennsylvania

10
Classroom Treatment of Psychotic Children

In the laboratory setting, applied behavior analysts have achieved significant success in modifying the behavior of autistic and schizophrenic children. Lovaas (1964, 1967; Lovaas, Bereich, Perloff, & Schaeffer, 1966; Lovaas, Freitag, Gold & Kassorla, 1965; Lovaas, Freitag, Kinder, et al, 1966; Lovaas, Schaeffer, & Simmons, 1965), Risley (1968; Wolf, Risley, & Mees, 1967), and Koegel (Koegel and Covert, 1972; Koegel, Firestone, Kramme, & Dunlap, 1974) utilized behavioral principles and procedures with psychotic children to develop appropriate social, verbal, and self-care behaviors and to eliminate disruptive, self-stimulatory, and self-injurious behavior.

These laboratory-based therapeutic efforts are impressive, but Lovaas, Koegel, Simmons, and Long (1973) reported that maintenance of treatment gains depended on posttreatment environment. In a one- to four-year follow-up of successfully treated psychotic children, they found that children who were returned to behaviorally trained parents maintained or improved on gains made during treatment, while children who were institutionalized regressed. These findings emphasize the importance of developing natural therapeutic settings that will facilitate the psychotic child's maintenance of treatment gains.

The original version of this article appeared under the title "Classroom Treatment of Psychotic Children" by Andrew W. Meyers and W. Edward Craighead, published in Behavior Modification Vol. 3 No. 1 (Jan. 1979) pp. 73-96 and is reprinted here by permission of the publisher, Sage Publications, Inc.

241

One obvious potentially therapeutic natural setting is the classroom. Here, effectiveness of behavioral interventions, specifically the use of teacher attention and token economies, has been well documented (Kazdin & Craighead, 1973; O'Leary & Drabman, 1971). Koegel and Rincover (1974) demonstrated that psychotic children could be maintained in the classroom by initiating one-to-one instructional sessions and gradually fading in the classroom stimulus situation. The question the present study addressed was whether teacher attention and token economy procedures can be successfully used in training and maintaining appropriate social behaviors of psychotic children as well as those behaviors necessary for learning in the classroom. In addition to observations of the children's behavior, extensive recordings of teacher behavior were made. This permitted direct confirmation of the manipulation of the independent treatment variables within the stated experimental design.

THE STUDY

Setting

The study was conducted in a special-education classroom, which was divided by a clear partition into two areas of approximately equal size (6m by 3m). One area was considered the "work area" and contained four students' desks, the teacher's desk, book shelves, a supply area, and a sink. The second area was a carpeted "free-play area" containing toys, a record player, and a sandbox. The daily class schedule consisted of nine 20- to 30-minute academic periods, each of which was followed by a free-play period of approximately 10 minutes.

Subjects

The special-education classroom consisted of four male children—Rob, Al, Irwin, and Seth—ranging in age from eight to ten years. At the age of five Rob had been diagnosed as an autistic child; he has subsequently been labeled ego-defective and childhood schizophrenic. Rod had undergone two years of play therapy, chemotherapy, psychiatric care, and the structured education setting. He was described by the school psychologist as unable to follow the classroom routine, possessing a limited attention span, poor peer relationships, and manifesting ritualistic behavior and inappropriate verbalizations. Classroom observations revealed that Rob engaged in a great deal of crawling, rocking, wandering, yelling,, and humming, as well as disturbing his and others' books and property. His speech was "understandable" and possibly typical for a boy his age.

Al was diagnosed as childhood schizophrenic and hyperkinetic. The school psychologist's report characterized Al as having poor social relationships, inappropriate and bizarre verbalizations, limited comprehension and abstract reasoning, and a confused orientation. Classroom observation revealed Al's awkward gait and unusual posturing. He engaged in a great deal of self-stimulatory behavior and skipping around the room. His speech, like Rob's, was "understandable." Therapeutic work with Al had centered on the classroom experience.

Irwin was diagnosed as autistic with idiopathic psychomotor retardation. Treatment had consisted of chemotherapy and the structured educational situation. Irwin was described by the school psychologist as hyperactive and aggressive, manifesting "strange" behavior and verbalizations. Observation revealed that Irwin engaged in a great deal of wandering, crawling, and isolate play. His verbalization consisted almost exclusively of babbling and screaming. Irwin attended school only half of each day (11:30–2:00)

Seth was diagnosed at various times as either childhood schizophrenic or autistic. He had undergone chemotherapy, speech therapy, and psychiatric care as well as the structured educational setting. The school psychologist described Seth as having extreme difficulty relating to others, and a limited repertoire of speech and social behaviors. Classroom observation of Seth revealed a great deal of mimicry, mechanical speech, humming, and yelling.

The entire class was characterized by an almost total absence of social interaction. All four children resided at home with their families.

Objective information on the students' intellectual abilities and academic functioning was unavailable. The students were considered untestable. In those situations where tests had been conducted, test-retest reliabilities were extremely low.

The teacher was a 22-year-old female with a half-year's experience teaching exceptional children. She possessed a bachelor's degree in psychology and was certified in both elementary and special education.

Rating Forms and Observers

Behavioral categories previously used by Madsen, Becker, and Thomas (1968) were modified for use in coding seven categories of inappropriate student behaviors and one category of appropriate behavior. Behavioral categories for coding student behavior are presented in Table 10–1. Behavioral categories for coding teacher behavior are presented in Table 10–2. These teacher behaviors were divided into those which occur before student behaviors—positive prompts, negative prompts, positive statements, and negative statements; those which occur after student behaviors—positive verbal feedback, negative verbal feedback, positive nonverbal feedback, negative nonverbal feedback, and ignore; and neutral behaviors with and without interaction.

Two rating forms were used, a Time-Sample Behavior Checklist (TSBC) for observing student behavior and a Teacher–Pupil Interaction Chronograph (TPIC) for observing teacher–student interactions. The TSBC employed the eight categories of student behavior recorded for five

Table 10–1
Behavior Coding Categories for Students

I. *Gross Motor*—Getting out of seat, standing up, running, skipping, jumping, walking, moving furniture, falling.

II. *Object Noise*—Clapping, tapping feet, pencil, or other objects, rattling or tearing paper, throwing or slamming a book. Rate only if you can hear the noise with eyes closed.

III. *Disturbance of Other's Property*—Grabbing or knocking away other's objects, work, or books, destroying another's property or pushing his desk or chair, throwing objects at another without hitting him.

IV. *Contact*—Hitting, kicking, shoving, pinching, slapping, striking, with object, striking with thrown object, poking with object, biting, pulling hair, touching, patting, etc.

V. *Verbalization*—Inappropriate conversation with another child, answering teacher without being called on, making comments or calling out, calling teacher's name to gain attention, crying, singing, whistling, screaming, laughing, coughing or blowing loudly. They must be inappropriate.

VI. *Isolate Play*—Neither initiates or responds to verbalizations with others, engages in no nonverbal interaction with others. Involved in some self-stimulatory behavior for over one-half of the rating period.

VII. *Other Inappropriate*—Ignoring teacher, doing something other than directed (such as playing with a pencil when he should be writing). Involved in an inappropriate task. Not rated when first six categories are used.

VIII. *Appropriate Behaviors*—Time on teacher-defined task including socially relevant behavior.

consecutive 10-second intervals followed by a 10-second break. Each TSBC observation consisted of four of these 50-second minutes on each child, resulting in 16 minutes of TSBC data for each set of observations. The TPIC was a ten-by-eight matrix form with the eight categories of pupil behavior along the abscissa and ten categories of teacher behavior along the ordinate (the category of neutral teacher behavior without interaction was marked outside the matrix). Teacher–pupil interaction was recorded by matching a particular row with a particular column (or column with row) and recording the initial of the pupil(s) with whom the teacher was interacting. A TPIC matrix marked 20 seconds of behavior, and each TPIC observation recorded six consecutive minutes repeated twice during each observation session.

Two sets of observations were taken daily, one in the morning (9:35–10:35 A.M.) and one in the afternoon (1:00–2:00 P.M.). One day's observation consisted of 8 minutes of TSBC observation on each child and 24 minutes of TPIC observation of the entire classroom. Within each set of observations the order of the two sets of TPIC observations and the

Table 10–2
Behavior Coding Categories for Teacher

PVF. *Positive Verbal Feedback*—Compliments, praise, verbal positive reinforcement, positive feedback (example: "Keep up the good work"). This
teacher response *must always follow behavior of child.*

NVF. *Negative Verbal Feedback*—Reprimands, negative feedback, derogatory
remarks (example: "You are not supposed to talk crazy"). his reponse
must always follow behavior of child.

PNF. *Positive Nonverbal Feedback*—Smiling, pleasant expression, positive
gesture, affectionate or complimentary pat, hug, or caress. This teacher
behavior *must always be in response to the behavior of the child.*

NNF. *Negative Nonverbal Feedback*—Frowns, grimaces, negative gesture.
Also pulling, dragging, shoving, pushing, restraining, or striking student.
This response *must always follow behavior of child.*

I. *Ignore, No Response*—Behavior or student is followed by no response by
teacher. Teacher turns away or gives student "dead-pan stare."

PP. *Positive Prompt*—A statement of negative expectations of requirements
that incorporates a reference to the negative consequences of the behavior for the student (example: "If you do that, you'll get a reward"). This
teacher response *always precedes child's behavior.*

NP. *Negative Prompt*—A statement of negative expectations or requirements
that incorporates a reference to the negative consequences of the behavior for the student (example: "If you do that, you'll get punished"). This
teacher response *always precedes child's behavior.*

PS. *Positive Statement*—Expression of expectation, encouragement, a command, instruction, or suggestion without reference to consequences. This
teacher response *must occur before child's behavior* (example: "You can
do it").

NS. *Negative statement*—Expression of expectation, discouragement, prohi-
bition, without reference to consequences (example: "Don't make any
noise"). This teacher response *must occur before child's behavior.*

N. *Neutral*—Questions or conversation without positive or negative valence
(example: "What did you get for Christmas?"), class announcements.

TSBC observations was randomized, as was the order of observation of
the four children.

Five undergraduate psychology majors were trained as observers as
part of their participation in a research course. The observers learned the
behavior coding categories for both students and teacher and became familiar with the mechanics of both the TSBC and TPIC. They then
received two weeks' on-the-job training in the classroom supplemented
by weekly discussion sessions on the use of the rating forms. The study
did not begin until observers agreement was above 80 percent on all
forms.

Procedure

A reversal of ABAB experimental design was employed in which each of the B conditions was a multiple baseline—one employing teacher attention, the other utilizing token reinforcement and teacher attention. The experimental conditions of the study were as follows: Baseline I, Baseline II, which included teacher training, Gross Motor Treatment I, Verbalization Treatment I, Reversal, Gross Motor Treatment II, Verbalization Treatment II, and Total Treatment.

BASELINE I.

The teacher was instructed to continue conducting her class as she always had. Two weeks of observations were taken to obtain baselines of student and teacher behavior and to identify target behaviors.

BASELINE II.

Since the teacher had been unsystematically using cookies to reward desired behavior and placement in the hall to punish undesirable behavior, a third week of baseline was added. During this week the teacher continued to conduct the class as she had in the past, except that she no longer employed her forms of contingency management.

Teacher training, consisting of five one-hour discussions, took place during the third week. Topics covered were the basic principles of behavior modification; relevant literature on behavior modification of the autistic child, teacher attention, and token reinforcement in the classroom; the design of the present study; the development of classroom rules of appropriate behavior; and desired teacher behavior during the first multiple baseline. The teacher was instructed that, *consistent with each treatment condition,* she was to define all classroom situations through the use of positive statements and positive prompts and to reinforce, with her attention all desired behavior with positive verbal and nonverbal feedback. She was further instructed to ignore purposely all inappropriate behavior and to minimize her use of negative statements, negative prompts, and negative feedback. Following teacher training, the teacher received additional instructions and feedback on her performance three times per week.

GROSS MOTOR TREATMENT I

The teacher was instructed to ignore all inappropriate gross motor behavior and to attend positively to all appropriate behavior incompatible with undesirable gross motor behavior. The classroom situation was defined by the following classroom rules that were repeated at the start of the day and immediately after lunch, augmented by positive prompts and positive statements throughout the school day:

1. Raise your hand in order to get permission to leave your seats.
2. During free time you must play on the rug.

The teacher was instructed to continue reacting to behaviors other than gross motor behavior as she had before treatment began. Gross motor treatment continued for three weeks.

VERBALIZATION TREATMENT I

While continuing treatment on gross motor behavior, the teacher was instructed to ignore all inappropriate verbalizations and to attend positively to appropriate verbalizations and all appropriate behavior incompatible with undesirable verbal behavior. The following rules were added to the classroom rules for gross motor behavior:

3. You must raise your hand to talk to me.
4. You may talk to each other without permission only during free play, arts and crafts, and cleanup.
5. During work time you must work quietly.

These rules were also augmented by positive prompts and positive statements. While maintaining treatment on gross motor and verbal behavior, the teacher attempted to continue reacting to other inappropriate behavior as she had before treatment. Verbalization treatment continued for four weeks.

REVERSAL

At this point the teacher-attention multiple baseline was discontinued due to difficulties in the classroom. The teacher felt that the students were not behaving as appropriately as they should, and so she informed the experimenters that she had departed from the instructions of the program. A formal reversal condition was instituted during which the teacher was instructed to react to the children as she had before treatment. During the one-week reversal the teacher took baseline data on inappropriate student behavior during the nine academic periods. She observed gross motor behavior, verbal behavior, and "other inappropriate" behavior (all other categories of inappropriate behavior were merged into a single category due to their low frequencies of occurrence) and "starred" those students who were totally appropriate during each academic period. The students were not aware of and did not receive the stars for her ratings. During reversal week the teacher received three hours of training in the use of token reinforcement.

GROSS MOTOR TREATMENT II

Charts for each student were placed in a prominent position on the classroom wall. At the end of each academic period the teacher placed a star on the charts of those students whose gross motor behavior had been totally appropriate. The free-time period that followed each academic period was made contingent on the student's receiving a "sitting-down" star for that period. "Goodies" (cakes, cookies, soda, or ice cream chosen by the individual student) were now dispensed in the morning (11:15 A.M.) and in the afternoon (1:40 P.M.). These goodies were first made contingent on the student's receiving one more star than he had received on the teacher's rating on the last day of the reversal condition. The criterion for receiving goodies was then raised each time the previous criterion was met. All four students reached ceiling after one week of gross motor treatment. During this week the conditions of Gross Motor Treatment I were also reintroduced.

VERBALIZATION TREATMENT II

Stars for appropriate gross motor and appropriate verbal behavior were now given after each academic period. Free time was contingent upon the student's receiving both a "sitting-down" star and a "being-quiet" star for each academic period. Goodies were contingent upon the perfect performance of gross motor behavior for all academic periods prior to the reinforcement period and upon the student's reaching a set criterion for verbal behavior. The criterion was determined by the student's performance on the last day of the reversal condition and then raised each time the criterion was met. All students reached ceiling after one week of Verbalization Treatment II. During this week the teacher differentially applied teacher attention to verbal behavior as well as gross motor behavior. The teacher was instructed to react to other inappropriate behavior as she had before treatment began.

TOTAL TREATMENT

The following rules were added to the existing classroom rules:

6. You must be quiet with the things you use.
7. You must be nice to each other.
8. You must pay attention in class.
9. If you want to use someone else's things, you must first ask that person.

The teacher was instructed to ignore all inappropriate behavior and to attend with positive social feedback to all appropriate behavior. She defined appropriate behaviors by repetition of the classroom rules, positive prompts, and positive statements.

At the end of each academic period "sitting-down" stars, "being-quiet" stars, and "being-good" stars were given to students who had emitted the corresponding appropriate behaviors. Free time was contingent on receiving all three stars for an academic period. Goodies were contingent on perfect performance in all three categories for all academic periods preceding reinforcement periods on that day. Total treatment continued for three weeks.

RESULTS

Interobserver Agreement

Two observers were present during all observations and reliability checks were conducted on 100 percent of the observations. Interobserver agreements for both the TSBC and TPIC were determined by dividing the number of observer agreements on recorded behaviors by the total number of agreements plus disagreements and multiplying this result by 100. The average interobserver agreement for the TSBC was 94.9 percent, with single day agreements ranging from 70 percent to 100 percent. The average reliability for the TPIC was 90.8 percent, with single day reliabilities ranging from 56.3 percent to 100 percent.

Student Behavior

Figure 10–1 shows the percentage of appropriate student behavior as defined by the TSBC for each of the eight experimental conditions. The percentage of appropriate behavior was calculated by dividing the number of ten-second intervals in which appropriate behavior occurred by the total number of ten-second intervals in that experimental condition. In the baseline conditions (I and II) appropriate behavior occurred respectively in 55.5 percent and 51.6 percent of the intervals observed. In Gross Motor Treatment I, during the teacher-attention phase of the study, appropriate behavior increased to 67.2 percent and in Verbalization Treatment I to 72.6 percent. Unexpectedly, appropriate student behavior continued to increase during the reversal condition to 85.4 percent of the intervals observed. In the token reinforcement period, Gross Motor Treatment II showed 86.7 percent appropriate behavior, 83.0 percent in Verbalization Treatment II, and 89.0 percent in Total Treatment. With minor variations, all four students revealed essentially the same pattern of behavior change as shown in Figure 10–1.

Figure 10–2 shows the percentage of inappropriate student behaviors for each of the eight experimental conditions. Inappropriate behavior is here divided into three categories: gross motor (gross motor category on the TSBC), verbalization (verbalization category on the TSBC), and other inappropriate behavior (object noise, disturbance of other's property,

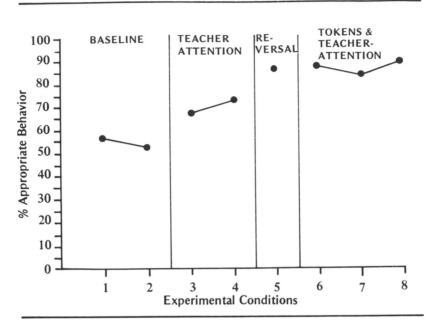

Fig. 10–1. The percent of appropriate student behavior for the eight experimental conditions: (1) Baseline I, (2) Baseline II, (3) Gross Motor Treatment I, (4) Verbalization Treatment I, (5) Reversal, (6) Gross Motor Treatment II, (7) Verbalization Treatment II, (8) Total Treatment.

physical contact, isolate play, and other inappropriate categories on the TSBC). This graph reveals that no multiple-baseline effect occurred during the teacher-attention phase of the study. Inappropriate verbalization and other inappropriate behavior both decreased during Gross Motor Treatment I (22.4 percent to 6.0 percent and 18.5 percent to 15.7 percent, respectively), but the treated inappropriate behavior, gross motor, actually increased from 6.4 percent to 6.7 percent of the observed intervals. The same pattern was apparent during Verbalization Treatment I; both other inappropriate behavior and gross motor behavior decreased (15.7 percent to 10.9 percent and 6.7 percent to 4.8 percent, respectively); while inappropriate verbalization increased from 6.0 percent to 11.7 percent. During the reversal condition inappropriate behavior declined across all categories. Gross motor behavior dropped from 4.8 percent to 2.5 percent, while verbalization fell from 11.7 percent to 7.4 percent and other inappropriate behavior decreased from 10.9 percent to 4.7 percent.

Within the token reinforcement phase of the study there was only a partial multiple baseline effect. During Gross Motor Treatment II gross motor behavior decreased from 2.5 percent to 1.0 percent. Simultane-

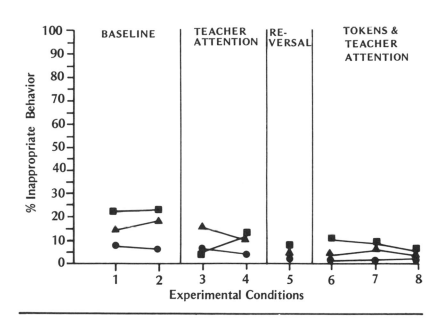

Fig. 10–2. The percent of inappropriate student behavior, divided into Gross Motor, (●—●), Verbalization (■—■), and Other Inappropriate Behavior (▲—▲) categories, for the eight experimental conditions: (1) Baseline I, (2) Baseline II, (3) Gross Motor Treatment I, (4) Verbalization Treatment I, (5) Reversal, (6) Gross Motor Treatment II, (7) Verbalization Treatment II, (8) Total Treatment.

ously, verbalization increased from 7.4 percent to 10.5 percent, but, contrary to the expectations of a multiple-baseline design, other inappropriate behavior decreased from 4.7 percent to 3.0 percent. In Verbalization Treatment II verbalization dropped from 10.5 percent to 9.5 percent of the time intervals observed, while the occurrence of gross motor behavior remained relatively constant at 1.1 percent. Other inappropriate behavior increased from 3.0 percent to 6.3 percent. Finally, during Total Treatment inappropriate verbalization and other inappropriate behavior dropped to 5.3 percent and 4.4 percent, respectively, while gross motor behavior remained relatively stable at 1.4 percent.

Teacher Behavior

Figure 10–3 presents the percentage of four categories of teacher behavior for each of the eight experimental conditions. Positive prompts, positive statements, positive verbal feedback and positive nonverbal

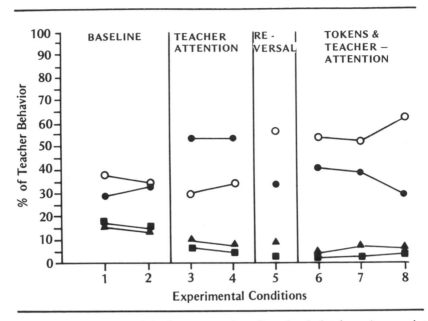

Fig. 10–3. The percent of the four categories of teacher behavior—Appropriate Behavior Appropriately Applied (●—●), Appropriate Behavior Inappropriately Applied (■—■), Inappropriate Behavior (▲—▲), and Neutral Behavior (○—○)— for the eight experimental conditions: (1) Baseline I, (2) Baseline II, (3) Gross Motor Treatment, I (4) Verbalization Treatment I, (5) Reversal, (6) Gross Motor Treatment II, (7) Verbalization Treatment II, (8) Total Treatment.

feedback occurring in conjunction with appropriate student behavior, and ignore occurring in conjunction with inappropriate student behavior are defined as Appropriate Behavior Appropriately Applied. The postive teacher behaviors occurring in conjunction with inappropriate student behavior and ignore occurring in relation to appropriate student behaviors are defined as Appropriate Behavior Inappropriately Applied. Negative prompts, negative statements, negative verbal feedback, and negative nonverbal feedback are defined as Inappropriate Behavior. Neutral behaviors with and without interaction are defined as Neutral Behavior. A category's percentage of teacher behavior was calculated by dividing the frequency of occurrence of that category in the particular experimental condition by the total frequency of teacher behaviors in the experimental condition.

As can be seen in Figure 10–3, the occurrence of appropriate behavior appropriately applied was uniformly low in Baselines I and II (28.8 percent and 32.8 percent), reached a high level in the teacher-attention phase (53.4 percent in both Gross Motor Treatment I and Verbalization

Treatment I), dropped during Reversal (32.9 percent), and then rose slightly during the token reinforcement phase (40.6 percent in Gross Motor Treatment II; 38.0 percent in Verbalization Treatment II; 28.3 percent in Total Treatment). Appropriate behavior inappropriately applied, inappropriate behavior, and neutral behavior all decreased from Baseline I to Baseline II (17.1 percent to 14.8 percent, 16.3 percent to 14.4 percent, and 37.8 percent to 34.8 percent, respectively). All three categories continued to decrease during Gross Motor Treatment I (7.3 percent for appropriate behavior inappropriately applied, 9.3 percent for inappropriate behavior, and 30.0 percent for neutral behavior), and both appropriate behavior inappropriately applied and inappropriate behavior stabilized at relatively low rates for the remainder of the study. Neutral behavior remained stable during the teacher-attention conditions (30 percent in Gross Motor Treatment I and 34.7 percent in Verbalization Treatment I) but rose to 55.9 percent in the Reversal condition. During token reinforcement neutral behavior accounted for 54.6 percent of teacher behavior in Gross Motor Treatment II, 52.5 percent in Verbalization Treatment II, and 62.7 percent in Total Treatment.

Reversal and Multiple Baseline

The data presented above raise two additional questions. First, why was there no multiple-baseline effect during the teacher-attention phase of the study and only a partial multiple-baseline effect during the token reinforcement phase? And second, why did no reversal effect occur during the appropriate experimental condition?

The first question was answered by reexamining the four categories of teacher behavior presented in Figure 10–3 in relation to specific inappropriate student behaviors. Teacher behavior and inappropriate gross motor behavior are presented in Figure 10–4, teacher behavior and inappropriate verbalization in Figure 10–5, and teacher behavior and other inappropriate behavior in Figure 10–6. Percentages were calculated by dividing frequency of occurrence of the category of teacher behavior occurring in conjunction with that inappropriate student behavior in that experimental condition. (i.e., if 20 teacher behaviors occurred in relation to inappropriate gross motor behavior and 10 of those teacher behaviors were appropriate behavior appropriately applied, then appropriate behavior appropriately applied accounted for 50 percent of teacher behavior occurring in conjunction with inappropriate gross behavior in that experimental condition).

As can be seen in Figures 10–4, 10–5, and 10–6, appropriate behavior appropriately applied increased for all three categories of inappropriate student behavior from Baseline II to Gross Motor Treatment I (7.7 per-

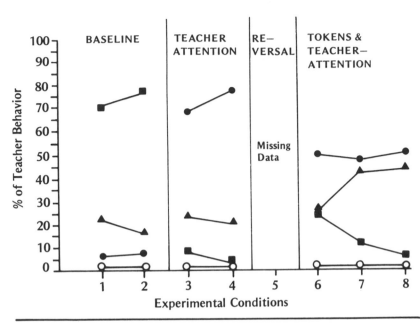

Fig. 10–4. The percent of the four categories of teacher behavior—Appropriate Behavior Appropriately Applied (●—●). Appropriate Behavior Inappropriately Applied (■—■), Inappropriate Behavior (▲—▲), and Neutral Behavior (○—○)—interacting with inappropriate student Gross Motor Behavior for the eight experimental conditions: (1) Baseline I, (2) Baseline II, (3) Gross Motor Treatment I, (4) Verbalization Treatment I, (5) Reversal, (6) Gross Motor Treatment II, (7) Verbalization Treatment II, (8) Total Treatment.

cent to 68.1 percent for gross motor, 16.7 percent to 41.4 percent for verbalization, and 0.0 percent to 13.4 percent for other inappropriate behavior). Simultaneously, appropriate behavior inappropriately applied decreased for all three categories of inappropriate student behavior (76.9 percent to 8.5 percent for gross motor, 66.7 percent to 40.0 percent for verbalization, and 25.6 percent to 19.5 percent for other inappropriate behavior). During this period both inappropriate and neutral teacher behavior remained relatively stable. So while treatment should only have commenced for gross motor behavior during Gross Motor Treatment I, it is apparent that the teacher actually began treatment on all three categories of inappropriate student behavior. The changes in more than one category of student behavior are not indicative of response generalization but are a function of the teacher's responding to other than the target behavior category. This same pattern of increased appropriate behavior appropriately applied and decreased appropriate behavior inappropriately

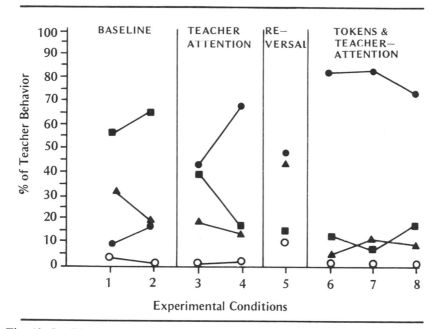

Fig. 10–5. The percent of the four categories of teacher behavior—Appropriate Behavior Appropriately Applied (●—●), Appropriate Behavior Inappropriately Applied (■—■), Inappropriate Behavior (▲—▲), and Neutral Behavior (○—○)— interacting with inappropriate student Verbalization behavior for the eight experimental conditions: (1) Baseline I, (2) Baseline II, (3) Gross Motor Treatment I, (4) Verbalization Treatment I, (5) Reversal, (6) Gross Motor Treatment II, (7) Verbalization Treatment II, (8) Total Treatment.

applied with relatively stable inappropriate and neutral teacher behavior for all student behaviors continued through Verbalization Treatment I.

In the token reinforcement phase of the study teacher behavior was only slightly more discriminative. During Gross Motor Treatment II appropriate behavior appropriately applied occurring in conjunction with verbalization behavior, which at this stage should have been untreated, reached its highest point, 89.9 percent of teacher behavior. Though appropriate behavior appropriately applied was 0.0 percent for the other untreated behavior (other inappropriate behavior), the discrimination in teacher behavior demanded by the multiple baseline design was certainly not manifested. Basically the same pattern of teacher behavior was revealed in Verbalization Treatment II and Total Treatment, though inappropriate teacher behavior did increase across all categories of student behavior.

To examine the question of the absence of any reversal effect, we again refer to Figure 10–3. While the percentage of appropriate behavior

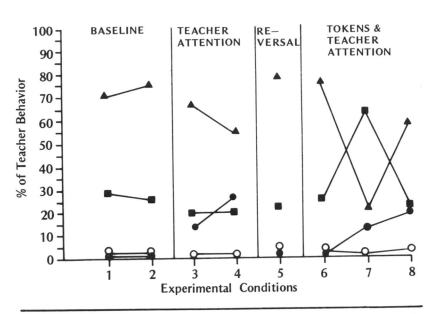

Fig. 10–6.   The percent of the four categories of teacher behavior—Appropriate
Behavior Appropriately Applied (●—●), Appropriate Behavior Inappropriately
Applied (■—■), Inappropriate Behavior (▲—▲), and Neutral Behavior (○—○)—
interacting with student Other Inappropriate Behavior for the eight experimental
conditions: (1) Basline I, (2) Baseline II, (3) Gross Motor Treatment I, (4) Verbalization Treatment I, (5) Reversal, (6) Gross Motor Treatment II, (7) Verbalization
Treatment II, (8) Total Treatment.

appropriately applied did indeed drop from treatment to reversal (53.4
percent to 32.8 percent), this decrease was not coupled with a concomitant increase in appropriate behavior inappropriately applied (4.9 percent
to 2.6 percent) or in inappropriate behavior (7.0 percent to 8.7 percent).
The increased teacher behavior occurred in the neutral behavior category
(34.7 percent to 55.9 percent), revealing that inappropriate student behavior received no additional teacher attention during the reversal condition.
This indicates that the so-called reversal condition produced no reversal
in teacher behavior, and that the teacher continued to follow the original
teacher-attention program.

DISCUSSION

The results of the present study support the findings of previous experiments that indicate that both the contingent use of teacher attention

(Madsen, Becker, & Thomas, 1968) and token reinforcement (O'Leary, Becker, Evans, & Saudargas, 1969) can reduce inappropriate classroom behavior. Student behavior improved from 51.6 percent appropriate during baseline to 72.6 percent appropriate during the teacher-attention condition. Behavior continued to improve through the token reinforcement phase, with 89.0 percent appropriate behavior in the Total Treatment condition. All categories of inappropriate student behavior showed concomitant decreases during the study. This supports Lovaas's (1966) assertion and Koegel and Rincover's (1974) evidence that behavior therapy techniques can be used successfully with psychotic children in the classroom setting.

The findings presented here indicate that a teacher can become an effective behavioral change agent in the classroom. During teacher attention the teacher significantly increased her appropriate behavior and decreased her inappropriate behavior. Inappropriate teacher behavior remained low during the token reinforcement phase of the study, while appropriate teacher behavior decreased and neutral teacher behavior increased.

These latter changes in teacher behavior may have been due to the teacher's increasing reliance on token reinforcement and difficulties involved in maintaining high levels of attention to classroom activities.

Additional evidence for the behavioral treatment of autism and childhood schizophrenia was produced by the interaction of student and teacher behavior. Despite the strictly defined experimental program, student behavior responded to the teacher's manipulations of the reinforcement contingencies rather than to the expectations of the experimenters or the observers.

Without the knowledge of the experimenters, the teacher independently restructured the experimental teacher-attention program, doing away with the reversal condition and the multiple baseline design. The failure to find any multiple-baseline effect seems clearly due to the teacher's indiscriminate simultaneous treatment of all inappropriate student behaviors in the teacher-attention phase of the study. The partial multiple-baseline effect observed in the token reinforcement phase must be attributed to both more discriminative teacher behavior and token reinforcement. The absence of a multiple-baseline effect within the teacher-attention conditions, however, should not be understood to mean that there was no positive effect from the contingent use of teacher attention; in fact, there was an increase in appropriate student behavior when the teacher contingently used teacher attention as social reinforcement for all student behaviors. Indeed, in examining the interactions between teacher and pupil behavior, one finds a remarkably specific student response to the operative contingencies of reinforcement.

These findings indicate the importance of recording change-agent behavior and change agent–subject interaction as well as subject behavior to confirm manipulation of the independent variables and utilization of the experimental design. Such detailed recording of teacher–pupil interaction, as permitted by the TPIC, allows clarification of the operative contingencies of reinforcement and of the resulting behavior changes.

Lovaas, Koegel, Simmons, and Long (1973) indicate that the development of educational settings that support the psychotic child's adaptive behaviors should serve to aid in the maintenance of previous treatment gains. The results of the present study support the systematic manipulation of environmental contingencies as a potentially effective intervention for maintaining psychotic children in the classroom and for creating classrooms that should facilitate the development and maintenance of the child's adaptive behavior.

REFERENCES

Kazdin, A., & Craighead, W. Behavior modification in special education. In L. Mann & D. Sabatino (Eds.), *The review of special education.* Philadelphia: Buttonwood Farms, 1973.

Koegel, R., & Covert, A. The relationship of self-stimulation to learning in autistic children. *Journal of Applied Behavior Analysis,* 1972, *5,* 381–388.

Koegel, R., Firestone, P., Kramme, K., & Dunlap, G. Increasing spontaneous play by suppressing self-stimulation in autistic children. *Journal of Applied Behavior Analysis.* 1974, *7,* 521–528.

Koegel, R., & Rincover, A. Treatment of psychotic children in a classroom environment; I. Learning in a large group. *Journal of Applied Behavior Analysis,* 1974, *7,* 45–60.

Lovaas, O. Control of food intake in children by reinforcement of relevant verbal behavior. *Journal of Abnormal and Social Psychology.* 1964, *68,* 672–677.

Lovaas, O. A program for the establishment of speech in psychotic children. In J.K.Wing (Ed.), *Early childhood autism.* Elmsford, NY:Pergamon, 1966.

Lovaas, O. A behavior therapy approach to the treatment of childhood schizophrenia. In J.P. Hill (Ed.), *Minnesota symposia on child psychology.* Minneapolis: University of Minnesota Press, 1967.

Lovaas, O., Bererich, J., Perloff, B., & Schaeffer, B. Acquisition of imitative speech by schizophrenic children. *Science,* 1966, *151,* 705–707.

Lovaas, O., Freitag, G., Gold, V., & Kassorla, I. Experimental studies in childhood schizophrenia. I. Analysis of self-destructive behavior. *Journal of Experimental Child Psychology,* 1965, *2,* 67–84.

Lovaas, O., Freitag, G., Kinder, M., et al. Establishment of social reinforcers in two schizophrenic children on the basis of food. *Journal of Experimental Child Psychology,* 1966, *4,* 109–125.

Lovaas, O., Koegel, R., Simmons, J., & Long, J. Some generalization and follow-up measures on autistic children in behavior therapy. *Journal of Applied Behavior Analysis,* 1973, *6,* 131–164.

Lovaas, O., Schaeffer, B., & Simmons, J. Building social behavior in autistic children by use of shock. *Journal of Experimental Research in Personality,* 1965, *1,* 99–109.

Madsen, C., Becker, W., & Thomas, D. Rules, praise and ignoring: Elementary classroom control. *Journal of Applied Behavior Analysis,* 1968, *1,* 139–150.

O'Leary, K., Becker, W., Evans, M., & Saudargas, R. A token reinforcement program in public school: A replication and systematic analysis. *Journal of Applied Behavior analysis, 1969, 2,* 3–13.

O'Leary, K., & Drabman, R. Token reinforcement programs in the classrooms: A review. *Psychological Bulletin,* 1971, *75,* 379–398.

Risley, T. The effects and the side effects of punishing the autistic behaviors of a deviant child. *Journal of Applied Behavior Analysis,* 1968, *1,* 21–34.

Wolf, M., Risley, T., & Mees, H. Application of operant conditioning procedures to the behavioral problems of an autistic child. In S. Bijou & D. Baer (Eds.), *Child development: Readings in experimental analysis.* New York: Appleton-Century-Crofts, 1967.

PART IV

In conclusion the authors wish to leave the reader with some direction as to the future education of children who exhibit severe maladaptive behaviors. Thus, the purpose of Part IV is twofold: (1) to familiarize the reader with popular thinking and possible trends in special education and (2) to suggest, from the authors' perspective, a viable means of circumventing in the future some of the present problems involved in the education of such children. In Chapter 11 the authors speculate about what might be the concerns in the closing years of the twentieth century, and in Chapter 12 an alternative is offered to avoid the current practice of classification/ segregation.

11
Future Trends in Education

In order to speculate intelligently about the future, we must rely on information regarding the past (Kanner, 1962; Kauffman, 1977) in combination with present concerns and trends (Stainback & Stainback, in press). In Chapters 2 and 3 the authors outlined some past and present issues and concerns relating to the education of children with severe maladaptive behavior patterns. By analyzing the past and present trends in education, we can speculate regarding the future by extending these trend lines in regard to what possibly may be expected in the future. From these speculated future trends, potential research concerns and areas of study and debate can be gleaned.

To be consistent with the trends mentioned in Chapters 2 and 3, the information presented in this chapter addresses the needs of children who exhibit severe maladaptive behavior rather than the needs of children assigned to traditional categories, such as seriously disturbed, autistic, psychotic, or schizophrenic. While many of the children in each of these categories do exhibit severe maladaptive behaviors (e.g., self-injurious behavior, aggressive behaviors, and/or withdrawal), the categories are neither indicative that all children so labeled will exhibit such behaviors nor that all children who do exhibit such behaviors are classified with one of these labels. In other words, not all children labeled seriously emotionally disturbed, for example, will exhibit the behaviors referred to in this chapter as being maladaptive, and other children not labeled emotionally disturbed, for example, severely/profoundly retarded, may exhibit such behaviors. Educationally, using the grouping "children who exhibit severe maladaptive behavior(s)" is relevant since these behaviors do share common programming procedures and concern. Traditional categorical groupings tend to be more educationally heterogeneous in regard to programming concerns and needs.

Before beginning the discussion of possible future trends, two major philosophical trends mentioned in Chapter 3 that are likely to have a tremendous impact on many aspects of future concerns need to be reviewed briefly. In the 1970s we have witnessed a swing away from segregated, institutionalized placements to more normalized community-based living and learning environments for children who exhibit severe maladaptive behaviors. "Normalization," deinstitutionalization," and "least restrictive environment," the terms that are used to describe this change, have become the objectives of increasing numbers of professionals.

A second major change relates to the growing popularity of behaviorism. Behaviorism, which involves the systematic manipulation of environmental variables to change behavior, espouses empirically verifiable principles of learning or behavior change. With the movements toward accountability and objectivity in education, some of the basic principles of behaviorism are being integrated into the teaching/learning process. As noted by Wayne and O'Connor (1979), "The number of programs using the behavioral approach has mushroomed in the past two decades" (p. 339).

From these two movements, considered both separately and in combination, many potential educational trends can be perceived in regard to the education of children who exhibit severe maladaptive behavior. Any discussion of the future, of necessity, is based on speculation, and the following discussion must be recognized as reflecting the authors' personal perspectives.

ENVIRONMENTAL FACTORS AS THE FOCUS FOR EDUCATIONAL RESEARCH

While the medical profession and social service agencies were primarily responsible in the past for the care and treatment of children who exhibited severe maladaptive behaviors, it is fairly obvious from recent events (c.g., Public Law 94–142) that education is taking on more responsibility for the treatment of these children. This trend is likely to continue. As a result, there will be more emphasis by educators as well as psychologists on how children learn not to exhibit maladaptive behaviors and how to exhibit adaptive or appropriate behaviors since *how children learn is the major concern of education*. This will be done from a learning model rather than a medical model perspective. The medical model of the past focused on a child's inner psyche or inner disabilities to change behavior. Under the learning model the concern will be with how environmental factors or factors outside of the child can be manipulated to change maladaptive behavior.

This is not to imply that some maladaptive behaviors are not caused by internal neurological disabilities or that medical studies into internal disabilities will not be a concern in the 1980s. What it does mean is that educators will be less involved in trying to determine underlying disabilities. They no longer will function as pseudo-medical specialists. They will function as educational specialists.

In short, in the future, educators will concern themselves less with within-child explanations for problems and more with where their expertise lies—in the teaching/learning process. This does not mean that educators should not be aware of the internal disabilities related to some behavior problems or that physicians should not be aware of the importance of teaching/learning influences on maladaptive behavior, but it does mean that education as a discipline, it its own right, is beginning to emerge as a powerful force to change the maladaptive behaviors of some children.

TEACHING SOME IMPORTANT BUT OFTEN FORGOTTEN APPROPRIATE BEHAVIORS

Children who display severe forms of maladaptive behavior tend to have deficits in some critical areas that have not been traditionally programmed for in the public schools. In the future educational programming in public schools will involve these "forgotten" areas.

Appropriate social, emotional, and attitudinal behaviors very often determine an individual's ability to be accepted and to adjust to community living, and it is in these areas that children who exhibit severe maladaptive behaviors are generally most deficient. They need to learn these skills to be able to function in the community. It has been suggested that systematic training of these skills in young children may serve to prevent at least some maladaptive behaviors from occurring in the first place (Schrag, 1972; Trower, Bryant, & Argyle, 1978). Future research will focus on the development and refinement of procedures and materials that are effective in teaching children appropriate social, emotional, and attitudinal behaviors.

Another area that will receive considerable attention in the formal educational process is the development of self-control teaching strategies. This has begun to receive attention in the literature (e.g., Polsgrove,

1979), and the importance of self-control to the success of individuals and the entire social structure in a community is being recognized by professionals and nonprofessionals alike. Some degree of self-control is critical to the successful adjustment of every child to the environment. While some children develop this skill incidentally, many do not, and children who exhibit severe maladaptive behaviors have considerable difficulty with it.

The focus of this discussion has been on the *development* of appropriate attitudes, emotions, social behaviors, and self-control. In the future stress will be placed on *building* or *developing* appropriate behaviors rather than only decreasing inappropriate ones. In some cases decreasing inappropriate behavior is a prerequisite to building behaviors; however, the objective should be on how to increase the abilities of the child rather than only on how to make the child tolerable by eliminating inappropriate behavior. By only eliminating behavior, the result of programming is a decrease in the child's behavioral repetoire with no development of skills that will enhance the child's ability to adapt to the community or to start growing on his/her own toward more healthy functioning. In short, whereas in the past the focus was on decreasing behaviors, in the future the focus will be on building behaviors, especially emotional, social, attitudinal, and self-control behaviors, for those children with severe maladaptive behavior.

BEHAVIORISM WILL BECOME MORE WIDELY ACCEPTED

While many strategies (e.g., ecological, psychoeducational, humanistic/open education, developmental) have emerged that educators can employ to change maladaptive behavior, two fundamentally different approaches still remain in the forefront—the psychodynamic and the behavioral approaches. Most of the strategies popular today can be traced to one or both of these. As pointed out in Chapter 2, therapists and teachers who follow the psychodynamic approach essentially believe that children who display severe forms of maladaptive behavior must feel secure and free to express their *inner* thoughts and conflicts and that gradually, as a result, they will, with the help of the teacher, come to understand and gain insight about themselves, their emotions, and their behaviors. On the other hand, those who follow the behavioral approach believe that many maladaptive (disturbed, disordered) behaviors are learned and that maladaptive behavior (learned or not) can be most effectively dealt with by clearly specifying the problem behavior and controlling the child's environment, more specifically, the antecedents and consequences surrounding the behavior. The current trend seems to be toward greater emphasis on the application of the behavioral approach.*

It appears that this trend will gain even more momentum in the decades to come. There will be a proliferation of work utilizing behavioral principles, especially with children who display severe forms of maladaptive behavior. While many individuals still adhere to the psychoanalytically oriented philosophy and concepts, which was by far the most widely accepted approach during the first half of the 1900s, more and more professionals are incorporating behavioral principles into their treatment and/or teaching strategies. Sometimes this is being done unconsciously. For example, many individuals are writing behavioral objectives, employing competency-based testing, task analysis, rewards and punishers, and/or keeping data on children's progress without considering the fact that they are following a behavioral orientation in their approach. In other words, behavioral principles have and are permeating many school activities and teaching approaches without being formally termed "behavior modification."

It is interesting to note that the principles of behavior modification are entering into our lives in numerous ways other than through school activities. For example, "weight-watchers" is utilizing many of the principles. In fact, Richard Stuart, a well-known behaviorist, is their psychological consultant. Many other businesses and organizations are also turning to behavior modification principles in their dealings.

Even many proponents of open education and psychoeducational approaches, which are basically modifications of psychodynamic beliefs, are using ideas from behaviorism, although some of them might vehemently deny it. But a careful review of their writings over the past several decades would indicate a gradual awareness of the importance of clearly stating what should be taught or what behaviors should be changed and reinforcing those behaviors (Kauffman, 1977). They may do this in less obvious ways than a die-hard behaviorist. For example, adherents of open education might smile, hug the child, show acceptance and warmth after appropriate behaviors are displayed without being exactly "data based" (scientific or objective) about what they are doing. Nevertheless, they seem to be more aware that smiles, warmth, and acceptance should be given after a child, for example, helps another child and should be avoided or not given after a child kicks another child, for example.

---

*We are very broadly referring to behavioral principles and not just the strict use of operant and/or respondent conditioning. Concepts from behaviorism are being integrated with many models for the learning process such as social learning theory, cognitive behavior modification, and precision teaching. We are speaking here in a generic sense about all applications of behavioral principles.

This discussion is not meant to imply that the future of special education or educational programming for children who display severe forms of maladaptive behavior will be constructed entirely from the research and writings of the behaviorists. Behavior modification is only a process or method of instruction or a way of changing the behaviors of children. There are many other variables that go into the education of children who exhibit severe maladaptive behaviors. For example, what should the objectives and curricular content be? Behavior modification is of little help in this regard. Behavioral principles might help in how to structure and organize the objectives and curriculum, but they are of little assistance in regard to what the objectives and curricular content should be.

Knowledge about various philosophies and value systems is needed to help determine appropriate educational objectives for children. Also, many ideas steming from ecological, humanistic/open education, and developmental theories and concepts have and will continue to be integrated into the education of children who display severe forms of maladaptive behavior. The overall trend, however, is likely to be toward more research and application of behavioral theory and principles.

DETERMINING POTENTIALLY EFFECTIVE REINFORCERS AND PUNISHERS

Researchers utilizing applied behavior analysis procedures (that is, behavior modification) are currently demonstrating that the severe maladaptive behaviors of some children previously considered "unteachable" can be eliminated or reduced and that appropriate or adaptive behaviors can be taught to these children. At the University of California Lovaas, Schaeffer, and Simmons (1965) eliminated the self-stimulatory behaviors of two young children labeled very seriously disturbed or psychotic. By using punishment procedures they were successful in getting the children not to self-stimulate. They would punish the children right after any self-stimulatory behaviors occurred by applying electric shock. They also taught these same children appropriate social interaction behaviors by removing the shock (reinforcing them) contingent upon social interaction. Other researchers have placed children in a state of deprivation for food and afterward required them to perform appropriate behaviors and/or to refrain from displaying maladaptive behavior in order to receive food reinforcers.

The use of such extreme techniques does present a problem, particularly from a humane and ethical viewpoint, but often it has been necessary to resort to extreme reinforcement conditions and punishers for those children who do not respond to conventional reinforcers (e.g., smiles, pats on the back) and punishers (e.g., elimination of recess time).

If a child, who exhibits severe maladaptive behavior, will only respond to very strong aversive punishers, such as electric shock, or reinforcers, such as food (under deprivation conditions), the teacher, who in the future will be required to teach these children in the public school setting, may be in trouble. Moral, ethical, and legal considerations are likely to deem such extreme punishers and reinforcers inappropriate for use in public school classrooms.

The logical question, then, is, What types of reinforcers and punishers can teachers use? The answer must await future research and experience. Some studies are now underway to find alternatives to extreme reinforcers. For example, psychologists (Rincover, Koegel & Russo, 1978) are exploring the use of sensory stimulation or sensory reinforcement for children who exhibit severe maladaptive behavior.

THE INFLUENCE OF CURRICULAR ACTIVITIES

To date, researchers have not been too concerned with the possible effects of various curricular activities on the frequency of severe forms of maladaptive behavior. This may be due to the fact that education has, in the past, played such a small, ancillary role in the treatment of children who exhibit these types of behaviors. In the residential setting often the basic physical needs of the children were met with little attention paid to their learning needs since generally these children were considered "hopeless."

With the continuing implementation of the normalization trend, these children will be placed in the public school setting in the future rather than in the traditional institutional facilities. Since curricular activities are an important part of any educational program, it can be expected that greater effort in the future will be made to determine the effects of various curricular activities on the frequency of severe forms of maladaptive behavior. While much of the work in the past, particularly of the applied behavior analysis variety, focused solely on the influence of consequent stimuli, in the future increasing amounts of attention will be focused on antecedent stimuli, and this will involve the influences of different curricular activities on maladaptive behavior. For example, do severe maladaptive behaviors occur more frequently when an individual is engaged in group participation or independent work, in repetitive drill or active thinking?

Keeping children actively engaged in learning new skills in a variety of curricular areas is probably the best way to reduce and/or prevent many forms of maladaptive behavior. When children are busy learning language, reading, arithmetic, writing, how to use leisure time, and appropriate social, attitudinal, and emotional behaviors, they have a reduced amount of time to engage in maladaptive behavior. From experience it is beginning to be recognized that a focus on building appropriate behavior is one of the best ways to avoid or reduce inappropriate behavior. Unfortunately, we have not always recognized or practiced this in the past. We have often devoted a considerable amount of attention on eliminating inappropriate behaviors without providing children alternatives for gaining stimulation from their environment(s).

In summary, it can be expected that in the future educators will spend more time on curricular activities that will involve how to build appropriate behavior rather than focusing undue amounts of time on how to eliminate or reduce maladaptive behavior.

REDUCED USAGE OF TRADITIONAL CATEGORIES

As has been pointed out throughout this volume, particularly, in Chapters 3 and 4, present educational categories (e.g., emotional disturbance, mental retardation, learning disabilities) are losing favor among many professionals. While these categories are designed to allow for more efficient communication, the categories do not actually provide any relevant educational information regarding what and how to teach.

There are, however, groups of children who require some environmental modifications, such as fewer distractions, smaller, and well-sequenced steps, more concrete examples, more repetitions and/or a slower presentation. Thus categorization that emphasizes the educational programming needs of children is becoming popular. Categories such as children deficient in language, children accelerated in reading, or children who exhibit severe maladaptive behavior are being used. As a result, educators will start to focus on the programming needs of children grouped according to such variables. Such categories may be composed of a wide variety of children with individual differences but who have an educationally relevant variable (or variables) in common, for example, a language deficit. While such children might be grouped for training in language, they will not necessarily be classified, labeled, and grouped with that group during the entire school day.

Thus, in the future we are likely to see educational classifications related to the relevant educational needs of children rather than along traditional, medically derived categorical groupings.

PROFESSIONAL ADULT INTERACTIONS

At present training teachers to work with children who exhibit severe maladaptive behavior generally concentrates on training the perspective teacher to program systematically and effectively for the development of objectives appropriate for the needs of each individual child. This focus met the skill needs of teachers in the past who remained in segregated classes and independently programmed for "their" children. Today, however, with the stress on integration and normalization, many skills needed by teachers are not systematically being met. The implementation of mainstreaming involves programs and procedures such as staffings, home intervention, interdisciplinary programming as well as normalized curriculum and experiences. Adult interaction skills play a major role in the formal educational process. Unfortunately, the breakdown in effective programming for children who exhibit severe maladaptive behaviors can sometimes be traced back to the breakdown of adult interaction. It is not uncommon to find in the school setting little communication or communication of poor quality among teachers, parents, and support personnel. This often leads to misperceptions, misinterpretation, and misunderstanding of programming needs. As a result, optimum learning opportunities for children cannot be initiated. Fortunately, there is a growing recognition of the problems of poor interaction among the personnel, including the parents, responsible for educating children.

In the future, systematic study will be required to identify precisely adult interaction skills needed by teachers of children who exhibit severe maladaptive behavior. This can be done by analyzing the desirable and undesirable behaviors in adult interactions. Methods of increasing desirable and decreasing undesirable behaviors in adult interactions will also constitute topics of future importance.

While some information is available on interpersonal interaction skills (e.g., Gutride, Goldstein, & Hunter, 1973), data specific to teacher training is needed. Teacher trainers are currently called upon to furnish training to perspective teachers to enable them to develop the interpersonal skills necessary to be effective teachers. Courses in "interdisciplinary skills" and "human relations" are being added to the curriculum. Research regarding some of the factors mentioned above (e.g., which behaviors should be taught and how to teach them) will need investigation to enhance and improve such offerings. In other words, more information regarding adult interaction skills will be needed in the future to insure the success of courses in "human relations" and "interdisciplinary skills."

LEARNING CHARACTERISTICS OF CHILDREN

Children do have different learning characteristics and skills. Knowing the learning characteristics of any child is important in designing an educationally relevant and appropriate program for that child. For example, some children during the learning process tend to be impulsive, which often results in quick and frequently inaccurate responding. Others tend to be more reflective and think through the learning problem, which generally results in slower but more accurate responding. Knowing whether a child is impulsive or reflective can aid the teacher in designing a program with objectives and activities that will enhance the efficiency of the child's learning style.

Knowing the learning characteristics of children who exhibit severe maladaptive behaviors is as important to their educational programming needs as for any child. These children often have difficulty in the learning process, so knowledge regarding their particular learning characteristics when used in program planning can increase their probability of success. More attention is now being given to the learning characteristics of these children. One characteristic generally common to children classified as autistic is overselectivity (Dunlap, Koegel, & Egel, 1979). Children who are overselective tend to pay attention to only a very small or restricted part of the information (or stimuli) available in the environment. These children "zero in on whatever has attracted their attention. But these children lack the capacity to 'zero out,' to expand their focus and comprehend the context of whatever they are focusing on" (Rimland, 1978, p. 80). As a result of the research findings regarding overselectivity, activities and materials are being developed and empirically verified to overcome and/or circumvent this problem.

While some work is presently being done regarding the learning characteristics of children who display severe maladaptive behavior, the future decade should see an increased emphasis on the impact of such characteristic on the learning process. Consideration of and programming for their unique learning characteristics could be critical to the potential success of these children.

CHILDREN INFLUENCE PARENTS

With the emphasis on keeping all children in the community setting, and preferably in the natural home environment, parent/child relations and interactions necessarily will be a popular area of concern. Appropriate and mutually rewarding interactional patterns in families that include children who exhibit severe maladaptive behavior are critical to the potential success of the normalization movement. In the past the focus of attention in parent/child relationships was almost exclusively on the influence of parental behaviors on the development of children. In many cases parents were found to exhibit inappropriate or undesirable child-rearing behaviors. As a result, it was often concluded that the child's troublesome behaviors were caused, at least in part, by the parents' behavior.

Current research, however, consistently indicates that undesirable parent behaviors or family interactions can result as a reaction to the maladaptive behaviors of the child as much as they may be a causative factor in the child's maladaptive behavior (Bell, 1968; Martin, 1975; Patterson, 1975). In other words, children who seem to have been born with difficult temperaments or behavioral styles can cause their parents to develop inappropriate or undesirable behaviors (Kauffman, 1977). It is not a one-way street. While parents influence the behaviors of their children, children also influence the behaviors of their parents. In short, it is now believed that children are born with a basic temperament or way of behaving (Thomas, Chess & Birch, 1968). Those born with difficult temperaments may cause parents who otherwise would be loving and accepting to become abusive, intolerant, negative, and/or hostile.

If the home situation of children with severe maladaptive behaviors is not properly monitored and controlled, such influences could be detrimental to the family interaction behaviors. If these influences are not addressed, normalization will fail. Initially, it will be necessary to conduct empirical analysis, testing, and verification of family interaction patterns and then develop methods of circumventing problems before they arise. Some work in this area has been done. For example, it has been demonstrated that parent training has been successful in modifying parental responses to their children in order to control the children's aggressive behaviors (Patterson, Reid, Jones & Conger, 1975).

Parents of children who display extremely difficult behaviors will need training in how *not* to let their children's behavior cause them to become negative, hostile, rejecting parents as well as training in how to *cope* with and *modify* their children's maladaptive behaviors. They will need the support and assistance of teachers and others. In the 1980s and beyond more emphasis on the best ways of providing support and training to parents of troublesome children will be recognized as a necessity.

RESEARCH IN NORMALIZED ENVIRONMENTS

There has been a trend over the past several decades for people other than highly trained researchers to become more involved in applied research in the public schools and other community settings. Techniques that have been found to be effective in changing severe forms of maladaptive behavior in research laboratories under highly controlled conditions are being tested by teachers, parents, and others through applied research in normalized settings. In the future greater stress will be placed on who carries out the research as well as where it is conducted. In addition to "experimenters" and "specialists" studying procedures for stopping head banging in a laboratory, for example, such procedures also will be studied by the teacher in the public school and/or parent in the home. Thus, in the future teachers and parents will be involved in applied research regarding possible ways or methods to change severe forms of maladaptive behavior. Whoever is intended to use a procedure will be called upon to keep data on the progress being made in order to evaluate the effectiveness of the procedure.

Frequently in the past a specialist or the developer, in a highly structured, unnatural setting, tested the effectiveness of a procedure, and teachers and others tended to take whatever the experimenter or developer said at face value. This will be less true in the future. The people for whom the procedure was designed to be used (e.g., teachers, parents) will test it. Data collection procedures and research and evaluation designs that parents and teachers can easily understand and apply in natural settings are now available (Kazdin, 1975).

In addition to new research ideas being tested in the normalized setting, replications of past research will become common. There is a vast body of research dealing with the education of children who exhibit severe maladaptive behavior that indicates procedures and materials that are effective. Much of this data, however, has been gathered by highly trained specialists in nonnormalized institutional or laboratory settings. Replications of this research in "normal" situations are needed to determine the usefulness of these procedures in normal settings.

There is no doubt that in the future empirical testing of methods for changing severe maladaptive behavior will be done by parents and teachers in public school classrooms, the typical home bathroom, community sidewalk, or wherever applicable. No longer will studies involving special implementers be accepted as providing final evidence that a procedure or activity is effective when used by community members in natural settings.

MORE EMPHASIS ON SINGLE-SUBJECT RESEARCH

One consideration of the research in the future concerning children who exhibit severe maladaptive behavior will involve the continuation and possible strengthening of a philosophical viewpoint regarding research designs. In the past group research designs (using preferably large numbers of randomly selected children) to determine the effectiveness of a procedure or applicability of a material were considered to be optimal.

The use, instead, of "single-subject designs" has been gaining momentum. A subject's behavior under experimental conditions is compared with his own (same subject's) behavior under nonexperimental or control conditions. Many researchers did not initially endorse this deviation from the traditional group design since with the small number of subjects, generally one, it was not possible to do any valid statistical analysis and generalization of the experimental procedures to other children could not be justified. After considerable debate two major concerns regarding single-subject designs were resolved for many researchers. One, the data from such designs could be visually analyzed and could stand alone (often pictorially represented in graphs). Second, children are so different (having individual needs and abilities) that there is value to knowing if a given technique works for a given child, even if the findings cannot be generalized to other children.

While data from single-subject research only demonstrate if a given technique either works or does not work for a given individual, professionals are increasingly recognizing that this is an important and worthwhile finding. Implications for trying the technique with other children is left to the discretion of the programmer. It is not automatically assumed that the technique should or will work with children other than those involved in the study, as is often interpreted from group design research findings.

This change in the direction of research has and will continue to have an important role in future trends dealing with children who exhibit severe maladaptive behavior. There is relatively a small incidence of children who exhibit such behaviors, and the large numbers of these children needed for group research are generally not available in the natural environment. Also, due to the severity of the handicap, techniques and procedures used to change these children's behaviors are generally rigorously systematic, detailed, and time-consuming, and it would be difficult, if not impossible, for a researcher to carry out such experimental conditions on a large group of children. Thus, it appears that single-subject designs will be involved in a growing number of the studies done in the future in regard to children who exhibit severe maladaptive behavior.

While the use of single-subject research designs is likely to increase in the future, there will continue to be a need for group research. A single-subject design is *not* necessarily always feasible or the best way to find answers to questions. Kazdin (1975) has provided an example of when it would be better to use a group design:

> For comparing the effectiveness of one experimental program with another, separate groups of clients are needed. Both programs cannot be given to one group, because the first program may make some relatively permanent changes in behavior. (p. 103)

Table 11–1
Projected Trends in Education

Trend	Impact
Environmental factors as the focus for educational research	Refocusing of primary attention from inner disabilities to how environmental factors outside of the child can be manipulated to change maladaptive behavior
Programming for community living	Attention to teaching appropriate social, emotional, attitudinal, and self-control behaviors to enhance chances of successful community living
Wider acceptance of behaviorism	Greater awareness and incorporation of behavioral principles into a wide variety of treatment and teaching strategies
Determining potentially effective reinforcers and punishers	Research by educators and psychologists and legal considerations to determine acceptable positive and aversive stimuli that can be used in classrooms
Research regarding the influence of curricular activities	Greater emphasis on antecedent stimuli including curricular activities to reduce inappropriate and increase appropriate behavior
Reduce usage of traditional categories	Focus of educational classification and groupings on the relevant educational needs of children rather than on traditional medically derived categorical groupings
Professional adult interactions	In addition to the adult–child interaction emphasis in education, greater attention to the adult-to-adult interaction skills
Learning characteristics of children	Increased attention to the learning characteristics of children that can be used to promote more option educational programming
Children influence parents	Greater emphasis in determining how children influence the behaviors of their parents and/or the family
Research in normalized environments	Greater stress on who conducts applied research and where it is conducted—emphasis on teachers and parents being involved in research conducted in classroom and home settings
More emphasis on single-subject research	Increased research in classroom settings with one to three or four subjects

CONCLUSION

Many changes in the education of children who exhibit severe maladaptive behaviors can be expected in the future. These future trends generally will flow from past and present knowledge and practices. For the reader's convenience, those trends that will have the greatest impact, in the authors' opinion, in the closing years of the twentieth century have been summarized in Table 11–1.

It is the speculated future trends, as well as past and present practice, that provide guidance in the development of objectives and goals for the education of children with severe maladaptive behaviors. Predictions about the future have a considerable impact on the progress of any field. As professionals, we must consistently look ahead and never allow ourselves to become satisfied with the present since such an attitude will result in loss of the momentum of progress and subsequent stagnation.

REFERENCES

Bartel, N.F., & Guskin, S. A handicap as a social phenomenon. In W.M. Cruickshank (Ed.) *Psychology of exceptional children and youth*. Englewood Cliffs, NJ: Prentice-Hall, 1971.

Bell, R. A reinterpretation of the direction of effects in studies of socialization. *Psychological Review*, 1968, *75*, 81–95.

Cartwright, G.P., & Cartwright, C.C. Definitions and classification approaches. In J. Neisworth & R. Smith (Eds.), *Retardation: Issues, assessment and intervention*. New York: McGraw-Hill, 1978.

Deno, E. *Educating children with emotional, learning and behavior problems*. Minneapolis: National Support Systems Projects, University of Minnesota Press, 1978.

Dunlap, G., Koegel, R., & Egel, A. Autistic children in school. *Exceptional Children*, 1979, *45*, 552–558.

Gutride, M., Goldstein, A., & Hunter, G.F. The use of modeling and role playing to increase social interaction among asocial clinical parents. *Journal of Consulting and Clinical Psychology*, 1973, *40*, 408–415.

Kadzin, A. *Behavior modification in applied settings*. Homewood ILL.: Dorsey, 1975.

Kanner, L. Emotionally disturbed children: A historical review. *Child Development*, 1962, *33*, 97–102.

Kauffman, J.M. *Characteristics of children's behavior disorders*. Columbus, OH: Merrill, 1977.

Lilly, S. *Children with exceptional needs*. New York: Holt, Rinehart & Winston, 1979.

Lovaas, O.I., Schaeffer, B., & Simmons, J.O. Experimental studies in childhood schizophrenia: Building social behavior by use of electric shock. *Journal of Experimental Studies in Personality,* 1965, *1,* 99–109.

Martin, B. Parent–child relations. In F.D. Horowitz (Ed.), *Review of child development research* (Vol. 4). Chicago: University of Chicago Press, 1975.

Patterson, G.R. The aggressive child: Victim or architect of a coercive system? In L.A. Hamerlynck, L.C. Handy, & E.J. Mash (Eds.), *Behavior modification and families.* New York: Brunner/Mazell, 1975.

Patterson, G.R., Reid, J.B., Jones, R.R., & Conger, R.E. *A social learning approach to family intervention* (Vol. 1). Families with aggressive children. Eugene, OR: Castalia, 1975.

Polsgrove, L. Self-control: Methods for children. *Behavioral Disorders,* 1979, *4,* 116–130.

Rimland, B. Inside the mind of the autistic savant. *Psychology Today,* 1978, *12,* 69–80.

Rincover, A., Koegel, R., & Russo, D. Some recent behavioral research on the education of autistic children. *Education and Treatment of Children,* 1978, *1,* 31–45.

Schrag, F. Learning what one feels and enlarging the range of one's feelings. *Educational Theory,* 1972, *22,* 382–394.

Stainback, S.B., & Stainback, W.C. Some Trends in special education. *Behavioral Disorders* (in press).

Thomas, A., Chess, S., & Birch, H. *Temperament and behavior disorders in children.* New York: New York University Press, 1968.

Trower, P., Bryant, B., & Argyle, M. *Social skills and mental health.* Pittsburgh, PA: University of Pittsburgh Press, 1978.

Wayne, M., & O'Connor, P. *Exceptional children: A development view* Lexington, MA: Heath and Company, 1979.

SELECTED READINGS FOR FURTHER STUDY

Deno, E. *Educating children with emotional, learning and behavior problems.* Minneapolis: National Support Systems Projects, University of Minnesota Press, 1978.

Rincover, A., Koegel, R., & Russo, D. Some recent behavioral research on the education of autistic children. *Education and Treatment of Children,* 1978, *1,* 31–45.

12
Disability Labeling/Segregation: An Alternative

Among the many present and future trends discussed in this volume, the trend away from disability labeling/segregated programming has to rank among the most noteworthy in terms of the overall influence it is likely to have in the future on the education of children who display maladaptive behaviors as well as public education in general.

As noted by Nicholas Hobbs (1974) after concluding a project on classification of exceptional children, "We seek, through analysis of the problem and alternative solutions to it, to maximize the utility of classification and to minimize its unfortunate consequences in the lives of children" (pp. 8–9). Since the completion of this project, while there has been some examination of the detrimental effects of classification and the subsequent segregation that it often leads to, there have been few attempts to propose alternatives to the present classification/segregation practices.

The first part of this chapter is devoted to background information about classification systems presently employed in special education and the problems inherent in such systems so that the reader can understand why there is a need to consider alternatives and have a basis for evaluating any proposed alternatives. In the second part of the chapter the authors suggest an alternative classification/educational programming system that points to one way of reducing the need for the category "behaviorally disordered" or "emotionally disturbed" and the subsequent segregation that often occurs. What is suggested could also stimulate ideas for reducing the need for other categorical groupings in special education.

279

PRESENT CLASSIFICATION SYSTEMS

Broadly speaking, within the field of special education, individuals can be classified as fitting into one of many disability categories—for example, behaviorally disordered, learning disabled, blind, or deaf. An individual can be further classified within a categorical group; for example, within behavioral disorders there are many possible classifications or categories—conduct disorder, personality disorder, neurotic, or psychotic. Classification can be done by the behavioral characteristics or symptoms of the individual, or it can be done by known or assumed etiologies.

The Reasons for the Systems

Currently, the goal of classification in special education is to establish categories to which children's behaviors can be reliably assigned. It is assumed that classification will permit special educators to select the best services and/or treatment for particular disorders or disabilities (e.g., mental retardation versus behavioral disorder, conduct versus personality disorder). This assumption is based on the belief that children who fit into various categories probably require differential treatment for a variety of reasons, including different etiologies. In addition, through classification it is hoped that knowledge in the field of special education will become more organized and refined and that communication between professionals will be easier.

The use of a definition/classification approach has also resulted from a concern on the part of professionals to have guidelines for determining whether a child has a "disorder" or "disability" that requires treatment. In education, after determining who has a "disorder," special services, which are designed to constitute educational treatment, are administered. Generally speaking, if an individual fits the definition of being "deviant," "disabled," or "disordered," he is entitled to special educational services, whereas if the individual does not qualify, the special services are not available to him. After an individual is classified as having a "disability" or "disorder" or "handicapping condition," he is usually further classified into the specific type that he has. As noted earlier, this is done so that the specific type of treatment or services the individual requires can be determined.

Premises of Current Educational Classification

The present educational approach to organizing information involving behavioral differences is being closely examined. The very premises on which the system is based are now under scrutiny, particularly those pertaining to current disability classification.

That a system serves as a communication device among professionals is the basic premise of any informational organization system. The present classification system does provide a shorthand means of transmitting information. This would also be true, however, of any well-organized informational system. It should be noted that a classification system can be well organized and provide a shorthand means of communication among professionals but still transmit information that is misleading and inaccurate. Goldstein, Arkell, Ashcroft, and associates (1976) alluded to this problem when they asked, "Are classification systems substituted for the real descriptions of children's characteristics to the extent that teachers and administrators are responding to labels rather than data as they portray children's educational needs?" (p. 55). Deno (1970) stated, "Many workers are now pointing out that the introduction of categorical constructs based on presumed child defects merely adds a cluttering, unessential administrative and conceptual layer which interferes more than it aids in realizing the goal of individual instruction for all children, handicapped and nonhandicapped" (p. 232).

A second premise is that the worth of an information organization system can be measured in terms of its utility to the individual classified. On this test of utility the present system breaks down. Many professionals now believe that more benefit is derived by the classifier than the individual classified. The classifier is provided with a shorthand means of information transfer whereas the classified individual generally gets negatively stereotyped. Present categories focus on the inappropriate behaviors (too much or too little) that an individual displays. Limitations rather than strengths are emphasized. The criteria to classify a child focus on limitations, such as low intelligence, inability to see or hear, physical limitations, or unacceptable social, attitudinal, and emotional behaviors. In short, children have been classified on the basis of what they *cannot do* rather than on their *capabilities*. As a result, there is a predesigned negative connotation associated with the category and thus a negative view of individuals associated with the category.

Proponents of the current classification system always contend that it allows the individuals classified the opportunity for special educational programming. As the present system operates today, however, the defined and classified categories generally being used (e.g., emotional disturbance, learning disability, mental retardation) are not programmatically specific enough (based on what needs to be learned) to be of any real benefit to teachers. Meyen (1978) believes that "teachers skilled in instructional planning and support personnel skilled in assessment and team planning will contribute to establishing a public school climate in which effective decisions can be made, ones which match instructional options with learner characteristics. If this is established, the need for eligibility criteria (i.e., definitions as a condition for program placement) will not be necessary" (p. 59). Lilly (1979) points out that "once this is done, the label is no longer necessary or useful for instructional purposes, since it has been replaced with far more specific information" (p. 40).

Not only are the categories, as presently structured, not useful for programmatic groupings, since they are not based on specific teaching/learning needs, they deny individuals *not* classified an opportunity for any chance of greater individualization according to their unique needs. As Pappanikou (1977) asserts, under the present system a child has "to be 'called deviant' in order to benefit from the concept of special education" (p. xiv).

Related to the problem outlined above is the repeated concern within the category of behavioral disorders to categorize only permanent or *chronic* conditions (Bower, 1969; Graubard, 1973; Smith & Neisworth, 1975). This denies the individual with a "transient" problem individualized or special services since he does not meet the criterion for being called deviant or disordered (i.e., he does not have a "permanent" condition). The denial of individualized training for a person who is considered to have only a "transient" behavioral difficulty might result in the development of a "permanent," more severe inappropriate behavior. There can be little hope, therefore, of preventing "permanent" problems if there is a failure to deal with "transient" problems. In short, most definitions of "behavioral disorders," within the present classification systems, require that a child display behavior patterns that deviate markedly from the expectations of others for a *long period* of time (e.g., Bower, 1969; Graubard, 1973) before that child can receive educational services to meet his/her needs. This denies individuals who have "transient" problems access to "special" services and works against a focus on the prevention of problems. The benefits of focusing on prevention of problems are well documented (Laub & Kurtz, 1978).

In an information organization system it is a must the information being transmitted be relevant in terms of dealing with, correcting, and/or modifying the condition described and delineated. The present system does nothing to enhance the selection of the *type* of treatment or "therapy" needed to correct the problem. Unlike the medical framework in which a wide variety of treatments are available, with some more applicable and successful with a particular physiological condition than others (e.g., biochemical, surgical, physical and occupational therapies), education has only one treatment available—the teaching/learning process. Although aspects of the process must be examined in terms of the learning characteristics of individual children to determine the objectives or goals, method of instruction, and materials to be used, the process remains the same—the teaching/learning process. As pointed out in Chapter 3, there is no unique educational process for use with exceptional children that is not used with "normal" children. *All* children should be evaluated in terms of their unique characteristics, and an individualized educational plan should be devised. *All children are unique,* not just those labeled "exceptional."

A fifth premise of the current classification system is that it helps to identify the child's problem. When confronted with a child who is not learning, the teacher's first questions are, "What is wrong with the child?" or "What are the reasons he is not learning?" The teacher wants the child diagnosed to determine his problem or defect. The teacher seldom requests that the instructional procedures be diagnosed for problems or defective areas. As Adelman (1971) so correctly asserts, "learning problems result not only from the characteristics of the youngster but also from the characteristics of the classroom situation to which he is assigned" (p. 529).

Lovitt (1967) has clearly explained the potential problem:

A teacher, for example, might seek diagnostic solace as a means of rationalizing his or her own programming inadequacies. Such a teacher, when finding a child who does not adapt to her program or choice of curricular materials, could have her programming decision greatly reinforced by a diagnostician who solves her dilemma with a report that the child is dyslexic or aphasic. As a result, when the child does not adequately perform, the teacher need only draw out her file and read the diagnosis to reassure herself that the student's poor performance is unalterably determined by some medical or psychological malady. Then no teaching obligation follows for altering the stimulus or consequence conditions of the program, nor is there any necessity for an assessment of possible errors within the teacher's management techniques. (p. 234)

Related to the tendency to look for causes within the child is the problem of "reification." Since the present classification system fosters the belief that the problem is always within the child, it indirectly fosters the reification process. This is the process whereby a label is initially used to describe a behavior pattern and afterward the label is used to explain why the behavioral pattern occurs. For example, Kanner (1943) labeled a behavioral pattern he observed in some children "autistic." But now the answer to the question as to why such children display the behaviors is usually, "The child behaves that way because he is autistic." A label that was initially used to describe behavior is now being used to explain the origin of behavior (Whelan, 1972).

Another basic premise of classification involves acceptance. Mac-Millan (1977) noted that public recognition of the classified individual helps others put the unusual behavior of the individual into perspective and results in greater acceptance. Acceptance of an individual designated as having a disorder may be quicker than if the condition is not publicly advertised. The problem with this logic becomes clear when this acceptance is analyzed. The quicker acceptances facilitated by a label is generally not acceptance as an equal but rather acceptance as an inferior or defective individual to be pitied. The social feedback given the labeled individual as a result of this "conditional" acceptance can be just as detrimental, if not more so, to the individual's perception of self-worth as nonacceptance. Another side effect of the acceptance factor is that acceptance of the disordered individual may generalize to acceptance of the unusual or situationally inappropriate behavior. Acceptance of inappropriate behavior is counterproductive to its modification generally due to the lower expectation of others and a subsequent decrease in the motivation of the individual designated as having a "disorder." Acceptance is important. Rather than allowing for conditional acceptance, however, the goal or objective should be the acceptance of every individual as having dignity and self-worth rather than acceptance of inappropriate behavior or an individual as one of less status or importance.

The last premise of the current classification system that we shall consider is that such a system facilitates the recognition of categories for monetary appropriations. As Deno (1970) stated, a de-emphasis on labels of children would diminish the "wellspring of sympathy" that has resulted in strong federal and state support. Although it is true that for years negative labels and the subsequent pity the labels evoked have resulted in substantial funding, research has revealed that these practices (i.e., disability labeling) have also resulted in such side effects as poorer self-concept, motivation, achievement, and possible overall success of individuals labeled in this manner (Stuart, 1970).

Now that we recognize the dehumanizing effect, can we continue to perpetuate these problems because it is an effective way to get funding by evoking sympathy and pity? Is it not possible for professionals to determine a means of communicating the monetary needs for more individualized training for *all* children without using "sophisticated insults"? Time, effort, materials, research, programming, all tied to monetary expenditures, are necessary to meet the needs of *all* children and adults including those traditionally labeled "disordered," "deviant," "idiots," "insane," and/or "disturbed." Ways to gain monetary support that are of benefit to *all* children, and not detrimental to any one group of children, must be determined.

In Table 12–1 the reader will find a brief summary of the premises upon which present classification systems rest. In addition, the reader will find in the table a review of the major problems inherent in disability classifications.

Table 12–1
Problems with Present Classification System

Basic Premises of Classification	Problems with Present System
Provides communication device among professionals	Provides misleading and inaccurate information
Provides benefits to individual classified	Classification more beneficial to classifier than classified
Allows the classified individual the opportunity for special programming	Educational categories being used (ED, MR, LD) are not programmatically specific enough to be of any real benefit in programming Present system categorizes permanent or chronic conditions only which denies individuals with transient problems individualized educational opportunities
Provides data to aid in correcting or modifying condition described	Does little to enhance the selection of *type* of treatment to correct the problem There are no unique educational (teaching/learning) processes to be used according to labels designated
Helps identify the child's problems	Ignores the interactive nature of the child and his environment; implies causation within the child
Helps others put the unusual behavior into perspective and results in greater acceptance	Acceptance generally quicker but promotes acceptance as an inferior rather than an equal Conditional acceptance leads too lower expectations that can result in poorer performance of the labelled individual
Promotes monetary appropriations	Monetary appropriations can not offset the dehumanizing effect of the labels used

While many professionals agree that the traditional categorical approach has several major limitations, changes will neither come quickly nor easily. Changes will come slowly since

> categorical address is too deeply entrenched in the social commitments of categorically defined special-interest advocacy groups in the structure of health, education and welfare programs at direct

service levels, in the staffing of teacher education institutions, in other professional training programs and in general public thinking. It may take a generation or more to achieve the basic shifts in how problems are defined and tackled even when the advantages of alternative approaches can be documented by research and demonstrations of effectiveness. (Deno 1978, pp. 39–40)

Despite this reality, we need to explore, suggest, and attempt change if problems with the traditional categorical system are to be overcome. The following section suggests an alternative to provide impetus for focusing on potential change.

PROPOSED CLASSIFICATION SYSTEM

Present knowledge and experiences are providing ideas for new and possibly more effective ways of dealing with the classification problems being faced by educators in the area of behavioral differences. Practices such as labeling children rather than conditions or knowledge, using negatively loaded terminology and stereotyping individuals have been recognized as detrimental. Goldstein and his associates (1976) recommended that "labels and systems of classification be abandoned in favor of more precise descriptions of individual children as they have implication for classroom interaction" (p. 55). Some professionals have attempted to outline possible ways of accomplishing this. For example, Hallahan and Kauffman (1977) stated the following:

If the traditional definitions and their resultant groupings of children are nonfunctional, what course should special education follow? It would be absurd (although not much more absurd than present practices) to assign children to classes randomly. If we are going to group children, why not do so because each one has, for example, about the same performance rate for arithmetic problems of a certain type? Does this not make more sense than to place children together because they all have IQs somewhere over 68 and all have reading and arithmetic disabilities to some unspecified character?

We suggest that children should be considered candidates for special education on the basis of specific social or academic performance deficits, and not judged solely on standardized test scores or clinical impressions. Children should be grouped for instruction according to their performance on remedial tasks. Such groupings would demand continuous assessment of the child's performance and flexibility in grouping children differently at different times, depending on the nature of the task and the child's progress. Chronological age, sex, and characteristic social behavior must be considered in grouping children for games and other social experiences, but specific academic skill must be the criterion for grouping for remedial academic instruction.

Yet there are several practical considerations that temper any enthusiasm for finding an ultimate solution to the problem of grouping exceptional children. First, children often must be grouped, especially in sparsely populated areas, as a matter of convenience or economic necessity. In such cases we must recognize that the children are being served in the same class or by the same resource teacher for administrative and financial reasons and not instructional purposes. Second, unless one has a great amount of flexibility in scheduling and a large number of children who can thus be matched very precisely on academic performance, the most effective remedial teaching will likely require one-to-one instruction. Finally, heterogeneous groupings of children complicate instruction for the teacher but present an opportunity for peer tutoring. (pp. 148– 149)*

The remainder of this section will expand some of the ideas of Hallahan and Kauffman (1977) by outlining a possible classification system that hopefully is fraught with fewer problems than the systems that have been used in the past. It is an attempt to move from the traditional categorical system in special education to one in which children are sorted and grouped on relevant dimensions.

The proposed system points to a way of reducing the need for the category "behaviorally disordered" or "emotional disturbed" for *instructional purposes*. Some of the overall basic ideas could apply to the reduced need for other categorical groupings in special education. This will become clearer to the reader after reviewing the proposed system. The proposed system is simply an extension of the existing classification system presently being used in "regular" education. Three areas of consideration are involved—training, task difficulty level, and departmentation.

Training

The first area of the system includes the categories in which training or education is required. Some of the broad categories being successfully used in schools today are spelling, reading, arithmetic, chemistry, typing, home economics, drafting, and so on. These categories are primarily of an academic or vocational nature. The systematic teaching of some other behaviors that are important to child development has sometimes been neglected. For example, little has been done to teach attitudinal, social,

---

*From "Labels, Categories, Behaviors; ED, LD, and EMR Reconsidered" by D.P. Hallahan and J.M. Kauffman, *Journal of Special Education*, 1977, *11*, 139–149. Reprinted by permission of authors and publisher.

emotional and self-control behaviors (Strain, Cooke, & Apolloni, 1976). When the behaviors of individuals who have been traditionally characterized as "emotionally disturbed" or "behaviorally disordered" are analyzed, much of the development of inappropriate behaviors displayed may have been avoided if the individuals were taught appropriate attitudinal, social, emotional, and self-control behaviors.

Unfortunately, systematic attempts in education to teach such behaviors are included in our present system only if an individual is provided a negative label. The "special services" for individuals labeled "behaviorally disordered" usually focus primarily on the development of self-control, social interaction, emotional, and attitudinal behaviors, generally in combination with academics, rather than predominately academics. If we could extend our regular educational offerings to include the development of appropriate social, attitudinal, emotional, and self-control behaviors, we could better accommodate the needs of all individuals without resorting to sophisticated insults as "emotionally disturbed" to obtain services and more importantly possibly *prevent* many of the problems in this area.

Training in socially and emotionally appropriate behaviors is important to *all* individuals. Areas such as appropriate attention-getting behaviors, tact, consideration of the feelings and perceptions of others, and a positive attitude toward one's self and others, if not learned, could be more detrimental to the success of every aspect of an individual's life, even more so than not being able to add! Despite the importance of these skills to reaching maximum potential (Lyon, 1971; Sandiford, 1936; Schrag, 1972; Thorndike, 1906), such skills are not currently addressed by the educational system in any systematic and organized way (Borich, 1971; Harbeck, 1970; Morse, 1971; Strain, Cooke, & Apolloni, 1976). The author's are not advocating that the curriculum for children who display severe forms of maladaptive behavior should *only* include teaching attitudinal, social, emotional, and self-control behaviors. Obviously such children need instruction in many other areas such as self-care, langauge and/ or reading, math, writing, career choices, and the use of recreational/leisure time. If children labeled as being seriously disturbed are to be educated in regular public schools, however, some attention will have to be focused on emotional, attitudinal, social, and self-control behaviors since major problems in these areas are often found among children who display severe forms of maladaptive behavior.

Task Difficulty Level

The second area of consideration for the classification system is the present use of task difficulty level. It too is being used in the "regular" educational system by the grading or level system (e.g., preschool, primary, intermediate, junior high, high school). There is little disagreement that academic and vocational skills need to be divided in accordance with difficulty. It would not be plausible, for example, for one teacher to instruct individuals in beginning to advanced mathematic skills in a single class with materials available to span the entire spectrum; similarly, it may not be plausible in all cases to teach all levels of appropriate attention-getting behavior, from the low level of reducing self-injurious behaviors and/or teaching very rudimentary social approach behaviors to pride in assigned duties and/or interactions in sophisticated political, social or economic debates. So classification of curricular areas including the additional attitudinal, emotional, social skill, and self-control areas would be done in accordance with task difficulty.

Departmentation

The third aspect of the educational system to enhance individualization in the schools is the more extensive use of the departmentalization approach for curricular areas typically used in the public secondary schools. If class placement based on assessed need in each categorical area (e.g., spelling, math, attitudinal, emotional/social skills) is arranged, such a system can accommodate the individual needs of students who are (1) at a beginning, rudimentary level, in one or more areas (e.g., math and attitudinal behavior) but are functioning at more advanced levels in other areas of study, (2) at a beginning level in academic areas but have more advanced skills in physical, vocational, and social areas, and even (3) particularly talented in one or more areas. By using such a system, classes according to level per curricular area can be arranged to fit the individual needs of each student without designating certain students as "disordered," "disturbed," "retarded," or "disabled." It should be noted that level appropriateness of classes may vary not only by designated or measured difficulty level in curricular areas, but also by age appropriateness. For example, a seven-year-old reading on a 1.1 grade level will require different materials than a thirteen-year-old reading at a 1.1 grade level. As Brown, Branston, Hamre-Nietupski, and associates (1979) have pointed out, if one goal of education is to minimize the stigmatizing discrepancies between handicapped students and their non-handicapped peers, it is our obligation to teach handicapped students the major functions characteristic of their chronological age, using materials and tasks that do not highlight the deficiencies in their repertoires.

In the proposed plan *all* children would be programmed into various levels and types of curricular classes throughout the day based on their individual needs while staying within the mainstream of education. Everyone would attend classes and receive instruction based on his or her ability to achieve and exhibit appropriate behaviors in a particular curricular area.

One premise of this proposed classification system is that these skills need to be recognized and systematically programmed for as a curricular area, since if they are only accepted as a part of other curricular areas they will, as they have in the past, become an ancillary concern rather than a primary focus of systematic instruction. While social, emotional, and self-control skills must be practiced in all other classes and life activities, this is not justification enough not to pay special attention to their development. Reading is also a skill used in most other classes and activities, such as reading directions, assignments, newspapers, and books for pleasure, enjoyment, information, and/or understanding. It is recognized and universally accepted that concentrated systematic instruction focused on reading skills is needed for *initial* development and refinement with transfer of skills being required and/or programmed into other settings. Educators do not leave the development of reading skills to chance or depend on these skills developing as part of other activities without designated and systematic instruction, although these skills are practiced and encouraged throughout all school and life activities.

Because of the importance of social, emotional, attitudinal, and self-control skills for achievement and success in later life, in education they too should receive concentrated attention with transfer, generalization, and practice in other activities specifically encouraged and programmed in.

Two additional points should be made. One, to the extent that systematic and organized instruction in emotional/attitudinal/social/self-control behaviors occurs as an integral part of all daily activities, the amount of designated time needed to concentrate on such skills will be lessened. The second point is that departmentalization, while having some benefits as outlined, also has some disadvantages, especially if carried to the extreme wherein children are required to switch or shuffle back and forth a great deal between classes. Although referring specifically to professional specialization rather than departmentalization, the following statements by Whelan (1977) are relevant:

> Good teaching fosters a positive relationship, and a child's life is enhanced from it. Further fragmentation of pupils' contact with an identifiable "my teacher" would obviate the possibility of establishing a facilitative learner–teacher relationship. A pupil would be left with a sequence of task points at which information would be exchanged, deleted and added much like a machine is kept running, and all of this would be done with the attendant lack of interpersonal relationships. (p. 66)

Basic Operational Strategy for the System

Let us assume that classification is to be done according to task difficulty per curricular area. General school groupings would then be divided according to a common variable(s), for example a chronological age range. The group could constitute the basic "class affiliation." This class would meet together for such sessions as homeroom or general activities, recess, study hall, lunch, and closing activities. During the other periods of each day *each and every* child would be assigned the classes that most appropriately meet the objectives for the child, taking into consideration his/her age, achievement level, social awareness, and other relevant factors. Other "class" members may or may not be in one or more of the classes. Each class structure would be based primarily on the objectives deemed needed by the students rather than by a classification of whether they are normal, mentally retarded, emotionally disturbed, chronically disruptive, culturally deprived, or physically handicapped.

In short, with such an arrangement, it would be easier to keep each child within the mainstream of education and society while providing greater individualization in programming for *all* children without the use of negative labeling. Each student would be exposed to a wide range of individuals who exhibit various behaviors by means of their "class affiliation" as well as the changing groups that they would interact with in the curricular areas.

AN ASSESSMENT OF THE PROPOSED ALTERNATIVE

The proposed classification system is an attempt to stimulate ideas to meet the challenge made by Meyen (1978):

> The most significant changes which could occur to resolve the definition/classification dilemma would be for public education to implement a continuum of educational and service alternatives, to individualize instruction and to eliminate the dichotomy between serving exceptional and nonexceptional students (p. 53).

The proposed system involves the classification of *categories of objectives or behaviors to be learned* rather than categories of children with problems. Classification of children is focused on what each individual needs to learn in the sequence of each category of objectives available within the educational classification system. This classification of children is done for every child in categorical learning areas (e.g. reading, math, attitude) rather than for selected children labeled "disordered" or "deviant." Classification and placement according to level in a categorical learning area is based on the needs of the child in the particular area and should be continuously assessed so that as a child gains expertise in a curricular area, he can move into the next learning level in the area. The child's chronological age and other relevant factors are taken into account when he is grouped with other children. The decision should not be based entirely on the child's functioning level in a particular curricular area, although this would be one of the primary considerations.

Stated another way, what is being advocated is the grouping of all children according to the instructional objectives to be learned. All children would be kept together in the mainstream of community life and schooling, with classroom arrangements and groupings made according to the specific needs of all children. This is not unlike what is done today for many children in some public schools. The only difference is that the authors are suggesting that the public schools "gear up" to accommodate all children including those traditionally labeled "disordered" by expanding curricular offerings (e.g., teaching of emotional/attitudinal/social/self-control behaviors) to meet a wider range of needs. It should be noted that the same approach could be advocated for children who have been traditionally labeled into other categorical areas such as severely mentally retarded. To accommodate these children, the schools will need to include curricular areas that meet the needs of these children, for example, "teaching independent eating skills."

In the authors' view, in the past the schools were not prepared or capable of teaching skills to children other than in traditional subject areas and the child who could not fit into this circumscribed curriculum was referred and designated "special" or "exceptional" or "handicapped" and taught by a "specialist" who was trained to teach attitudes or eating skills or beginning reading to a ten-year-old, for example.

The authors are not proposing that a few selected children be sent off to a "specialist" within the building for a designated hour or so each day to get their attitudes and/or social behaviors "fixed." As stated previously, what is being advocated is the teaching of appropriate attitudinal/emotional/social/self-control skills be added as a curricular area within the public schools as is reading, math, social studies, etc. Attitudes, emotions, and so forth can be operationally defined and systematically taught. The technology is now available (Gardner, 1977; Strain, Cooke & Apolloni, 1976).

It is recognized that most schools at the present time make an effort to foster such behaviors. What the authors are proposing is more designated attention be given to this so that "all" children can have their needs met within the mainstream. Currently, if a child's attitudinal emotional, and/or social behaviors get too far out of line with the expectations of others (e.g., parents, teachers), he is referred to and usually labeled as "behaviorally disordered" or "emotionally disturbed" and sent to a "specialist" (special teacher, psychiatrist, and the like) to get his attitudes "fixed." This approach has not been found to be very successful. The success rate of preventing as well as correcting such problems would probably be much higher if the focus were on establishing an environment within the mainstream that could foster and maintain appropriate emotional, attitudinal, social, and self-control behaviors. As pointed out by Holland (1978), and expanded on in Chapter 3, the solution to making lasting changes in behaviors cannot rest in the specially arranged contingencies in the special setting. Unfortunately, the special educator or psychologist often misses the point. He/she attempts a technical fix in the clinic or special classroom for a problem such as extremely aggressive behavior or the failure of the child to interact with others. But outside the clinic or special classroom all those conditions prevail that maintain the behavior in the first place and the behavior gradually readjusts to these conditions when the child is no longer required to function in the special setting.

The authors are not suggesting that the alternative classification system outlined in this chapter is the ultimate solution to the current problems related to grouping children for instructional purposes. We realize that the proposed system is also fraught with potential hazards, although hopefully fewer than the current system. For example, such a system could be inappropriately implemented to increase homogeneity to the degree that some positive heterogeneous factors are eliminated in the prescribed groups. Any proposed system is likely, however, to possess possible dangers and disadvantages. We must start considering alternative classification or organizational systems to overcome the numerous problems we face in the present system since it is not likely that the schools could function efficiently and effectively without some organizational structure. As Hallahan and Kauffman (1977) pointed out, "It would be absurd (although not much more absurd than present practices) to assign children to classes randomly" (p. 148).

Many educators are beginning to recognize that providing children with special needs disability labels and segregating them from their peers, teachers and friends is not always in their best interest or anyone elses. We hope this text has been informative regarding why this is so and has stimulated the reader, as writing the book stimulated us, to search for possible solutions. Hopefully, these solutions will focus on ways of meeting the special needs of all children.

REFERENCES

Adelman, H.S. The not-so-specific learning disability population. *Exceptional Children,* 1971, *37,* 528–533.

Borich, G.D. Accountability in the affective domain. *Journal of Research and Development in Education, 1971, 5,* 87–96.

Bower, E.M. *Early identification of emotional handicapped children in school* (2nd ed.). Springfield, IL: Thomas, 1969.

Brown, L., Branston, M., Hamre-Nietupski, S., et al. A strategy for developing chronological age appropriate and functional curricular content for severely handicapped adolescents and young adults. *Journal of Special Education,* 1979, *13,* 81–90.

Cartwright, G.P., & Cartwright, C.C. Definitions and classification approaches. In J. Neisworth & R. Smith (Eds.), *Retardation: Issues, assessment and intervention.* New York: McGraw-Hill, 1978.

Deno, E.N. Special education as developmental capital. *Exceptional Children,* 1970, *37,* 229–237.

Deno, E.N. *Educating children with emotional, learning, and behavior problems.* Minneapolis: National Support Systems Project. University of Minnesota Press, 1978.

Foster, G.G., & Salvia, J. Teacher response to label of learning disabled as a function of demand characteristics. *Exceptional Children,* 1977, *43,* 533–534.

Gallagher, J.J., Forsythe, P., Ringelheim, D., & Weintraub, F.J. Funding patterns and labeling. In N. Hobbs (Ed.), *Issues in the classification of children* (Vol. II). San Francisco: Jossey-Bass, 1976.

Gardner, W.I. *Learning and behavior characteristics of exceptional children and youth.* Boston: Allyn & Bacon, 1977.

Gillung, T.G., & Rucker, C.M. Labels and teacher expectations. *Exceptional Children,* 1977, *43,* 464–465.

Goldstein, H., Arkell, C., Ashcroft, S.C., et al. In N. Hobbs (Ed.), *Issues in the classification of children* (Vol. II). San Francisco: Jossey-Bass, 1976.

Graubard, P.S. Children with behavioral disabilities. In L.M. Dunn (Ed.), *Exceptional children in the schools (2nd ed.). New York: Holt, Rinehart & Winston, 1973.*

Hallahan, D.P., & Kauffman, J.M. Labels, categories, behaviors: ED, LD, and EMR reconsidered. *Journal of Special Education,* 1977, *11,* 139–149.

Harbeck, M.B. Instructional objectives in the affective domain. *Educational Technology,* 1970, *10,* 49–52.

Hobbs, N. *The futures of children: categories, labels, and their consequences.* San Francisco: Jossey-Bass, 1974.

Holland, J.C. Behaviorism: Part of the problem or part of the solution? *Journal of Applied Behavior Analysis,* 1978, *11,* 163–174.

Kanner, L. *Child psychiatry.* Springfield, IL: Thomas, 1943.

Laub, K.W., & Kurtz, P.D. Early Identification, In J. Neisworth & R. Smith (Eds.), *Retardation: Issues, assessment and intervention.* New York: McGraw-Hill, 1978, pp. 243–267.

Lilly, S. *Children with exceptional needs.* New York: Holt, Rinehart & Winston, 1979.

Lovitt, T.C. Assessment of children with learning disabilities. *Exceptional Children,* 1967, *34,* 233–239.

Lyon, H.C. *Learning to feel–feeling to learn.* Columbus, OH: Merrill, 1971.

MacMillan, D.L. *Mental retardation in school and society.* Boston: Little, Brown, 1977.

Meyen, E. An introductory perspective. In E. Meyen (Ed.), *Exceptional children and youth.* Denver: Love Publishing, 1978.

Morse, W.C. Special pupils in regular classes: Problems of accomodation. In M.C. Reynolds & M.D. Davis (Eds.), *Exceptional children in regular classrooms.* Washington, DC: U.S. Office of Education, 1971.

Pappanikou, A.J. Introduction. In A.J. Pappanikou & J.L. Paul (Eds.), *Mainstreaming emotionally disturbed children.* New York: Syracuse University Press, 1977.

Sandiford, P. *Education psychology: An objective study.* New York: Longmans, Green, 1936.

Schrag, F. Learning what one feels and enlarging the range of one's feelings. *Educational Theory,* 1972, *22,* 382–394.

Smith, R.M., & Neisworth, J.T. *The exceptional child: A functional approach.* New York: McGraw-Hill, 1975.

Stone, A.A., & Stone, S.S. (Eds.) *The abnormal personality through literature.* Englewood Cliffs, NJ: Prentice-Hall, 1966.

Strain, P.S., Cooke, T.P., & Apolloni, T. *Teaching Exceptional Children.* New YorK: Academic Press, 1976.

Stuart, R.B. *Trick or treatment: How and when psychotherapy fails.* Champaign, IL: Research Press, 1970.

Thorndike, E. *The principles of teaching.* New York: Longmans, Green, 1936.

Whelan, R.J. What's in a label? A hell of a lot! In *The legal and educational consequences of the intelligence testing movement: Handicapped and minority group children.* Columbia: University of Missouri Press, 1972.

Whelan, R.J. Human understanding of human behavior. In A.J.Pappanikou & J.L. Paul (Eds.), *Mainstreaming emotionally disturbed children.* New York: Syracuse University Press, 1977.

SELECTED READINGS FOR FURTHER STUDY

Brown, L., Branston, M., Hamre-Nietupski, S., et al. A strategy for developing chronological age appropriate and functional curricular content for severely handicapped adolescents and young adults. *Journal of Special Education,* 1979, *13,* 81–90.

Deno, E.N. Special education as developmental capital. *Exceptional Children,* 1970, *37,* 229–237.

Deno, E.N. *Educating children with emotional, learning, and behavior problems.* Minneapolis: National Support Systems Project, University of Minnesota Press, 1978.

Hallahan, D.P., & Kauffman, J.M. Labels, categories, behaviors: ED, LD, and EMR reconsidered. *Journal of Special Education,* 1977, *11,* 139–149.

Index